Taking the Long View

Taking the Long View

Three and a Half Decades of General Synod

Colin Buchanan

CHURCH HOUSE PUBLISHING

Church House Publishing
Church House
Great Smith Street
London SW1P 3NZ

Tel: 020 7898 1451
Fax: 020 7898 1449

ISBN-13 978-0-7151-4098-7
ISBN-10 0 7151 4098 1

Published 2006 by Church House Publishing

Typeset by RefineCatch Limited, Bungay, Suffolk
Printed in England by MPG Books Ltd, Bodmin, Cornwall

Contents

Contents

Acknowledgements

This book has been written almost entirely from official sources, private documents, my own records, and (occasionally) personal memories. Small parts have been checked with relevant individuals, and I owe a debt for their careful informing or checking to: Bishops David Atkinson, Peter Dawes, John Dennis, David Hope, David James, the late Hugh Montefiore, Michael Turnbull and Wilfred Wood; and to Gordon Kuhrt, Martin Davie, Diana Murrie, David Williams and their assistants in Church House, Westminster; and also to Michael Hodge and Vasantha Gnanadoss of General Synod members. But my debt runs on to those who elected me to Synod (especially those who held me to account) and those who have stimulated, instructed and occasionally infuriated me within the life of General Synod. They have all had a part in forming this idiosyncratic book.

Two people, however, read the whole text in draft. One was Colin Podmore, erstwhile on the staff of the Council for Christian Unity, and currently secretary of the Liturgical Commission, and an exceedingly well-informed and able historian. His careful annotating of the major draft has led to very useful improving and polishing of it. The text was referred to him by Kathryn Pritchard, who as commissioning editor took on this book on behalf of Church House Publishing (a route into print which I had never anticipated) and has herself been superb as a tough negotiator with a wayward author. A comparison of the numbers of footnotes at the foot of pages on the one hand and the numbers banished to endnotes on the other betrays exactly the relative force which author and publisher respectively were able to bring to bear upon each other. I greatly honour her skills.

The account remains, for better or worse, genuinely mine, and nobody else's.

Veni, dixi, scripsi.

Preliminary

Reading this book may prove far more rewarding if the inside of General Synod (a club with its own distinctive rules and customs) does not baffle the reader. Being directed to the Synodical Government Measure 1969 will prove as helpful as being asked to read the rules of cricket in order to learn how to play the game. A broad understanding can be gained from a recent helpful book by Colin Podmore, a member of the secretariat of General Synod – *Aspects of Anglican Identity* (Church House Publishing, 2005), especially chapters 7 and 8. The points I make below are those which obtained during the 35 years I have endeavoured to cover in this book, though various changes occurred with the new Synod in autumn 2005.

There are three Houses of Synod, Bishops, Clergy and Laity, with roughly 50 members of the House of Bishops, 260 of the other two Houses. Capitals are always used here for the three Houses, whether 'House of' appears before, e.g., 'Clergy' or not. Other references will say, e.g., 'bishops' without a capital. Synod meets in a 'group of sessions' for two, three, four or five days at a time, twice or three times a year. The actual meetings since 1970 are tabulated in Appendix B. Synod functions under fairly strict standing orders, and most of its business is generated from the Standing Committee (since 1998 the Archbishops' Council), or from individual Boards, Councils or (since 1998) Divisions, though with virtually open access for the House of Bishops to bring business. 'Ordinary' members (and I write as a genuinely back-benching ordinary member) can affect the business in several ways.

1. They can in theory speak once in any debate (but they are wise to send in their names in advance, stating their reason for wishing to, and even then they may not be called by a chairman with a long list of people wishing to speak).

2. They can move an amendment to various kinds of motion – but not to a motion to 'take note' of something, nor to various stages of legislation (including, obviously, final approval).

3. They can table up to three questions at each group of sessions, and ask one supplementary to the answer they get to each, and can also ask a supplementary to the answer to other people's questions. I got in three questions in almost all the 80 or so groups of sessions I attended.

4.   They can take a motion through their diocesan synod and bring it to General Synod on behalf of their diocese – and diocesan synod motions are usually brought before General Synod after a short delay.

5.   They can table a Private Member's Motion of their own, and it is displayed in the coffee-bar area for members to add signatures, and one or two are debated at most groups of sessions, starting with those with the highest number of signatures. Usually it has taken around 160 signatures to bring a PMM into debate.

They may also move points of order (e.g. to pass to next business, or to test whether there is a quorum, 20 per cent, present in one or another House); and they can thus also affect the way a vote is counted (see below). In between sessions they may correspond with the secretariat (or with each other!); and they may send in suggestions to Revision Committees (also usually given capitals here), and in some cases may appear before them.

Standing orders are tuned for different categories of debate (e.g., there are specific standing orders for liturgical business), and in theory the chairman chosen for any particular debate is specially briefed – even trained – for that kind of business.

In early years General Synod met residentially in the University of York twice in each quinquennium, but more recently has always had its July group of sessions there, and has often met only once a year in London. There is provision for corporate worship.

A note on Synod voting

Voting is recorded in one of two ways (with the numbers 'for' always given first, and the numbers 'against' second). If there is one set of figures given (e.g. 132–99), then it refers to a vote of the whole Synod, unless its context shows it is of a different body, e.g. the House of Bishops on its own. If there are three sets of numbers (e.g. 24–10; 110–92; 78–144), then the voting was by Houses and is reported in the order: Bishops; Clergy; Laity. In such cases, one House opposed will defeat the motion. Voting by Houses is required at final approval for various forms of business, but can always be required under standing orders if 25 members support it, by standing in their places after one member has requested it. For some legislation (as, e.g., final approval of liturgical material – and of the ordination of women) a two-thirds vote in favour is needed in each House, and a 'yes' vote, if it does not reach two-thirds of those voting, is still a defeat. If no figures are mentioned, the result was immediately visible on a show of hands and the motion is simply reported as having succeeded or been defeated.

The *Report of Proceedings*

All Synod's proceedings are recorded verbatim in the published *Report of Proceedings*, for which each group of sessions provides one volume. I have drawn frequently upon these volumes in the pages following, and have not given references, as it is easy, once this source is known, to find any particular speech, or vote, or point of order. On the whole, the verbatim record shows a very high degree of accuracy.

Abbreviations

Synodical language

ABM	Advisory Board for Ministry
ACCM	Advisory Council for the Church's Ministry
ASB	Alternative Service Book
BMU	Board of Mission and Unity
BSR	Board for Social Responsibility
CAC	Crown Appointments Commission
CACTM	Central Advisory Council for Training for the Ministry
CBAC	Committee for Black Anglican Concerns
CBF	Central Board of Finance
CCU	Council for Christian Unity
CME	Continuing [i.e. post-ordination] Ministerial Education
CMEAC	Committee for Minority Ethnic Anglican Concerns
CNC	Crown Nominations Committee
CW	Common Worship
FOAG	Faith and Order Advisory Group
GOE	General Ordination Examination
JIC	Joint Implementation Commission [for Anglican–Methodist Covenant]
MERE	Mission, Evangelism and Renewal in England Committee [of Board of Mission]
NIFCAT	Nurture in Faith and Catechism working group
PMM	Private Member's Motion
RTP	Regional Training Partnership [of theological institutions]

Other ecclesiastical language

ACC	Anglican Consultative Council
ACO	Anglican Communion Office
AEE	Areas of Ecumenical Experiment
ARCIC	Anglican–Roman Catholic International Commission
BCC	British Council of Churches
BEM	*Baptism – Eucharist – Ministry* (= WCC Lima Report)
CAPA	Council of Anglican Provinces in Africa
CCBI	Council of Churches of Britain and Ireland
CHN	Community of the Holy Name
CIBC	Church of India, Burma and Ceylon

CMS	Church Missionary Society (since 1992, Church Mission Society)
CRE	Commission on Racial Equality
CRRU	Community and Race Relations Unit
CSI	Church of South India
CTE	Churches Together in England
DDO	Diocesan Director of Ordinands
ELLC	English Language Liturgical Consultation
ECUSA	Episcopal Church (USA)
FiF	Forward in Faith (opponents of women's ordination)
FITC	*Faith in the City*
GRAS	Group for Rescinding the Act of Synod (opponents of FiF)
GROW	Group for Renewal of Worship
IALC	International Anglican Liturgical Consultations
IASCER	International Anglican Standing Commission on Ecumenical Relations
ICET	International Consultation on English Texts
LCD	London College of Divinity
LEP	Local Ecumenical Project (latterly Partnership, but Project in the 1980s)
LGCM	Lesbian and Gay Christian Movement
LHLG	Latimer House Liturgy Group
MORIB	Movement for the Reform of Infant Baptism
MOW	Movement for the Ordination of Women
NEAC	National Evangelical Anglican Congress/Celebration
PiM	Partners in Mission
SDMTS	Southern Dioceses Ministerial Training Scheme
SPG	Society for the Propagation of the Gospel
STV	Single Transferable Vote
URC	United Reformed Church
WCC	World Council of Churches

Introduction

We cannot do anything against the truth.

(2 Corinthians 13.8)

You may like to know a minimum about Colin Buchanan to understand what he has been up to.

This is a fairly personal book. It records 40 years of cut and thrust in the Church of England's General Synod and kindred bodies, as I have seen it, experienced it, and on occasion handed it out myself. Much is told from my personal standpoint, and the selection of themes derives from my own involvement. It is not autobiography, but an attempt (as in my other writings) at accurate journalism. With that point clear, the reader may be well advised to skip the rest of this Introduction and plunge into the book. The timeline in Appendix B relates my life skeletally to the meetings of Synod. But I also contribute a little more background here to add perspectives to the scenes in the following chapters.

From undergraduate days I engaged in theological controversy. Entering Lincoln College, Oxford, in 1955, I was alongside various ordinands and other students reflecting the then current Anglo-Catholic hegemony in the Church of England. I, a convinced evangelical, was being confirmed and then selected for ordination training while there, so, although reading classics ('Mods and Greats'), I had to know Prayer Book, Articles, and Reformation history to offer a credible apologia for my position. Then in my final year, when I chaired the Bishop Jewel Society, a passing word from one Noel Pollard led me to run study groups on the 1549, 1552 and 1662 Communion services. These equipped me at Tyndale Hall, my theological college in Bristol, to get '10 out of 10' in the ordination exam worship paper – which began to mark out my future. I found myself, unusually for an evangelical, with a church, ministry and sacraments agenda as main theological interests. In 1961, the year I was ordained deacon, I was a founder-member of the Latimer House Liturgy Group (LHLG), which later became the Group for Renewal of Worship (GROW).

In February 1963, during my curacy in Cheadle in Chester Diocese, the 1956–63 Anglican–Methodist Conversations reported, with the centrepiece of their proposals the 'Service of Reconciliation'.[1] I gave it a hostile review in the *Church of England Newspaper*, armed men sprang from the ground for the fight, and I was in the thick of national events. Then in 1964 I was appointed liturgy lecturer at the old London College of Divinity, and, before I started and thus still in my curacy (and under 30 years of age), I found in my hands one day a letter from Michael Ramsey. To my amazement he was inviting me to join the Liturgical Commission. He wrote: 'The Archbishop of York and I are keen that on the Commission there should be not only depth of liturgical knowledge, but also varieties of theological outlook.' Those close to me said it was pretty clear which of these I was.* The appointment to LCD began that summer and I was also asked to the British Council of Churches (BCC) Faith and Order Conference at Nottingham that September, and was pressed by some evangelical London clergy to run for Convocation that Autumn.† I was not elected, but my synodical appetite was whetted, and my pilgrimage with the Single Transferable Vote (STV) was begun also. I also ran in a by-election in 1967, but, with a single vacancy, no evangelical could have been elected in London. Instead I used the experience to learn more about STV.

Another feature of my own life, which indirectly bears upon the rest of the story here, is that I became involved in various evangelical networks, which led to my helping draft the initial document which went to the famous Keele Congress in April 1967. I drafted texts on worship and on ecumenism, and, though they were carefully amended at the Congress, in substance they emerged very close to my original drafting.[2]

By the time 1970 came, I was itching to be on the General Synod starting that autumn. LCD was moving in August to Nottingham, but I had a sabbatical, and was allowed to precede the College to Nottingham, get licensed, and, by a margin of four days, become a candidate in Southwell Diocese for election to

---

* I later discovered that my appointment stemmed from John Wenham (then vice-principal of Tyndale Hall) writing an article for the church press, saying that it was not surprising that evangelicals opposed most proposals for change in the Church of England, as they were fairly firmly excluded from participating in drafting them. He then thought twice about sending it to the press, and instead sent it to the Archbishops. He got a courteous reply, and one of them asked him to suggest names – he put mine in, citing that GOE result in worship, and thus I got invited and the invitation started to mark out my future.

† Marvellously, in those bad old days one did not need a licence in the province of Canterbury to run for election in a diocese. The particular election was of historical interest as being the last time the Convocations were being elected in double harness with a Parliamentary election. Those elected that autumn were to have a six-year stint, and then start to observe the five-year cycle in time with the House of Laity in the General Synod.

General Synod.* This time I succeeded, and then represented Southwell clergy from 1970 to 1985. I was active in Synod, a member of the Liturgical Commission, Revision Committees and working parties, as will appear in the later chapters. In 1978 I became principal of the College, when Robin Nixon died suddenly in early middle age[3]; and I not only chaired GROW, but ran a publishing house, Grove Books, which published and marketed the Grove Booklets GROW produced. From January 1975 until December 2003 I edited the monthly journal *News of Liturgy*, which has been a reliable source in writing this book.

Everything changed in 1985. Hugh Montefiore invited me to become Bishop of Aston.† As in 1970, I now joined a new synodical constituency – this time of suffragan bishops of Canterbury province – four days before the list closed for election to Synod. History, however, did not repeat itself; and I was defeated.‡ Then I was dropped from the Liturgical Commission – but put on the Doctrine Commission.§ I also joined the Inter-Church Process, seeking ecumenical agencies to succeed the BCC after its planned demise. I shadowed the activities of General Synod, which I hope comes through in this book. But in general I was being sidelined nationally, and I simply swallowed and addressed my job as a bishop in Birmingham. This, however, was also not without risk.

In 1988-9 I chaired an inter-church committee to bring Desmond Tutu to Birmingham for a Christian Celebration of the city's centenary. Our ecumenical organization was stretched to the limit, and we were hit by racist

---

* It was a terrible scramble. The then Bishop of Southwell left under a cloud the day I arrived in Nottingham, and licensing had to be done via the Archbishop of York. It was by sheer accident I opened *Church Times* one day and discovered the date when the Convocations were to be dissolved only about a fortnight away, and before the date set for my licensing. Finally the suffragan bishop worked it for four days before the closure, and I had to leave a Liturgical Commission meeting to get to Nottingham for this five-minute ceremony. Much has hung on this 'chance' also since.

† It was a great surprise. I had opposed Hugh fairly regularly in General Synod, admittedly in rather secondary matters, and had prevailed. Two of these instances are reported on pages 35 and 91. But Hugh, though imperious, did not just want 'yes-men' around him. I was helped into accepting the appointment by Roy Williamson, who as chairman of St John's College Council exercised his trusteeship by bidding me go. See page 142 for a feature of my consecration.

‡ Wonderfully, Clifford Longley wrote in *The Times* that my defeat was a 'freak result' of the voting system. I got some small satisfaction by sending a letter saying that any fool defends a voting system by which he has been elected (Parliamentarians do this with ease), but I was defending as fair a system under which I had just been defeated – and defeated not as a 'freak result' (which is virtually impossible), but simply because, in sober if unwelcome truth, not enough voters wanted me.

§ I complained to Hugh, who said, 'But doctrine is much more important than liturgy.' 'True,' I replied, 'but in liturgy we are forming people's doctrine for decades ahead, whereas the Doctrine Commission will get a two-hour debate on its reports, and they will then be pigeon-holed forever.' Hugh acknowledged this as true.

propaganda, partly from the apartheid regime in South Africa ('Tutu shakes hands with Mandela'), but some from the Tory minority on the city council. I was told we had lost a six-figure sum, and had to turn to Birmingham Diocese to fund the last weekend. I was placed in a position where I could not but offer my resignation, and it was promptly accepted and I was out.[4] Michael Turnbull, Bishop of Rochester, rescued me. I had a year and more in a kind of exile.

An assistant bishop can become a voter in the suffragans election, if his diocesan bishop nominates him to the diocesan House of Bishops. In 1990 Michael Turnbull helpfully took this step, and I became not just a voter, but also a candidate – and then, elected sixth out of the six successful southern suffragans, entered the House of Bishops when still out of a job. Soon after, I became incumbent of St Mark's, Gillingham, the first ever incumbent in the House of Bishops. Back in Synod, I was invited to join, of all things, the Standing Orders Committee. I found this underwhelming and declined. I was dropped from the Doctrine Commission, and not restored to the Liturgical Commission, but was nominated for the Council for Christian Unity – and that did strike me as a charter to be useful. The CCU in turn sent me as their representative to the Committee for Black Anglican Concerns (CBAC), where Wilfred Wood had just been succeeded by John Sentamu as chair. It was a chance to conserve some of my Birmingham inner-city experience. In 1995 I served on the Revision Committee for alternative eucharistic prayers – only to see a good job destroyed by the new Synod in early 1996.

In October 1995, still an incumbent, I was again elected sixth out of six among the southern suffragans, and this time was elected by the Synod to CCU. I had recommended that the House of Bishops should have their own representative on CBAC (now being renamed the Committee for Minority Ethnic Anglican Concerns, CMEAC), and the House duly nominated me for it. Bishops were asked to volunteer to chair liturgical Revision Committees, as *Common Worship* drafts would be coming. I duly volunteered – but the Initiation Services Revision Committee to which I had already been appointed (as an ordinary member) ran for almost the whole of that quinquennium, and that *may* have accounted for why I was not asked to chair another one.

In 1996 Roy Williamson, having followed the new consultative process, invited me to become Bishop of Woolwich, and I gratefully completed my stipendiary time back as a working bishop. In 2000 I again ran for election by the southern suffragans. Being now 66, I stated in my electoral address that, if voters preferred a bright young suffragan, he would probably become a diocesan after two years, whereas I could virtually promise four. I got in now on the first count, and used my seniority to provide some low-key leadership to the suffragans' constituency. I was still a back-bencher in Synod itself and in the House of

Bishops – and, of course, time ran out in July 2004, and I was gone. I had been on the Synod 29 of its 34 years of life.

This outline shows that my memories (and indeed archives) go back before Synod began in 1970. I have followed the historic unfolding and organic development of many issues, several for 40 years and most for over 30; and I now find members (and even officers) of Synod ignorant of its history or misconceiving historical causes and effects. I report chronologically here most of the themes with which I have been closely identified. In two cases – Chapter 2 on 'Open communion' and Chapter 12 on 'The ordination of women' – I was not greatly proactive. But these changes were so significant for the Church of England, and so dependent upon Synod's decisions, that they had to be included. With other themes I have tried to sketch my own theological approach, and have then told the story from my own standpoint. It was inevitable that liturgy feature strongly, and so Chapter 3 on 'The Liturgical Commission and liturgy in Synod' provides an unfolding backdrop to Chapters 4–7, four chapters on liturgical subjects. However, the issue of children in communion, the theme of Chapter 5, has not in England been entrusted to liturgists. Apart from that one needed backdrop, most chapters have a 'stand-alone' character and can be read in any order – and cross-referencing using the index to General Synods and the timeline in Appendix B enables readers to relate one theme to another. In the course of it all, I have mentioned many people by name.[5] In almost every case, I have viewed them with affection and as colleagues, even if I disagreed profoundly with them. I would not want disputes over issues and policies to be read as personal attacks – no, I report a Christian Synod.[6]

I would also not want any reader, friend, or latterday member of Synod to misunderstand my participation. There have been great debates not reported here. The debate that stamped itself into memories was on nuclear weaponry in 1983.[7] I have kept my powder dry when I have trusted the main speakers. I may not have spoken, but I have not ducked big issues. I have been there, been voting, and usually been reporting to my constituency. One such instance came when in 1973 a young tutor, Oliver O'Donovan, began the Grove Ethics booklets with *The Christian and the Unborn Child*, confronting the still recent 1967 Abortion Act. In 1974, bolstered by his writing, I moved an amendment to strengthen a synodical motion about tightening the Act. But my major endeavours for a just society have lain in promoting multi-ethnicity, and in advocating proportional representation by STV.[8] My proactive role in Synod has been more often that of seeking a more biblical stance for the Church of England itself.*

---

* One tiny initiative on which I originally drafted an account in an extended appendix in this book has been dropped to save space. I questioned Archbishops in 1974 and 1980 as to when they would follow the call of the 1968 Lambeth Conference and ensure we denied 'My Lord' and 'Your Grace' further currency. Their replies were not unequivocal. There is much else in the episcopal subculture which needs pruning.

Finally, I must emphasize that the work of ministry goes on in Christian lives, including mine, without being swamped by Synod. I, a synodical enthusiast, yet had over 97 per cent of my working days spent elsewhere! Ministering as a bishop in two major inner-city, multi-ethnic, relatively deprived contexts, I have not only organized, pastored and evangelized, but have frequently been at the interface of church and community.[9] This began with the Handsworth riots and their outcome in 1985; it ran through to my Woolwich days, to such activities as supporting Drop the Debt, confronting the Church Commissioners about their policy for rents on the Octavia Hill Estate in Walworth, picketing a British National Party (BNP) march in Bermondsey, backing the campaign for a directly elected mayor in Lewisham, and identifying with the Residents Association of the Ferrier Estate in opposing Greenwich Council's plans for the regeneration of their estate. The path led, via bringing Desmond Tutu to Birmingham, to arriving in South London in the wake of the Stephen Lawrence murder in Eltham. I have been an unprominent member of the Urban Bishops' Panel as they have set in motion the national Commission on Urban Life and Faith which has, as this goes to press, just published its far-reaching report, *Faithful Cities*. I would hate anyone to think that my church concerns in Synod, occasionally 'niche' concerns, had blinded me to the needs of a Christian witness in our secular society.[10] As you read on, please do not misunderstand my priorities.

Oh yes, and remember I am not telling it the way it was. No one on earth can do that. I am telling it the way I have found it.

1

The Synod

It . . . seemed good to the Holy Spirit and to us.

(Acts 15.28)

No, not just a talking shop, and certainly not much like Parliament – could it be a Christian assembly?

On 4 November 1970 I marched in procession into Westminster Abbey at the inaugural Communion service of the General Synod. Technically, I was an elected proctor in the Lower House of the Convocation of York. This, however, made me in reality a member of the Clergy of the General Synod on the day of its formation. The Queen was present, and at the end of the service her Lord High Chancellor, Lord Hailsham, a member of Ted Heath's cabinet, trumpeted Her Majesty's writs to convene the Clergy Convocations.[1] She herself made a formal Declaration that we were now joined with the House of Laity in the General Synod of the Church of England. So we adjourned for lunch, and duly met in the Assembly Hall of Church House, still, if my memory serves me, clad in formal academic dress. The Synod was inaugurated by the Queen and the Archbishop of Canterbury, Michael Ramsey, doing a measured pas de deux round each other on the platform, not leaving it entirely clear, at least to an innocent observer, which was host and which was guest.[2] So I was launched upon my 29 years as a member of that Synod. I became deeply engaged right from the start, always with a sense of responsibility in having been elected, always valuing the privilege of being there. If I had regularly to groan at the frequent blindness of majorities who, despite my helpful interventions, continued in perverse policies, I also learned quickly to lick any wounds and come back for more. For the truth is, I loved it – and revelled in Christian vision-forming, and argument on the way.

The origins of Synod

How did the General Synod of the Church of England come about in the first place? Well, in a nutshell, a Church with a national organization needs to govern itself. Until 1920 the Church of England was in effect a semi-detached department of state, and its sole governing body was Parliament. Yet from the early nineteenth century, as the Church of England found a positive identity distinct from being merely the citizenry of England, the inappropriateness of Parliament as the source and guardian of Church legislation had become very clear.[3] The Convocations of the Clergy, which had in effect been paralysed since 1717, were revived in 1852 (Canterbury) and 1861 (York) and these representative bodies could approach the government with requests, but had little power to make their own policies effective. Serious decision-taking needed a way to bring together bishops, clergy and laity to form a single body with the requisite powers.

That major change came in 1920. The Church Assembly, composed of the Convocations (with a reformed membership) and a House of Laity, received powers to devise Church legislation.[4] Parliament would still legislate, for the change was to be an amelioration *within* the establishment, not a change *from* it. But Church laws were now 'Measures' – and they were to be drafted and revised within the Assembly, and finally approved by Parliament by a single reading in Lords and Commons. Parliament could not amend Measures, only accept or reject them in their entirety. Indeed, within a few years the House of Lords flexed its muscles and vetoed the formation of a Diocese of Shrewsbury, and in 1927–8 the House of Commons twice vetoed a new Prayer Book. But on the whole the leaders of the Church reckoned they had a good solution – the Assembly had a representative character and real power to create Church legislation by its own processes of drafting and revising.

Within the Assembly, however, a restiveness arose in the House of Laity. The Convocations retained a large privilege in relation to doctrine, and sole power of passing Canons, that is, the internal rules of the Church of England (these go via the Home Office to the monarch for the Royal Assent prior to being 'promulged'). Further, as the Convocations and the House of Laity often met separately, legislative and other business often came last to the Laity. In the 1950s they fought their way into being consulted about revision of the Canons, and they then got into the provisions of the Canons actual powers for their House (and for parochial church councils) in the authorization of alternative services. Nevertheless, they were still handicapped, as, when liturgical revision began (from May 1966 onwards), the Convocations could make textual changes at will, and then send services on for approval by the Laity as a final stage. If the Laity then wanted further changes, they had to go back to the Convocations asking them to accept the changes and return the texts again. Trouble was reduced by informal conferencing together (the best example came in April 1967[5]), but a single Synod, somewhat smaller in size, with the three Houses, Bishops, Clergy and Laity, sitting and debating together and holding powers jointly, was the screaming need. Synodical government was being negotiated from the early 1960s, and the Synodical Government Measure 1969 finally brought the General Synod into being.

Realities of Synod

In the Synod which I joined in 1970 the Bishops had 43 members (suffragans and Europe came later); the Clergy 250+ (43 *ex officio* archdeacons, and 15 deans and provosts elected among themselves, and 192 elected by the licensed clergy of their dioceses); and the Laity 250+ (all elected). Wonderfully, elections were done by the Single Transferable Vote (STV), and thus the voters broadly got what they wanted – you can't 'beat' STV.[6] The age of the House of Clergy was coming down – and, as younger clergy arrived, there was a visible group of undefensive evangelical clergy elected amongst them. The House of Laity on the other hand had much in common with the pre-synodical House of Laity in Church Assembly, but that previous experience had given a certain anti-clericalism to their debates, and they had now to forget that adversarial role of redressing the follies of the Clergy.* There was extra needle in it, because the House of Laity had gained energetic and able evangelicals in 1960 and 1965, whereas the Convocations were dominated by an old-fashioned catholicism. But from 1970 we were all going to be together three times a year for five years, and had to learn how to learn from each other.

Newly elected members of Synod face a sharp learning curve. They can come without experience in 'lower' Synods, or having never seen a chasuble, or astonished that any parish does not have a weekly parish Communion. They can come assuming that their music (be it Merbecke, Taizé, A & M or *Mission Praise*) is *the* Anglican music. They can come used to parish budgets in six figures – or to those with barely five. They can come from the countryside or the inner city. They have to discover the rest of the Church of England in the microcosm which has been elected.

Members do learn and shake down together, and a five-year term (hereafter called a quinquennium) is a fair period for action to happen. Good management has always needed an eye to the calendar to get important decisions taken within the life of one Synod. For example, the decision in February 1976 to provide an Alternative Service Book dictated a slightly crammed timetable: all the ASB services had to get final approval in November 1979 for the ASB to be published in 1980, beyond any chance of a Synod elected in autumn 1980 blocking it. Thus it would not figure in 1980 election manifestos.[7] In passing, I find it extraordinary to contemplate governing bodies, such as the Methodist Conference or the General Assembly of the Church of Scotland, which meet

---

* Quite apart from liturgical matters, note the frustration recorded on page 107.

annually, *with a largely new membership each time they meet.* Getting accustomed to speaking in a large assembly in order to change minds takes time. People who come only once are unlikely to be sufficiently *au fait* with the conventions or sufficiently confident to speak compellingly in their brief time. Thus the platform (and not least the 'civil servants') has an improperly powerful position in such assemblies. In our case, the five-year span and the three (sometimes two) meetings per annum have usually meant that big decisions are rarely put to the first gathering of a newly elected Synod.

I press this further. Even a five-year period has limitations. This book is intended to portray the longer term – the organic development over decades of policies and action. I seek to provide a 40-year memory to those who themselves have only a five-year or ten-year one. This can apply to the officers of Synod as well as the members.

How Synod differs from Parliament

Shaking down together does not mean that people have to agree with each other, or that they have to lose or lessen their convictions. They are there to debate; and Synod gives the engaging chance that, each time you stand, you might change *one* mind. What a contrast with Parliament – I always found it reassuring to visit the Commons gallery. Rarely does anyone speaking there expect to change anyone else's mind – and because members neither expect nor desire to have their minds changed, they have no need to listen to each other – so the small percentage of the House who wish to speak sit around and wait their turn, the big guns reappear near voting time, and members troop through the lobbies, uninformed, as the whips desire them to. The occasional mild dissent can be expressed by absence (perhaps through 'pairing'), and only the keenest observer would spot it; the rare major desertion to the opposite lobby by some of the governing party is headline news.

This difference seems to me fundamental. There are no party whips in Synod, no predetermined votes, no buttoned-up results. Minority standpoints, if well based, are always worth taking; sometimes they win the day a year or two later, even if savaged when first presented.* Paul has a word for synods: 'Speaking the truth in love, we must grow up in every way into him who is the head, into Christ' (Ephesians 4.15). We are to tell it the way it is (at least as we see it), to engage with others' arguments, and yet to love each other enough to go on to share with him or her at the Peace in the Eucharist and over coffee after the debate – all that, yes, but we are also to be unsparing of weaknesses in others'

* Chapter 5 below reports a reform which first came before Synod in July 1971, where the side of the angels has only just prevailed in February 2006!

advocacy, of errors in others' logic, of bias in others' judgement. Too many speakers arrive with prepared speeches and insufficiently engage with others' arguments – close engagement is the ideal.* And Synod is arranged with an eye to getting results, not by a majority of one on a snap vote, but via a series of procedures to arrive at the form of action which has the nearest to a consensus behind it, after argumentation is complete.

Although there is no 'government' and 'opposition', yet there is naturally a great advantage lying with the management. Documents backing up policy recommendations are circulated in advance. Major speeches ('from the platform' – whether or not it is a literal 'platform') by hand-picked able advocates introduce resolutions, and the movers of them have a chance to reply also at the end of the debate. Amendments from the floor can usually be resisted by the main speaker if he or she does not want them, and prevailing from the floor against the platform does require some uphill battling. For myself I have really only held the platform once – the drone's brief, though productive, flight.[8] For the rest of my 29 years, while much official business has been acceptable to me, I have always been responding to it, never promoting or moving it. And there has been much which I wished to correct or even defeat, so I have ample experience of trying to resist, delay, amend or deflect the platform on its course – and that is not easy.† I have sometimes introduced myself as an espouser of lost causes – and that represents my strong belief that in Synod you go for God's truth and its current application as you see it, whatever forces are stacked against you. I have, I fear, done worse than espouse lost causes, I have at times helped lose them, and that is a risk to which anyone who speaks with less than perfection is always open. Indeed I have sometimes expressed my support for the ordination of women as the outcome of listening for ten years to those opposed.

Synod also differs from Parliament in its understanding of its decision-taking. With various forms of business (as, e.g., with liturgical forms or with change of relationships with another Church) a two-thirds majority in favour is needed in each of the three Houses; and in almost any business any 25 members on their feet can ask for a count by Houses – and then a motion lost in any one House is lost in the whole Synod.[9] Furthermore, some major items are designated as

* I have occasionally put into a 'request to speak' (a written note delivered before a debate) an indication that I would like to speak late on in order to address earlier arguments – though this ran a risk of someone moving the closure early.

† While I have frequently felt frustrated at this inbuilt advantage of the 'platform', I have tried to accept patiently my regular 'back-bench' role. To be honest, the task my old Adam would love to have done once – but never did – would have been to answer questions. I suffer from the persuasion that 21 years of interactive theological teaching had geared me to giving deft answers to probing supplementaries.

'Article 8' business, which means such an item is sent to the dioceses, and a majority of diocesan synods, voting by Houses themselves, must support that change or it cannot proceed. Other business also may be referred to dioceses by Synod, and, if so, when the business comes back, the diocesan voting figures (often with further motions or other comment attached) lie before the members of Synod when they vote. Diocesan synods may send to Synod motions for the reform or improvement of the Church of England. I have myself moved a motion in my deanery synod, then in diocesan synod, and then moved it (successfully!) in General Synod.[10] I always urge those with grumbles not to write to the papers, but to take a motion to their PCC or deanery synod and gather support for it. This may actually impact the public life of our Church. I submit that, while Synod can occasionally go into a separate orbit of its own, it is organically rooted in its constituents' lives in a way to which the Westminster politicians have no parallel at all.

Synod differs from Parliament not only in its processes but also in accountability.[11] Electors should know how their representatives exercise their trusteeship. Diocesan synods have reports from General Synod, sometimes with questions. Diocesan journals have reports. Synod members sometimes have link-deaneries to which they report. I have always myself sent a letter at intervals to my constituents (initially Southwell clergy, latterly suffragan and assistant bishops of Canterbury province). Such reporting – like this book – has not been a detached account of Synod's business, but has outlined what I have personally been doing, sometimes including the purblindness of the platform, or the gullibility of the members, as I perceived them. In my 14 years in the House of Bishops, I was also each year at three separate meetings of that House apart from full Synod. Suffragans receive the papers of the House, so would know what decisions had been taken, whereas I sent a more personal missive, not only reporting my own synodical infighting, but also sometimes seeking to discover their mind on particular issues.[12]

The House of Bishops

There has been a suggestion that the Bishops fix a 'line' (like parliamentary whips), and then stick to it against all comers. That would be hard to demonstrate – Chapter 8 below shows how, in relation to the original Anglican–Methodist Scheme, General Synod began its life with bishops in locked-horns struggles over the Scheme. Bishops often disagreed with each other in public thereafter – most notably, of course, as Chapter 12 shows, about the ordination of women. It is a pleasure to report that, in my own 14 years in the House, I recall no occasion on which I had to be other than I am. Certainly, a bishop taking a minority line was morally bound to warn the House. On one famous occasion the House agreed to stick to a procedure, of which I had some doubts, but reckoned that a common front was the best approach.[13] On another occasion some bishops opposed the House's own business in Synod, without having warned their colleagues when the business was before the House.[14] Arguably, in the early years the Bishops generally were not sufficiently concerned with the Synod's business, and at later stages clues emerged as to why this might be.

In the 1970s we still had large numbers of bishops who had been 'formed' episcopally in the pre-synodical era, and not all welcomed the different procedures of the all-in-one-chamber Synod. Yet two of the leading senior ones, the bishop who ordained me, Gerald Ellison, and the last pre-synodical bishop to survive in office in the synodical era, David Say, actually gave themselves to the processes very well.[15] In later years, I reckoned I could detect a different distinction to be drawn between two sets of bishops. One set had in earlier life run for election to the House of Clergy, and thus valued their place on Synod, even though now there ex officio. The other set had never been near Synod before, but were now parachuted in as diocesan bishops. This latter set might well consider Synod a burden, with processes designed to inhibit rather than facilitate their tasks. Suffragan bishops were first seated in the House in 1975, are elected by their fellow-suffragans and value their opportunity highly.*

In my House of Clergy days, I occasionally called for a count to check a quorum in the House of Bishops. I did not do this randomly (yet it was tempting when few bishops were visible – and always caused merriment as the cry went round the tea rooms and bishops scurried in to friendly but taunting jeers). In the 1970s I was deeply involved in liturgical revision – and the House of Bishops provided the text for final approval. It grieved me then (and has often since) to see bishops neither sending in amendments, nor present at debates, but then flexing hostile muscles at penultimate or ultimate stages. So I called for a count of the Bishops when I thought they ought to hear a debate on a subject where they held powers at a later stage. Yet a quorum is only 20 per cent – i.e. nine bishops in 1970–75, and, since the suffragans joined, 11. An awful lot of bishops have been free to neglect Synod business.

The Bishops have a rota to sustain the quorum, though it still sometimes fails. I have tried myself to be present for around 75 per cent of Synod's time, sometimes for more. But the church press – and, yes, the national press – occasionally prints photos of bishops on their Synod bench with their eyes closed. In November 2000 I wrote to *The Times*:

---

* Yet one of those rare occasions of no contest (only three candidates) occurred with York suffragans at the 2000 election. Faces ought to have been red about that.

Sir

I figure in your picture of three bishops at the Church of England General Synod in your issue of 17 November, though I was not myself the one who appears to be fast asleep. I therefore take the opportunity to ask you (as I have previously asked the ecclesiastical press), when publishing such photos, to indicate clearly who was speaking and on what topic at the time. If I am speaking in Synod, I must take responsibility myself for keeping people awake. Correspondingly, if members do sleep, someone else is largely responsible – and, I submit, the guilty need naming. Oh yes, and bishops have no escape – we have to remain and sustain a quorum, so even a sleeping member makes a useful contribution to that.

I devised an axiom, 'A sleeping suffragan is better value than an absent diocesan'. And Synod still provides plentiful wordy cures for episcopal insomnia.*

The Archbishops' Council

In the mid-1990s there was a commission, headed by Michael Turnbull, enquiring how the National Institutions of the Church of England might work more efficiently. The prospectus developed that, when a new management structure, centred in the Archbishops' Council, came into being, far-reaching decisions would be taken far more easily. It often sounded as though Synod itself would become impotent – left to do little more than rubber-stamp others' policy decisions. Well, it went through, and the Archbishops' Council started life in January 1998.[16] My impression is that the Archbishops and others with experience of the old Standing Committee have found life slightly easier in the new system, and, if so, I am glad for them. My own experience was that it made very little difference to the powers and dynamics of Synod; and that was a relief. There is much greater threat in the reduction of numbers, which cut the total from a maximum of 581 to a maximum of 486 in October 2005; in the reduction from three meetings to two in the year; and in the constant cutting down on the length of speeches from the floor, by decision on the day if not by altering Standing Orders (though, to be fair, there is currently some cutting of the platform speeches too).

A word too on finance. Diocesan treasurers have always been cost-conscious in my experience. It is easy for dioceses to view 'central' spending as a whole as

---

* A happy opportunity came in February 2004, when, in a Synod emptied after some momentous debate, I raised a point of order that I think had no precedent: 'Mr Chairman, can you check whether there is quorum in *any* of the three Houses of this Synod?'

something of a luxury in comparison to their diocesan necessities, and thus seek to cut it. I have three hesitations:

1. It is diocesan treasurers themselves who most usually view central spending as excessive. But General Synod budgeting comes after consultation with exactly those persons as a group – and I suspect that bringing them together produces a corporate negativity which is bigger than the sum of its parts.

2. Dioceses make central contributions of around 3 per cent of their budgets (probably 80 per cent goes on stipends); and, if half of that 3 per cent is earmarked for ordination and equivalent training, which no one wants to cut, then only the other half is open to serious negotiation. So in any one year if that half is reduced by, say, 10 per cent, then the saving is 0.15 per cent of the diocesan outgoings, or £1,500 in each £1 million. And that is frankly peanuts. Yes, strict scrutiny is needed, and no feather-bedding, but dioceses should be willing to pay what Synod costs to run, and underwrite the service the central secretariat gives to the Church of England.

3. Dioceses need to evaluate very carefully what Synod gives them, and, if dissatisfied, not call for reductions 'across the board', but identify the points of supposed waste.

The finance factor gives me the opportunity to plug the real need for the dioceses to engage closely with Synod. The representatives on General Synod must not only sustain contact with their constituencies, but must bring them into 'shadowing' the work of Synod, picketing it with diocesan motions, instigating the questions asked by their representatives, and making the 'centre' as accountable to the Church at large as possible.

But what has it been like?

Remember, I have been a back-bencher. I have never even seen the agenda or the minutes of a Standing Committee or an Archbishops' Council meeting. I have had the privilege of being in the House of Bishops, but, as in Synod itself for all but one item in 1978-9, I have never introduced official business; in synodical chess I have only played black to careful gambits by white – and that limits one's freedom. I have tried in Appendix A to portray some characters to illuminate the pages where they come into the story which I tell; but I offer here some more random recollections as glimpses of the Synod in action.

Michael Ramsey was an unsynodical figure. (Christopher Wansey, a strong disestablishment man, was his cousin and would refer in Synod to 'Cousin Michael', usually, I think, to the great man's embarrassment.) I have a happy memory of Ramsey in the chair of Canterbury Convocation when Christopher Wansey tried to move an amendment to the Ten Commandments. 'No,' said Ramsey. 'God gave them to Moses and we cannot amend them.'[17]

When Synod began, I believe, the original division of the Standing Committee into three subcommittees (policy, business and appointments) was engineered so as to give Michael Ramsey, in his inalienable role as chair of the full Committee, as little as possible to do. On one occasion the chair of Synod called on him to move the adoption of the report on the agenda; the Archbishop was slumbering; his chaplain prodded him and said something like, 'You're on, Archbishop'; and he bumbled to the rostrum and said: 'Er, I move whatever it is I am supposed to move.'

The Synod loved him. When we first went to York in July 1971, I sat up in the raked seats and there below me was Michael Ramsey on the bench at floor level, presumably sitting where someone had arranged for him, but at a right angle to the platform and actually out of sight of even the corner of the chairman's eye. I said to my neighbour, 'I think we may yet see the Archbishop fail to get called' – and that is exactly what happened: he stood in his seat at the right moment, and the chairman never saw him. After the next speech he had to lean forward and wave to get attention, and then he was graciously called. It was also said that, when we shared communion in Heslington Church, in those early days the greeting of peace went from one to another in what the liturgists called the daisy-chain effect. It went round the church and the last person in the front row stepped forward to greet the Archbishop, only to be met by a firm declining of the proferred hand, 'It's *been* here.'

And time would fail me to tell of Canon Bryan, who, resisting the diocesanization of glebe, told us how he had in the past ploughed his own glebe; of Ronald Jasper, chairman of the Liturgical Commission, who one day told the Synod (without consulting any of the Commission) that if the Synod took some stated course of action (or inaction), 'The whole Commission will resign', and the Commission members in Synod stared at each other in wild surmise, lest his threat be welcomed as a promise; of the man behind me who, when the House of Bishops blocked something everybody else wanted, was on his feet shouting, 'Resign! resign!'; of Michael Baughen (when still in London) chanting to Anglican chant 'I am so happy' and 'I am so miserable' to demonstrate the identical timbre of each when so chanted; of Peter Dawes, when on ACCM and trying to pin the closure of Brasted pre-Theological College on the House of Bishops, first of all moving the reduction of ACCM's own budget by £1 – as a penalty for giving the House of Bishops inadequate advice –

and secondly waving a £1 note (which shows how long ago it was) to make good the shortfall himself; of David Smith, the Bishop of Bradford, in the debate to add 'and Leeds' to the title of the Diocese of Ripon, expressing an intention of changing his own diocese to 'Bradford and Bingley'; of the resemblances between secretary-generals and Sir Humphrey; and yet, as with that list in the Epistle to the Hebrews, these were they who made policies, persuaded doubters, defeated amendments, declined alternatives and brought results.

Perhaps future generations, surrounded by so great a cloud of witnesses, will run the synodical race set before them with equal celerity.

Some changes for the future

I have not settled for Synod-as-it-is, and thus disengaged my critical faculties. But I go strongly with the large canvas of Synod (bar my final point on the next page), and offer only narrow-focus suggestions for internal change. My final tintacks about the future of the slimmed-down Synod are three. Firstly, I grieve at the cut of numbers of elected suffragans in Canterbury province from 6 to 4. I would, wouldn't I? There was an 'unkindest cut', for in 1999 it was proposed to give the Bishop of Dover an ex officio place in the Bishops, as the *de facto* diocesan of Canterbury. In the minimal debate we had, I said I feared that further down the line his presence in the Bishops would be an argument for squeezing the number of elected suffragans. In the event, when reductions were first proposed, the Dover point was not made – and in July 2001 I carried in Synod an amendment to retain six elected southern suffragans.* But when the proposals to reduce them still came to Synod from the Revision Committee, I was doubly frustrated, for I had funerals (one a clergy wife, one a rural dean) at exactly the moment these proposals came to Synod for debate and decision in February 2003 and 2004. In each case I missed just one hour, and that one hour deprived me of participating and trying to retrieve the losses. I never missed Synod time for funerals at any other point in my life.

Secondly, I think an STV way of choosing Private Member's Motions is desperately needed (the present system is, in effect, the corrupt 'multiple Xs').

And, thirdly, I would like to see the Diocese in Europe severed from the Church

* The unkindest cut was that it was the Bishop of Dover himself, one Stephen Venner whom I highly respect in his own person, who chaired the Steering Committee and, safe in his own *ex officio* seat which I reckoned I had given him, administered the *coup de grâce* on such as me – and not only reduced the elected suffragans to 7 in total, but, incomprehensibly, divided them as 4 in the south and 3 in the north, when there are 50+ electors in the south and 20+ in the north. Even a 5–2 split would leave it easier to be elected in the north than in the south – but probably the answer is to make the whole country one constituency.

of England and united in a lightweight province with other Anglicans on the continent. We could (and should) give it a dowry; we might well be able to offer it other continuing services and links; but we would cease to pretend it was somehow 'in' England, would leave it out of our 'national' Church governing body, and would free ourselves of all the exceptions which it has driven into our synodical (and establishment!) rules.[18]

But, those slight reforms noted, on the larger canvas we need to escape the last grasp which a godless Parliament and a Prime Minister who happens to lead the largest party in the House of Commons still have upon us.[19]

A rationale for the Synod and for a one-nation unit of Church government

What can be said for a Synod theologically?[20] In the simplest terms the Church of God is, under God, to be self-governing, self-regulating, self-directing. There are scriptural precedents not only in the Council of Jerusalem (Acts 15), but in the ways in which St Paul expects local churches to organize their own lives, including dealing with error. In the whole of 1 Corinthians, there are no clergy or named leaders responsible for sifting through his letter and then implementing it – no, the whole church is expected to take action as an entity. The members are not free to act on whims, for they are to recognize God speaking to them in the letter – and so God's word is to impact them corporately. We find within the New Testament the beginnings of a 'connexionalist' Church – where local congregations so belong to each other that they make common decisions for the common good, and make local decisions with an eye to each other. Obviously, the Council of Jerusalem reckoned it was proclaiming a worldwide gospel to unite Jews and Gentiles. But even in Corinth, if there is a church in the port of Cenchrea (Romans 16.1) and a church in Priscilla and Aquila's home (Romans 16.5), then action taken (as, e.g., about sexual misbehaviour or litigiousness or even the conduct of the assembly) would involve some 'central' corporate decision, and presumably consistent local application. Paul also bids them make a collection for the 'saints in Jerusalem', and in 2 Corinthians he cites to the Corinthians the Macedonians' response to the same call. So there is an inter-city, catholic, purview to their decision taking. If we put this into legal or 'canonical' terms, we are very near to a constitutional linkage between congregations with an overseeing 'governing body'. In broad terms this is 'connexionalism'.[21] Ministers with oversight of more than one congregation are regularly known as bishops, and their decision-taking councils are synods.[22]

The origin of diocesan bishops is not very clear. There may be some seminal biblical evidence in the role of Titus in Crete (Titus 1.5) – a sub-apostolic person in a semi-settled quasi-episcopal role. But, at any rate, when the Church of the early centuries addressed a heresy, it was the bishops from across the world who constituted an Ecumenical (i.e. 'worldwide') Council. Though the statements of the first four Councils defined the doctrines of the Trinity and Incarnation, Anglicans believe neither bishops nor Councils to be infallible. Firstly, those early bishops only got it right after much buffeting from 'the floor'. We must not be starry-eyed about bishops in the Early Church – in the fourth and fifth centuries congregations might shout down an erring bishop.[23] Secondly, the Anglican Reformers retained the credal formulations *not* because they were framed by Councils, *nor* even because they had been believed for over a thousand years, *but* because 'they may be proved by most certain warrants of holy Scripture'.[24]

So much for early Councils. The development of our own synodical pattern has a strong pragmatic element. Henry VIII by parliamentary action reformed the Church in his nation, became head on earth of *ecclesia anglicana*, and laid the groundwork for Article XXXIV in 1571 to state, 'Every particular or national Church hath authority to ordain, change, and abolish, ceremonies or rites of the Church ordained only by man's authority'. There could be no variation from parish to parish (across the parishes, 'uniformity' had to reign), but the highest level of decision-taking (previously the Pope) would now be the sovereign nation. In the event, Henry was providing for a governable unit embodying the connexionalist character of the Church of England, but with limits on it. The changes of the nineteenth and twentieth centuries, shedding Ireland and Wales, and slowly providing for representative Bishops, Clergy and Laity together to take responsibility for the life of the Church of England, represent an appropriate, if not always smooth, evolution from Tudor times.

The Bible gives no particular sanction to the political nation as the appropriate decision-taking unit for ecclesiastical government. Arguably the New Testament identifies both indvidual congregations and the worldwide Church as the body of Christ, with perhaps a hint of embryonic dioceses. So can a connexionalist church properly function on a limited *national* basis? My own answer, partly pragmatic, is 'yes'.

First, such a church is manageable. The travel and communication needed since 1970 to administer the Church of England centrally, and to handle relationships of the centre with the dioceses, have been relatively easily accomplished. We are used to it and it may seem obvious – but the only real model of a single worldwide autonomous church, viz. the Church of Rome, 'manages' by a top-down process which is contrary (I hope) to our ecclesiology and not very credible in its own workings. If a system is not to be taken over by its own officers, then Synod members need to be able to oversee them and call them to account.

Secondly, such a church enables true lay participation. It is reasonable to expect *some* lay persons to be active in their parishes, dioceses and General Synod. Such a participation stretches those who can manage it – for being 'active' involves not just attending meetings of one's synods, but also taking part in committees and ingesting quantities of often uninviting literature. No doubt the laity elected to General Synod are not 'typical' Anglican lay people – for, if typical, they would, I fear, be limited in their commitment, passive in their energies, and complacently ignorant in their theology. Those who seek election are bound to have both energies and some goals (or at least desires) for the future of the Church of England – and are elected for those reasons. Lay people do exist who can credibly take a live part in three 'tiers' of Church government, whereas a fourth (e.g. in Rome!) might well be impossible.*

Thirdly, such a church can function with one system of law (and currency). There are some untidy edges to the Church of England's boundaries – a separate diocese in the Isle of Man, part of a diocese in the Channel Islands, and an almost alien institution in the diocese in Europe.[25] With those exceptions, the Church of England has developed a standard expertise for living with the laws of the land, including charitable financial provisions, employment law, building regulations, etc.

Fourthly, it can address its own nation. When the Synod, or the Bishops, or other central bodies call upon the government to do, or not to do, something which is in prospect, they do so speaking as Christians of England with a clear stake in what our government decides. This speaking from within a nation to the leaders of the nation has been vital to Anglicans in other parts of the world (think of Tutu addressing Botha and Gitari addressing Daniel Arap Moi) – it is not an establishment point; it is more a prophetic one.[26]

Fifthly, it gives realistic goals for ecumenism. Other denominations have come up with a similar answer to ours (though the 'four nations in one United Kingdom' – plus Eire – has set ecumenical agencies some difficult problems). It

---

* If I am right about this, then it is not surprising that two other vague internal contenders to be units of church organization – the deanery and the province – are non-starters in terms of energies. As there are virtually no finances belonging to them, they also lack any pretence at real powers, and that is just as well. The Convocations have a shadowy continued existence. When I was first elected to the Lower House of the Convocation of York, we were still summoned to York twice a year (and indeed met from 2 till 4 on one afternoon, then from 10 till 12 the next morning, thus writing off over 24 hours of our time for a minimum of conferring). We robed in our Convocation dress; we marched through the streets of York; we had a Latin litany; and almost our sole business was our own standing orders (like debating when to meet or whether to use Latin). I do not recall us ever addressing anything useful, except for electing a prolocutor (who joined the Standing Committee) once every five years – until the first time we had a 'special reference' to us of an item coming for Final Approval (see p. 91 below). And that was in London during Synod time.

is thus in principle going with the grain to talk with the Methodists about union. Quite apart from doctrinal issues, it would be structurally much less easy with the Roman Catholics, whose only decision-making unit is the worldwide Church – in and through its Pope.

Anglicans are left with the question of international relationships, and they have been proving tricky. A church with the same boundaries as its nation is in danger of falling for the national culture, conventions and customs as being 'givens', even as revealed from heaven, without any questioning. For us the historic establishment of the Church of England has reinforced a sense that English institutions and our 'way of life' are in fact God-given. Certainly, our own adapting to them can invoke incarnational theology as justification. But the caution is that, though we are not free of the state as the 37 other Churches of the Anglican Communion are, there must be a constant vigilance, a recollection that the gospel may well be counter-cultural, and that the people of God may need to prophesy to their nation. We ought, of course, to be seeking that freedom for ourselves too.[27] We do need to sit somewhat loosely by our own country's culture, rallying calls and blindspots. The gospel bids us be internationalists far more than nationalists, and a Synod must constantly recall this. There are inevitably limitations for a Church organized on a single-nation basis, and some Anglicans at intervals understandably itch for a supra-national single *locus* of authority for the whole Communion. We rightly lack that, yet certainly need a great sense of international responsibility and readiness for consultation.[28]

2

Open communion

Welcome one another, therefore, just as Christ has welcomed you.

(Romans 15.7)

Once we excommunicated non-conformists; now we don't; here's how we changed.

Who should be admitted to 'our' communion tables? How far must they agree with us, or jump through our hoops? We know the Church of Rome's answer – but what has been the Anglican one? The subject came at the very beginning of the Synod, and I had little active involvement in it. But its outcome underlies a large amount of later ecumenical interchange, for, back in 1971–2, the Church of England was changing its character by synodical action in a far-reaching way, and this change, startling at the time, has been taken for granted ever since.

In the 1662 Prayer Book the confirmation rubric retained the substance of 1552: '*And there shall none be admitted to the holy Communion, until such time as he be confirmed, or be ready and desirous to be confirmed.*' In 1552 there had been no exceptive clause, but a requirement that '*he can say the Catechism and be confirmed*'. The differing forms expressed the Reformers' desire that young people should have some understanding of the Christian life before admission to communion. The requirement of confirmation was a rule-of-thumb way of measuring that people were prepared. However, the conventional practice for centuries was that people should be mature (the 1604 Canons indicated 13 to 15 years old) and be instructed – higher considerations than the availability of confirmation. The confirmation rubric was for the Church of England, and 1662 viewed the whole country as 'C/E' – dissent was nowhere anticipated in the text, so excluding dissenters was not in view. After 1662 dissenters were not even 'desirous' of being confirmed, but some would receive communion in the parish church for the sake of unity.[1] After the Test Act of 1673, some received communion in the Church on an occasional basis *in order to qualify for public office*. In Queen Anne's reign, the Occasional

Conformity Act of 1711 was introduced to halt that practice – but it did not forbid communion to the unconfirmed, nor disqualify from office such communicants. No, it forbade them *to return to their conventicles* on pain of disqualification for office and being fined. All this could have been avoided if the confirmation rubric had been read literally and the unconfirmed disqualified in the first place.

There were also Anglicans who were 'desirous' but not confirmed. The 'desirous' category probably arose in 1662, because for two decades few had been confirmed, and the bishops had to catch up with ministering confirmation. So the parish clergy could admit to communion those who were 'ready'. This became a norm in some places – confirmation was unknown in America until 1784. No Bishop of Winchester visited the Channel Islands for over a century and a half after 1662. And some bishops did not visit their dioceses anyway – for, apart from difficulties in travel, because bishops could not retire, at any one time several would be fairly incapacitated. The availability of confirmation in any borough was often problematical.[2]

In the nineteenth century two interdependent major changes occurred, one doctrinal, one logistical. Doctrinally, the rise of Anglo-Catholicism from 1833 onwards distanced dissenters further from the Church of England. Logistically, while first-generation Anglo-Catholics did not make much of confirmation, after 1850 confirmation became far more readily available. The coming of the railways was central to this geater accessibility, but also dioceses were divided through Victoria's reign, bishops were able to retire from the 1860s, and suffragans were consecrated from 1870 onwards.

In June 1870 Dean Stanley invited the Revisers of the New Testament for the Revised Version of the Bible to a special Communion service in Westminster Abbey when they began their work. They included a Unitarian and other (orthodox) non-conformists. All received communion together, but in Canterbury Convocation a fortnight later objections were raised about not only the Unitarian but also unconfirmed dissenters – probably the first occasion of such objections. Archbishop Tait, no friend to Anglo-Catholics, distinguished firmly between the two categories in answering a 'memorial' from T. T. Carter on behalf of 1,529 clergy of the Church of England. This mentioned 'teachers of various sects' (sic) and specifically cited the confirmation rubric. Tait stated that he could not understand how a Unitarian could have been invited or taken part. He continued:

> But some of the memorialists are indignant at the admission of any
> Dissenters, however orthodox, to the Holy Communion in our Church.
> I confess that I have no sympathy with such objections. I consider
> that the interpretation which these memorialists put upon the rubric
> to which they appeal, at the end of the Communion Service, is quite
> untenable.[3]

Thereafter Anglo-Catholics were committed to standing with the memorial,
and, as Puller and Mason started to up the doctrine of confirmation in
subsequent years, so the rightness of excluding the unconfirmed from
communion was reinforced. Memories of pre-1870 custom died almost
overnight. The reverse implication also attained currency – Anglicans should
receive communion only from episcopally ordained clergy.[4]

One very sharp contention grew from this new stance. In 1913 a missionary
ecumenical conference was held at Kikuyu in Kenya, chaired by J. J. Willis, the
Anglican Bishop of Uganda. W. G. Peel, the Bishop of Mombasa (Kenya), also
took part. It ended with communion in a Presbyterian church building; it was,
however, a Prayer Book service with Bishop Peel presiding, and all (except
Quakers) receiving communion. Frank Weston, Bishop of Zanzibar, whose
Anglo-Catholic principles were deeply offended, delated the Anglican bishops
for heresy and schism to the Archbishop of Canterbury, Randall Davidson, their
metropolitan. Weston was totally confident that only the confirmed could be
administered communion. Davidson had been Tait's chaplain and biographer,
and had little sympathy with Weston's charge that such hospitality was
'propagating heresy and committing schism'. He referred it to the Consultative
Body of the Lambeth Conference. This met in July 1914, but published no
findings as World War I started. Finally, Davidson published them himself, with
his own lengthy memorandum, in spring 1915. Neither the Consultative Body
nor Davidson disapproved of the 'open' communion (knowing there was ample
precedent), but they advised Anglicans to refrain in the future.* Anglican
leadership was accepting that the norm was exclusion.

It ran and ran. The general Anglican view till around 1960 was that the
unconfirmed should not communicate at our services, and we should not at
non-episcopal services.[5] Thus at the 1958 Lambeth Conference, the report on
Church Unity and the Church Universal said, about relationships with
Presbyterians:

---

* The findings were pithily summarized by a wit: 'The event at Kikuyu was eminently pleasing to
God, and must on no account be repeated.'

It must, however, be recognized as a fact that Anglicans conscientiously hold that the celebrant of the Eucharist should have been ordained by a bishop standing in the historic succession, and generally believe it their duty to bear witness to this principle by receiving Holy Communion only from those who have been thus ordained.*

I discovered in the 1950s that only the doughtiest evangelicals showed any knowledge of history. Church Society circulated to parishes bold placards: 'In accordance with the historic practice of the Church of England, we welcome communicant members of other Churches to join us at the Lord's Table.'[6] But such parishes were exceptional – and were resented. The placards provoked a delation, as 50 members of the Lower House of Canterbury in October 1966 presented a *gravamen* to the Upper House, asking (as the *reformandum*) that the Bishops would censure the Declaration as 'not consonant with the doctrine and discipline of the Church of England'.[7] This indicates both the Anglo-Catholic weighting in the Convocation and the lack of corporate memory. I was in the gallery, aghast; but no action ever resulted.

In the 1950s, the Church Assembly concentrated on Canon Law revision, to which Geoffrey Fisher had devoted his archiepiscopate (1945–61). The Canon Law Commission had reported in 1947.[8] In their draft Code, Canon 21 ('Of the Holy Communion') reproduced the confirmation rubric: '2. No person shall be admitted to the Holy Communion until such time as he be confirmed, or be ready and desirous to be confirmed.'

The Church Assembly processed draft Canons as a very thorough, long-running, mincing-machine. By 1958 this provision about admission to communion came in a later Canon ('On the Receiving of Holy Communion'), along with an exceptive clause, to admit 'an individual baptized communicant member of a Church not in communion with the Church of England to meet occasional or pastoral needs, or the admission of a baptized person in danger of death'.

Despairing at this mincing process, in 1961 32 notable Anglican theologians addressed an open letter to the archbishops, calling for a principled practice of intercommunion with Churches with which we were addressing reunion. This gained considerable publicity, and opened the question in the country, but

* *The 1958 Lambeth Conference Report* 2.44. This section was chaired by Falkner Allison, then Bishop of Chelmsford, but earlier (1945–50) principal of Ridley Hall. I asked him in later years how he had agreed such a sweeping statement, asserting such a questionable common conscience of *all* Anglicans. He replied, 'We only said "some Anglicans".' Not having the text to hand, I shrugged, letting his faulty memory stand with his faulty theology. In fairness, the paragraph allowed that admitting Presbyterians to Anglican Eucharists would not be as cataclysmic as would Anglicans attending Presbyterian ones.

hardly affected the inching of the draft Canon through the Assembly. Broadly, the Convocations wanted to keep exceptions down to a minimum, while the House of Laity not only wanted the exceptions wide and welcoming, but also wanted the admission of guests entrenched as a normative principle. But the initiative (and, until the coming of General Synod, the ultimate powers) lay with the Convocations. By spring 1964 the draft Canon B 15 ('Of the Receiving of Holy Communion') which was sent by them to the House of Laity included a section 4:[9]

> Nothing in these Canons shall be deemed to forbid the admission to the Holy Communion at the discretion of the Minister
>
> (a)   of a baptized person in instant danger of death, or
>
> (b)   subject to the general direction of the Bishop of an individual baptized communicant member of a Church not in communion with the Church of England, to meet occasional and particular pastoral needs.

The Laity's response was so critical that a fresh treatment was needed. When new Convocations had been elected in autumn 1964, there was appointed a joint Archbishops' Commission on Intercommunion, chaired by the Bishop of Bristol, Oliver Tomkins.[10] Its task was: 'To consider the theological and practical aspects of Intercommunion with reference to the relation of the Church of England to other Churches and the making of rules for Admission to Holy Communion under Canon B 15.'

They were meeting now against a background of a prospective Anglican–Methodist 'reconciliation'.[11] The theological argument had changed to whether (on the more 'catholic' theory) sharing communion is a fruit of reunion, or whether (on evangelical views) sharing communion is normal for Christians, and is a means towards reunion. Putting the debate thus went beyond simply saying that the unconfirmed are only half-Christians. The new Commission was weighty and representative in its membership, lengthy in its deliberations, and highly responsible in its 1968 report.[12] Centrally it made recommendations about intercommunion – i.e. about churchly relationships between different confessional families of Christians. In passing, however, it addressed individual participation across denominational frontiers. Paragraph 171 concerned Anglicans receiving communion elsewhere: 'Here the principles which we have set out in paras 159–167 still apply and the individual should feel free to receive communion if his conscience allows and when he knows he is welcome.'[13] This contrasted with the previously prevalent attempts to bind consciences to 'catholic' principles.

On the issue of Anglicans offering hospitality, the report proposed a new draft Canon ('Of the Admission to Holy Communion'); and this, after clauses dealing with Anglicans and members of Churches 'in full communion', went on (Clause 3): 'The General Synod may by regulations provide for welcoming baptized and communicant members of other Churches ... who desire to receive the Holy Communion.'[14]

This was unique among the Canons being drafted in the 1960s, for it was obviously going to run on into the post-1970 days of General Synod – and that was so far recognized that 'General Synod' actually appears in its text in the Clause 3 quoted above. The Convocations initiated the preparation of a Measure,[15] a Canon, and draft regulations to be proposed under the Canon. For the time being, the bland old draft B 15 ('Of the Receiving of Holy Communion') was enacted in 1969 – the confirmed should receive the sacrament regularly and the minister should teach the people so.

In 1968 the Lambeth Conference met in London. The bishops tackled this issue totally differently from their predecessors.[16] Resolution 45 opened the door for non-Anglicans to receive communion in Anglican churches, and Resolution 46, handling Anglicans receiving elsewhere, contained:

> The Conference recommends that ... to meet special pastoral need, such [i.e. Anglican] communicants be free to attend the Eucharist in other Churches holding the apostolic faith as contained in the Scriptures and summarized in the ... Creeds, and as conscience dictates, to receive the sacrament, when they know they are welcome to do so.[17]

This loosened the tightness of 1958. Underneath it, greater weight was being given to baptism as a basis of both unity and admission into communion, and correspondingly less to confirmation.

In 1969 I was working with Graham Leonard, Bishop of Willesden, to combat the 1968 Anglican–Methodist Scheme.[18] After our letters to the Convocations in May and July 1969, the two of us wrote a joint essay for *Theology* in October 1969, 'Intercommunion – Some Interim Agreement'.[19] While we wrote against a background of the conventional expectations of middle-to-high Anglicans (don't forget that *gravamen* of only three years before), we were opening the door much wider than the convention would have required. Our hesitation was not now simply, 'Have the visitors been confirmed?', but rather, 'What kind of ecclesial belonging to us and with us does their wishing to come to communion with us represent?' This was a start, and in *Growing into Union* itself in May 1970, the four of us demonstrated that we viewed water baptism as fundamental to sacramental life, but did not view confirmation as fundamental at all.[20]

So in autumn 1970, General Synod inherited this one unfinished issue in the new Canons. Firstly, the Measure to permit the Canon had received General Approval at the last session of the Church Assembly in July, and it came to Synod for a revision stage that November. After marginal retouching it read as follows:

A MEASURE
PROPOSED TO BE PASSED BY
THE GENERAL SYNOD OF THE CHURCH OF ENGLAND
To provide for admission to the Holy Communion

1. The rubric at the end of the Order of Confirmation in the Book of Common Prayer (which reads 'And there shall none be admitted to the Holy Communion until such time as he be confirmed or be ready and desirous to be confirmed') shall not prevent the General Synod from making provision by Canon and regulations for the admission to the Holy Communion of other baptized persons.

2. This Measure may be cited as the Admission to Holy Communion Measure 197.

During the debate Michael Ramsey cited the centenary of the original 'Revisers' Communion', and both questioned the received legal advice and aligned himself with Archbishop Tait, quoting with approval the extract on page 24 above. The Measure was accepted, and in February 1971 received final approval. It went on to the Ecclesiastical Committee of Parliament, where processes were slow, but they duly found it 'expedient', and it went through both Houses of Parliament in early 1972, and received the Royal Assent on 10 February 1972. This cleared the way for the Canon.

Synod debated the draft Canon in February 1971. Its provisions in Clauses 1 and 2 were for the existing confirmed persons, or those 'ready and desirous', or visitors from any Church in full communion. Clause 3 gave the General Synod power to make regulations about admitting 'other baptized persons', just as the intercommunion report had recommended. So Gerald Ellison, Bishop of Chester, proposed it. But Professor Geoffrey Lampe delivered a coup.* He persuaded the Synod not to accept the draft Canon for Revision, but instead to instruct the Canon Law Commission to provide a new Canon in which guests would be admitted to communion not by secondary 'regulations', but by the primary entrenching in the text of the Canon of 'Baptized and communicant members of other Churches who are in good standing in their own Churches.' This passed

---

* I recall this with enormous pleasure. The Lampe proposal was absolutely right, but it was also the first defeat of the platform in the life of Synod. While it has stuck in my memory, going back to read the *Report of Proceedings* again, for the first time in 30 years, has added to the pleasure.

21–10; 121–93; 159–42. The House of Clergy, it seemed, was not being carried overwhelmingly.

The Canon then came in draft form to the July 1971 Synod. The Canon Law Commission had slipped in, after 'other Churches' in Lampe's proposal, 'which subscribe to the doctrine of the Holy Trinity'; and they had retained the clause, 'any other baptized persons authorized to be admitted under regulations of the General Synod'. Why keep the clause, when it was not needed now for guests? Ah, but a new issue was dawning and the Commission had anticipated it – and Gerald Ellison spelled it out.[21] The vote on General Approval (27–8; 124–81; 165–46) showed a slow gathering towards the Canon.[22] The Revision Committee merely added 'immediate' to the 'danger of death' clause (not discussed here), and Synod had a Revision Stage in November 1971. No amendment was carried; the Canon was complete. It gained the Royal Assent after the Measure, and was promulged on 9 July 1972, the first Canon to emerge from synodical government.

No official proposals ever touched Anglicans receiving communion in other Churches. But in 1970 the corporate atmosphere was changing. Anglicans, at least in General Synod, were learning that there were no rules nor even agreed conventions in this field. Individuals could develop their own practice in accordance with their own theology and convictions. This was wonderfully portrayed for me in autumn 1971, at my first residential Assembly of the BCC, in Scotland. The Kirk hosted a communion service at Dunblane Abbey. Michael Ramsey was sitting two or three rows in front of me. Would he receive communion? And yes, he did. So the liberty of conscience applied even to a fairly 'catholic' Archbishop of Canterbury. The floodgates were open – it would be difficult for Anglicans even to pretend thereafter that they had churchly limits.

I submit that, since B 15 A went through in July 1972, the Church of England has been a different Church with open borders to other Christian Churches. It recognizes baptism alone as the sacrament of initiation. It recognizes the baptism of other Trinitarian Churches as true baptism. And it therefore puts up no denominational barriers which are treated as necessary parts of Christian initiation. The Church of England has breathed a different atmosphere, and appeared to others as a different animal, since that Canon in July 1972. A new backdrop has appeared behind our life, and has affected our understanding of much that happens in front of it.

Internally this Canon set much in train for the Church of England. One obvious issue was the admission of unconfirmed children to communion. Regulations under the Canon have been slow.* But externally the change was enormous.

---

* See Chapter 5 below. My adjective 'obvious' is not borne out by its subsequent history.

From 1972 on all special deals about reciprocal intercommunion became redundant. The Church of England could no longer negotiate careful theological frameworks to provide it – it was already there.[23] We had with a jump reached the end of a road while people were still talking, and the radical practice was already the everyday experience. Areas of Ecumenical Experiment (now Local Ecumenical Partnerships) were just beginning to spread.[24] They could encourage sacramental mixed bathing without having to get exceptive or defensive clauses into their constitutions, or check whether they had episcopal smiles or frowns. And, amusingly, a Commission on Reciprocal Intercommunion, which had arisen in the late stages of the Convocations debating *Intercommunion Today* in 1969 and 1970, produced its thorough report (GS 155) in early 1973 – in the light of history, far too late to be of use. It had an interesting bleat about Anglicans receiving communion in the Free Churches:

> If they [official acts of bodies of Anglicans participating in Free Church communions] happen they must be formally authorized, unless we accept the view that we are already in communion with all other Christian bodies who are willing to receive us ... Such a presupposition in regard to the Free Churches would be a departure from all previous Anglican practice and from the basis on which discussions with these Churches have been entered upon.[25]

Their bleat captures precisely what had happened – a 'departure'; a departure which B 15 A had precipitated, had now undercut all other 'formal authorization'. Synod did debate this report in July 1973 – and even recorded a motion that we approved of Anglicans receiving communion in other Trinitarian Churches, and also approved of Anglicans not doing so. Certainly the Church of England had no rules on its own members receiving communion elsewhere.[26] But in terms of reciprocal agreements the report was a beached whale. B 15 A had so thrown open the ecumenical door that it was ludicrous for a Commission to offer conditions whereby other people might borrow a key to it. There was nothing left to debate. The pre-1972 position has now been forgotten as totally as the pre-1870 one had been. The Church of England is a fundamentally changed institution through the breaking of barriers by Canon B 15 A in 1972.

3

The Liturgical Commission and liturgy in Synod

Return, O Israel, to the Lord . . . Take words with you . . . and say . . .
(Hosea 14.1–2)

The way we worship is the way we believe – so there's plenty of action needed to change it – both behind the scenes on the Commission, and in front of house in Synod (and I've been in the middle of quite a bit of it).

This chapter gives a backdrop to Chapters 4, 6 and 7. The worshipping life of the Church of England, which is how 98 per cent of its adherents actually experience the Church, has changed vastly in half a century. Virtually all such changes originated in the Liturgical Commission and were screened and altered by the General Synod. So some grasp of the Commission's work should help in understanding the role of Synod.

The Liturgical Commission was formed in December 1955 as an Archbishops' Commission (these were pre-synodical days). Archbishop Geoffrey Fisher attended the first meeting and made clear its work was to be allocated by the Archbishops. The chairman until 1960 was Colin Dunlop, Dean of Lincoln.[1] The story of the first ten years – i.e. before the days of the Prayer Book (Alternative and Other Services) Measure 1965 – is told in Ronald Jasper's semi-autobiographical *The Development of Anglican Liturgy 1662–1980*. During that time the Commission published two reports of some substance: *Prayer Book Revision in the Church of England*, a resource for the 1958 Lambeth Conference; and the first liturgical text: *Baptism and Confirmation*.[2] When the latter was attacked in York Convocation, the chairman resigned, and was succeeded by Donald Coggan. He became Archbishop of York soon after; and was supposed to have arranged that the bishops would be consulted, and be broadly in support, before texts were published.

In Donald Coggan's years the Commission addressed minor tasks, such as occasional prayers and thanksgivings. It had a shake-up in membership in 1962 (and three-year periods of appointment began). I arrived myself mid-term in

September 1964, when the Commission was newly addressing a eucharistic order.[3] In 1964, the Assembly passed the Prayer Book (Alternative and Other Services) Measure, and the path to authorization of rites came in sight. The policy was still to delay publishing texts until they could be debated and authorized. But then the Measure went through Parliament in March 1965, and the archbishops named 1 May 1966 for it come into force. Before that, the relevant Canons would be enacted and promulged – and now proposed texts could be published.

The Measure had been tightened over the years and it defined exhaustively which services had 'lawful authority' – i.e. without remainder and without any episcopal say-so. So the 1928 services, widely used on that supposed say-so, themselves needed authorization under the provisions of the Measure and Canons, or would become starkly illegal. Geoffrey Fisher had earlier anticipated a Schedule of Agreed Amendments permitting 1928 variants on 1662; but in 1964 the lawyers advised that the Measure required whole services to be authorized. The Commission was asked to edit the 1928 services (which would have aroused old battles), but we declined, saying 1928 was not our work, and (in effect) we had better things to do. The published *Alternative Services: First Series* said in an unsigned note that they were 'the result of long consideration by the Bishops, and of consultation with some members of the Liturgical Commission'.[4] This latter apparently meant Ronald Jasper himself in great haste.[5] Then, when authorization began in May–June 1966, 1928 confirmation was unexpectedly defeated in the House of Laity by an undetected phalanx of evangelicals.[6] In a packed House the Series 1 communion (not 1928, but 'interim rite') and burial (a slightly edited 1928) then just scraped their two-thirds majorities against this phalanx's distrust about petitions for the dead.[7] The two-thirds were ready to vote through existing services that way, but, when it came to new proposals from the Commission, they were weary of handling services confrontationally. From then on majorities were not going to override conscientious minorities; they sought unitive ways forward.[8] That was how they handled the draft Series 2 services in 1967–8.

Modern language and Series 3 communion

Addressing God as 'you' came fast in the late 1960s around the English-speaking world. In 1968 the Commission published *Modern Liturgical Texts*, including our translations of the Lord's Prayer, Creeds, Gloria in Excelsis, among others, which we submitted to the ecumenical agency beginning that year, the International Consultation on English Texts (ICET).[9] We included a modernized text of Series 2 initiation services, and a one-man (i.e. Geoffrey Cuming) translation of Series 2 communion. In early 1970 ICET produced a semi-definitive report, *Prayers We Have in Common*. The Commission reckoned to include these in our projected first modern text, Series 3 communion. This delayed by 18 months the publicizing of the 'you' form liturgy, and we incurred hostility, which could have been absorbed earlier. On the Commission David Frost, a Cambridge English don, insisted that 'modern' did not necessarily mean 'colourless' or 'lacking in imagery' – and composed prayers to demonstrate this.[10] Later, with two Cambridge Hebraists, he produced the modern psalter which, after a switchback progress, became in the ASB 'The Liturgical Psalter'.

In late 1974 the Church of England (Worship and Doctrine) Measure went through Parliament, to come into force on 1 September 1975.[11] 'Alternative' services could now run for any length of time.[12] In 1973 a working party had been appointed to consider a comprehensive worship book, and Synod had also called for a debate about continuing without such a book. The working party reported for a Synod debate in February 1976, recommending a single Alternative Service Book (ASB). I opposed commissioning this book, deploring the lack of the other debate Synod had desired. I urged costing the projected ASB by 1978 and taking a decision then. I was rubbed out by John Habgood replying that my amendment was 'impossible ... improper ... and ... unnecessary.' Whew! So I lost my amendment then, and again a year later. The ASB proposal rested upon the notion that Anglicans brought their Prayer Book to church with them, and needed now a new book to carry similarly. I reckoned the habit had died, and would not revive, and history proved me right.

While the Commission initiated new texts, synodical experience taught that Revision Committees held enormous power thereafter. David Silk and I, who together found agreed ways forward on the Commission, at intervals, when the Bishops urged unwelcome changes, muttered, 'Well, we will let that go now, but sort it out at Revision Committee.' We had some slightly cynical confidence that later the Bishops' members or minds would have changed.[13] Our confidence was well placed.

In 1975–80 the three synodical stages of each service (with a Revision Committee between the first and second) began to overlap each other. Series 1 and 2 communion services were brought together in a 'Series 1 and 2 Revised' in 1976.* Series 3 marriage, calendar and lectionary, ordination and initiation services went through in 1976–8. Series 3 communion, authorized since 1973, was to be revised in 1978–9 after actual usage. For standard texts, like the Lord's Prayer, this revision would establish definitive forms (other services would be adapted to include them). All needed final approval in November

---

* This was the ancestor of Rite B in the ASB, and of traditional language texts in CW. It was only authorized by 105–52 in the House of Clergy – and Geoffrey Cuming, being lame, had baulked at climbing steps to the 'no' door in York. In London the rite would have perished!

1979, allowing a year for production.[14] I served on the Steering Committee for all these (except calendar and lectionary), and chaired it for the revision of Series 3 communion.

The Synod originally approved an ASB in two formats – one with the Sunday eucharistic readings printed in full, the other to have simply references (and some 600 fewer pages). John Habgood, the Bishop of Durham, chaired a working party to implement the publishing of the book. Without reference back, they unilaterally scrapped the shorter version – asserting a better deal with the publishers. But ultimately Synod required two versions anyway, with or without the Liturgical Psalter. The under-700-pages edition would have made me much happier. Where people already had Bibles or duplicated Bible passages with which to follow readings, then the 600 unwanted pages of rainforest were a desperate waste.[15]

One wonderful procedural absurdity lived long in memories, not least in the House of Bishops. At the Revision Stage of calendar and lectionary in February 1978, a Mrs Adcock, vexed that few women appeared in the third division of worthies (St Peter etc. being in the premier division), moved amendments to add five more. Two went in, three did not – but Josephine Butler, the social reformer, lost by 117–120. Cyril Bowles, that most reasonable of bishops, at final reference to the House of Bishops, cited the split vote in Synod, and asked the Bishops to reinstate her. They did – by 22–21! So in July 1978 Synod was to give final approval to a name it had rejected (and could not now amend). Sir Norman Anderson, the chairman of the House of Laity, told the Bishops that, if they did it again, he would vote against their whole package, however important. For years thereafter 'Remember Josephine Butler' became a doom-laden reminder to bishops to mind their synodical ways.

A transitional Liturgical Commission 1981–6

Ronald Jasper's Commission did less as its major work passed into Synod for authorization there. Ronald himself worked on production of the ASB, 'the Church of England's greatest publishing event in four hundred years'. The Commission did in 1980 produce services for use with the sick (and two flanking provisions – Blessing of Oils and Reconciliation of a Penitent).[16] Then in autumn 1980 it was over; Ronald retired; a new archbishop had begun; a new Synod was elected. The ASB was launched on 10 November 1980 amid an air of semi-exhaustion with liturgical revision. The decade ahead was for using the ASB. So what kind of Commission and what tasks were to come?

The Archbishops appointed Professor Douglas Jones of Durham as chairman. He had been the prolocutor of York Convocation and had chaired the Revision

Committee on the ordinal. But he was a surprising choice – neither bishop, nor liturgist, nor even now a member of Synod. He was a Canon-residentiary of Durham, interested in defending traditional liturgy, and ensuring that actual uses of it (as in Durham cathedral) were kept legal. The Commission had occasionally to rejig these priorities of his; though he was not alone, and, having let the original Series 1 communion (i.e. the Interim Rite) perish in 1980, the Commission and the Synod found themselves under pressure to reintroduce Series 1 during that quinquennium. The Commission declined to recommend any revival. But the House of Bishops decided to respond, and in February 1984 Hugh Montefiore, Bishop of Birmingham, moved on their behalf an oh-so-cautious motion, giving the Synod the chance to ask the House of Bishops to introduce Series 1. 'Series 1' had an emotional ring to it – Margaret Hewitt told the Synod that she had had to abandon her place of worship in Exeter in 1980, as her incumbent had scrupulously given up Series 1! I opposed vigorously, and later wrote that I 'undertake to lay on a demonstration antique Rite B, fully lawful, which the lover of the Interim Rite could only distinguish from the text of his heart by the use of a microscope'. A vote of 28–1 in the House of Bishops contrasted with 91–80 in the House of Laity, and the Bishops licked their wounds and never came back.

To be fair to Douglas Jones, he not only did not encourage the House of Bishops about Series 1 (we all on the Commission ensured that), but he engaged with a programme centred on Lent, Holy Week and Easter, and encouraged the right people to work on it.* From the early 1980s language had to be gender-inclusive – i.e. 'man' and 'mankind' were now read as gender-specific, a phenomenon from which the ASB had been free. The change happened quite rapidly in secular spheres as well, and by 1983 the ASB was looking dated (and, of course, to some users even offensive). *Lent-Holy Week-Easter* provided the first services drafted on the inclusive-language principle.

But how were these seasonal services to be authorized? They were not 'alternative' to anything in the BCP, so did not need those two-thirds majorities.[17] Were the Archbishops to authorize them under Canon B 4? But that would illegalize every other Holy Week use anywhere, as B 5 only allows local discretion where Convocations or Archbishops have *not* authorized services. I take some credit for our solution – that the Bishops would 'commend'

---

* There was also a small report on Concelebration, which evoked a splendid Grove Worship Booklet (no. 82, still in print) by John Fenwick, *Eucharistic Concelebration*. Douglas Jones, co-opted to York Convocation, also won applause for an answer to a question in Synod in November 1983 about Coronation oil! His magisterial reply included the rare and arguably useless information that in 1953 the monarch was anointed with an oil compiled from a secret formula containing 'oil of orange flowers, of roses, cinnamon, jasmine and sesame with benzoin, musk, civet and ambergris'. With information like that made public, how can anyone doubt the value of Synod?

such services. Local creativity remained lawful, but 'commended' services boasted *some* standing (and were published) as Church of England services. The synodical convention for processing such rites emerged: the House of Bishops would submit them to Synod for a single 'take note' debate, airing ideas for retouching the services. Written submissions would be received also, and the Commission would sift, and perhaps marginally revise, the drafts, before the Bishops finally 'commended' such rites.

I was one of the few survivors from the Jasper Commission, and in 1985 I was asked to draft the strategy document to wind up our five years and usher in the next. It became, after retouching by the Standing Committee, *The Worship of the Church* (GS 698). I proposed that the ASB's ten years be extended by five more, giving time to assess how the texts were doing, and revise them. The Standing Committee preferred a ten-year extension, and (granted the way the Bishops [and others] wasted time in following years) Parkinson's Law supported them. I mention my proposal defensively, lest anyone suppose that, being of the ASB vintage, I wanted to put up the shutters and block its ever being revised again.

The Stancliffe years, 1986–2005

In early 1986, when a 15-year rule was invented, I was dismissed from the Commission under it.* Colin James, newly Bishop of Winchester, became chairman, and David Stancliffe, then Provost of Portsmouth, held a key role, and succeeded to the chair in 1993, just before becoming Bishop of Salisbury.[18] The ten-year extension to 2000 for the ASB in 1985-6 gave perhaps 13 years to expand, revise and supplement existing rites for a new range to be authorized and published by 2000. The Commission's membership was kept relatively stable through those 15 years.

The first quinquennium exhibited typical Stancliffe in *The Liturgical Ministry of the Deacon*. Few evangelicals would have given this time on the agenda.[19] Nor, in my judgement, would Ronald Jasper. There followed *Making Women Visible*, consolidating the approach to inclusive language pioneered in *Lent-Holy Week-Easter*.[20] Meanwhile two different weighty strands of work began. One, partly responding to *Faith in the City*'s strictures, was to provide resources for 'services

---

* I confess I occasionally detect in myself a suspicion it was invented to dismiss me, but that may simply signify my hubris at the time – that I thought they could not do without me. But at the time I also had other evidence, in that Donald Gray, who had done 18 years, had been reappointed – and, naturally, I pointed this out. They promptly dismissed him, thus exploding any conspiracy theory, and suggesting rather the alternative theory. Donald immediately returned as a 'consultant', being chair of the interdenominational Joint Liturgical Group, and thus was better able to forgive me for knifing him.

of the word', along with its own sacramental proposals, Rite C.[21] These were published in November 1989 as *Patterns for Worship*. The other strand reinforced seasonal provision for 1 November to 2 February in *The Promise of His Glory*.[22] The Bishops were to 'commend' these, and straightforwardly did so with *Promise*. But *Patterns* encountered problems, partly because its eucharistic material could not be 'commended', and needed to be authorized.[23] After some delay, Synod found itself authorizing 'A Service of the Word', merely an outline structure, in 1993.[24] Then in 1995 the House of Bishops 'commended' a revised *Patterns*, solely for non-eucharistic usage, and it was amplified in 2002.

In 1994–5 the Commission asked the Synod for decisions on (a) whether to have 'one book or many?' and (b) whether 'traditional language' services should be included. The answers were, respectively, 'many' and 'yes'. The first was a non-question, as, if everything authorized or 'commended' had been collected in one book, it would have had around 3,000 pages – and books were giving way to new technology (and I said so). The second question was a trap, and the Commission misled the Synod to invest heavily in 'traditional' material in the main *Common Worship* (*CW*) book. As this book (a mere 850+ pages) was hardly a congregational one, it was absurd to load it (for cosmetic purposes?) with hundreds of 'traditional language' pages – thus ensuring that for both price and convenience (and in the face of electronic customizing of texts) it never would be scattered around congregations. They inconsistently (but rightly) omitted to do the same with *Pastoral Services*.

In 1995–2000 we gained (what I had wanted in the 1970s) a separate treatment of the Lord's Prayer.[25] We had a short synodical fight about the Psalter.* We had a fascinating long-running debate on the Greek preposition *ek* in the Nicene Creed! I fought unsuccessfully the omission of section numbers from services – a totally daft policy decision of the Commission and the Publishing Group. We also passed a provision in 1997–8 for bishops to allow off their own bats the continuance of services which had lapsed (see Canon B 2 (3)). I contested this, as it clearly transgressed the text of the Worship and Doctrine Measure – but I was simply told that the lawyers had allowed it, without being told their basis. The *CW* collects had (and still have) an extraordinary Prayer Book atmosphere to them, and that provoked Wakefield Diocese to persuade

---

* The Psalter from the Commission was derived from the American Prayer Book, the Psalter of which had had inclusive language since the 1970s. The Americans had waived all copyright considerations so it passed into use in, e.g., the Franciscan *Celebrating Common Prayer*, which was widely used. It was further polished for use with *Common Worship*, and Jane Sinclair, as the Commission's resident Hebraist, saw off attempts in Synod to authorize an inclusivized version of the MacIntosh-Frost Psalter in its place. Quite irrelevantly I note that the only point where the Psalter is *not* inclusive is, following the Americans, in verse 1 of Psalms 14 and 53: 'The fool has said in *his* heart "There is no God"' (my emphasis). Had Jane smiled secretively and hoped no mere male would notice?

General Synod in 2001 to commission simplified alternative collects. Other major *CW* components are discussed below in Chapters 4 and 6, lesser ones in Chapter 7. In the post-2000 era the ordinal and rites of reconciliation figure in Chapter 7, but omitted here are *Daily Prayer*, which, after two years of experiment, reached hardback form in 2005, and *Times and Seasons*. In 2005 the Commission defied financial trends in getting a new appointment created: a National Worship Development Officer (with some resemblance to Mark Earey's role as Praxis National Development Officer in 1997–2001). The appointed officer, Peter Moger, has nevertheless an uphill task to fulfil. Finally, David Stancliffe's own time was done. He has left a deep mark. A new Commission has different faces addressing different tasks.

4

Baptism and Confirmation

Repent, and be baptized . . . and you will receive the gift of the Holy Spirit.

(Acts 2.38)

Think of all the problems there are in baptism – and in confirmation – and you'll find we faced most of them over 40 years, and some are still there.

The confirmation issue

The discussion of open communion in Chapter 2 shows how confirmation grew in significance in Anglicanism as the Anglo-Catholic movement took it aboard – and as, in the latter part of the nineteenth century, it became regularly available around every diocese. The 'Mason-Dix line' taught that baptism in water was only half-initiation, and that confirmation provided the second and completing half – indeed the half within which the Holy Spirit was given. This doctrine was at odds with the Thirty-Nine Articles, and not easy to square with the Prayer Book confirmation rite. But it was dominant in Anglicanism from 1890 to 1970, and in that time Acts 8.14–17 got incorporated into confirmation texts in various countries, as in the 1928 'proposed' Prayer Book. From 1928 to 1966 English bishops regularly confirmed with the 1928 rite, and their sermons often reflected the (wholly exceptional) Acts 8 passage. We still suffer today from the fact that the first new liturgical texts for initiation, *Baptism and Confirmation* (1959), arose in that Mason-Dix era. The structure created then has been difficult to discard, and has obscured right through to the present the more biblical doctrine that sacramental initiation is complete in baptism. This has ensured a kind of running battle for 40 years. Alongside it, I have been concerned that baptismal texts should spell out the true character of Christian discipleship, even if infant baptism was given indiscriminately in many parishes.

The 1959 texts suspended the whole concept of the 'archetypal' service upon the 'recovery of the worship of the Primitive Church which was the aim of the compilers of the first Prayer Books of the Church of England'.[1] Gregory Dix had died in 1952, but his Mason-Dix line, outlined above, ran strongly till 1970. The Commission wrote that 'From every point of view . . . Baptism and Confirmation must be viewed as two parts of one whole.'[2] This was teaching that the rebirth signified in water-baptism needed 'completion' by the coming of the Spirit in confirmation. The Reformers' emphasis upon a renewal of baptismal vows was marginalized in this almost unprecedented two-staging sacramentalism.[3] The 1959 texts now abandoned Acts 8. But the heading before the bishop's prayer was '*the prayer for the sending of the Spirit*', and the text had the 1549 'Send down from heaven upon them thy Holy Ghost', where 1662 had had 'Strengthen them ... with the Holy Ghost'. In confirmation on its own, the bishop's introduction included, 'These persons have been baptized ... instructed ... and ... come with repentance and faith to receive the Spirit.' The readings were Joel 2.28,29,32 and Acts 1.3-9 and John 14.15-17 – teaching that confirmation is the candidate's personal Pentecost. To make this compatible with 1662 involves special pleading, and the Commission's own citing of 'the Primitive Church' disregarded such compatibility. The bishops on the Commission (Colin Dunlop and Henry de Candole) were almost certainly using 1928, including Acts 8.14-17, in their own confirmations. The 'two halves of one whole' theology easily predominated.

On the Commission Eric Milner-White and Ernest Evans dissented, favouring the existent (not of course legal) 1951 'York rite' for infant baptism.[4] Milner-White carried the attack into the 1960 York Convocation debate, waving his York rite as he did so, and was viewed by the Commission as having acted treacherously towards them. When I joined the Commission in 1964, his memory was still execrated – and no dissent of mine could match his enormities.* There were other criticisms, particularly about the founding of Christian baptism on John's baptism of Jesus.[5] The two dissentients opposed the infant rite simply because their York rite had been ignored.[6] But for me, the doctrine of confirmation presented the greatest problem. Knowing some of its Anglican history, I believed the Mason-Dix line to be erroneous and dangerous.

After 1960 the Commission left baptism and confirmation aside, until 1966, when, as the Alternative Services Measure came into force on 1 May that year, the 1928 services were to be authorized as Series 1. The Convocations accepted them all with the required two-thirds majorities on 9–10 May 1966; but, when the services went to the Laity on 10 June, that House vetoed the 1928 confirmation by 129-72 (i.e. with less than two-thirds in favour). The speeches attacked the 1928 rite as having escalated the doctrine of confirmation beyond what the Scriptures and Anglican formularies warranted, and the members used their muscle. They incidentally put the bishops themselves on the spot. With any other service, it was parish clergy who might break the law – but with

* I once asked George Addleshaw, one of the few other Commission members in York Convocation, whether he had been present at this event. 'Present?' he said. 'I was the victim offered up for slaughter.'

confirmation bishops took their own decision, and their use of 1928 was deeply entrenched.[7] But any supposed episcopal power to authorize rites had been removed by the Measure, so, if they continued using 1928 off their own bats, they would, in effect, trash all the new legal procedures. Lambeth was rumoured to have sent round an edict telling bishops to keep the process credible – 'stick with 1662 alone for confirmations'. Bishops muttered, and complained in their diocesan newsletters, but took the point, and for 15 months scrupulously used 1662. There even existed stories about bishops hesitating to preach or sing hymns, as 1662 is silent about them.

Series 2 initiation

Losing Series 1 confirmation moved Series 2 services of baptism and confirmation up the Commission's priorities.[8] Ronald Jasper placed the 1959 rites on the table to be minimally adjusted (which I found frustrating). In June 1966 I submitted a memorandum about its overstated doctrine of confirmation; and, when Ronald was absent, Douglas Harrison from the chair dismissed my memorandum and tried to move straight to next business – and I had to ask why someone submitting a memorandum was not allowed to speak to it! Discussion with the judicious Geoffrey Cuming, newly on the Commission, was more fruitful – he drafted an Introduction which dropped the 'archetypal' and 'two parts of one whole' language, and merely said, 'The Commission here presents four services of Christian initiation' and listed them. The Introduction did claim varying theologies had been met, but the text, while keeping baptism-and-confirmation in one service for adults, softened the 1959 Mason-Dix line. The central line of the bishop's prayer became 'Send forth upon them thy Holy Spirit'. The renunciations gained a cross-heading 'The Decision', which I welcomed (I suggested 'The Conversion', but was not taken seriously). The infant baptism rite acquired a cunning lead-in: 'Those who bring young children to baptism must affirm their allegiance to Christ . . .' The concealed issue was to identify the antecedent of 'their' – i.e. was it 'Those who' (as many parishes understood it), or was it 'young children' (which I, believing in vicarious affirmations, would defend)? There was also a new pastoral Preface to the infant rite telling the officiant to ask the parents and sponsors whether they would bring the child up 'within the family of Christ's church'. The readings at the confirmation-only service now repeated the baptismal ones.* I slipped in Joshua 24 (about renewal of vows) in the alternative readings we offered. In sum, by September 1966 I reckoned the Commission had 'heard' me more than

---

* The Ezekiel 36 passage, which had been in the 1959 'archetypal' rite, was filleted so that its denunciation of idols disappeared, as requested by Kenneth Ross, the vicar of All Saints, Margaret Street. Mervyn Stockwood twitted him that he was trying to avoid denunciation of the idols of Margaret Street.

when I was forced into dissent over the Eucharist just six months before.[9] I therefore included a bracketed note, not of dissent, but of strong preference: '(The Rev. C. O. Buchanan would have desired the services more clearly to express that the work of the Spirit in sacramental initiation is complete in baptism.)'

If the Eucharist was slow going through the Convocations and Laity, baptism and confirmation were swift. They were discussed at the Liturgical Conference in April 1967, and, with the bishops restive over their 1662-only situation, the confirmation-only service was fast-tracked, and was authorized in September 1967. Authorizing a derived rite in advance of its source was odd, but the others followed unamended, perhaps unscrutinized, in February 1968. In early 1968 also *Modern Liturgical Texts* included a modernized (but otherwise unrevised) text of the Series 2 initiation services.[10] Once published, it languished for nine years, before Series 3 texts appeared.

Ely

The year General Synod began, 1970, was the watershed year for initiation theology, and retaining rites structured on pre-1970 principles was unhelpful. Geoffrey Lampe had challenged Dix et al. in *The Seal of the Spirit*, but was a lone voice until 1970. Then the field visibly changed. Jimmy Dunn's book, *Baptism in the Holy Spirit*, addressing charismatics' exposition of Scripture, both dealt magisterially with the charismatics, and also demonstrated that the 'confirmationists' (as he dubbed them) are equally unscriptural. A very interesting complement was Charles Whitaker's second edition of his *Documents of the Baptismal Liturgy*; he now provided an Introduction, demonstrating that there was no generally used primitive 'integrated rite' current throughout the Mediterranean region in the first four centuries.[11] Furthermore, the four authors of *Growing into Union* agreed, 'we cannot regard those who are to be baptized as adults as needing any ceremony other than water-baptism before entry into the communicant life, provided that the bishop is presiding.'[12] The theological change was reinforced by the Ely Commission in *Christian Initiation: Birth and Growth in the Christian Society*. This said the Church of England should clarify that sacramental initiation is complete in baptism, and, in respect of the test case of this, recommended:

1. A person baptized in adult life be not subsequently presented for the rite of Confirmation since commitment and commissioning for responsible Christian life and service are adequately declared in the rite of the Baptism of adults.

2. The first Communion of such a person be administered wherever possible by the bishop.[13]

The Ely Report, after a first airing in Synod in July 1971, then hung fire till Peter Cornwell introduced his 'working paper' (GS 184) to the Synod in February 1974.[14] He had distilled the Ely material into recommendations to Synod, but unhelpfully dodged the hot potato of 'sacramental initiation complete in baptism'. The debates in February and July 1974 led to a reference of questions to dioceses. I got involved in two ways before it went to the dioceses, and once after it came back.

My first intervention was in February 1974, on a matter I have hardly mentioned here – the qualifications for infant baptism. The Bishop of Ely was to move that baptism should be available to the children of all parents 'who request it and are willing to make the requisite promises'.[15] Peter Cornwell's report (rightly or wrongly) said:

> At present there is a conflict between the Church's official baptismal policy and the promises as presented in Series II Baptism Service. Canon Law supports Baptism on request, but an authorized experimental service of the Church frames promises which would move us in the direction of a more selective policy.

This reflection on Series 2 baptism took the 'those who' view of the antecedent of the 'their' in the ambiguity I have described. By an amazing coincidence, Series 2 initiation services needed their licence renewed (to run to 31 December 1979) on the night before this Ely debate on qualifications for infant baptism. I therefore argued that previous night that, if we followed Cornwell, we should either terminate Series 2 services immediately (and so protect 'official baptismal policy ... Baptism on request'), or, if renewing the services, should the next day accept my amendment about a more 'selective' policy. Thus 'I would rather we had a thumping vote against it [renewing the licence] to-night, than found ourselves facing in two different directions at once.' Well, Synod is Synod (and fudge is fudge) – they renewed the licence of the services.

Next day came the motion to provide baptism for the children of all 'who request it and are willing to make the requisite promises'. I duly moved an amendment, which noted that the Cornwell report distinguished two different views and, accepting his analysis, preferred that parents should show some 'evidence' that they would fulfil their promises. The chair (Margaret Hewitt) ruled this out of order (as negativing the motion) *after I had spoken to it*, and I had to produce a fudged variant of it – and Synod, predictably inconsistent with the night before, blocked it and accepted 'all who request it [etc.]'.* However, the issue was going to the dioceses, along with the question of a 'thanksgiving'

---

* I was procedurally ambushed – see my account in *Infant Baptism and the Gospel: The Church of England's Dilemma*, Darton, Longman & Todd, 1993, pp.126–7n.

or a 'blessing' after childbirth, and the question about children and communion (see Chapter 5). So I could address it further in my diocese.

In July 1974 I moved a following motion to send to the dioceses (along with the other matters) the Ely recommendation that confirmation be abolished for those baptized as adults. My motion quoted the extract on page 42, but lost out because Synod had not had to engage with 'sacramental initiation complete in baptism', which underlies it. The Bishop of Ely, Ted Roberts, gently backed me, but antipathy rose like an almost visible cloud from the bishops in the front row at York, teaching me that bishops tend to oppose changes affecting confirmation. A suspicion always lurks that they fear that changes to confirmation would mean that bishops would be less needed in the parishes – and, like all pastors, they arguably have a need to be needed. At any rate, Synod unsympathetically defeated my motion.

All this delayed revision of Series 2 initiation.[16] But the dioceses picked over the issues, preferred 'thanksgiving' to 'blessing' for the non-baptism of infants, and on children and communion produced the confusion reported in Chapter 5. They were not asked about qualifications for infant baptism, but were free to comment. I seized my chance, and moved in my deanery:

> That this Synod, endorsing the forms of interrogation in Series 2 and
> draft Series 3 Infant Baptism Services, desires that there should be a
> re-examination of the conditions upon which infants are accepted
> for baptism.

It went through the deanery synod, then through Southwell diocesan synod, and on to General Synod as part of our response to the reference to the dioceses. In General Synod I moved it on Southwell's behalf in November 1976, and treated the conflicting points in debate as, by their very confusion, demonstrating the need of a re-examination. The 'endorsing . . .' phrase linked liturgical rites with policy, unlike the 1974 oddities. General Synod bought it (170–151), and Standing Committee commissioned a one-man report. This report, *Infant Baptism: A memorandum by the Rt. Rev. E. G. Knapp-Fisher* (GS Misc 59), had the doubtful merit of being written by an ageing Anglo-Catholic who had been long out of the country, and stood far from our initiation debates. It had predictable traditionalisms – 'There are at least some grounds for asserting that the rigorist position tends to sectarianism.' It also ventured on to ground beyond its commission, betraying Knapp-Fisher's 'Mason-Dix' vintage (he was born in 1915) in: 'It seems clear that from New Testament times baptism with water was accompanied by a laying-on of hands as an integral part of Christian initiation.' Clear indeed! Nothing could have been less clear – and had he read the relevant literature? We were far beyond that 1970 watershed, but he had not yet reached it.

Worse, however, than the deficient Knapp-Fisher memorandum was Standing Committee's failure to report back. They circulated the document without scheduling a synodical debate. I reckoned this left the matter of qualifications for infant baptism strictly *sub judice*, as unfinished business, and corresponded at intervals with the secretary-general to that effect.[17] So the promising Ely Report of 1971 ended six years later in barrenness: by then Synod had lost sight of Ely's central theme, that baptism is complete sacramental initiation; it had dismissed the abolition of confirmation for those baptized as adults; it had messily abandoned the admission of children to communion (see Chapter 5); and it had failed to grapple with the basis for infant baptism. The tiny tadpole of a positive outcome was that the dioceses wanted a thanksgiving after childbirth – but this did not need an officially authorized service, and the 'pirate' Grove Booklet rite had been in use for five years.[18]

Series 3 initiation

However, the Commission could now publish Series 3 initiation services (GS 343). One gain came from the 1967 Latimer Monograph – the uniting of adult and infant baptism in a single service (a true 'archetype'), though confirmation obviously still accompanied it. Uncertainties about infant baptismal vows were settled by the drafting already published in the draft 1975 infant baptism rite – 'You must answer both for yourselves and for these children.'[19]

We also had to grapple with an existing misuse of the adult service. Bishops who revelled in 'the full rite' were finding themselves with, say, 20 candidates for confirmation, of whom 3 were to receive baptism first. If the bishop took the 3 to the (west end) font after the Decision, and duly blessed the font there, he would then ask affirmations of faith from 3 at the font and from 17 still in the front row of the nave. The answer of Mervyn Stockwood, Bishop of Southwark, was to alter the order, have them all affirm their faith in the front row, then march the three off to the font, say the blessing over it, and baptize them easily. But the Commission deplored separating the profession of faith from baptism. Bishops had not yet embraced the practice (which is in 2005 used regularly and not found difficult) of marching confirmation candidates to the font with baptismal ones, and interrogating the lot there. The Commission would not yield (our Introduction shows that to sustain the principle we even preferred a temporary font at the front, which many clergy would abhor, to shuffling the order). Then we found bishops proposing to meet us by blessing a ewer of water at the front and interrogating all the candidates together there, then marching off with ewer and baptismal candidates to baptize them at a west end font. This seemed to us idiocy, and we stuck to our guns, simply providing an opening note that 'the precise ordering of the service and the place of baptism should be determined by consultation between the bishop and the parish priest.'

I was still fighting for 'sacramental initiation complete in baptism'.[20] The Introduction to the services now recorded a march in theological history, even if not a change in practice:

> in 1958, the 'Mason-Dix' line was more widely accepted than is now the case. The 1958 structure has been retained in both Series 2 and Series 3 services: and this *structure* still suggests that baptism is a preliminary to be dealt with so that the service can proceed to confirmation – the real climax. We do not think that the *wording* of the service supports this suggestion. Nevertheless the suggestion is there . . .
>
> Recent debates on initiation did not directly touch the question of initiating adults in this two-stage manner . . . But problems do arise when attempting to justify the confirmation of adults who have just been baptized: and the number of such people is increasing. Some members of the Commission feel the time has come when this issue must be faced.[21]

These paragraphs contrast wonderfully with what Knapp-Fisher was drafting at the same time (see p. 44). Whether they put down a sufficient marker for my doctrinal concerns is doubtful, but at least we now called in question the 1959 structure as well as individual lines of text. Confirmation could hardly be removed from adult initiation simply during the revision process, so airing a concern was all that could be done.

The General Approval stage came in Synod in November 1977 and the package was remitted to a Revision Committee, chaired by a figure rarely seen in Synod: yes, Mervyn Stockwood himself. A great host of amendments came in – around 350 specific proposals. Several proposed abolishing confirmation for those baptized as adults. The Revision Committee did not think itself competent to effect this; but it took aboard many other proposals, and reported to the Synod with rewritten and even restructured texts. A subtle change was made in the bishop's confirmation prayer, in which the crucial line became 'Let your Holy Spirit rest upon them', clearly dependent upon Isaiah 11, from which the characteristics of the Spirit in the rest of the prayer are drawn. A structural change was moving the signing with the cross to come at the end of the Decision. This delivered it from the old suspicion of being confused with the act of baptism, and grouped together the different references to evil – first the renouncing, then the injunction to 'fight . . . against sin, the world, and the devil', and finally the prayer for God's protection against the powers of darkness.[22] A most controversial change was the permission in the opening notes for the use of oil at the signing with the cross in baptism and at the laying on the hand in confirmation. A tiny novelty was the provision in emergency baptism that a child could be baptized without being given a name.[23]

The revised text was scheduled for debate in July 1978. This brought Mervyn Stockwood to the residential Synod at York, in breach of his vow of abstinence from Synod – but the business was postponed. In November 1978 he introduced the revised texts as his maiden speech from the platform. He was enthusiastic about oiling people – which he claimed he did, *inter alia*, to over 300 clergy on Maundy Thursday. He made mention of Greek athletes oiling their muscles, a reference which recurred 20 years later.[24] He played into the hands of Peter Dawes, who had an amendment to delete the permitted use of oil. Peter Dawes quoted the Commission's Introductions to both the 1975 draft infant rite (which Synod had not debated) and the present services, both of which said the Commission was ready to consider including anointing, *providing that good theological explanations of its meaning accompanied it.* He complained that the permission was now there *without* any reasoning or explanation, and 'I think that the Bishop of Southwark gave four explanations and Prof. Lampe three more – seven in all ... does it not become meaningless?' He grieved at a circular from the Catholic Group, which said that, if deleting the oil were carried, they would vote against the whole service. Realistically, he recognized they might raise a blocking one-third in one House, and so, bowing to the threat, he reluctantly would not move his amendment. I cannot but agree with him: 'I see no reference to the use of oil in initiation in the New Testament'; I had voted on the Committee against permitting anointing – and its acceptance in 1978 became the thin end of a very oily wedge.

One non-baptismal issue came in under cover of 'initiation'. GS 343 included, with the Thanksgiving for the Birth of a Child (that tiny outcome of the Ely years), prayers to be used after a stillbirth or neonatal death. The Bishop of Winchester, John V. Taylor, proposed to add a prayer to be used after an abortion. The Revision Committee rejected it, and he went to full Synod. The Synod recognized the moral ambiguity implied in authorizing such a prayer, and defeated it in two Houses of the three.[25] Series 3 services gained final approval (29–0; 180–3; 146–10) in February 1979, and ran for 17 months before being adapted into the ASB in November 1980.[26]

Policies for infant baptism

During the 1980s General Synod had various cracks at the WCC's 'Lima document', *Baptism, Eucharist, and Ministry.* This reinforced the unease expressed in the 1970s about the lack of Christian standing of many parents bringing infants for baptism.[27] It led Roger Godin in 1985–90 to table a Private Member's Motion reiterating the Lima warning against 'apparently indiscriminate baptism'. He moved it in November 1988; it was adjourned till February 1989, and was then amended to include warnings against both indiscriminate and rigorist practices.[28] It then (unsurprisingly?) was passed without much dissent, and Standing Committee built consideration of it into its commission for a one-man report on initiation. This duly emerged in spring 1991 as *Christian Initiation – A Policy for The Church of England: A Discussion Paper* by Canon Martin Reardon (GS Misc 365). It particularly focused on issues of baptismal policy, and Martin received submissions from several eminent baptismal reformers, and included them in his report.

However, when the big debate came in July 1991, the forces of reaction rose. I compared them in *News of Liturgy* to a buffalo charge. The motion was (oddly) that there should be no change in the Canons! The buffalo charge on behalf of this inaction swept away all contrary voices. Gordon Kuhrt, still then an elected member, courageously tried to draw out the kinds of discipline which even keeping the Canons implied – but the buffaloes swept him aside. For my part I was back on Synod by then, but I sensed the futility of resisting, and, as I wanted to be heard properly in the afternoon (see next chapter), I rolled out of the buffaloes' path. The Canons were duly not changed.[29]

Common Worship initiation

The Liturgical Commission contributed to that July 1991 debate an unhelpful document, *Christian Initiation and its Relation to Some Pastoral Offices* (GS Misc 366), criticized in Chapter 5 below.[30] The Commission was working towards the year 2000 with a notion that 'initiation' was a good umbrella title, or even an undergirding principle, to hold together a range of different services. They produced in 1994 drafts which went to the Bishops suggesting that under 'Initiation' should come not only Thanksgiving for the Gift of a Child, Baptism and Confirmation, but also Catechumenate, the Renewal of Baptismal Vows, Reception from Other Churches, Healing Ministry, and Reconciliation of a Penitent – and some blank but numbered sections for other items also.[31] The Bishops were cool about the Reconciliation of a Penitent, and confined the task to services revising the ASB initiation services and services with the sick – still a very full package. The drafts restored the Apostles' Creed (said by the whole congregation), retouched the baptismal affirmations to give three renunciations and three adherings to Christ, optionally postponed giving candles to the end of the service (and therefore 'candling' the newly confirmed alongside the newly baptized), and brought in anointing, sprinkling of confirmation candidates, 'clothing' and a new section, called 'The Commission', to come straight after confirmation. The first debate came in July 1995, as that quinquennium ended. Michael Saward, at his last ever Synod, was less than persuaded the

Commission had it right – 'while sin may not have gone, 16 other items of significance, including repentance, have gone from the ASB rite.' The rites received General Approval then, but the Revision Committee's work was delayed until early 1996, so that Synod members newly elected in the autumn could make submissions.

I was on the Revision Committee. We quickly decided to present baptism and confirmation as a totally distinct set of services, separated from wholeness and healing, which could follow after an interval, when we had done baptism and confirmation. As in 1977–8 there were submissions about abolishing confirmation for those baptized as adults; and, as then, the Revision Committee could not actually effect it. Amazingly, the optional anointing now found a rationale – yes, the oiling of athletes! Much of the Committee's energy went on getting right the variants needed when infants are baptized. In the questions to parents and sponsors, 'You must answer both for yourselves and for these infants' had gone. So the rubric made clear that only the candidates were being addressed, and they would reply by the vicarious responses of the sponsors. The text had prior questions about whether the parents and sponsors of infants would 'support them in the way of Christ', but this seemed too vague to several of us, and we pressed for more specific visible belonging to the Church, and the one question became two pointed ones – will sponsors 'walk with them in the way of Christ?' and 'help them to take their place within the life and worship of Christ's church?' The baptismal reformers believed the full implications of baptism should appear in the rite (not least to assist with preparing parents and sponsors), even if particular families showed little sign of grasping the significance. They regained in these questions some of the ground they had lost when the Commission revised the ASB rites.

In two Revision Stages in Synod little change was made.* Final approval came in November 1997. There was some unease, relating probably to the complexity and the increased character of symbols in the rite, and 55 members voted against, compared with 13 in 1979.

In July 2000, Synod debated a Liverpool diocesan synod resolution about infant baptism. It was amended (by another Liverpool person) and passed as follows:

> That this Synod, believing that baptism provides a unique missionary opportunity for the Church,

---

* Nigel McCulloch, Bishop of Wakefield (previously of Taunton), helped get 'proud' deleted before 'rebellion': 'In Taunton ... they know exactly what is meant by proud rebellion because they will immediately look back to that glorious day when the citizens of Taunton proclaimed the Duke of Monmouth King ... If Judge Jeffreys could not get them to reject their pride, neither will this service.'

(a) recognize that enquirers should be offered relevant preparation from the Church which relates to life and commend the use of material already widely available;

(b) urge all churches to examine ways to help the journey of faith that is marked at baptism to continue; and

(c) encourage PCCs to discuss and prepare a baptism policy in consultation with the bishop to be made available to enquirers.

I took advantage of this debate both to air the liturgists' dilemmas in drafting baptismal services and to expound the Canons as not giving any right in law to baptism on demand. But in fact both the original and the amended form of the motion were almost pointless, as they required no action and pinned no responsibilities anywhere. I do not recall that either I, as a working bishop, or the parishes of my area ever received any nudge, push, question or coaching from General Synod on the subject. So there was not much point in Synod 'urging' or 'encouraging' simply by raising hands in the chamber. Nor is it surprising that we heard nothing – Synod was assured during the debate that the cost of passing the motion was 'nil'.[32]

And the confirmation issue remains

The otiose use of confirmation for those baptized as adults remained. The Revision Committee, as in 1977–8, had not viewed themselves as competent to excise it. They had, however, got the chairman, John Hind, then Bishop in Europe, to take a lengthy memorandum to the Bishops in June 1996, asking them to address the subject. In November 1997 I made a long speech about this at final approval, and got nods from David Hope, Archbishop of York, during the speech, and overt agreement from David Stancliffe in his reply to the debate. I wrote to David Hope after the Synod and asked for his help in pursuing the matter in the Bishops. He replied, mentioning that David Stancliffe had put in a condition that bishops should administer the adult baptisms (which was no problem to me), and saying he would bring my letter to the Standing Committee of the House.

Confirmation and its relation to baptism nevertheless did not come on the House of Bishops' agenda. I wrote twice in the following years, urging that not only did the initiation services we had authorized cry out for a re-examination of confirmation, but the whole issue of admitting children to communion on the basis of their baptism required it too. As bishops were administering confirmation week after week and had never discussed its meaning (and thus their sermons!), was it not timely, or indeed late in the day, to look at our doctrine of confirmation?

The Standing Committee of the House twice declined my proposal. It is difficult to know whether the House as a whole would prefer to march on in a kind of twilight. But it is almost certain that no serious change will be handled without the full consent of the House – and how much better that the Bishops should initiate it!

5

Children in communion

> We were all baptized into one body ... we who are many are one body, for we all partake of the one bread.
>
> (1 Corinthians 12.13; 10.17)

Are children members of the Church to share in our feast – or not? It was a long slow march, but we got there.

Background

What qualifies Christians to be communicant? In the New Testament all the Church shared communion together, and in 1 Corinthians 10 Paul demonstrates from the Exodus and wilderness experiences that *all* the baptized are also communicant. But does this not pose a problem when, on a sound basis, we baptize infants?

The Reformers made confirmation the door to communion in order to provide instruction of candidates.[1] Anglicans thereafter did not expect children to receive communion until they were catechized, if not confirmed. In the early twentieth century many parishes still offered communion only at 8 a.m. on Sundays, and sometimes by 'staying behind'. Children would rarely, if ever, be present. Yet the developing sacramentalism of other parishes also rarely suggested that children should communicate, as the classic mid-morning Sunday high mass was a non-communicating occasion, and parents and children alike would not go up to the rail. Coming, fasting, at 8 a.m. was the way to receive – without the children.[2] As confirmation became more readily available throughout England in the second half of the nineteenth century, the pressures in catholic circles were towards getting children confirmed younger, to admit them to communion at, say, 10. But the 1604 Canons anticipated 13 as the age for confirmation, and in 1900 12 to 13 remained the normal age.

The doctrine that confirmation is the second, completing, half of sacramental initiation prevailed from around 1890 until 1970. So strongly did it run that, when Convocation reports on initiation began in 1940, there was open discussion of separating renewal of baptismal vows from confirmation. This

52

would enable the age of confirmation to go down, even to uniting it with infant baptism, and admission to communion would follow.[3] Evangelicals (let alone the Reformers) would have viewed this as a thorough corruption of confirmation. The reports discussed admission to communion prior to confirmation, but never as a live option. In the 1954 report three 'Mason-Dix' advocates urged that sacramental initiation should be seen as baptism-confirmation-communion in an 'integrated' unity.[4] They launched a trouble-some word – 'disintegration' of the primitive rite.[5] Without recommending the whole pattern for infants, they teed up the argument to go that way. The main report did not clearly adopt a Mason-Dix line, but mentioned the first serious modern theological challenge to it – Geoffrey Lampe's *The Seal of the Spirit* (1951).

But, in the following years, there was less theological pressure for younger children to be communicant. The growing parish communion movement brought parents and children together into a main Sunday morning Eucharist. The Pope relaxed the fasting rules in 1951, and even Anglicans who looked to Rome then happily received communion at 9.30, 10.00 or 10.30. Children were not to be left in a pew when parents went up to a rail – and got taken along, and received a 'blessing'.[6] At intervals there surfaced a sense that the children were still deprived, and a slow groundswell developed in parish communion circles. Parish & People articulated the question in the 1950s.

Evangelicals never had unconfirmed children present at communion in the 1950s, and were quite unaffected by the practical argument. Yet, as they sought a more confident doctrine of infant baptism (their classic Achilles heel), so they encountered the logical assertion deployed by Anabaptists, that 'arguments for infant baptism are also arguments for child communion'. Intended to lure evangelicals *away* from infant baptism, by the 1960s this was planting an idea impelling them *towards* child communion.

The Keele Congress in April 1967 expressed this:

> 74.   We call for further theological study as to whether the age of discretion is always the right time for admission to Holy Communion. Some of us would like the children of Christian families to be admitted as communicants at an early age, provided that there is adequate baptismal discipline.[7]

I was not technically a signatory.[8] But I was encouraged in my own advocacy. In 1968 I wrote in a mild Anglo-Catholic journal:

> It is difficult to defend the present method of admitting to communion, and ... instead we ought to abandon it ... In simple

terms the baptized person is a Christian, and the Christian is a communicant. Thus a baptized babe is in principle admissible to communion *with his parents* . . . For evangelicals this again would require the rehabilitation of communion to a central place.[9]

This passing remark in a lengthy essay drew a major attack by Roger Beckwith in *The Churchman* in spring 1971. His article became a rallying point for adherents of a traditional discipline.

The synodical processes of the 1970s

In many ways 1970 was a watershed year, theologically as well as synodically; the theology of confirmation was changing fast (see Ch. 4), and changes in practice began elsewhere in the Anglican Communion.[10] American children arrived, already communicant, in England.[11] Canonically, in 1970 we still had no rule. The draft code of Canons in 1947 had incorporated the confirmation rubric, but that did not appear in the otherwise virtually complete code of 1964 and 1969. So that one text was still *sub judice* in 1970, and possibilities for baptized young children perhaps still remained open.

The Ely Report, *Christian Initiation: Birth and Growth in the Christian Society* was published in June 1971, and went straight to Synod members for debate in July. It was based throughout on a theology of baptism as complete sacramental initiation (Geoffrey Lampe was a member, but the Commission agreed unanimously). They recommended chiefly that: 'The Church should make explicit its recognition of Baptism as the full and complete rite of Christian initiation.'[12]

Confirmation was a serious point of mature commitment to Christ, and not a necessary gateway to communion for children – and, interestingly, quite unnecessary for those baptized as adults.[13] The July debate was solely to 'take note', was brief, and was affected by protests about insufficient time to digest the report. Christopher Wansey's desire to abolish infant baptism also skewed it. Only the Bishop of Ely ('for') and an evangelical layman ('against') even mentioned admission of unconfirmed children to communion. After the debate the issues went into purdah.

All, however, was not lost. A later debate the same day handled the draft Canon B 15 A 'Of admission to holy communion'. The Bishop of Chester (Gerald Ellison) introduced it, and the main interest lay in open communion towards other denominations. But a benign forward look had led the Canon Law Commission to write in a Clause 1(c) providing a category for admission of 'Other baptized persons in accordance with regulations made by General Synod'. Gerald Ellison's speech on this (totally forgotten till the third millennium) included:

Clause 1(c) gives power to the General Synod to admit other persons to communion by regulation, if it is so minded. The Commission recommends the insertion of this sub-clause for two reasons. First, we do not yet know what may be the outcome of the report on Christian Initiation ... It is possible that if paragraph 121 of that report is implemented, some adjustment in this Canon would be necessary. That may well be some time ahead [*sic* – COB], and rather than delay the passing of this Canon till the Synod has decided ... we advise the Synod to proceed with this Canon, but to provide powers by regulation ...

The text stayed in the draft, became an authorized Canon in 1972, and remains unchanged – though regularly forgotten – to this day.

The Ely Report included one area – thanksgiving for the birth of a child – about which the Doctrine Commission was also reporting. The Standing Committee needed to unify the treatment and asked Peter Cornwell to write a one-man report, digesting issues into a shape for decision-taking by Synod. His report, *Christian Initiation*,[14] identified as an issue 'sacramental initiation complete in baptism', but also introduced an element alien to Ely – the option of uniting confirmation with baptism, even for infants, and rendering them admissible to communion by that route from earliest infancy. The proposal, though possibly guileless, was highly controversial. If the renewal of baptismal vows and personal commitment to Christ is integral to confirmation, then the 'confirming' of infants without mature commitment bowdlerizes received Anglican confirmation. Ely was strong on mature commitment; Cornwell made circumventing it an option. Therein lay trouble.

The Cornwell Report came to Synod twice in February 1974 – once for Synod to 'receive' it, once for decisions about policy. The issue of 'sacramental initiation complete in baptism' had fallen out of sight. Other baptismal issues dominated, but Derek Palmer on behalf of the Standing Committee moved that baptized children could be admitted to communion prior to confirmation, and that the dioceses should be asked whether they would support this. However, he indicated he would be happy to accept an amendment by the Bishop of Durham, John Habgood, and we could see how the wind was blowing. The amendment came, an end bit was deleted, and the amended motion was passed:

That this Synod, recognizing that there are divergent theological understandings of Christian Initiation within the Church:

(i)   accepts the principle that full sacramental participation within the Church may precede a mature Profession of Faith;

(ii)   invites the Standing Committee to ask the dioceses if they would support a reordering of initiation practice according to this principle by one or more of the following means within the continuing framework of training for the Christian life:

(a)   admission of baptized persons to the Holy Communion at the discretion of the parish priest in consultation with the Bishop, followed by Confirmation at the hands of the Bishop;

(b)   uniting the laying on of hands and/or anointing with oil to Baptism, followed, after due preparation, by admission to Holy Communion at the discretion of the parish priest: and subsequently providing an opportunity, where appropriate, for a solemn affirmation of baptismal promises accompanied by a further laying on of hands;

and to report their views to the Secretary-General by April 1975.[15]

Derek Palmer's accepting of the Durham amendment made it almost impossible to overthrow, but I watched helplessly as the Ely issue became complicated by the alternatives in that amendment.

The issue went to the dioceses and trouble ensued. The document referring the issues (GS Misc 34) asked diocesan synods to consider three successive motions – the first about the principle of 'accepting that full sacramental participation within the Church may precede a mature profession of faith'; the second and third embodying the two Durham alternatives. The diocesan synods fumbled badly. I suspected at the time that opposition to the principle would unite: (a) evangelicals (who had not yet bought the notion); (b) people of all shades who wanted the principle, but feared they would get an unacceptable way of implementing it; (c) traditional catholics; and (d) those who frankly found it muddling. This last group is illustrated by sample diocesan returns – York synod had only 20 clergy and 29 laity in favour of the principle (with 41 and 39 against), but 50 clergy and 45 laity in 'support' of the first alternative (with only 29 and 25 against). Similarly Birmingham lost the first motion in all three houses, but carried the first alternative overwhelmingly. A motion had to carry all three Houses, and so in Lichfield, for instance, it passed in clergy and laity but was lost because the bishop abstained – and in Norwich the principle and the first alternative were carried very strongly in both clergy and laity but lost through the vote of the bishop, Maurice Wood.[16] The cumulated return was impenetrable:

Motions	Yes	No
On the principle	20	18
On the first alternative	14	22
On the second alternative	4	32

Oddly, more dioceses favoured change than supported either of the alternatives – and, as the Lichfield voting makes clear, it was the more paradoxical because the 14 in favour of the first alternative included synods which had voted *against* the principle![17]

The result, when Synod debated these muddled figures in July 1976, was predictable. The principle was debated, but the Standing Committee warned that it was divisive; and it was opposed that day by its normal opponents (as, e.g., Professor Roy Porter and Bishop Maurice Wood), but also, because of the inadequate mandate, by the heavyweight Bishop of Durham who had devised the 1974 motion. He revealed little heart for the concept (though he enjoyed telling us the phrase 'full sacramental participation preceding a mature profession of faith' had come to him in the bath at the Athenaeum*). For the next 19 years he threw his weight against similar proposals. Only one speech was in favour (the children themselves had no representatives[18]). The principle went down (17–27; 83–132; 86–112). Alternative ways of implementing the principle fell with it; and instead we passed a meretricious fallback:

> That diocesan bishops, in consultation with their Synods, be invited
> to make wider use of the discretion already allowed by Canon B 27,
> so as to admit young children to Confirmation when so requested.

This was 'meretricious' because it incited bishops to wrongdoing with a misleading smile. It *was* wrongdoing – we had wrestled with how to raise the minimum age of confirmation, and, frustrated, were instead invited to lower it (permissively). And it *was* misleading – though originated by the guileless Ronnie Bowlby – because Canon B 27 does not include 'discretion' (or an equivalent) anywhere, and requires candidates to be of 'age of discretion', and able to 'render an account of their faith according to the Catechism'. Where was the charter for 'widening' discretion?

Marvellously, few bishops actually followed it.[19] I never heard of one consulting his synod. Given a choice between substantial error and contentless gesture, I'll

---

* The location is not a key to character (as it was when Brian Brindley died at the Athenaeum during a seven-course dinner to celebrate his seventieth birthday). John Habgood travelled by bus in London and in steerage on the train; and told this against himself, for amusement and not self-advertising.

settle for the gesture any day. But Synod members went home believing they had salvaged something, when they had risked prejudicing the future terribly.

Outside the Synod pressures were building up. A literature was arising.[20] In Southwark and Manchester, Ely encouraged bishops to give an (illegal) go-ahead for 'experiments' which, once begun, were clearly irreversible.[21] Leaving overseas Anglicans aside, in Britain other Churches – notably the Church of Scotland and the Methodist Church – were moving in this direction. An academic undergirding was also developing.[22] And by 1980 the WCC was convening a worldwide interdenominational consultation about the one question, 'Should children be admitted to the Eucharist?'[23]

The 1980s: Knaresborough, Boston and Lambeth

Could Canute's veto hold back the waves? Dioceses that had voted heavily in favour in 1974–6 were disappointed and wanting to salvage the situation. Thus Winchester, having voted 63–10 (clergy and laity together[24]), had awaited the General Synod go-ahead, and was deeply frustrated at the outcome. Winchester synod passed a new motion in 1981:

That this Synod

(a)   confirms its resolution passed in November 1975 and supports the proposed admission of baptized persons to the Holy Communion at the discretion of the parish priest in consultation with the bishop, followed at a later stage by confirmation, subject to the adoption by the incumbent, the parish and the family concerned of guidelines approved by this Synod;

(b)   requests the General Synod to review its resolution of July 1976 disallowing the admission of baptized persons to the Holy Communion followed at a later stage by Confirmation; and in the light of a growing demand for such an option, urges the General Synod to permit the introduction of this change in certain dioceses for a period of twelve years as a pilot experiment.

This motion joined a queue at General Synod, and, although it might be defeated, the Board of Education asked the then Bishop of Knaresborough, John Dennis, to convene a working party, of which I was a member, to consider it. We first met in 1982, and then, when the Winchester motion was accepted by General Synod, we were reinforced and charged with fulfilling the remit of the motion.

The Winchester motion was moved in February 1983 by Robert Teare more or less as (b) in the wording of the diocesan synod motion above. He described two parishes where unconfirmed children received communion – at the insistence of the children themselves. He emphasized the dismay when Winchester's heavy vote in favour in 1975 had been simply rejected by General Synod. Some speakers stuck to an old-fashioned two-staging initiation, even adding, almost irritably, that 'Ely', dismissed less than seven years before, should not be reopened, and Winchester had no right to bring it back. But John Dennis cited the evidence already gathered by the working party, that in at least 18 dioceses 'some form of experiment' existed. John Habgood did not speak; and a positive spirit prevailed. An amendment deleted the second half of the motion and the Synod then passed (228–104):

> That this Synod requests the Standing Committee to review the General Synod's Resolution of July 1976 disallowing the admission of baptized persons to the Holy Communion followed at a later stage by Confirmation.

The Standing Committee remitted this, via the Board of Education, to the Knaresborough working party. Now we were following a charter, and were not just shadow-boxing against a contingency. We addressed the Bible, the Early Church and the Reformation. We included a learned appendix on confirmation in the Reformation era. We accepted that sacramental initiation is complete in baptism, and provided a true pastoral outworking of it.[25] Our summarized findings were:

> We conclude:
>
> (a)   that Baptism with water, in the name of the Holy Trinity, is a complete sacrament of Initiation into the Body of Christ;
>
> (b)   that Confirmation is not an absolutely necessary prerequisite for the admission of persons to Holy Communion;
>
> (c)   that it is desirable, both for clarity of principle and for effective pastoral practice, to permit the admission of baptized persons to Holy Communion, before Confirmation;
>
> (d)   that Confirmation should remain in the Church of England as a sacramental means of grace to accompany an adult profession of faith.
>
> We recommend:
>
> (a)   that a regulation along the lines of the draft appended to this

chapter be approved by the General Synod of the Church of England;

(b)   that the Standing Committee be requested to ensure that parishes are assisted to discuss, formulate and implement an appropriate policy and to develop effectual educational strategies for Christian growth.

The recommended draft regulation, to be made under Canon B 15 A (1C), was duly set out in an appendix and is important in the light of later history. A further appendix suggested 'Guidelines' for parishes, on such issues as a minimum age, keeping a register, and restraining services of 'admission'. Our draft regulation gathered dust for 19 years, as all discussion oscillated between either illegal connivance or the overkill of canonical change. No one read Canon B 15 A.

On Knaresborough our unanimity may have led us erroneously to believe all was well. I once said: 'Are we too much of one mind? Ought we not to get opponents to engage with us before we publish?' Others thought this unnecessary, as it would be difficult among disparate people to find a representative view. We saw little literature from such sources, and really believed we were catching the Church of England, if not on flood tide, at least on a securely rising tide. We were in for some nasty shocks.

Here I need to divert. Donald Gray (England) and David Holeton (Canada) had arranged a first International Anglican Liturgical Consultation in July 1985 in Boston (Mass.) on the theme 'Children and Communion'. I got the Knaresborough report (duplicated) to the Consultation, and also persuaded Brian Davis, the leading practitioner from New Zealand, to attend. Three days of hard work produced the Boston Statement.[26] Our recommendations were:

1.   that since baptism is the sacramental sign of full incorporation into the church, all baptized persons be admitted to communion;

2.   that provincial baptismal rites be reviewed to the end that such texts explicitly affirm the communion of the newly baptized and that only one rite be authorized for the baptism whether of adults or infants so that no essential distinction be made between persons on basis of age;

3.   that in the celebration of baptism the vivid use of liturgical signs, e.g. the practice of immersion and the copious use of water, be encouraged;

4.   that the celebration of baptism constitute a normal part of an episcopal visit;

5.   that anyone admitted to communion in any part of the Anglican Communion be acknowledged as a communicant in every part of the Anglican Communion and not be denied communion on the basis of age or lack of confirmation;

6.   that the Constitution and Canons of each Province be revised in accordance with the above recommendations; and that the Constitution and Canons be amended wherever they imply the necessity of confirmation for full church membership;

7.   that each Province clearly affirm that confirmation is not a rite of admission to communion, a principle affirmed by the bishops at Lambeth in 1968;

8.   that the general communion of all the baptized assume a significant place in all ecumenical dialogues in which Anglicans are engaged.

The Consultation ended in euphoria at these far-reaching recommendations and our plans to publish them.

But all went wrong in England. Publication of Knaresborough was inexplicably delayed. A new Synod was elected in October (and I was not[27]), and Knaresborough was not in the papers circulated. The Board of Education held it back incomprehensibly until the last second. I asked the secretary-general to circulate the Boston Statement. He declined on cost grounds, so that too was lacking. The newly elected Synod, with only three days to read Knaresborough, had a 'take note' debate. David Lunn, Bishop of Sheffield, led off, warning about 'laying aside part of our inheritance'. Others wanted children to be communicant earlier, but to lower the age of confirmation. The mood was heavily distorted by the rip-roaring (newly elected) John Sentamu, with a maiden speech distinguished (the only time in his life) by being simply wrong. What would Third World Anglicans think if the Church of England undermined confirmation? And how he remembered his own confirmation: 'a great day for celebration. A goat was killed and chickens were slaughtered, so that we could celebrate.' Others muttered that the bishop's place in initiation would be damaged. It was unlike 1983, and the doubters induced a count on 'take note' (263–106). The report went to the Bishops with no 'steer' from the Synod.

The Standing Committee of the House of Bishops then simply sat on Knaresborough (and Boston) for a whole quinquennium. The Synod never saw it again, and advocates tried instead to stir their own diocesan synods. To questions asked in General Synod, the answer was to wait until after the 1988 Lambeth Conference. However, diocesan concerns were helped by the Board of Education's report, *Children in the Way*. Its compilers wrote:

4.32 General Synod received the Report *Communion before Confirmation?* in 1985. We have not thought it appropriate to repeat the arguments here, but we suggest this is an urgent matter for the Church to resolve, bound up as it is with the wider issue of the status of children and their place in the Church.[28]

This 1988 report was sent to the dioceses, so the prevaricating response to questions was now that Knaresborough would have to wait until diocesan returns were in. The returns came to General Synod in July 1990, and seven dioceses had passed motions seeking admission to communion of unconfirmed children. But a silent struggle ensued – bishops saying there was no great demand from their parishes, despite these motions. Parishes hung fire, without encouragement from their leaders, and hesitating to admit unconfirmed children to communion, when they might then be rejected elsewhere. A national framework was needed – not just individual parishes becoming adventurous.

In the background there were the ACC and the Lambeth Conference. The ACC in Singapore in April 1987 (ACC-7) reflected on trends round the Communion, mentioning Boston and Knaresborough, but by resolution only called for study.[29] So how would it come to Lambeth 1988 as a serious issue for the Communion?

The Lambeth planning of 'Mission and Ministry' included liturgical renewal.[30] The Blackheath preparatory seminar disregarded the ACC and fed nothing relevant into the Conference.[31] At the Conference the group on liturgy affirmed, 'Baptism by water is the scriptural sacrament of once-for-all initiation into Christ and his Body.'[32] We asked that the Boston Statement and the ACC's questions 'should be widely circulated throughout our Communion'. Needless to say, no one in General Synod's management thought that applied to us. However, Brian Davis moved a private member's resolution (no. 69), which the Conference accepted:

> That this Conference requests all Provinces to consider the theological and pastoral issues involved in the admission of those baptized but unconfirmed to communion (as set out in the report of ACC-7), and to report their findings to the ACC.

The leadership of the Church of England was immune to this also. Yet here there was a rising tide of diocesan motions, some – e.g. in York and Liverpool – passed *against* the mind and advice of their own diocesan bishop. And yet bishops (perhaps different ones) were still saying, 'I do not find any desire for this.'

The 1990s: Three paces forward and two back

Somehow Knaresborough was, after five years, on the Bishops' agenda when I arrived in the House in October 1990. The diocesan motions had some impact. Martin Reardon's report particularly focused baptismal policy.[33] The responses to *Children in the Way* were still around. The Bishops had sought the help of the Liturgical Commission, and Kenneth Stevenson and David Stancliffe wrote a curious document, *Christian Initiation and its Relation to Some Pastoral Offices*.[34] They outlined 'Three routes to Christian Faith and Practice':

1. Infant baptism – confirmation at age of discretion – participation in communion.

2. Adult baptism and confirmation together, leading to participation in communion.

3. Staged rites – which would take into account lapsing and restoration, with renewal of baptismal vows.

I call this 'curious', for not only is 3 not an alternative to 1 and 2, but an add-on to them, but also the very question at issue, admission of the unconfirmed to communion, is simply not focused, but is treated in passing as a variant on 1. The document did not help.

The Bishops scheduled the major debate for July 1991. John Habgood drafted motions in January, which we agreed (28–17) to take to Synod. There Michael Adie, Bishop of Guildford and chair of the Board of Education, moved:

That this Synod

(a)   affirm the traditional sequence of Baptism–Confirmation–admission to Communion as normative in the Church of England;

(b)   accept that within this sequence Confirmation can take place at an early age when this is deemed appropriate by the parish priest and the bishop;

(c)   agree that experiments of admission to Communion before Confirmation should be discontinued at a rate which gives due regard to the pastoral difficulties in individual dioceses and parishes;

(d)   ask the Liturgical Commission to prepare a series of rites described as Route Three in GS Misc 366 for the renewal of baptismal vows, for the reception of members of another Church and for reconciliation and healing;

(e)   ask the House of Bishops in consultation with the Board of Education and the Liturgical Commission to prepare a paper on patterns of nurture in the faith, including the Catechumenate.

If the Knaresborough issue was fudged or ducked previously, here it was nakedly faced – and brutally vetoed: (a) stated the tradition, (b) took us down the wrong route, and (c) was a final nail in a coffin. Yet Michael Adie, whose Board had produced Knaresborough, was to wield this guillotine against it – and he spoke in Synod instead as though his motion was simply raising a question and introducing a seminar. There was incredulity among the dioceses whose motions said just the opposite. There was on parade a predictable plethora of weighty amendments, and marvellously, the most crucial one, Brian McHenry's, succeeded (252–161) in deleting section (c) – and this greatly qualified the overall thrust. I myself moved an amendment: 'at the end of paragraph (a) *add* "without prejudice to the various provisions of Canon B 15 A."' I wanted to keep the Canons in play. Michael Adie would accept it, but it was defeated by the floor by 155–190. Michael Baughen, Bishop of Chester, got in a request for a service of adult commitment, and so the amended motion was carried. The first diocesan motion followed. Peter Lock (Rochester) moved:

That this Synod request the House of Bishops to prepare draft regulations that enable children to be admitted to Holy Communion before confirmation, so that discussion can take place within the Church and conditions for such admission, if any, can be considered.

The voting was tight, and a count revealed 7–34; 112–105; 116–102. So the formal position remained unchanged. But surely the House of Bishops had received a message?

I departed to Toronto, where IALC-4 (with 60 members from 19 provinces) addressed Christian initiation and produced an 8,000-word Statement ('Walk in Newness of Life') and seven recommendations, including:

c. Baptism is complete sacramental initiation and leads to participation in the eucharist. Confirmation and other rites of affirmation have a continuing pastoral role in the renewal of faith among the baptized but are in no way to be seen as a completion of baptism or as necessary for admission to communion.[35]

The brilliant Toronto sky had two small lingering clouds. First, two of our Church of England Commission, Mark Dalby and Colin James, Bishop of Winchester and chair of our Commission, dissented from this recommendation.[36] Secondly (as always) would anyone in England take the international findings seriously? In January 1993 the Primates and ACC in their joint Resolution 18 urged

> the provinces . . . of the Anglican Communion to study and reflect on 'Walk in Newness of Life' . . . with a view to further discussion of the issues it has raised at a future meeting of the Primates and the Anglican Consultative Council.

But, once again, not a hint was heard in England.[37] Suffragan bishops made noises in regional meetings of bishops, and resolutions went to the Standing Committee of the Bishops. But nothing was done.[38]

The Bishops had two further possible reasons for delay. One was the Culham College enquiry into the actual use in parishes that had started the practice. The report of this, *Communion before Confirmation*, was published in 1993, and displayed a high degree of enthusiasm for the changed practice. The other delaying factor was NIFCAT (the Nurture in Faith and Catechism working group), arising from (e) in the 1991 resolution. Michael Vasey drafted the brilliant *On the Way*, at breakneck speed, in 1995. Michael outlined five central features of confirmation – none of which was admission to communion.[39] The theological point was getting through.

John Habgood retired in 1995, and that June the annual meeting of all the bishops (suffragans included) revealed overwhelming support for taking the issue a stage further. The House of Bishops agreed and the minute read:

> The House . . . affirms that confirmation remains an essential part of Christian initiation within the tradition of the Church of England, although in anticipation reception of Holy Communion may be permitted in carefully defined circumstances, and where children thus admitted are able to discern the significance of the Sacrament.

This was drafted to carry the doubters, but the logjam was released, and the House set in motion the production of agreed guidelines (GS 1212). I got in my submissions, but the document which the House's Theological Group produced still insisted that the inherited tradition remained 'normative', but 'nevertheless regards "communion before confirmation" as permissible in certain circumstances'.[40] Synod members in November 1996 detected a 'grudging' tone: but the House of Bishops was going to commend such proposals only if key words like 'preparation' and 'nurture' appeared in them. The Bishops' advertised speaker, Stephen Sykes, might have proved even more reluctant than the drafted guidelines, but he was unwell, and David Stancliffe introduced them instead. He enthused the Synod beyond what the guidelines said. He did say that real change would need canonical change, and the guidelines were provisional. I again expounded lawful change by adopting regulations *under* the existing Canon, but this was, as usual, ignored.[41] I also slipped in the following:

> One of the problems ... is that those who are suffering from exclusion have no voice. When half of the persons in the Church of England who wished to be ordained could apparently not be ordained, they formed a pressure group and they now are being ordained – and you will know that, Madame Chairman![42] However, at this point we are talking about those who, by definition, cannot band themselves together and form a pressure group at all. We are the trustees for their need to be one with us in Communion. I hope we will take that trusteeship extremely carefully.

The Synod, with some tiny reservations, agreed the guidelines at that November 1996 session; and the House of Bishops retouched the text accordingly in January 1997 and issued them as policy.

So we were there – or the children were – 30 years on from the beginnings. But the Bishops were acting uncanonically, when a canonical route lay under their noses. Instead of seeking a regulation of Synod, they had acted on powers they did not possess. I, who wanted the outcome, had hesitated to rock the boat on behalf of the other Houses; and the Clergy and Laity had supinely let the House of Bishops get away with illegality. Few, I fear, had looked at Canon B 15 A (though it was printed in GS 1212); the mindset was that Canons have to be changed to change anything (note David Stancliffe's own remarks); and no one wanted to revise Canons for an interim move which would be reviewed a few years further on. Synodical memories are woefully short.

Afterwards: Lambeth, Bristol and Dover

I have written about Lambeth 1998 elsewhere.[43] There Section 3 drafted a statement on liturgy. Section 4 slew it, possibly because it advocated admission of the unconfirmed to communion. In para. 3 (on baptism), after endorsing the Lambeth 1988 and Toronto Statements, we had written:

> – Baptism formally admits to holy communion, so the onus of proof lies upon any who would delay admission until the baptized have fulfilled further qualifications.

> – Confirmation stands as a pastoral office, and this raises a question as to how far it should be treated as a part of initiation. It is appropriate for the personal affirmation of baptismal vows for those

baptized as infants and now come of age, and it is valued by bishops and candidates alike for the pastoral role the bishop thus fulfilled towards the laity of the diocese; but it is less appropriate for receiving baptized Christians from other denominations or for adding after the baptism of an adult, and such practices should be radically re-examined.[44]

So we lacked the backing of the Lambeth Conference; but the guidelines in England bid fair to inaugurate a growing practice. Yet General Synod had more rounds ahead. In November 2000, the Bishop of Bristol, Barry Rogerson, moved on behalf of his diocesan synod:

That this Synod request the House of Bishops to initiate a change in canon law, thereby enabling this Synod, on behalf of the Church of England, to decide whether to retain the inherited norm of 'confirmation before communion' or to change its practice to affirm the norm, for those who have been baptized, to receive Communion before confirmation, rather than leave it to individual diocesan bishops and parishes to make the decision.

This motion was weasel-like. The whole country was to have a single pattern ('norm') of admission to communion. The guidelines called the traditional pattern 'the norm', but allowed an alternative. Barry Rogerson wanted a norm to be mandatory without exceptions – and hoped that the existing norm would stand, and exceptions cease. I cannot imagine what change in the Canons he anticipated, but I fear he had not referred to their text. His speech disregarded all Canons, whether existent or projected, and was largely concerned with resolving what he saw as a problem in having two alternative practices alongside each other. My amendment was:

Leave out all the words after 'request' and *insert* the words 'the Archbishops' Council, after consultation with the House of Bishops, to introduce into this Synod draft regulations for the admission of baptized but unconfirmed children to Communion under the provisions of Canon B 15 A 1(c) which states "[there shall be admitted to the Holy Communion] any other baptized persons authorized to be admitted under regulations of General Synod", so as to encourage norms of national practice in this respect.'

I once again had to work on two fronts at once – procedurally, to get the Synod to focus on what the Canons actually said; and substantially, to protect, extend and, if possible, entrench the admission of unconfirmed children to communion. New members of Synod might well be led by the nose; but there was little history of old members ever actually reading the Canon. So I both quoted the Canon in my amendment, and pressed the secretariat (successfully) to distribute copies of Canon B 15 A to the members of Synod.*

Well, I lost the amendment, and the Bishop of Dover, Stephen Venner, moved:

> *Leave out* all the words after 'request' and *insert* the words 'to continue to monitor the implementation in dioceses of its 1997 guidelines on Communion before confirmation to report back to Synod by 2005, with a recommendation as to whether changes in canon law are required as a result of developing practice and understanding in the Church.'

This was a good fallback, and Stephen Venner made a telling point that there had been no monitoring in the 1997 guidelines. The Synod bought his amendment, so the outcome of it has run on. The year 2005 became a serious focus for work to be done by Diana Murrie, the National Children's Officer of the Board of Education. However, even Stephen, with Canon B 15 A under his nose, was moving an amendment partly about the Canons, without mentioning Canons anywhere in his speech. The unhappy myth that the revision of Canon Law might well be needed was further prolonged.

Diana Murrie brought a preliminary draft of her report to the House of Bishops in June 2004, my own last meeting of the House. The notion that change, to be lawful, required a change in Canon Law still haunted her report. However, the text of Canon B 15 A was also there, and for the first time I found the flow going with me. The legal adviser, Stephen Slack, solemnly opined not only that the guidelines were *ultra vires*, but also that the Regulations route was possible under the Canon (no one, of course, remembered why the provision had originally been put in the Canon). Regulations were duly drafted during Winter 2004–5, and in July 2005 were put before General Synod for discussion. The 2005–10 Synod amended and approved regulations in November 2005 and February 2006.

And the children will receive communion.

---

* I did 'confess', slightly *sotto voce*, that the Bishops had acted 'extra-canonically' in issuing their guidelines, adding that the registrar, Brian Hanson, stated that the House had not been acting on his advice! He had advised Regulations of Synod, while not quite telling the House that Guidelines would be *ultra vires*.

6

Eucharistic prayers

When he had given thanks, he broke it and said ... 'Do this in remembrance of me.'

(1 Corinthians 11.24)

Jesus gave thanks over the bread and cup and told us to. But what should be in a Great Thanksgiving?

In the early 20th century, when 1662 was the only lawful communion rite of the Church of England, many wished to replace its Prayer of Consecration with a 'Long Prayer'. A regular contender was the Interim Rite, in which, after the eucharistic opening dialogue ('Lift up your hearts' etc.), Preface and Sanctus, Humble Access was removed and the 1662 Prayer of Consecration followed immediately – and then itself ran on (somewhat as in 1549) to what was, in 1662, the post-communion Prayer of Oblation.[1] Gregory Dix in the 1940s castigated his Anglo-Catholic friends for thinking this provided a 'Catholic' rite. Instead his 'fourfold action' gave a central place to 'Giving Thanks' and thus increased the quest for a totally revised (rather than rejuggled) 'Great Thanksgiving' (or eucharistic prayer). Nevertheless, the Interim Rite ran on in anglo-catholic circles.

A different precedent occurred in the Church of South India (CSI) in 1950, where their committee members were the first liturgists to compose a liturgy with Dix's book open in front of them. They produced what was much more visibly a Thanksgiving, and it pioneered responsive acclamations (over and above the opening dialogue and Sanctus) from the congregation.

Series 2, 1964–7

When I joined the Liturgical Commission in early summer 1964, the draft eucharistic prayer sent me had no hint of 1662's 'grant that we receiving ... may be partakers', nor of 'his [Christ's] one oblation of himself once offered, a full, perfect, and sufficient sacrifice, oblation and satisfaction for the sins of the whole world'. It did have an anamnesis (the paragraph responding to 'Do this in remembrance of me'), which said, 'we offer unto thee this bread and this cup'. This made the Eucharist an offering of the elements to God, a concept foreign to Bible and Prayer Book.[2] I may have been innocent as an evangelical in my reading and my use of the Prayer Book, but opening this mailing was like being parachuted onto another planet. If the rest of the Commission were to go with Arthur Couratin's drafting, then how could I resist? I could hardly say that inhabiting his planet was not part of my charter and we should simply decamp back to a safe Reformation one. I had 12 months to get my mind straight, for the Eucharist was then beginning a new venture for the whole Commission.* (I can still hear Mervyn Stockwood saying, 'Mr Chairman, I have been on this Commission for nearly ten years and I am still waiting for us to give one day, simply one whole day, to the Eucharist. When can we do that?') So I sorted out that, while I was unafraid to dissent, I would dissent only over that which I could not in conscience say, and would not take such a stand over things I wanted to say which were missing. With Arthur drafting, and following his own half-concealed agenda, I was forced to respond critically to texts which were starting nowhere near how I would have drafted them. I was preaching in Durham in November 1964, so I asked Arthur if I could call on him, and spent a morning with him (and learned much of my trade as a new liturgy teacher from him). His drafting policy was that evangelicals had 1662 and professedly were happy with it, and therefore alternative services had to cater rather for Anglo-Catholics. I could detect the run-on from Gregory Dix in this, but I could not assent to such a policy (though the supposedly evangelical Douglas Harrison and Cyril Bowles on the Commission obviously had bought it, and thus the Commission as a whole backed Arthur).

The first Series 2 services were published in December 1965. Most services in the volume were finished and signed, but the eucharistic rite was printed as an unsigned draft, an interim indication of our thinking. My opposition to 'we offer unto thee this bread and this cup' could not be overtly registered. The Commission met with the members of the Church Assembly at a Liturgical Conference in February 1966 – and found middle-to-high people, perhaps the Parish Communion constituency, standing up, almost ecstatically, applauding our draft eucharistic rite, and asking for it quickly. The message was clear – it would be completed when the Commission met in March. But I tried it out on a younger evangelical clergy conference at Swanwick in March 1966 – and their opposition was almost total.

At the Commission's meeting, the text was finalized and adopted. I cited the

---

* I was sufficiently out on a limb and sufficiently distrustful of where Arthur was going to ensure I did not miss even a minute of the Commission's business. On one occasion, when I was playing rugby and the kick-off had been later than planned, I had to leave the match at half-time to be sure I did not miss the beginning of the Commission's business.

evangelical opposition to it. Douglas Harrison in his peppery way condemned 'the rise of neo-calvinism in the Church of England' as appalling – he almost called for its suppression. I asked the others to amend to 'we give thee thanks over this bread and this cup', but only Austin Farrer would support me. So the existing text went through as Series 2 communion.[3] I formally dissented.[4]

How then to follow up the dissent? The text was being published in order to be debated in the Joint Convocations in May. Helped by Frank Gough, manager of the Church Book Room Press, and Roger Beckwith, librarian of Latimer House, I wrote at breakneck speed a 14-page booklet, *The New Communion Service – Reasons for Dissent*. It was published in about three weeks and posted to all members of the Convocations before they met, and I recall the timbre of excitement and apprehension, when, as a very young member of the Commission, I sat in the gallery of Church House, looking down to where a high proportion of members, right up to Michael Ramsey himself, had the green booklet of dissent visible in front of them.

In the debate Cyril Bowles had been briefed to see me off, but Eric Kemp and others expressed concern about going ahead without full support. They asked the Archbishops to set up a small group to draft an agreed anamnesis and report back in October. The group produced some clumsy wording, in which Michael Ramsey in October claimed to see the different hands in sequence in one sentence. The Convocations rejected it and went back (with their inbuilt Anglo-Catholic majority) to 'we offer unto thee this bread and this cup'. Jim Hickinbotham asked, in this last resort, for alternatives – and the Convocations allowed, 'we give thanks to thee over this bread and this cup' as an alternative. The text was reprinted with alternatives to go to the Laity in February 1967, but the Laity, fresh from painful conflict over Series 1 services, said they wanted new texts to be such that all could use, and they rejected polarizing alternatives.[5] Could the eucharistic prayer therefore go to the next Liturgical Conference in April 1967? In April a series of straw votes produced no agreement, until Ronald Jasper proposed a variant on 1549 ('with this bread and this cup we make the memorial of his saving death, etc.'), a text which I had suggested in my booklet might offer a unitive solution.* The House of Laity members present said they would go with it; the Convocations took the message (reluctantly in many cases – having seen the one that got away), and next day amended the text, and sent it to the Laity to approve on 7 July. The Laity authorized it overwhelmingly for use from 7 September 1967.

---

* I have vivid memories of Maurice Wood, one of the very few evangelical proctors, grabbing me during a tea-break at this Conference and saying, 'Can we go with this?' – to which I replied, 'I think you had better, lest worse befall us.'

Series 3, 1968–73

As it transpired, Ratcliff died at the end of June 1967. Arthur Couratin was already dispirited by losing his coveted text, and Ratcliff's death depressed him further. When the Laity authorized the amended text, he threw in the towel, resigned from the Commission, and virtually went into opposition. As a result, a completely new start dawned for Series 3, with different leading players. The passage to modern language in Series 3 is recounted in Chapter 3. For a revised eucharistic prayer in spring 1970 Ronald Jasper asked me to begin a three-cornered correspondence with him and Kenneth Ross, of All Saints, Margaret Street. Could I make positive recommendations about a paragraph with which I had lived and slept and agonized over for six years? We quite quickly had this result:[6]

> Therefore, heavenly Father, we do this in remembrance of him: with this bread and this cup we celebrate his perfect sacrifice made once for all upon the cross; we proclaim his resurrection from the dead and his ascension into heaven; and we look for the fullness of his coming in glory.

Astonishingly, Kenneth died two days after registering agreement – but the text was there. I made a separate contribution to it, by suggesting to Ronald we turn passives into active imperatives. Texts drafted to read as:

> Grant that we may be renewed by your Holy Spirit and filled with your grace and heavenly blessing

became

> Renew us with your Spirit, inspire us with your love, and unite us in the body of your Son, Jesus Christ our Lord.

We were feeling our way (without precedents, it must be remembered) into a modern liturgical English. And I, out from under Arthur's shadow, could make positive proposals knowing that the Commission would 'hear' the points being made. The coming of Geoffrey Cuming, Charles Whitaker and David Frost had contributed to this sense of entering a new era, where we were not entrenched in previous fortified positions.[7] We were also stepping up congregational responses. So we had acclamations (with **bold type** and 'lining out' for congregational texts):

> **Christ has died**
> **Christ is risen**
> **In Christ shall all be made alive.**

The Series 3 text was getting a both unitive and fresh look to it. And being elected to Synod in autumn 1970, I would be able to engage with the process further down the line.

Series 3 communion was published as a white booklet in September 1971.[8] Synod debated it in November in the first Revision Stage under standing orders of the time. It was Synod's (perhaps the whole Church of England's) first encounter with addressing God as 'you'. A very turbulent first stage hardly reached the eucharistic prayer before the debate was adjourned. The Liturgical Steering Committee that winter corresponded or met with members who had further amendments to move. Proposals came back to the Commission itself, and we approved certain projected changes. Meanwhile, following the publication of the ARCIC-1 Agreed Statement on the Eucharist on 31 December 1971, in February 1972 Synod asked the House of Bishops for a theological evaluation of the rite.[9] Thus in July 1972, at the second Revision Stage, there was a report from the Bishops as well as one from the Liturgical Steering Committee. Much of the attention focused on the 'New Testament Decalogue' (which the Bishops had moved from the main text to an appendix), the Creed and the Lord's Prayer. The eucharistic prayer was marginally retouched, and, wonderfully, on behalf of the Bishops Donald Coggan moved 'Christ shall come again' for 'In Christ shall all be made alive'. He said we ought to be equally clear about each of the three affirmations: 'Are we all clear about the form in which he rose, or ought we to say "Christ has passed away. Christ survives in some form or another"?'

David Jenkins was not in Synod then, and the amendment was passed. And a slight adjustment of the anamnesis followed, to read 'we celebrate and proclaim [his death, resurrection and ascension]' instead of providing the different verbs with different objects. I, with 1 Corinthians 11.26 in mind, was not wholly comfortable with this arrangement – but how much better than the patched-up bare minimal 'make the memorial' with which we had survived in 1967! I think it fair to say that on the Commission we were keen to get away from 'memorial', and in the country many of us had picked up negative lay reaction also. Except for particularly tuned Anglo-Catholic ears, 'memorial' sounded the wrong note. We gave provisional approval to the text. Then in November 1972, at Final Approval, there was no debate, and it passed 27–0; 148–10; 123–9. We had united Synod, and the texts were authorized for a four-year period from 1 February 1973.[10]

Rite A, 1976–80

In 1975 the Worship and Doctrine Measure came into force, and in 1976 Synod adopted the plan for a hardback worship book. The policy was to revise Series 3 communion in the light of use, and give it a definitive and defining place in the resultant book. The Commission put out questionnaires, and discovered from nearly 30,000 that came back that, of those using Series 3, around 90 per cent liked it throughout – save for the Lord's Prayer.[11] In 1976 Ronald Jasper asked four of us, including me, to take on liaison with four bishops so that, as we retouched the text (the Bishops had asked – fatal words – for a 'light revision'), we would keep them supportively on board. We agreed to send to the Bishops no fewer than six eucharistic prayers, including one ecumenical one from the Joint Liturgical Group, and one in which I had invested deeply, a highly responsive one. But, as the timetable for revising Series 3 started to run, we had a significant crisis. In February 1978 the House of Bishops decided not only to cut down our six (not out of doctrinal doubt, but to save difficulties in revision), but also to reject our proposed anamnesis text:

> Therefore, heavenly Father, we remember his offering of himself made once for all upon the cross, we proclaim his glorious resurrection and ascension, and as we celebrate with this bread and cup his one perfect sacrifice, we look for his coming in glory.

At that meeting of the House of Bishops, in a random moment Ronald Jasper said something like, 'Well, if you don't like it, we shall have to go back to "make the memorial".' 'Yes,' said the Bishops, 'let us do that.' Ronald accepted this a little too quickly, though that does not quite emerge in his account.

The Commission had planned a one-day meeting in London on 27 February, a meeting I had myself urged, lest we be confronted (as we now were) with problems from the Bishops. I could not get there till lunch-time, and on arrival was told that Derek Pattinson, the secretary-general, had come to the Commission that morning to report the Bishops' decisions, including this reactionary redrafting of the anamnesis. The Commission appeared to be in gloom, saying to me, 'We are going to have to lump it.' I was not prepared to do so. I diverted the afternoon session's agenda, pointed out to Ronald that we personally signed texts published in our name, and that I was not prepared to sign what the Bishops were apparently telling us we had to. The Commission at large took new heart, and, as we were meeting in Church House, asked Derek Pattinson to return and hear us – which he did. We absolutely rejected any return to 'make the memorial' from the Series 2 anamnesis for any Series 3 prayer. On this basis, we got a further liaison meeting with the four bishops on 7 March, stuck to our guns, and persuaded them to get the agreement of their House by post to a slightly amended text, very near to the existing Series 3. So publication proceeded, and the text was on course for a General Approval stage at the July 1978 Synod.

This was 'Series 3 Revised' (itself to be revised in the synodical process), but I call it 'Rite A', as it shortly became. I was myself asked in late February 1978 to chair the Steering Committee, and therefore in July I introduced the service to General Synod. I had a rare opportunity to spread myself in a speech from the platform, and I took it enthusiastically. The 12 months till the end of the Revision Stage in July 1979 were the only time I officially had a platform role in Synod – the drone's brief flight. The service received General Approval.

The Revision Committee was to meet through the autumn, under the chairmanship of Cyril Bowles. Members of Synod submitted something like 1,200 amendments, mostly from people with genuinely modest improvements.* I had had experience with the other Series 3 services, of every member submitting an amendment being allowed to attend and to move the actual amendment to the particular text on the table. Anticipating the size of the problem, I introduced a different steering procedure. The Steering Committee met in advance of the Revision Committee, considered the multiple proposed amendments, and then produced by assimilation what I called a 'mainstream' text.[12] This was tabled for the Revision Committee, with a noting of amendments which were met by its drafted form, and proposers of amendments would then be asked if they wished to persevere with their proposal. Even so we met 15 times that autumn.

In the process, the Revision Committee made structural changes in the presentation of the eucharistic prayers. In the Commission's text proposed to Synod, the retouched Series 3 eucharistic prayer was the sole one printed in the text, and modernized forms of the Series 1 and Series 2 prayers came in an appendix. These two were brought into the main text as alternatives on equal footing with the one already there. George Timms promoted the idea of saying something about being built into a living temple, and the Committee helped him draft it, and located it in the First Eucharistic Prayer, the one derived from Series 3. Furthermore, the now famous Beckwith-Brindley submission was made, and the Committee decided it could give it a fair wind. The Beckwith half was the request for a modern-language 1662, for which he had already provided a precedent.[13] What he did not know – though Brian Brindley who was on the Committee did – was that the Committee was already making provision for this, so that Brian had readily engaged in such 'horse-trading' (Roger Beckwith's own term for the deal). The other half of the horse-trading was Roger Beckwith's support for a 'Brindley' eucharistic prayer adapted from the Roman Catholic Eucharistic Prayer II, itself drawn from Hippolytus. The 'deal' was put forward to the Revision Committee by the two of them jointly; but overtly on a 'one for me and one for you' basis, a polarizing in options which, as

---

* I described this – and Ronald Jasper quoted it – as worthy of a place in the *Guinness Book of Records.*

a policy, was contrary to the whole basis of the Commission's work in liturgical revision, and was unacceptable to the Committee. So, while setting out the 1662-type in full without demur, we retouched the 'Brindley' prayer to make it usable by such as me. We had to look hard at one novelty, 'We bring before you this bread and this cup', and, gulping, I reckoned I could use and commend it. The sticking point was a 'second epiclesis' which went, 'send your Holy Spirit on all that your church sets before you' (a version of 'upon the oblation of your church' in Hippolytus). We changed that into 'Send the Holy Spirit on your people' – and the rite was acceptable to the whole Committee. At a late stage, the Committee agreed (4–3 with some abstentions) on a trimmed-down prayer for use with the sick – and the package went to Synod for its Revision Stage in February 1979.

The Revision Stage had its moments – quite a few of them. In February and July 1979 together, we revised the text in full Synod for a total of 19 hours. This must set a record (uniquely the Synod Notice Papers came out on A4); and it reflects around 200 amendments submitted, and another 100 or so our Steering Committee drafted. Many of course fell; quite a few were consequential on others for consistency; and a good proportion went through on the nod. I had my typewriter at Synod (no laptops in 1979), and each evening typed battle orders in listed form, distributing responsibility for answering amendments between David Silk, Cyril Bowles and myself. We regularly met amendments from the floor, in a way which I have not seen since, by saying something like, 'The Steering Committee has drafted amendment no. XX which follows the next three on the Notice Paper; if the Synod is disposed to defeat the amendments from the floor, then our own amendment will give the movers of them a large part of what they are seeking.' We left the opening Notes till last, as, once everything else was fixed, we could well help some people by permissions given in the Notes. We made allies of the Synod rather than polarizing from them, not just shouting down minorities, but finding unitive ways through.

We reached halfway through the eucharistic prayers in the February Revision Stage for Rite A, and then adjourned till July. We had a cliffhanger over a tiny word. In Series 3 – and in our initial revision of it – the narrative of institution began with the conjunction 'for', not the relative 'who'. The Revision Committee reverted to 'who'. Geoffrey Cuming, for the First Eucharistic Prayer, in February moved a return to 'for'.[14] He lost 116–117. I was myself distracted by business and did not vote – but would have supported him. I therefore in July gently encouraged him to move his identical amendment in the Second Prayer! He did so – and this time lost 82–85. 'For' passed into history.

Ronald Jasper got George Timms's 'living temple' lines moved from the First Prayer (and Jean Mayland got them inserted into the Second), and the Series 3 'Renew us by your Spirit [etc.]' was restored in the First. We had a wonderful debate re the consecratory epiclesis in the Brindley prayer – 'word' (as an instrument of consecration) was deleted and 'Spirit' replaced it – by 97–96! In the same prayer there was an attempt to remove 'memorial' (on which the Commission had turned its back since the white Series 3 in 1971). I defended its retention in the Second Prayer and presence in the (new) Third – and it was indeed retained.

The four Eucharistic Prayers emerged from the Revision very nearly as they had entered it, and still set out as options within the main text. Much of the great fuss in Synod lay elsewhere in Rite A – an interesting contrast with the struggles of both the 1960s and the 1990s. Rite A duly received Provisional Approval with one vote against.* It was authorized at Final Approval in November by 33–4; 207–10; 150–23. It came into use on 1 April 1980 (as a booklet) before becoming the backbone of the ASB on 10 November 1980.

Rite C, 1989–92

The clock moves on. I came off the Commission in 1986, and the new Commission, taking *Faith in the City* seriously, took steps to address the liturgical needs of Urban Priority Areas. The outcome was *Patterns for Worship*, published in report form in November 1989. It included an outline Eucharist, Rite C, which, as simply a structure, took a little over two pages. For the eucharistic prayer, those in Rite A could be used – or one of the four new ones in section 8 which provided 'building blocks' for constructing liturgical services. These four were recognizably in developed continuity with Rite A, but more varied in their emphases and provided a range of possible congregational responses (which had been presented in almost identical form, with identical cue words, in Rite A's four prayers). Prayer C was a 'mini-canon' concluding with the Sanctus. Prayer D was little more than a matrix, into which the major seasonal or thematic thanksgivings elsewhere in *Patterns* were to be inserted. All four had a 'consecratory epiclesis' *after* the narrative of institution and the anamnesis. This was a real novelty in the Church of England (bar 1928!), but the order was defended by a separate document by David Stancliffe and Kenneth Stevenson (GS Misc 333) which started to promote the concept of a 'Trinitarian

---

* My last speech, moving Provisional Approval on the last morning of Synod, contained two points of some passing interest. Firstly, in reminding the Synod that most time at the Eucharist is given to local uses and choices (as, e.g., in hymnody) I spoke of 'the time taken for the kiss of peace, which is quite extensive in some places'. The shorthand-writer (who always had some trouble keeping up) recorded 'the time taken to kiss a priest, which is quite extensive in some places', and it stands thus in the *Report of Proceedings*. Lest it intrigue historians in decades ahead, I now correct the, perhaps unwelcome, impression given. Secondly, in conclusion I said: 'It has been a great joy to have been allowed out above ground once in our lives, like a drone with its own brief life, and then to perish forever, as is now likely to happen.' In my case, it did. (I am convinced I actually said 'one brief flight' but this is what is on record.)

structure' – i.e. a Preface and Sanctus addressed to the Father, a run-up to the narrative of institution and anamnesis, which sets out the saving work of the Son, and an epiclesis which invokes the Spirit. When a preliminary 'take note' debate took place in Synod in February 1990, Mark Santer criticized the wording in prayers B and C, where the Holy Spirit was asked to 'show' the elements to be the body and blood of Christ – a curious novelty.

The general welcome for virtually all of *Patterns* meant that the Commission could tidy up everything needed for 'A Service of the Word', and the liturgical building blocks could be available in user-friendly form, 'commended' by the Bishops rather than authorized. That policy needed the 'Service of the Word' to be authorized, and that was done through the months of 1993 relatively uncontroversially. The eucharistic prayers were handled separately – the Commission retouched them and brought them to the Bishops in January 1992, to start a full authorization process for them, simply as additional eucharistic prayers for Rite A. If they were authorized before 1995, they could be used and then amended further in the run-up to the time when the ASB's licence would expire in 2000. At a late stage of their editing, General Synod in November 1991 amended and passed a Coventry diocesan motion that:

> This Synod, welcoming the initiatives taken by other Churches, request the House of Bishops as soon as possible to introduce proposals for Eucharistic Prayers suitable for use in the Church of England at services with children present.

This motion lurked around the Synod and its Revision Committees through the rest of the story.

When the retouched four Rite C prayers came to the Bishops in January 1992, they were roundly attacked by two heavyweight traditionalist bishops – I think on the grounds of being too venturesome, though it stuck in my memory more in the form, 'These are not close enough to the Prayer Book.' Suddenly the House was sending prayers back to the Commission with a totally unhelpful label 'Not acceptable – please do better'. And the Commission genuinely addressed the task, and came back again in January 1994 with five somewhat different prayers. The House did not favour introducing them to Synod. It seemed to have no idea of timetable implications of delay. Instead it decided it would go round in a circle, simply asking the Synod members whether they would like the Bishops to introduce these prayers. The House then went even less decisive (I said in the Synod debate that they had been 'in a state of delicious indecision for years over this issue'). So its motion for the July 1994 Synod uselessly asked the Synod to 'invite the House of Bishops to reflect further ... on the eucharistic proposals'. Pete Broadbent rescued the process with an amendment (itself further amended) asking the Bishops actually to 'introduce ... up to five Eucharistic Prayers, at least one of which should be suitable for when children are present'. The amended motion was carried, and the Bishops got a substantial 'steer'.

Delicious indecision was succeeded by clear-cut stupidity. In October the House of Bishops decided to send just two eucharistic prayers to Synod (expressing desire for one more for use with children present). They sent them with no introduction – again unprecedented. Synod did not learn why five had been reduced to two, nor why it was those two, nor even, more neutrally, were they enlightened by an introduction to the characteristics of those two. The two prayers were in fact both shaped with an epiclesis invoking the Spirit upon the sacramental elements *after* the narrative of institution and the anamnesis. Here was the House of Bishops introducing prayers on a totally unprecedented basis, without a word of explanation. Thus Trevor Lloyd, who as chairman of the Steering Committee introduced them, had to make liturgical bricks without any episcopal straw, but he gave us good guidance, including a theological commendation of this 'Trinitarian' shape.[15] I slipped in the following about the epiclesis calling the Spirit onto the elements:

> I cannot get past 'Pour out your Holy Spirit over us and these gifts'; I can never look at it or say it, as I occasionally have, without thinking about custard. (I am sorry if I have ruined it for everybody else here now!)

Later in the debate Pete Broadbent opined about this particular text, 'I am not sure it will survive after Bishop Buchanan's *bon mot* about custard.' The two prayers were approved with much hope they would be improved (and perhaps multiplied) by the Revision Committee to which they were remitted.

I was on the Revision Committee. We met in January 1995, and began by reinstating all the five prayers we had debated in July. One was now adapted to be child-friendly. It was a good Committee – and I persuaded them to add further a responsive form of the First Eucharistic Prayer in Rite A. That was welcomed as still being 'Western' and not having gone over to the Trinitarian shape. So the six prayers came to Synod in July 1995, and there was not one motion for recommittal to the Revision Committee (which was how the standing orders of the 1990s operated). The prayers would therefore simply move on to the House of Bishops for the final reference before coming back to Synod for Final Approval.

But that Synod was over. A new Synod was elected in the autumn. The prayers were coming not to the November meeting, but to the February 1996 one. The Bishops, with some agonizing over how their two prayers had returned as six, approved them, and they went to Synod for Final Approval. They were only proposed to run until 31 December 1998. But at that February Synod trouble struck. New members had not seen the prayers before. Old members forgot they had seen nothing wrong with them in July. Jeremy Haselock, from the Revision Committee which had produced the prayers, now asked us to reject them (the one for use with children was 'thin to the point of anorexia'). Bishops themselves also stood up and made criticisms not previously heard – Mark Santer said two of them called in question our ecumenical commitment to the ARCIC process. The six prayers were a package, so people with complaints about just this one or just that one would vote against the package – and those persons cumulated into a substantial blocking third in the Laity. It failed to get its two-thirds majorities, losing by 25–10; 164–44; 135–81. The House of Laity had defeated it, but if just two more bishops had voted against, the House of Bishops would have defeated its own business.[16] The Bishops were indirectly responsible somewhat earlier in the process when, as shown, they irresponsibly sabotaged the 1990–95 timetable.

New Prayers for the *Common Worship* Eucharist

The Commission and the House of Bishops then let the existing plan for a revision of Rites A and B go forward in Synod in July 1996, independently of new eucharistic prayers. So a new separate item of eucharistic prayers became requisite. A light-hearted seminar about the nature of such prayers was held in Synod in July 1997, and in October texts were approved to start their passage towards *Common Worship*, not immediately via Synod, but by circulation to 'experimental' parishes. The first three (still virtually untouched in *CW* Order One) were the four from Rite A, but with the First and Second conflated. To my horror, in conflating they brought from the Second Prayer the very features of Series 2 which we had been superseding in Series 3. This meant both looking 'for the coming of your kingdom' and (worse) 'make the memorial'. This last was staggering, but the Commission, I assume, neither knew the history I have recounted above, nor perhaps would have taken the stances we took. I fought this one unsuccessfully until it came out still in this less desirable form in *CW*.[17] Prayer D was the one ascribed to James Jones's family, and I have been happy with it. Prayer E went back to sending the Holy Spirit 'upon us and these gifts', and in the anamnesis had 'We set before you the bread . . . and cup'. Prayer F caused few problems. In my speech in July 1998 at the General Approval stage and in written submissions I urged that the problems in Prayer E needed sorting, and that we ought to have a more responsive prayer. The Bishop of St Albans, Christopher Herbert, (chairing the Revision Committee) acknowledged that 'set before' now came also in 'offertory' prayers (see the final section of this chapter), and consistency was needed. The Revision Committee changed this to 'bringing before', which I could accept. My complaint about invoking the Spirit upon the gifts the Committee answered by saying that there was precedent in the prayers rejected in February 1996, but at the first Revision Stage in July 1999 I had to point out that this was erroneous, as our Revision Committee had in 1995 already revised it – and the Synod duly referred the text back. The Committee had turned down flat my request for a truly responsive prayer, but the Synod, against the Steering Committee's wishes, referred that matter back to them, 180–143. We also got a partial return to one of the rejected prayers of 1996, Richard Harries, the Bishop of Oxford, asking for the phrases about a mother tenderly gathering her children to come at least in a Preface.

Time was running out. The Revision Committee struck out the invocation of the Spirit on the elements; bumped up Richard Harries' request into a full Prayer G; and quickly addressed the responsive prayer they had not wanted, and it came out as Prayer H. A ghastly procedural tangle at the next Revision Stage in November was rescued by suspending standing orders, and Prayer H reached its final form just in time to be approved in Synod on 28 February 2000, agreed by the Bishops and returned, within the whole Order One, to be authorized on 1 March (28–0; 175–1; 164–17). To my relief I can use them all with a clear conscience, and to my joy, after efforts going back to the 1970s, we have in Prayer H a succinct yet profound truly responsive eucharistic prayer.[18]

A note on offertory and 'laying the table'

A sensitive drafting point in eucharistic revision has been the placing of the bread and wine on the table. In pre-Reformation use this was called the offertory, but Cranmer's liturgy changed the meaning of 'offertory' and made it mean simply a collection of money. It belonged in the ante-communion, as, for three hundred years on the many Sundays when there was no communion, there would still be ante-communion – and a collection. Obviously, laying the table still occurred (though Cranmer in 1552 provided no guidance), but then in 1662 it was directed before the prayer for the Church Militant. In the nineteenth century Anglo-Catholics, following Roman use, began to call it the offertory, and thus muddled the terminology in English.

Gregory Dix, in promoting the 'four-action' shape, identified the preparing of the table with the first dominical action (Jesus 'took' bread and wine), and so built offertory into that fundamental scheme. He proclaimed the marching up of lay people with the elements to be 'their liturgy'! The 1958 Lambeth subcommittee on liturgical revision bought this and recommended, 'The Offertory, with which the people should be definitely associated, to be more closely connected with the Prayer of Consecration.' This was implicitly calling the preparation of the elements the 'offertory', and explicitly making it 'the people's liturgy' and the first of Dix's four actions.

Arthur Couratin went with this entirely, though the cross-heading in Series 2 was 'The Preparation of the Table', not 'The Offertory'. Ronald Jasper steadily led the Commission in a different direction – and the cross-headings in Series 3 and Rite A display a Preparation of the Table (which we would have compared to the disciples going ahead to prepare the room), and then a separate provision, clearly the first of the dominical actions, for 'The Taking of the Bread and Wine', prior to the Eucharistic Prayer – and no provision for any 'taking' or manipulating of the elements during the narrative of institution. In the text we sent to Synod we reckoned we had the shape clarified – and had never used the word 'offertory'.

However, the Revision Committee for Rite A hit an extraordinary clash, as various submissions wanted to incorporate in the Preparation section the Roman Catholic offertory prayers, including 'through your goodness we have this bread/wine to offer'. This was exactly what other members did not want. The first lot would not settle for variant texts (personally I would have been ready to say, 'We have this bread/wine to share'), but we could not give them the Roman texts. The Revision Committee drafted a cunning provision:

THE PREPARATION OF THE GIFTS

32   *The bread and wine are placed on the holy table.*

33   *The president may praise God for his gifts in appropriate words to which all respond*
   Blessed be God for ever.

Here was a response without a versicle – a liturgical near-absurdity. But our wisdom soon appeared. In the Revision Stage in February 1979 an evangelical amendment was to delete section 33, while an Anglo-Catholic one was to print out the Roman offertory prayers. How were we to see them both off? I defended the above text with the following argument:

> There are those . . . who are accustomed to seeing a Cheshire cat . . . when they go into the garden, and there are others who . . . never find a Cheshire cat on the branches of their trees. We have tried to put them together, and the result is that you have here the smile in the main text . . . those who have never seen a Cheshire cat . . . while they may be slightly puzzled to see a smile above a branch . . . nevertheless will not stop or be hurt or worry . . . but will simply pass by on the ground that the atmospherics are slightly odd. On the other hand, those who are well accustomed to Cheshire cats will recognize that there is only one thing that this smile could ever possibly fit and will have no difficulty at all finding and feeling and coping with the

Cheshire cat which undoubtedly is there behind the smile. Thus, all will be perfectly happy.

Both kinds of amendment fell away.* Rite A kept a clearly defined rational order at this transition point in the liturgy.

When *Common Worship* was in prospect, the Commission presented in July 1996 GS 1211, a draft revision of Rites A and B without eucharistic prayers (for the six reported above had just been defeated). At the Preparation of the Table they had a retrogressive rubric: '*The president may take the bread and wine*' – a dominical action which does not belong in the Preparation. A jumble of prayers in an appendix, 'Prayers when the Table has been Prepared', included a full text of the Roman offertory prayers, though with 'to offer' changed to 'to set before you'. I think Michael Vasey had advised that, with this small change, the text need be invisible no longer. To my mind, the change was all too small – in the Old Testament 'set before' clearly means 'offer'. It was so used in the reply of the Archbishops to Leo XIII's attack on Anglican orders, where they professed that 1662 retains eucharistic sacrifice, on the grounds that we 'set' the elements 'before' God (though it would be difficult to find anything in the 1662 text to warrant this). Christopher Herbert, who chaired the Revision Committees for both the rite and the eucharistic prayers, agreed in debates that consistency was needed; but somehow it never came to actual changes to provide the consistency. The jumble in the appendix meant that the 1 Chronicles 29 passage (of offering money) was printed in the middle of texts provided for the bread and wine, which took us right back to Couratin's drafting in 1966.

I made my submissions, but got little change. The Revision Committee came to Synod in November 1997 with Jeremy Fletcher steering this text:

THE PREPARATION OF THE TABLE

THE TAKING OF THE BREAD AND WINE

[Rubrics about a hymn and gathering gifts]

The table is prepared and bread and wine are placed upon it.

The president takes the bread and wine now or during the eucharistic prayer.

One or more of the prayers at the preparation of the table . . . may be said.

---

* *English Churchman* reported that I had compared the presence of Christ in the Eucharist to the smile on the Cheshire cat (!); but the Lewis Carroll Society wrote and said they had heard I had made learned reference to his works in Synod, and could they have the text.

I put down a motion to refer it back to sort this out. In my speech I said:

> The Liturgical Commission ... made a right mess ... the Revision Committee have improved it but it is still muddled ...

> Now ... come back with a clean answer ... Like Paul before Herod Agrippa I say to Jeremy Fletcher, 'Jeremy Fletcher, do you not know *The Shape of the Liturgy*? Surely you know it, you have been schooled in it ...'

Jeremy Fletcher responded, laughing, and, I think, knowing he had a poor case. Synod carried my motion, and the Revision Committee had to think again. Their revised text was not challenged at the second Revision Stage, so is printed on page 175 of the main *CW* Book. Note the change of text and order in the last two rubrics:

> *The table is prepared and bread and wine are placed upon it.*

> *One or more of the prayers at the preparation of the table may be said.*

> *The president takes the bread and wine.*

The 'taking' is now properly next before giving thanks. Although a note on page 333 allows it to come during the eucharistic prayer, the norm is much better placarded.

The Revision Committee left the appendix of prayers in a jumble, but a tiny gain was made when the Bishops at the final reference grouped the prayers by themes and put the money ones, including 1 Chronicles 29, first.

But, oh, would it not be much better to do without such prayers, and just lay the table, then take bread and wine and give thanks?

7

Six other liturgical issues

> Where two or three are gathered in my name, I am there among
> them.
>
> (Matthew 18.20)

*Over the years I have been in several side-skirmishes over secondary issues
in liturgy – and six of them get a mention here.*

1 Petitions for the departed

The New Testament has neither precedent nor precept for asking God to be
gracious to the departed. To the bereaved Thessalonians Paul simply gave
eschatological answers, without a hint that they could usefully pray for them (1
Thessalonians 4.13-18). Such petitions nevertheless grew down Christian
history, and helped develop the doctrine of purgatory. The Reformers repudiated
purgatory as 'a fond thing vainly invented' (Article XXII), and they purged their
liturgies of all petitions for the dead. This exclusion continued through the
seventeenth and eighteenth centuries, but did not satisfy the Anglo-Catholics
of the nineteenth. In time petitions for the departed were inserted
(controversially) into the 1927–8 Prayer Books, and passed into use, as the 1928
services gained a doubtful currency. When the 1928 texts came for
authorization edited as Series 1 in 1966, the House of Laity very nearly defeated
them on the grounds of the petitions for the departed.

When I joined the Commission in 1964, Series 2 burial service, laden with
petitions for the departed, was virtually completed. I asked not to be a
signatory. Later the House of Laity declined in 1969 even to debate it, as the
Convocations had refused to accept compromise texts. However, the issue had
reappeared in Series 2 communion, and my dissent in March 1966 specified the
(optional) petition 'Remember those who have died in faith ... and grant them
a share in thy eternal kingdom.'[1] However, after the Liturgical Conference in
April 1967, all concerned opted for the final text: 'Hear us as we remember
those who have died in faith, and grant us with them a share in thy eternal
kingdom.' Series 2 communion was then authorized.

Facing a near deadlock between the Convocations and the Laity, the
Archbishops in 1968 referred the question to the Doctrine Commission under

Ian Ramsey. In the Commission's report, *Prayer and the Departed*, the mutual engagement of Anglo-Catholic and evangelical theologians resulted in a scaling down of the conventional 'catholic' texts.[2] The Commission avowedly sought texts which all could use, and thus proposed:

> May God in his infinite love and mercy bring the whole Church, living and departed in the Lord Jesus, to a joyful resurrection and the fulfilment of his eternal kingdom.

> We commend to God almighty this our brother N here departed.

> We commend all men to thee, that in them thy will be done . . .

The Liturgical Commission brought these texts (in 'you' form) into Series 3 communion, and they went unscathed through General Synod to Final Approval on 7 November 1972.

Prayer and the Departed was debated in Synod the very next day. I reported a battle the Commission had had with the lawyers who insisted that all prayers to be used in Series 3 burial must be printed out – whereas I had been urging (for pastoral as well as doctrinal reasons) a simple rubric saying: '*Here suitable prayers are used; a selection is in Appendix X.*' We defeated the lawyers, and drafted accordingly.[3] However, such restraint was unwelcome to both archbishops, and Michael Ramsey attacked the *Prayer and the Departed* proposals ('It reminds me a little of the kind of beverages sometimes produced in the forlorn hope they will satisfy both teetotallers and others'). Synod addressed a following motion:

> That this Synod, while recognizing that there are some members of the Church of England who would not wish to use prayers for the dead, realizes nevertheless that there are many others who value the use of such prayers and who wish them to be included in our liturgical services, provided that they are clearly optional.

They rejected an amendment seeking unitive texts and passed the motion above: 19–1; 149–32; 90–61. But the Laity had again revealed a potentially blocking third, which gave pause to implementing the motion. Series 3 burial joined Series 3 communion much more on the unitive lines, and both, duly adapted and revised, were authorized within the ASB with little controversy.

In the subsequent two decades the *Common Worship* texts followed in the ASB footsteps. The Commission ran lunch-time fringe seminars on prayer and the departed for invited participants in two successive July Synods in the mid-1990s, and drafted fairly unitive *Common Worship* funeral texts with provision for officiants to add further material as they saw fit. These sailed through the Revision Stage without any challenge, and they appear in *Common Worship: Pastoral Services.*

A side-issue has been the rising profile of All Souls Day (or 'Commemoration of the Faithful Departed'). The liturgical texts have escaped the worst medievalisms, but any distinction between 'saints' on 1 November and 'faithful departed' on 2 November is difficult to endorse.* Yet each stage of revising calendars has raised the profile of All Souls a fraction more. I have learned to appreciate the pastoral usefulness of an annual commemoration of those who have died during each year – but there are parishes (and indeed crematoria) which employ any date that seems suitable, without having to theologize about distinctions between the first two days of November.

2 Absolutions

Services for the sick were controversial in the 1960s because of reservation. The Liturgical Commission did not address them until 1979–80. Reservation is handled in Section 6 below. But a different matter was squeezing me.

The Visitation of the Sick in the BCP included the 'indicative' absolution ('I absolve thee from all thy sins') particularly for the dying ('*if he humbly and heartily desire it*'). The 1549 rubric had said, '*the same form of absolution shall be used in all private confessions*', but this disappeared in 1552. The warning exhortation about communion was also drastically changed from 1549 to 1552:

1549	1552
come to me, or some other discreet and learned priest, taught in the law of God	come to me, or some other discreet and learned minister of God's word
that of us (as of the ministers of God and of the church) he may receive comfort and absolution	that by the ministry of God's word he may receive comfort and the benefit of absolution
such as shall be satisfied with a general confession not to be offended with those that do use . . . the auricular and secret confession to the Priest	[No equivalent section]
not judging other men's consciences	

---

* Back in the 1960s Kenneth Ross, being vicar of All Saints, Margaret Street, used to tell me how necessary it was to give John Stott at All Souls, Langham Place, 'proper' chance to celebrate his Feast of Dedication. I always found John Stott dry-eyed about the lack.

This comparison and Article XXV show that in 1552 'secret confession' as an ordinance had ceased, and private 'counsel', with 'absolution' through 'the ministry of God's word', had replaced it – and no specific text or forms were provided. The indicative absolution remained only for the sick, who were assumed to be dying. Article XXV of the Thirty-Nine Articles declared that the so-called sacrament of Penance had arisen from the 'corrupt following of the apostles', and most official documents of the sixteenth and seventeenth centuries asserted that there were only two sacraments – baptism and the Lord's Supper – and thus precluded ranking Penance as a sacrament. Canon 113 of 1604 bound any cleric to whom someone came and in confidence 'opened his grief' to respect that confidentiality totally (this being provided in a context where, with this exception, all church officers are bound to 'present' to the 'Ordinary' – i.e. the bishop – the crimes and misdoings in their parish). The Canon does not call this the 'confessional', let alone 'penance'; it does not refer to 'absolution' (but to 'spiritual consolation'); and it does not employ terms like 'seal of the confessional'; but it sets up a proper relationship of confidentiality, such as any mature pastor, counsellor or spiritual director would observe. When the Canons were being revised in the 1960s, along with Canon B 29, which rounded up the teaching of the Prayer Book, it seems that people could not agree on how to phrase the requirement of confidentiality, and they simply reprinted this extract and kept it in the Code.

However, the 1960s were facing a changed Church of England scene. There was now a strand in English church life which was pressing a Roman pattern of 'the confessional', and drawing upon the indicative absolution from the 1662 Visitation of the Sick as the formal putting away of the penitent's guilt. And a question therefore hung over the scene: could, or should, the Church of England give more official recognition, and perhaps regulation, to this ministry?

Thus, after more than two decades of passing by the issue, in 1980 the Commission proposed *The Reconciliation of a Penitent* (GS 472) as an 'alternative service', and not only institutionalized that which the BCP had left open and informal, but also included that indicative absolution. This text is highly misleading as to the forgiveness of God, and Hugh Craig and I both dissented. It was grievous to me to do so, as it was 14 years since my dissent over the Eucharist, and I had meantime become viewed as a positive player, truly seeking creative and unitive ways into the liturgical future. My steering Rite A through General Synod in 1978–9 had, I think, increased this impression. But now it was all to be scuppered, as the Commission, rather like in 1966, wanted to go ahead without taking a conscientious minority into account.

I prepared for the inevitable confrontation by asking synodical questions (linked with *News of Liturgy*). The February 1981 interchange went:

COB: Is it permissible for a priest of the Church of England to minister absolution to a penitent privately with any form of words he chooses under Canon B 5(2)?

The Secretary-General (Derek Pattinson): Canon B 5(2) relates to occasions for which no provision is made in the BCP. Given the provision for this ministry in the BCP, I do not think that the priest is free to use any form of words he chooses under Canon B 5(2), but is caught by Canon B 1.

COB [Supplementary]: Can the Secretary-General tell us what provision is made in the BCP for private absolution of healthy penitents?

The Secretary-General: I have studied both the exhortation and the particular form of confession and absolution to which Mr Buchanan is drawing my attention, and I cannot see anything actually in the words of confession or absolution which in fact says anything about the person concerned being sick.

He had marvellously avoided the BCP context. I corresponded with him, and with permission printed his replies in *News of Liturgy* in May 1981. In July I pressed further:

COB: . . . would he now indicate:

(i)   whether he holds to his view ... that legally the only available (and thus legally requisite) form of Absolution to be used in private for a physically healthy penitent is that ... in 1662 for the Visitation of the Sick?

(ii)   to what service in the BCP the proposed 'Reconciliation of a Penitent' is, within the meaning of the Worship and Doctrine Measure, an alternative?

The Secretary-General: [After a lengthy statement of researches] I hold to the view that the 1662 Book makes provision for the reconciliation of a penitent by the reference to that ministry in the Communion Exhortation and then makes specific provision for particular occasion in the Visitation ... [Mr Buchanan interprets the formularies differently.] I am reluctant to say that the words are not capable of the interpretation which he gives them. But I am in no doubt at all that they are capable of the interpretation which I have given them ... [and we proceed with authorizing the service on that interpretation]

So there it was – in July 1981 no one could be absolved in private except by a priest using the indicative ('I absolve thee') BCP form. No informality, no choice of scripture, no extemporary praying with each other could legally absolve. Lawyers and secretary-general had spoken: the case was closed.

The service then started its progress through Synod at that same group of sessions. At that General Approval stage, I raised three objections of principle:

1.   Synod should not 'authorize' forms of private ministry as public worship, and the rite was not 'alternative' to any BCP service. How could a rite for reconciling a healthy sinner come as an 'alternative' to visiting the nearly dead?

2.   Apparently, whatever Synod did, the form would remain in use anyway, so the exercise was futile.

3.   I had dissented from this text – and claimed the right to seek to improve 1662 today. 'It apparently locates in the priest's power that which is God's alone.'

I continued that throughout the 1970s Synod and the Commission had sought unitive ways forward, eschewing a 'one for you and one for me' set of alternatives such as we now had.

Donald Gray chaired the Steering Committee (which, paradoxically, I was on). He replied (*inter alia*), 'we are talking about a public service, a public ministry, which must have the support and authority of the Church ... It cannot be left to a merely casual approach.' But, I responded, calling private counsel 'public worship' was stretching both words and ideas, and the Church of England had never since 1552 authorized official texts for declaring God's forgiveness in such contexts – and, by definition, such ministry was not, within the meaning of the relevant legislation, a BCP service for which an 'alternative' would have to be authorized by the full procedure. In essence, each minister gets on with such ministry, and uses whatever means and whatever words the need and the context require.

The Commission's text went to the Revision Committee, and returned a year later, still with two absolutions. One contained, 'you are absolved from all your sins'; the other was rewritten, not now akin to the BCP Visitation text, but still providing:

> By his authority committed to me
> I absolve you from all your sins.

How could we remove *ego absolvo te* from this? Jim Duxbury proposed replacing both absolutions with the 'precatory' form from the Eucharist, and lost (59–249). I sought to delete the second absolution and, when this failed, to amend 'I absolve you' to 'you are absolved'. I began my speech, 'I am now at the end of my road' – and again emphasized that, contrary to scare stories, no one would be deprived of anything if they went with me. This amendment failed also.

In November 1982 the House of Laity rejected a different offshoot of services for the sick, the blessing of oils. They then requested a 'special reference' for the reconciliation rite, requiring that in February 1983 two Upper and two Lower Houses of Convocation and the House of Laity would all vote separately on it before final approval in Synod. This was a rare power retained to the five Houses separately, and it was the first such exercise of the power since synodical government started – and indicated, even before the debate was joined, that unusual trouble was anticipated. On arrival in Westminster for the February Synod, we found on our seats a 'legal opinion' of the registrar, Brian Hanson. This reinforced Derek Pattinson's 1981 interpretation – more a judgement of policy than of law? York Convocation in the separate reference voted 7–3 and 42–15, and I then moved a following motion, 'That this Convocation does not believe that official authorization is necessary for the use of the proposed "Reconciliation" Rite' – and lost by 32–33! Meanwhile Canterbury Convocation approved the draft rite (23–2; 93–27), but the Laity voted 96–55 – so would two-thirds be in favour the next day?

The final conflict in Synod came the next day. John Bullimore quietly shredded the legal opinion – the proposed rite was demonstrably not 'alternative' to the 1662 Visitation. Hugh Montefiore, saying he had the previous night in Convocation quoted eight commentators on John 20.23, threw down a gauntlet – who could show from Scripture, tradition or reason the error of 'I absolve you'? Michael Saward replied that the eight commentators had not actually backed priestly absolution. I took Hugh head-on – on Scripture, we cannot believe the apostles thought they had to establish confessional boxes across the world; on tradition, the ministry at issue was a medieval, not a patristic, development; and on reason, we are constantly told that the priest does not *really* absolve, only communicates or declares God's forgiveness – but, contrary to reason, we are not allowed to put that reality into the text, where the misleading *ego absolvo te* is non-negotiable. The debate is worth re-reading. There resulted 35–6; 157–49; 124–75. The House of Laity, with less than two-thirds in favour, had defeated it.

There were run-ons. I suppose that in pastoral practice nothing changed one whit. Then the Commission, in its *Lent–Holy Week–Easter* services, produced a form of absolution containing 'I declare that you are absolved from your sins'. Note not just the text but also the context – for these were *not* alternative services, but were simply 'commended' by the House of Bishops, on Brian Hanson's advice, *as outside the range of 'alternatives'*!

Then Terry Knight moved a successful Private Member's Motion in November 1984:

> That this Synod requests the Doctrine Commission to prepare and publish a report examining the theology and current practice of *The Reconciliation of a Penitent* in order to assist the Synod in any future consideration of this matter.*

I supported this motion. Would that it had indeed gone to the Doctrine Commission, but instead, with a controversial issue facing them, Standing Committee incomprehensibly asked for a one-man report.[4] I cannot think the author was briefed, and his report, *The Reconciliation of a Penitent: A Report by Professor John MacQuarrie* (GS Misc 258) serenely set out a 'Catholic' approach. I wrote in *News of Liturgy* in February 1987:

> he writes ... almost as a scholar who will give some basic information to ignorant souls who ask for it ... Their controversies have barely impinged on him, though ... hearsay has reached him, telling him that some good folk are unhappy about 'Ego te absolvo' ... so odd a stance that he is not disposed to take it seriously.

Wonderfully, MacQuarrie concluded: 'Now that the practice ... is so widespread ... it is natural that thought should be given to drawing up an appropriate liturgical form.' He had not been briefed, knew *absolutely nothing* about events, and presumably consulted *nobody*.

Terry Knight's next Private Member's Motion, passed in November 1987, asked the Bishops, in the light of the MacQuarrie Report, to reintroduce GS 530. The Bishops hesitated, consulted the Liturgical Commission, and in October 1988 produced this minute:

> The House accepted the Commission's advice that ways be sought to re-open consideration of the wider issues in a less technical context in due time, rather than precipitate further controversy by reintroducing to the floor of Synod, unamended, a report which had already been rejected.

---

* A long preamble about Canterbury Convocation's discernment that there is a collective mind in the Church of England I got deleted by amendment, not only because York was not necessarily mindful of Canterbury, but more because Canterbury had inadvertently omitted to tell us what this collective mind was.

Apparently the Church of England can get on perfectly well without an official rite, however strident the pressure that we need one is when a vote is coming up. After 1988 the run-on was intermittent. In 1993 the registrar required *A Service of the Word* (basically just a structure outline) to have pages of absolutions added to it at Revision Stage – they could not be left to local or extemporary provision but must be authorized. But in 2000 he had changed his mind again (or failed to notice what he was allowing), as, in *Common Worship: Pastoral Services*, in 'Ministry at the time of death', the absolution on p. 221 is simply 'commended (see p. 404[5])'. Thus any form of absolution is allowable in informal contexts, and private ministry lies beyond the control of authorized texts.

The final stages came with *Rites on the Way and Reconciliation and Restoration* (GS 1546) in 2004. The new registrar, Stephen Slack, openly disagreed with Brian Hanson's legal opinion of 1983. The introduction says all the rites are for 'commendation'. Various absolutions (including *ego absolvo te*) are printed, but their context has now changed.[6] In Synod I sketched a warning in July 2004 against trusting in lawyers. The texts were duly commended by the House of Bishops and published in January 2006 in the new edition of *CW: Christian Initiation*.

What about practice? If the biblical promises of the forgiveness of God through Christ are oft-times ministered by one lay person to another, does or should this particular 'priestly' discipline, used in only a small proportion of parishes, have any entrenched place in the life of the Church of England at large?

3 The Lord's Prayer

The recent Church of England history of the Lord's Prayer is complex. I wrote it up to 1994 in *The Lord's Prayer in the Church of England*.[7] I summarize that briefly here.

In early 1968 the Commission produced modern language drafts, *Modern Liturgical Texts*,[8] including two translations of the Lord's Prayer and a commentary justifying the linguistic choices. Austin Farrer produced this section, perhaps his last published work. Our texts went to ICET, and they published substantive recommendations in early 1970 in *Prayers we have in Common*. We were to incorporate ICET forms into Series 3 services, to be authorized in them. The ninth line of the Lord's Prayer read 'Do not bring us to the test.' Series 3 communion had trouble over this in February 1972, but professors of theology at Oxford and Cambridge resisted a return to 'temptation'. The Steering Committee tried again. Ronald Jasper knew ICET planned replacing 'the test' with 'time of trial', and successfully proposed that in July 1972. The ninth line then ran 'Do not bring us to the time of trial.'

Questionnaires in 1976–7 showed Series 3 users as 90 per cent happy generally, but split 50–50 over the Lord's Prayer, because of that ninth line.

For the ASB in 1978–9, such texts were to be settled within a revised Series 3 communion (other services would be adapted). John Habgood, chairing the group overseeing the publishing, led the Synod in November 1977 to seek a single modern text of the Lord's Prayer as the norm (171–148). For the revised Series 3 communion the Commission proposed 'Let us not be led into temptation.' The Revision Committee wrote a rubric '*The Lord's Prayer is said in the following or a traditional form*', and printed the ICET 'Save us from the time of trial.' In full Synod John Habgood moved that we return to two alternatives (not in parallel columns, 'a typographical disaster'), but I, chairing the Steering Committee, persuaded the Synod to resist that. They then restored 'Lead us not into temptation.'* That went into the ASB. I hoped that this text, itself indefensible, would enable lovers of the old to transfer painlessly to the new. However, the widespread subsequent inertia about transferring, which the next two decades exposed, suggested a different analysis; namely, that the votes which had assimilated the modern to the ancient were of people not intending to use the modern.

Then in July 1987 John Bickersteth, Bishop of Bath and Wells (once dubbed in Synod 'The Bishop of Stonehenge'), in his last appearance before retirement moved a Private Member's Motion to delete the modern text altogether and substitute an ancient one. Colin James, chairman of the Commission, carried a reconciling amendment to put both in parallel.† This should have led to the parallel texts coming before Synod for General Approval, with revision stages and a Revision Committee. But an indulgent registrar, Brian Hanson, advised the Standing Committee of the House of Bishops that no synodical steps were needed, as the rubric permitting a traditional form sufficiently authorized them now to print it out in parallel with the modern text – and it was so. We had obviously been taking otiose decisions about printing only one text in 1979!

This minor idiocy during my absence from Synod alerted me about the revision processes pending for *Common Worship*. However, in 1994 the Commission published *Language and the Worship of the Church* (GS 1115), containing clear commendation of both the modified traditional and a modern version. General Synod in July 1994 was asked to agree that:

---

* Amusingly, while the Synod clearly wanted 'Lead us not into temptation', no one in that amendment-hungry assembly had tabled it. I provided it as a fall-back myself – and got it, without personally wanting it.
† This was John Habgood's 'typographical disaster' – but he now supported it.

> The ecumenical texts ... should be adopted in all subsequent
> services authorized for use in the Church of England, with the
> following provisos:
> [(a) and (b) re the Creeds]
>
> (c)   that discussion should be initiated with the other Churches in
> England and Wales to determine whether to adopt the ASB
> ['Lead us not into temptation'] or the ICET/ELLC ['Save us from
> the time of trial'] version of the Lord's Prayer ...
>
> (d)   that both the modified traditional and an agreed modern
> version of the Lord's Prayer should be used in the Church of
> England.

We agreed this. But if those agreeing it thought we had fixed a policy which
later decisions could not undo, we were deceiving ourselves. We never received
a report of the 'discussion' which was to be 'initiated'.

My Grove Booklet was published in January 1995. This time the Commission
provided what I had unsuccessfully urged in the 1970s: a separate report on the
Lord's Prayer (GS 1271), with a full revision process solely for the text and
rubrics of the one item. At General Approval in February 1998 David Stancliffe
proposed and advocated forcefully the ELLC text, 'Save us from the time of
trial', in tandem with the modified traditional text. It went to a Revision
Committee. I wrote in to urge printing solely the ELLC text and permitting the
ancient by rubric (as originally authorized in the ASB). The Revision Committee
rejected this, and at Revision Stage I tabled a reference back to delete the
ancient text.

Too late I discovered I was fighting the wrong battle – the ELLC wording itself
was in danger. In July the Revision Committee brought the ELLC version back to
Synod, but a frontal attack on 'time of trial' by Tony Thiselton* found David
Stancliffe unresistant ('I have no particular vested interest in which way we
go'). We never heard about consulting other denominations. The Revision
Committee had to reconsider lines 9–10. I could hardly join battle, as my own
motion about only one text was to come, and that extract was referred back. I
moved my own reference back, deploying irresistible argument – e.g. that
parishes printing their own texts would make the choice themselves – against
an immovable Sarum. I lost – but was more disconcerted about the Thiselton
effect on the ELLC text. The scenario of 1979 was repeating itself – lovers

---

* Tony Thiselton was, I judge, unaware of the February 1972 professorial dismissal of 'temptation'.
Not that he would have wavered.

of the ancient were keeping 'their' line 9 in the modern text, even if not intending to use it.

In November 1998, the Revision Committee provided the ASB text in a left-hand column, the modified traditional in the right-hand, and the ELLC text below them, to be authorized – but for an uncertain location. So I moved an amendment to interchange the ASB and ELLC texts in the threesome, giving ELLC priority. I ventured this:

> The Bishop of Salisbury, whom I greatly respect ... but who is very much in favour of 'Save us from the time of trial' when I talk to him out of this assembly ... has actually been corrupted, and is a goalkeeper who has been bribed to let goals through.

I was defeated (so was an amendment to delete ELLC), and the three versions, as tabled, were referred to the Bishops.

The Bishops duly approved (29–6). In November 1999 David Stancliffe came to carry the Synod for two alternatives in the main text, ELLC floating elsewhere. At Final Approval no amendments were possible. So I tabled following motions, one for if it was defeated (vain hope), and one for if it succeeded – which it did (34–1; 180–5; 158–35). So I moved:

> That this Synod ask the House of Bishops to reconsider the priorities of presentation in modern language texts of the Lord's Prayer and then report to Synod urgently if the Roman Catholic Church in England and Wales gives official sanction to the international (ELLC) text in any authorized English-language rites that it publishes.

I stated this was mild. I further tried to rescue 'time of trial', as not simply eschatological (I had had several times of trial myself and said so). I scored an empty debating point: 'The Bishop of Salisbury was fairly convincing in his reply [to the main debate] but he was equally convincing when he was proposing the ELLC text earlier in the procedure.'

Rome of course had not then spoken, and the ELLC text might then have been part of the English proposals to Rome, so my motion was plain sense.[9] However, David Stancliffe was unable to reply – a procedural motion took us to next business (214–135). My attempt collapsed.

4 Vesture

In February 1988, Peter Hobson, a Manchester cleric from a good college, proposed a Private Member's Motion:

That this Synod invites the Standing Committee to introduce a draft amendment to Canon B 8 so as to give legitimate channels of expression to the desires of some congregations for their ministers on occasion to conduct divine service without wearing the customary vesture.

The short debate reads like a conversation between loquacious stone-deaf persons. Replying to it, Peter Hobson said:

I had a letter ... from Mr John Vanheems. He sent me a catalogue. I think he thought I had not come across his accoutrements before. 'Dear Mr Hobson, I hope you will allow us to continue in business a few more years at least. We are already struggling, but some of us have wives, mortgages, kids in school, etc., and really need the work just now.'

A nice thought – ecclesiastical robemakers asking us to buy out of pity. But in fact, as Peter Hobson added, he was not proposing to make discarding robes mandatory. His motion was still lost.

I had a go when the liturgical Canons were being revised in 1992–3. In the debate on General Approval in July 1992, I opined that, 'The Canons in relation to liturgical worship strike me as the most classic instance of the Church of England tithing mint and anise.' I proposed to the Revision Committee various relaxations, and then visited them. In one marvellous instance, my proposal that the president of the Eucharist should not invariably have to wear one of the specified vestures split the Committee 7–7, but Pat Nappin, the chair, decided against me. I went to the floor of Synod, and in February 1993, spoke in the debate:

[There was a point in the Revision Committee] where the Bishop of Winchester said to Miss Nappin 'Madam Chairman, there are times in the life of the Church of England when bold and revolutionary steps are needed' – I did not think that I would ever hear the Bishop of Winchester say such words, but I could have predicted, I suppose, what came next – 'but, Madam Chairman, this is not one of them.'

So I moved an amendment that ministers should wear 'appropriate vesture' (naming surplice and alb as traditional use) but without including a specific requirement. I was seen off by dubious argument from Colin James, and, without 40 supporters for continuing debate, my effort lapsed. David Butterfield proposed 'normally' to be added to 'shall' about vesture at the Eucharist, and he found the 40 supporters and had a genuine debate – but lost. The revised liturgical Canons were approved.

The next attempt was in November 2002 by Southwell Diocese (though the Bishop of Southwell spoke ambiguously):

> That this Synod ask that a Canon amending Canon B 8 be introduced to give ministers discretion by agreeing with church councils to dispense with the provisions relating to the vesture of ordained and authorized ministers during the time of divine service.

The debate was impassioned – both sides sure that they were forwarding mission, outreach and the kingdom of God. An amendment to include permission from the diocesan bishop was turned down. Once again, the supporters had to shout (unheard) that they were not trying to abolish robes. The debate concluded with the delightful mover, Andrew David, singing the same three lines to different tunes to make his point, and urging members to 'be part of an exciting, historical moment in the Church of England'. Not so – Southwell lost: 7–24; 69–118; 98–92.

Here I have a kind of confession to make. I have regularly taught that no omission of robes is uncanonical, disloyal, or non-Anglican. On any analysis, wearing vesture is of no substantial importance, and Canon B 5 allows the officiant to make such changes at his or her discretion. In the Reformation era the authorities acknowledged that robes were a small matter, but then asserted that disobedience in a small matter is itself a big matter. It has been my belief that B 5 allowed us to treat a small matter *as* a small matter, and therefore that parishes can relax about this matter. However, as I show in a footnote, my belief has been first challenged and then deemed legally incorrect, and in all honesty I need to acknowledge that, and do so.[10]

5 The Ordinal

Modern Anglican ordinals began with the Church of South India rites authorized in 1958, and the 1958 Lambeth Conference recommendations that the laying on of hands should be *with prayer* – a formula somewhat honoured in the breach in 1662. The CSI drafting had been assisted by Edward Ratcliff, who also advised in the derivative drafting of the ordination rites proposed in the (ill-fated) 1968 Anglican–Methodist Scheme.[11] These rites got widespread support – the major problem being the excision from 1662 of 'Whose sins you forgive, they are forgiven, whose sins you retain, they are retained.' John 20.19-23 was the gospel reading, and retained Jesus' words without applying them so literally to the actual candidate.

There were no Series 2 ordination rites, but a Series 3 project began in 1976 for inclusion in the ASB. The Liturgical Commission's report in 1977 (GS 327) placed the laying on of hands securely within the ordination prayer, and amended the text 'Take thou authority' at the giving of the Bible, lest it appear actually to effect the ordination. The prayer formula at the laying on of hands was (through pressure by the Bishops):

> Send down your Holy Spirit upon your servant N, whom we now ordain in your name to the office and work of a priest in the Church.

The Bible was given with these words:

> Receive this Book, a token of the authority which you have received . . .

On the fast-working Revision Committee in Autumn 1977, David Silk and I, reckoning on short episcopal memories, restored (in GS 327A) our preferred:

> Send down the Holy Spirit upon your servant N, for the office and work of a priest in your Church.

We had a wry laugh at the juxtaposition (shown above) of 'Book' and 'token' and changed that too. We had no opening Notes, but were pressed by Brian Brindley and others to include vesting, anointing, delivery of paten and chalice, giving of staff (and ring) to new bishops and 'concelebration' of newly ordained priests and bishops with the presiding bishop. We produced in GS 327A some restrained Notes about vesting and giving 'symbols of the priest's or bishop's office' after the giving of the Bible. We made a very positive addition, 'or Presbyters', to the title 'The Ordination of Priests'.

At the Revision Stage in February 1978 Brian Brindley got two additions into the Notes. The first stated, 'It is appropriate that the newly ordained should be invited by the bishop to exercise their new ministry in the course of the service.' By this he intended the deacons to lay the table and the priests to 'concelebrate'.[12] I never discovered what he thought bishops should do. His other amendment, after retouching, specified 'paten and chalice' and 'pastoral staff' in the 'symbols of office' Note.

These rites ran from 1978 to 2005, and fitted well with Rite A and with Order One in *Common Worship*. But bishops often uncritically assimilated the process to previous 1662 procedures. Many still sat to ordain, so that, *in the midst of a single prayer*, candidates were marching up individually, kneeling to receive the laying on of hands, standing, bowing, walking away (possibly backwards) and then being followed by the next one. Similarly the bishops, seated or standing, loved wearing mitres although they were now praying.*

As *Common Worship* began, the ASB ordinal's licence was extended by five years. Some small permissions were smuggled in by an amendment during the authorization of services. The presentation of the candidates could come at the very beginning, and the giving of the Bible at the very end. I was insufficiently alert to this latter point, and *News of Liturgy* carried no mention of the change (see GS 1432B). So thoroughly had I overlooked it that I (along with everyone else) treated the permission to give the Bible at the end as an innovation in the drafting of a *CW* Ordinal in 2003. At the meeting of diocesan liturgical secretaries that year Paul Bradshaw spoke of the Commission making the end-point the place where the giving of the Bible was not only permitted but was actually printed. To those who feared this disruption, it was a relief when the text published in January 2004 in GS 1535 had the giving of the Bible printed in the usual place. The report's introduction treated the end position as an innovation, and offered seductive reasoning to commend it ('more prominent and more closely associated with the sending out of the newly ordained'). The text also expressed a partisan and, in my judgement, deeply unsatisfactory Salisbury preference about *how* the Bible is given:

> In some dioceses a large Bible is presented to each of the newly ordained in turn; in others, individual copies of the Scriptures are handed over to them. The symbolism of the act may perhaps be more clearly seen when the first of these two practices is followed . . .

The text removed words said to the newly ordained individually as the Bibles are given, in favour of a corporate formula said once to all of them.

When David Stancliffe moved General Approval in February 2004 he spoke of the option of giving the Bible at the end as an innovation (one he was sure many would welcome). I again missed the trick – there were several other battles to fight.[13] But Christina Baxter denounced the option roundly and elicited no answer from David Stancliffe when he replied to the debate. I did make this side-point:

> I distrust the extra ceremonies[14] he is bringing in. As the Bishop of Salisbury has mentioned practice in both Portsmouth and Salisbury, which has been happening illegally, it seems, up to now, and as he seems totally unbothered whether it is in the book or not, I do not

---

* I note in *News of Liturgy* (January 1981) that Robert Runcie stood to ordain bishops on an occasion I attended. But it did not last, and later both he and George Carey sat. York consecrations were done much more cleanly.

see why he has to put it in the book now – because, obviously, other people will do it.

The fact that anointing and footwashing were already in use (largely, I suspect, in Salisbury) was acknowledged in the introduction to GS 1535. At any rate, the rites were generally approved and went to their Revision Committee. While the text was there, the Archbishop of Canterbury put the giving of the Bible at the end at a couple of consecrations of bishops, avowedly to assist the Revision Committee to get the feel of the change. I appeared before them in the first months of 2004, but this was only to handle early questions, like the use of 'presbyter' – and the restoration of the rubric about the royal mandate at the consecration of bishops!* When I came off Synod in July 2004, I continued a correspondence with the Revision Committee. One point they took was cautiously to increase the use of 'presbyters' in place of 'priests'.

At the Revision Stage in February 2005, references back were attempted from the floor, and, importantly, John Cook's one to delete the option of giving the Bible at the end succeeded (129–112). No hint was given that it was already permitted. The Revision Committee then rejected Synod's request, and reported back in July 2005 keeping the option at the end. They opined that, as less than half the Synod had voted, 'it was hard to assess the mind of Synod as a whole'. I have never heard a Revision Committee ever adopt such a way of undermining a reference to them before – and, as a matter of fact, a vote of 240 people is not untypical of much business in Synod. They rejected the argument I had raised, based wholly upon our work in the 1970s, citing the parallel between the liturgies for marriage and for ordination which had determined our revision of texts 25 years before – the ring (or rings) in marriage followed the mutual taking, but was a 'sign' subsequent to the marriage, and similarly the giving of the Bible followed the laying on of hands with prayer, and was a 'sign' subsequent to the ordination – yet belonged with it as closely as the ring did with the marriage. The committee report (GS1535Z) rejected the argument on the grounds that *the ring is totally integral to the act of marriage*, and so there is no analogy.† I believe this to be bad in law, but could get no opinion from the

---

* I found this appearing before the Committee somewhat humiliating. On the first occasion those of us who wished to speak to some part of the business were simply asked to come at 1.30, and we would find out the timetable. I sat the whole afternoon for the sake of about two minutes' interaction with the committee. There was even a point where in my written submission I had especially asked that something should *not* be changed, but, when it came up, the chairman ruled that, as I had made no proposal for change (which is why the Revision Committee existed), I could not speak to the matter! I do think we did better by people appearing before us in the olden days.
† They went further in an overkill to demonstrate that the giving of the Bible is not the 'matter' of ordination, wonderfully tracing this back to the Nag's Head Fable. In Synod Tony Thiselton described this as 'an irrelevance, a red herring, a straw man, a rhetorical ploy of less than hypothetical or theoretical significance'.

registrar, and wrote to *Church Times* to say so. So the Committee kept the option of giving the Bible at the end in the text – and again never stated it had been permitted since 2000.

At the Second Revision Stage in July 2005 Christopher Hill, Bishop of Guildford, mentioned almost in passing that the position at the end had been permitted since 2000 (and he had used it there). Kenneth Stevenson, Bishop of Portsmouth, said (as he had said in passing in February) that he also had been giving the Bible at the end; no other speaker referred to the point; but some of the head of steam went out of the attempt to remove the option, and it went down. The Bishops finally restored the ASB individual words accompanying the giving of the Bible to each; and the rites then went through overwhelmingly at Final Approval.[15] But structuring in such options (options, that is, for the ordaining bishops, not options for the candidates) is almost calculated to remove some of the commonality which an ordinal for 44 dioceses ought to have.

6 Reservation

I first spoke in Synod at its first meeting in November 1970, about reservation of consecrated elements, as someone had requested regulations governing it. I put down my marker, that reservation was illegal, and for that reason would not admit of regulations. In 1972 I wrote what I believe to have been the first ever positive statement by an evangelical about 'extended administration'.[16] I was thus able to recommend and support the provision, authorized in 1982, for communion of the sick using extension (though evading the word). Distribution around homes or hospitals more or less directly from a celebration has become widely acceptable.

However, permanent reservation, though I lived with it in many parishes as a working bishop, still seems to me wrong, fostering an unwarranted concept of a localized presence of Christ. When, in the late 1990s, Synod handled services of communion from reserved elements, led by lay persons or deacons, I voted against. One of my problems was that the House of Bishops had been urging that children, to be communicant, ought to be present when the Eucharistic Prayer was said – and now we were taking the opposite view that adults did not need it. At a deeper level it disturbed the balance of the Church of England. I wrote in *News of Liturgy* (August 2000):

> those who want to reserve . . . say to those who don't 'Do not be dog-
> in-the-mangerish – just because you do not want extended
> communion, surely you should not mind us being able to use it?' But

the non-reservers are not . . . allowed to say back 'Do not be dog-in-the-mangerish – just because you do not want lay presidency, surely you should not mind us being able to use it?'

The rite passed in July 2000 (38–2; 137–34; 131–64). The House of Laity figure, where the noes were within a whisker of a blocking one-third, caused a gasp. The Archbishop of York, David Hope, who was in the chair, then promised the Synod that (as a following motion for which there was insufficient time had requested) the House of Bishops would review the decision and report back within five years. But this did not happen.

8

Anglicans and Methodists

Has Christ been divided?

(1 Corinthians 1.13)

Well, Geoffrey Fisher restarted it all in 1946, and the pace has varied from slow and halting to visibly static – and still has a long way to go. But here is the record.

How do separate denominations of the Christian Church ever reunite? In my time – and throughout my time – the question for Anglicans has largely centred on the Methodists. So can we unite with the Methodist Church? Many apparent obstacles confront us, such as: actual separate structures, an Anglican superiority complex, and the Church of England's 'special relationship' with the State. But the besetting theological problem from 1946 to the present day has been the issue of bishops and invariable ordination by bishops.

The necessity of bishops

Since 1662 the Church of England has ruled that only bishops can ordain other ministers, and that ministers ordained by other methods cannot be recognized as ministers by us. Methodism, arising in the eighteenth century, has not had bishops, so its ministers have not been recognized as presbyters by us. Then from 1833 onwards the Anglo-Catholics promoted apostolic succession (the *Tracts for the Times* literally said to clergy, 'magnify your office') and completely unchurched Churches without bishops. This further distanced Methodists from us, and even made them glad not to be Anglicans.[1] The 20th century had an entrenched division to address.

The absolute necessity of bishops in the historic succession and of ordination by bishops remained the presenting issue. Even when Anglicans have not believed this was revealed from heaven, they have still *acted* as though it had been. And presenting issues, even if many reckon them secondary, cannot be ducked. In conversations with Baptists, a presenting issue is infant baptism. With Roman Catholics, it is papal authority.[2] Between Anglicans and Methodists in England, it has been episcopacy. People cannot dub it 'secondary' and then be impatient of protracted wrestling over secondary issues – if reunion itself is a primary matter, then we have to address any presenting issue that hinders it, rather than dismiss it as insignificant.

First steps

Conversations in England began after the 1920 Lambeth Conference issued its 'Appeal to all Christian People' (citing the 1888 'Lambeth Quadrilateral' as a basis). In 1923 a conference was held with non-episcopalians at Lambeth Palace, and the Anglicans typically stated about Free Church ministers:

> It seems to us to be in accordance with the Lambeth Appeal to say ... that the ministries which we have in view in this memorandum, ministries which imply a sincere intention to preach Christ's Word and administer the Sacraments as Christ has ordained, and to which authority had been solemnly given by the Church concerned, are real ministries of Christ's Word and Sacraments in the Universal Church.

> Yet ministries, even when so regarded, may be in varying degrees irregular or defective.[3]

There, in a nutshell, was, and is, the problem. True ministries, real ministries, ministries abundantly blessed by God; but (the sting in the tail) yet defective – and thus, from an Anglican standpoint, ministries by those disqualified as ministers. But suppose Methodist ministers are unconvinced by this, and take their call, their ordination, and their existing gospel responsibilities seriously. How then are the structures of two Churches to join?

The Church of South India

One answer dawned on the world scene in 1919, when conversations began in South India between (largely indigenous) Indian Christians from the Anglican, Methodist and South India United Churches.[4] By the early 1930s they had agreed that the whole united church should become episcopal at union, that new bishops should be consecrated from among the presbyters of the uniting Churches by existing bishops, that existing presbyters should equally become presbyters of the united episcopal church without further ordination or supplementing of ordination, and that ordinations should thereafter be episcopal. That is what CSI means when invoked as a pattern in this chapter.

Agreed by the early 1930s? Yes, but Anglicans around the world attacked the Scheme at this very point of recognizing Methodist and SIUC presbyters *as* presbyters in the united church, without a bishop laying hands on them. The Anglo-Catholic missionary society, the Society for the Propagation of the Gospel (SPG), withdrew support from any missionaries entering CSI. Kenneth Kirk edited the massive *The Apostolic Ministry* (1946) marshalling vast theological arguments against it. The Anglican province itself, the Church of India, Burma and Ceylon (CIBC), included many who hesitated to consent. Thus there were great delays, but finally the CIBC Synod agreed, and the Churches united on 27 September 1947.[5] Anglo-Catholics led heavy attacks on CSI at the 1948 and 1958 Lambeth Conferences, and other conversations (notably in North India, Pakistan and Ceylon, but with broad hints to England) were told not to imitate South India, but somehow to 'episcopalianize' all clergy from the start.

The Anglican–Methodist Scheme, 1956–70

In England Geoffrey Fisher's post-war Cambridge sermon restarted everything in November 1946. The Church of England, he said, cannot unite with others for three good reasons:

1.   We are disagreed among ourselves;

2.   We are established;

3.   We are the nodal point of the Anglican Communion.

So, would the Free Churches 'take episcopacy into their system' and try it out themselves? Ten years on, conversations began with the Methodists, and they reported in February 1963.[6] The Anglicans were unanimous; four of the twelve Methodists dissented. The report had a strong strand of catholicism in its statements on Scripture and tradition and on priesthood and sacraments, but gave most trouble by its Service of Reconciliation. Bishops were to lay hands on all Methodist ministers, and Methodist ministers on all Anglican ones, and an ambiguous prayer would be used, after which all ministers would be in good standing in both Churches. Evangelical Anglicans, who had, typically, not been represented on the conversations, disapproved, and the Latimer House Doctrine Group, which I was in, provided reasoned argument against the Service of Reconciliation (citing CSI).[7] For Methodist ministers to accept episcopacy for the future without calling in doubt their existing ordination was sufficient (and the laying on of hands by Methodists on Anglicans was clearly spoof). We did seek visible organic unity – but not on these terms. This is important, as Anglicans are often told they rejected the Methodists in this period, when it was the Scheme, not the Methodist Church, which was unacceptable. Our group sought a one-stage scheme instead of the vague promise and postponing of hard decisions involved in the two stages of the report.

The first decision was by the Convocations. Their Anglo-Catholic weighting meant they asked only, 'Is the Service of Reconciliation sufficient to ensure that Methodist ministers are episcopally ordained?' After reference to the dioceses, the Convocations in 1965 said 'yes' and, with the Methodist Conference 78 per cent vote in favour, the two Churches then set up the Anglican–Methodist Unity Commission. Methodist dissentients were excluded, but Jim Packer, convenor of the Latimer House Group and editor of our published criticisms of the Scheme, was appointed to the Anglican team, while sustaining his opposition to the Service of Reconciliation.

The Unity Commission made its final report in two parts, the Ordinal and the Scheme, in 1968.[8] Jim Packer, while improving the doctrinal chapters, still opposed the Service of Reconciliation and dissented from it. The two stages were still there, and stage two was still pretty misty.

My own Area Bishop of Willesden, Graham Leonard, was opposed, saying that no bishop could with integrity administer what had to be an ordination, while forbidden to call it an ordination. Other determined Anglo-Catholics went with him. Early in 1968 I told him that I thought that he and I had more in common than the Scheme's proponents allowed – they reckoned to gain by dividing us. I pinned him down for serious leisured conversation, and finally in October spent a whole evening with him. He reckoned that CSI 'had integrity' – this (over against calculated ambiguity) moved him. Could we take this further? He wanted to include his theological consultant – Eric Mascall. I responded by nominating mine – Jim Packer.[9] And we were in business – with time against us. Four of us met and addressed a letter to the Convocations before their first vote in May 1969, and another before the final vote in July 1969. We stated that we were nearer to each other than any of us was to the Scheme, and we predicted a full agreement between us, which raised some hollow laughs.[10] The House of Laity, with strong evangelical membership, had no powers, but in June by a narrow majority they requested the Convocations not to proceed on such a split basis.* The Convocations then defeated the Scheme – narrowly. The vote reached a two-thirds majority in each House, but missed the three-quarters majority needed overall. The Methodist Conference voted by 78 per cent for 'provisional legislation', and were constitutionally due to vote finally a year later – meantime leaving the Scheme half-alive.

We four spent a day together each month in autumn 1969 to write a book, finishing with 24 hours in January 1970. I became secretary, setting drafting timetables, chasing others to write, and drafting myself where they lagged. In

---

* Also in June 1968 all licensed clergy were asked, 'Will you take part in the Service of Reconciliation to inaugurate Stage One?' They answered 9642–5621 in favour, a highly divisive reconciliation.

theological discussion we reached an agreement on integrating ministries, a parallel to CSI. Eric Mascall said he viewed the relationship of the ministry to the body of the Church as an organic structure to which people ordained in other ways could not belong. I suggested that a good model of an organic structure is a biological family, but that, if a child were adopted from outside the structure, this built up the biological family structure rather destroying it, and the adopted child was treated identically to a birthed child thereafter. Eric went with this; and Jim and I agreed a fairly strong statement on episcopacy, and on ministry and sacraments; and we were there.* Robin Brookes at SPCK was publishing it; we delivered the manuscript in mid-January; and it was published in mid-May as *Growing into Union: Proposals for Forming a United Church in England*. The four of us agreed the whole text (except two doctrinal appendixes by two persons only[11]). It had a dynamic effect. As an extraordinary bonus Michael Ramsey invited us to spend a day going over the book with him. He had marked the margins of his copy and led us through chapter by chapter asking us probing, but genuinely questing, theological questions. He was deeply committed to the Scheme, and was not going to abandon it, so finished the day saying he would exhort others to read our book before rejecting it! But we, having had an amazing theological seminar, welcomed his reconciling spirit of enquiry when we were largely being battered in public.

'Clarifying' the Scheme – and ending it, 1970–72

Growing into Union was timely, as the Scheme lingered on. The Methodists were treated to a blistering attack on our book before their 1970 Conference.† Unsurprisingly the Conference finally endorsed the Scheme, and thus asked our Synod at its inauguration, 'What are you going to do about our embracing of the Scheme?' Standing Committee brought a report in February 1971, and Synod asked for the Scheme to be clarified and brought back again.

The idea of 'clarifying' the Scheme begged two enormous questions. The first was the typical assumption of single-minded zealots who have lost a vote that everyone who voted 'our' way knew what they were doing, but those who voted against must have misunderstood the Scheme – and thus might come to a

---

* I love driving an opposed position to its logical outcome, and I drafted an extensive appendix, 'A Bog of Illogic or The Service of Reconciliation and the Law of Non-Contradiction'. After 36 years I confess my own hand in this. The appendix went through without emendation – and was attributed by readers to Eric Mascall, one of the happiest indirect compliments I have received!

† Six Methodist leaders wrote an extensive, but clearly hasty, critique of *Growing into Union* in the *Methodist Recorder* on 4 June 1970. We responded in time for Conference with *Growing into Union and Six Methodist Leaders* (Grove Books, 1970) – drafted, agreed, proofed and printed so fast that Eric Mascall opined (incorrectly) that I had resorted to the black arts. But, oddly, I could not persuade the Conference bookstall to display it.

better mind. The other enormous question begged was the assumption that a Scheme deliberately staked upon unresolved ambiguity could be 'clarified' and remain itself.

So, after the February 1971 Synod, a fast-working working party was appointed – and the four authors of *Growing into Union* appeared before it (though without effect). The working party reported (with predictably little changed) three months from starting work. I got a critique published and around to Synod members.[12] In July 1971 Synod debated giving the 'clarified' Scheme provisional approval and sending it to the dioceses. The most constructive amendment came from Cyril Bowles, Bishop of Derby. He would have invited the Methodists to become episcopal by unilateral action while going on working with us at a full scheme. He lost by 5–36; 89–133; 93–121 (virtually a 40–60 split). The 'clarified' Scheme was sent to the dioceses (35–2; 140–81; 132–80 – more like 65–35) – and at Final Approval Synod was going to need not only a two-thirds majority in each House, but a 75 per cent majority overall. Amid much whistling to keep up courage, the dioceses responded with a 68–32 split, but there was a widespread sense of going up a *cul de sac*. Open communion in the Church of England was at the same time making the Scheme unnecessary for intercommunion.[13] Sure enough, on 3 May 1972, Michael Ramsey, acknowledging only a miracle would achieve 75 per cent, introduced the Scheme in a relatively laid-back seminar-style way – and lost by 34–6; 152–80; 147–87 – an overall split of 65.8–34.2 per cent. The end had come. I sorrowed for those who had set their hearts on it – not least Michael Ramsey himself – but the Church of England had not really faced hard questions, and both Churches had been salvaged from a prospective appalling mess.[14]

The whole 1963–72 period has been mythologized as the time we led the Methodists up the garden path and – mixing the metaphor – abandoned them at the church door. The myth has distorted much ecumenical thinking since. I return to it later.

The CSI 25 years on

That Scheme had no sooner departed than an unexpected cross-current flowed. In September 1972 CSI would be 25 years old. How could the Church of England mark the occasion? The Faith and Order Advisory Group (FOAG) proposed celebrating by moving the relationship on by a millimetre. Previously, episcopally ordained clergy of CSI could preside at Anglican Eucharists only by not doing so in other denominations in England.* Now – wonderfully – Synod

---

* Defensive? Or plain batty? No, simply an instance of how grudging was any recognition at all in 1950 and 1955.

could lift that restriction. Eric Kemp, moving the resolution, said that FOAG had considered:

> whether we could do as some other parts of our Communion appear to have done; namely, to declare that we are in full communion with the Church of South India while maintaining our rules intact, which would mean . . . a practical limitation. That was what the first draft of our Report outlined; but . . . It seemed to some to be a mere playing with words.

Ah, but suppose the *substance* of full communion could be delivered? Over the horizon on a white charger rode that dangerous radical Robert Runcie, Bishop of St Albans. His amendment read:

> That this Synod, recognizing that the Church of South India is an episcopally ordered Church and believing it to hold all the essentials of the Christian Faith requests the House of Bishops to consider how the Church of England and the Church of South India can now be joined in a relationship of full communion.

His 'now' sounded urgent. He referred generously to *Growing into Union*, and secured his amendment by 24–8; 93–75; 114–60.

What would the Bishops bring us? Well, the documents for February 1973 told us Runcie was returning to *cancel it all*. Geoffrey Lampe, John V. Taylor (general secretary of CMS, not then on Synod) and I sent round a 1,200-word memorandum asking Synod members to reject the report. We wrote:

> 'Now' was the key word in the St Albans' amendment of last July . . . The situation is now clear, however – any meaningful 'full communion' does require legislation, and the Bishops are not proposing it . . . The Church of South India is apparently absolutely fine, except that we cannot change our position to turn such approval into action. The Synod is solemnly to 'resolve to enter into full communion with the Church of South India' and then regulations follow which amount to entering into NOTHING . . . a bogus bit of window-dressing.

I also put down amendments. Robert Runcie rose blushingly to torpedo his own initiative, 'without any desire to disguise the movement – some may even think the wobbling – of my own mind'. We did receive the report and reached the resolutions, one recognizing CSI as 'a true part of the Church universal'; a second 'to enter into communion with CSI subject to regulations'; a third that the present law *is* the 'regulations' (hence the Lampe-Taylor-Buchanan picketing above); a fourth for more theological work; and a fifth to review these resolutions not later than 1975. I had an amendment to the second to give full recognition to all CSI presbyters without distinction. Runcie switched from principle to practicalities – 'The presbyters concerned ... would be few in number, now of advanced age, and ... unable to speak English ... not a very realistic thing' – and saw me off. In the fifth I sought to substitute 1974 for 1975. Only one thing remained to review; it would not take two years. I lost the amendment by 110–117.

Well, at least 1975 was fixed. Yet nothing was done. In February 1975 I asked questions and got no answer. In July 1975 I spoke on the report on the agenda and got no reply. In the new Synod in November, I made the first speech on the agenda, asking when the review would be. Ah, Standing Committee had decided not to do it. Another resolution of Synod had disappeared into the ground at management's behest.

Momentum restarted . . . and lost: Ten propositions and the covenant

How was momentum for healthy union now to be regained? In 1972 the Congregationalists and Presbyterians formed the United Reformed Church (URC), constitutionally committing themselves to seeking further union. So they asked for 'talks about talks' with other Churches, and, with General Synod's approval in 1973, a Churches' Unity Commission was formed from eight Churches. It produced in early 1976 'ten propositions' on church unity for evaluation by late 1977. The propositions were woolly, little more than 'motherhood and apple pie' – you were bound to vote for them.[15] However, number 6 contained a discernible 'covenant' (a term from the 1964 BCC Faith and Order Conference):

> We agree to recognize, as from an accepted date, the ordained ministries of other covenanting Churches, as true ministries of word and sacraments in the Holy Catholic Church, and we agree that all subsequent ordinations to the ministries of the covenanting Churches shall be according to a Common Ordinal which will properly incorporate the episcopal, presbyteral and lay roles in ordination.

The word 'episcopal' was crucial, presumably meaning that participants would get bishops, and 'recognize' implied a parallel to CSI. So the propositions stood near to Geoffrey Fisher's call 30 years before for non-episcopal Churches to 'take episcopacy into their system' and see how they got on with it – and with us.

Synod debated the propositions in July 1976, and in February 1977 sent them to the dioceses. The Archbishop of Canterbury, Donald Coggan, then instigated a historic High Leigh Conference to look (among other things) at leading Anglicans' attitudes to incorporating presbyters of non-episcopal Churches into a threefold order without actual or pretend ordination. Canon Wallis, a notably hardline Anglo-Catholic, testified that he could now for the first time contemplate such an incorporation; and David Brown, Bishop of Guildford, and chairman of the Board of Mission and Unity (BMU), acknowledged a 'conversion' (his word) also. Then Synod got a positive response from the dioceses (it *was* motherhood and apple pie) and in July 1978 approved 'covenanting with other Churches on the basis of the Ten Propositions' (38–6; 161–55; 168–31), though with some caveats. We required a 'distinctive sign' of incorporation of ministers, which, the speeches agreed, would best *not* be the laying on of hands. I revelled in speaking in favour.

Four other Churches concurred, and in Autumn 1978 a Churches' Council for Covenanting was formed, with nine Church of England representatives.[16] They drafted a covenant, including liturgical provision for its inauguration with mutual welcoming of Churches, consecration of bishops, and incorporation of presbyters.[17] But three Anglo-Catholics dissented, arguing: first, that not all URC provincial moderators would become bishops at the outset (which suggested indifference about episcopacy); secondly, that it was not clear that all presbyters would be expected to attend the incorporating event (so some would escape the 'distinctive sign'); thirdly, that the whole thing might be a backdoor way of letting in women clergy.

This dissent led to a divided vote, even on 'take note' (the only motion), in July 1980: 35–2; 113–70; 138–45. The next Synod in February 1981 fixed the voting needed at Final Approval as two-thirds in each House. Separate votes on the three topics identified in the dissent mentioned above passed easily, though on the second and third without a two-thirds majority in the House of Clergy. Provisional Approval followed, and it was referred to the dioceses.

It came back in July 1982 with even more question marks. The BMU's report, *Towards Visible Unity: Proposals for a Covenant – Commendation for Final Approval* (GS 534), showed that voting in other Churches had not been overwhelming, though strongest in the Methodists. The diocesan returns (in GS 533) were around two-thirds in favour. In the Synod debate David Silk charged that defects in the form of prayer at inauguration and piecemeal 'reconciliation by post' (his words outside Synod) disqualified it. Other opposition was hardening against any backdoor for women ministers. For my part I wanted to call on David Brown to reply to the debate acknowledging that Final Approval was not actually *final*, and promising to take care of David Silk's issues in the Measure which would necessarily follow. I was not called to speak, so my tactic remained unspoken. David Silk afterwards conceded that he would have had to 'think hard' if the Bishop had indeed so responded. I reflect now that the women ministers issue would probably have determined the House of Clergy vote anyway. The result fell short of two-thirds in that House: 38–11; 148–91; 154–71.

Ecumenical Canons and priesthood

Ten years on from the old Scheme's demise, the covenant was now also dead. What hope of progress was there? The Standing Committee's answer (as was mine and that of many on Synod) was to shelve national initiatives, and unilaterally address helping Local Ecumenical Projects (LEPs). The 1964 BCC Faith and Order Conference had proposed Areas of Ecumenical Experiment (AEEs). Many experiments since had included Anglicans – illegally. Perhaps we could take helpful steps, without having to agree both contents and timetable with other Churches.

The Standing Committee asked the BMU to set up a working party to look at local unity. Cyril Bowles, Bishop of Derby, chaired it and David Silk and I were members – the old firm from steering Rite A.[18] Our Derby report in early 1984 provided for ministers of other denominations to baptize and assist at the distribution of communion and fulfil other roles in existing parishes, under a Canon B 43. We also defined areas (not necessarily parishes) where, once designated as LEPs, the rules on ministry and worship would be suspended, and other provision by the diocesan bishop would replace them. We asked ourselves what constituted an Anglican Eucharist: president? congregation? building? liturgical rite? We finally said merely that a Eucharist with a non-Anglican president should *not* be described as Anglican. All this came in Canon B 44.[19]

These draft Canons gave the first official Anglican acknowledgement of the very existence of Free Church ministers. I added a note of dissent re B 43, to enable such ministers to preside at Anglican Eucharists as guests on occasion, just as they could preach, baptize, and so on. I put this down initially as a Private Member's Motion:

> That this Synod believes it theologically acceptable and pastorally and ecumenically desirable that presbyters of the main non-episcopal Churches in England, and of the Church of South India and other overseas Churches which are in communion with the main non-episcopal Churches in England, should be allowed and authorized to preside at the holy communion in the parishes of the Church of England and in such ecumenical contexts as this Synod may in future determine, provided that:
>
> (a)   such presbyters acknowledge that they exercise their ministry

under the authority of the respective Anglican bishop and receive written authorization from him;

(b)   that the congregations where they minister approve and desire their ministry;

(c)   that they do not by such means (unless further provision is made) become presbyters of the Church of England, or become entitled to financial or constitutional benefits attached to being clerks in holy orders of the Church of England,

and requests the Standing Committee to take action to give legal expression to this belief.

Debate on the Derby Report was delayed till November 1984. By then my motion with 140 signatures in support was running fifth in the list, so I turned it into an amendment – thus ensuring it entered the debate, though under the handicap of losing the chance to reply. Anglo-Catholics had also dissented, so my amendment appeared as balancing theirs, and Robert Runcie declared he was 'anxious to squeeze out both wrecking and libertarian amendments'. My thrust was that in 1971 we had recognized Free Church communicants, but not their ministers (see Ch. 2 above). Now we were recognizing the ministers *as* ministers, and thus accepting their eucharistic presidency was consistent and principled. I lost by 5–27; 55–124; 75–96. Derby passed by 34–0; 142–43; 136–37 – over 75 per cent in all. In July 1985 General Synod sent it to the dioceses. The returns in November 1986 showed each House of every diocese in favour, mostly by upwards of 80 per cent in each House. General Synod gave final approval in July 1987 with only nine votes against in three Houses together. Parliament concurred in 1988, and the two Canons were duly adopted by Synod and promulged. Methodist (and other) ministers were now true and acceptable ministers of word and sacrament in LEPs, though of more doubtful standing when ministering in their own denominations and in other ecumenical relationships with us.[20]

The priesthood of the ordained ministry

A different approach came in 1983. A lay member, Jim Fairlie, put down a Private Member's Motion:

That this Synod,

(a)   aware of the different, and deeply held, convictions existing within the Church of England ... concerning the nature of the ordained priesthood,

(b)   noting that this difference of conviction has lain behind various divisions of opinion on major issues in recent years,

(c)   sensitive to the ecumenical implications of the word 'priest' and

(d)   believing that a thoroughgoing study of the theology and functions of the ordained priesthood is urgently needed,

welcomes the study of various aspects of Ministry currently being undertaken in response to the ARCIC and Lima documents, and requests the Standing Committee to consider in particular how progress can best be made towards agreement on the ordained priesthood within the Church of England itself.

In his speech in July 1989 he urged more internal doctrinal grappling within the Church of England: 'I recall addressing two deanery synods on the Covenant, and I used the word "presbyter". At the first synod, considerable relief was expressed that the word "priest" was disappearing. At the second considerable regret was expressed.'

He made reference to an earlier gutsy speech of David Edwards, who said:

the opposition . . . particularly the leaders of the Catholic group, have a duty to work out their theological position far more carefully . . . For example there has been no major restatement of the Anglo-Catholic theology of the ministry for almost 40 years, although in this period Roman Catholic thinking has undergone great changes.

Jim Fairlie had touched a real nub in the ambiguity of the word 'priest'. The Synod passed his motion. The Standing Committee asked FOAG for a report.

FOAG duly produced *The Priesthood of the Ordained Ministry* to clarify what distinctive 'priesthood' belonged to the ordained ministry.[21] It was a fascinating example of second-rate Anglican methodology. A short, early, accurate, chapter 4 on the New Testament concluded 'No priesthood is attributed to the distinctive ministry' (para 52, p. 28). Then the final chapter 13 on 'The Priesthood of the Ordained Ministry: A Contemporary Expression' in three short pages managed by tortuous steps to achieve a total U-turn:

Bishops and presbyters . . . participate [in the priesthood of Christ] in a different way . . . the difference is this, that their ministry is an appointed means through which Christ makes his priesthood present and effective to his people.

> Although the terms 'priest' and 'priesthood' are not used in the New Testament with reference to the work of the Church's special ministry, nevertheless in the way they have been used ... they indicate *essential* aspects of the ministry of bishops and presbyters.[22]

Whew! That *essential* here is theological effrontery, asserting that a concept, nowhere found in the New Testament and self-evidently contrary to the Epistle to the Hebrews (as FOAG had shown), is essential to our understanding of ordained ministry.* I dissected the report in *News of Liturgy* in August 1986, as self-contradictory and specious.† But I was not on Synod.

In November 1986 Henry Chadwick moved in Synod: 'That this Synod welcomes Chapter XIII of GS 694 as a contemporary Church of England expression of the Anglican understanding of the priesthood of the ordained ministry.' Synod was alert. Peter Dawes moved as an amendment after 'Synod': 'views Chapter XIII of GS 694 as inconsistent with Chapters I–IV and asks the House of Bishops to give consideration to this issue.'

Battle was joined. The amendment was just lost (in a very full Synod) by 224–207 – and the report was thereafter dead in the water. A successful amendment removed everything after 'as' in the motion's first line, and substituted 'a stimulating contribution towards the development of', and it then passed by 318–137. The report has *no* standing as a contemporary authoritative statement, but, being in print, it has survived; and it has astonishingly been quoted as authoritative, when the debate and its verdict have been lost to memory.

After 1990 – Anglican–Methodist relationships again

In April 1991, back on the Synod, I was nominated to the Council for Christian Unity (CCU). The agenda concentrated on the Meissen and Porvoo conversations, the former with the Lutheran-and-Reformed Church in Germany (EKD),[23] the latter with the Nordic and Baltic Lutheran (and episcopal) Churches. Both had great value, but I distrusted CCU's apparent standstill in England itself. After two years of probing, I submitted a motion for CCU's meeting in May 1993, 'that this Council wishes to open direct talks with the Methodist and United Reformed Churches with a view to the quest for organic unity'. Mary

---

* I spoke with an episcopal member of FOAG (who, I strongly suspect, had drafted this chapter). He conceded (as he also did in Synod): 'You can let the word "priest" go, so long as you hold to the reality which it expresses.' When I asked, 'Oh, what is that reality?' I got no answer. I recalled the philosopher discussing the presence of an invisible pink elephant in the college quad – easier to assert than to define, locate or verify.

† Specious? Well, yes, it even twisted Protestant and Reformed writers into backing its thesis.

Tanner, secretary of CCU, urged us to postpone this until Porvoo negotiations were over, and I reluctantly accepted that, and CCU agreed by 9–2:

> that this Council should take steps to bring forward to General Synod, subsequent to the debates on the *Porvoo Common Statement* and the Moravian Conversations and in the light of those debates, a motion, backed by supporting documentation 'that this Synod wishes to open direct talks with the Methodist and United Reformed Churches with a view to the quest for visible unity in England.'

To my surprise, very soon after this, the Methodist Church made a unilateral approach to us. Their General Purposes Committee wrote in March 1994 asking CCU to 'join in preliminary talks . . . to consider whether we share a common goal of visible unity'. I do not think anyone in position to bring any leverage to bear took any notice of the Council's motion above. Instead the Executive Committee of CCU (which I was not on) consulted with the Standing Committee of General Synod and recommended acceptance to CCU. The Executive Committee picked six men, largely Anglo-Catholic, for the talks. There were no evangelicals. I protested to Mary Tanner. She replied, 'Oh, well, yes, we need a woman – could you find an evangelical woman?' I protested at the serious unfairness of this, but, protesting, suggested Vera Sinton from Wycliffe Hall staff – and she joined the team. Mary also said to me, 'It is very difficult to find evangelical theologians for ecumenical conversations' – and I, slightly thrown, replied, 'Mary, I have sat here with you for years and have you never thought of asking me?' But she hadn't.*

The preliminary talks report, *Commitment to Mission and Unity*,[24] was to identify issues for formal negotiations, and also addressed the question, 'Is this the right time for formal conversations?' On balance, they concluded now was the right time and formal conversations should be entered.[25] The report outlined big issues and made two substantial recommendations:

We recommend that

[1–4 on procedure]

5. formal conversations address the issues identified in Chapter III.

6. formal conversations prepare a Common Statement as described in Chapter IV, including a Declaration of mutual recognition and solemn commitment, in order to enable our two churches to take significant steps on the way to visible unity.

---

* Well, to be scrupulously fair, I led a tiny team for a one-day meeting with – of all people – the Mennonites. I think that in one room we met with all the Mennonites in England. We did not formulate a Scheme.

Point 5 included grappling with matters of substance. Point 6 would probably be little more than cosmetic. This contrast was of significance, and should be borne in mind in the next few paragraphs. However, *Commitment to Mission and Unity* did include a sketched (and bizarre) proposal for integrating ministries, so in 1997 I tried to anticipate correcting this on CCU itself. I drew on existing pointers.

In April 1996 I had participated in the Meissen theological talks (I gave a liturgist's paper on the reform of the ordinal in 1550, 1552 and 1662).[26] We identified the same old problem restricting us from the full communion which was imminent with the Porvoo Churches; the Germans lacked the historic episcopate. We reported:

> on the English side it will have to be clarified what further steps
> would need to be taken (including consideration of . . . the existing
> legal obstacles) to accord such recognition to the episcopate of the
> churches of the EKD as to make possible unrestricted interchange of
> ministries.[27]

Obviously only one change is needed in the legalities – 'recognition' of ministers outside the historic episcopate. Non-recognition in the Canons is 'the existing legal obstacle'. The next steps (though totally clear) 'will have to be clarified'. But would anyone actually do anything? Could it be linked with Anglican–Methodist reconciliation?

Later in 1996 an ecumenical agreement for the mutual recognition of ministers began in South Africa. Anglicans, Methodists, Presbyterians and Congregationalists shared in joint celebrations, and emphasized that recognition involves true acceptance of each other's ministers to preside at communion. I tried to get this closely examined in the CCU, but in vain.

Germany had a problem. South Africa had an answer. In fact, as shown above, we had had an answer in England in 1978–82 – but no one seems to have remembered that. So in spring 1997 I moved in CCU that we should bring to Synod (along with *Commitment to Mission and Unity*) proposals for truly recognizing under defined conditions the ministers of non-episcopal churches. Heavyweight consultants from FOAG appeared advising CCU that this would be 'imprudent'. I got a reduced motion through CCU asking for a special study of 'ways in which we could extend such recognition'. This, as far as I know, was remitted to FOAG. Meanwhile George Carey in the July 1997 debate on *Called to be One*[28] said he looked for changes to put ministers of non-episcopal churches on equal footing with those episcopally ordained. I asked him to press the chairman of CCU. I asked at CCU meetings and of CCU staff what had happened to our own CCU motion about such recognition – and I wrote several documents myself to fuel the discussion. But nothing ever happened. There was a vast history (much of it outlined in this chapter) – going right back to South Indian beginnings in 1919 – but CCU doors were closed. If FOAG ever had it on their agenda (and I was always assured they had), they never addressed it.

Formal conversations and implementation, 1997 onwards

When CCU prepared for the *Commitment to Mission and Unity* debate in November 1997, I expected formal conversations to address those major roadblocks. The original draft motion we saw said, 'We do not seek a Scheme', and I got that limitation deleted in CCU's own discussion. So I spoke in Synod hoping for a Scheme which addressed problems. But I was adrift from the actual document we were debating – the motion was only that a Commission should 'prepare a Common Statement' – i.e. act on recommendation 6 from the report (printed on page 117) (recommendation 5 being quietly ignored, which I should have realized). This left us with the motherhood–and–apple-pie affirmations, and easy assent. The Methodists duly concurred in June 1998. A Commission was to be set up.

I wanted to be on this Commission, but instead was asked to lead four Anglicans in three-way 'informal conversations' with Methodists and the URC. During 1999–2001, we trilateral conversationalists were in theory privy to all documents of the formal Commission. But nothing of substance came: only a Statement had been commissioned. Sure enough, the formal Commission's report, *An Anglican–Methodist Covenant*, published by both denominations in December 2001, skipped the difficult issues of recommendation 5 – and it was motherhood-and-apple-pie again. The report did include muddled counsel about the ordained ministry. Paragraph 153 reads 'The Church of England believes that there is a distinctive priestly ministry which is derived from Christ himself and which is exercised by those ordained priest.' Two paragraphs then simply quote the most controversial passages of – yes, you guessed it – *The Priesthood of the Ordained Ministry*, as though they had some standing. Yet, despite this 'distinctive' Anglican doctrine, they levelled the playing field a few paragraphs later: '157 We believe that there is a common understanding of the presbyterate and that this provides a sound foundation for the eventual interchangeability of presbyteral ministries.'

So, despite all the tangles, with one bound Jack was free. Yet, if 157 was to be believed, why was the interchangeability only 'eventual'? The summary of the covenant was seven affirmations and six commitments – all *jejune* ('We commit ourselves to continue to welcome each other's baptized members ... We commit ourselves to listen to each other ...').

What happened to the trilaterals I introduced above? We reported some useful, if inconclusive, things about matters the URC had raised, eldership and conciliarity, in *Conversations on the Way to Unity 1999–2001*.[29] But the Formal Conversations had provided nothing with which to engage, and our non-Anglican members wanted to publish when ready, well before the Formal Conversations were. So our recommendations did not relate to the Formal Conversations or their report. We did recommend that the three Churches should 'explore together . . . what further steps would be necessary to make an English covenantal relationship between them', but without reference to the Formal Conversations. So I dissented, seeking to give the URC a chance to join the Anglican–Methodist relationships when the covenant came before the Churches in summer 2002.[30] I might as well not have bothered. I asked Ian Cundy, Bishop of Peterborough, who chairs CCU, when and how I might introduce the report at CCU, and was told I would not be needed. The report got a kind passing mention in GS 1462, the CCU document that introduced the Anglican–Methodist covenant, but it went nowhere. It was pointless to have recommended *anything*. This was a classic fob-off; I was a fool to have hoped anything of it.

Well, the Methodist Conference accepted the covenant in June 2002 (with worries about the Church of England and women bishops[31]), voting first in the light of 'previous experience'.[32] General Synod in July was to send it to the dioceses (though it recommended no substantial change to either Church). In the debate the chair called a succession of Anglo-Catholics, who each said (very nearly in these words) that a covenant which involved no change was fine, but they could not promise future approval if the covenant did get some content. I sent in my name and was never called. Genuine enthusiasts did pitch in, and it was good to hear David Hope, Archbishop of York, urging a much faster grappling with real issues. The covenant went to the dioceses with some ill-based euphoria attached to it.

Eight years on from the Methodist approach we faced first a year with the covenant in the dioceses, then a vote to create a new commission to give content to it. The two Churches were being led into exactly that which 'previous experience' had told them to avoid. The way for a courting couple to walk a long garden path and finally come unstuck is by making initial soft cooing noises and delay facing hard questions. And this is *precisely* what this whole process involved. If the Formal Conversations had recommended a Scheme addressing hard questions of ministry, authority, structures, Church and State, etc., garden paths would not have been in view. The issue is *not* who *votes* first, as the mythology taught, but *in what order* the hard and easy questions come. The earliest that tough recommendations can come in the current state-of-play is in 2008, after a 14-year courtship of sweet nothings; and, if recommendations prove difficult to accept then, history will probably say we deceived the innocent Methodist maiden yet again. Let the reader – and the Synod member – beware.

I run ahead. When the covenant came to Southwark Diocese in 2002–3 we had scope to address General Synod. Our ecumenical committee drafted a following motion for the Bishop's Council to take to the diocesan synod:

> That this Synod, having voted in favour of the Anglican–Methodist covenant, believes that such a covenant entails a movement towards the interchangeability of presbyteral ministries, and calls upon General Synod to take steps to effect that change.

Our diocesan synod well saw that the covenant on which we voted had no content, and we could give it some. For an actual change in relationships, we would target the actual point of experienced need. Our synod voted by 99–18 in favour, with two Methodist chairs of Districts there to welcome it.

A next round of voting

So to General Synod in July 2003. CCU was asking Synod to give final approval to the covenant and 'authorize the setting up of a joint implementation commission' (JIC). The report from CCU (GS 1513) stated JIC's terms of reference and added 'including any following motions which may be passed'. CCU's motion was passed by 332–32, and Synod thus accepted the affirmations and commitments, and JIC was to 'monitor and promote the implementation of the Covenant'. Yet, without actual content described, implementation looked almost meaningless. Perhaps our Southwark motion could help.

I came on, made my speech, and moved the Southwark motion with a changed last sentence: 'and request the Joint Implementation Commission to bring forward recommendations in order to bring about that change'. JIC would then have a specific task to fulfil. Ian Cundy, the chair of CCU, opposed with three complaints: (a) the motion ignored bishops and deacons; (b) the Methodists were not ready for interchangeability of presbyters; and (c) that this kind of matter 'should not come to Synod hanging on the coat-tails of a main motion'. Peter Forster, Bishop of Chester, said it was 'singling that [interchangeability] out as a clerical agenda'. But an enthusiastic woman presbyter backed it whole-heartedly. I replied that a following motion was the official way for dioceses to affect the process (see the terms of reference quoted earlier); that Methodists have no bishops, and deacons are covered by Canon B 43; and that Ian Cundy's opposition was 'nit-picking'. The two bishops had not impressed the Synod, and Synod passed the motion 137–119, and it went to the JIC.

Implementation?

The JIC was constituted with a five-year life, but to give an interim report in two years. That interim report, *In the Spirit of the Covenant*, came for debate in July 2005. It surprisingly admits: 'It was only at a comparatively late stage that the Formal Conversations realized that the proposals ... were of a covenantal nature, and called for covenantal language to express them.'[33] Was it that the Formal Conversations realized late how very slender their proposals were, and invoked covenantal language to dignify them, or that JIC is now embarrassed at handling a covenant, to which no virtually no content can be found? An interesting chapter about biblical covenants is followed in the report by 'Developing a Lifestyle'. This shows good progress in relationships in some places on the ground, though much would have come about anyway, given the right people with the right relationships (as, for instance, between David Sheppard, Derek Worlock and John Newton in Merseyside in the 1980s and early 1990s). The report then deals with three specific matters – the bread and wine of communion, lay presidency of the Eucharist, and the interchangeability of ministers. The JIC does not solve these, nor make them easier to solve, and it quibbles about the Southwark motion, which, as shown above, was supposed to be part of their terms of reference (wonderfully, they say CCU 'supported the thrust of it', a most remarkable way of recording CCU's opposition to it).[34] One presumes that, in their 2008 final report, they will present 'solutions', recommending to the Churches *actual necessary changes* to their laws or constitutions.

Methodism may yet unilaterally jump the (not yet loaded) gun. For many years the Connexion has been moving towards becoming episcopal, by means not suspended upon anything done or promised by the Church of England at all. The JIC report then does raise a question – even half a solution – about interchangeability of presbyters (even those ordained by other presbyters before the Church became episcopal) in such a context.[35]

But if all hangs on the covenant, and we are to name our problems and solve them years after we have sworn faithfulness to each other, then 2008 is the earliest date for solutions. Will we then hear how to unite, or only how to make life sweeter in proximity to each other? The report is not clear about this. And 2008 means it is 14 years from that original Methodist approach before *anybody* actually recommends *anything* difficult – and, presumably, more like 20 years before anyone *does* anything difficult.

At the July 2005 Synod the report was commended for study, prayer and action. The garden path stretches ahead. But perhaps the Methodists will get bishops by themselves before the covenant produces any change.

9

Roman Catholic relationships

When Cephas came to Antioch, I opposed him to his face.

(Galatians 2.11)

Rome has amazing claims to be the one true church – but over 35 years a joint commission has explored that and the findings have in recent years been controversial.

How do Anglicans relate to the Roman Catholic Church today? There are, of course, flourishing informal relationships – but what about the official position? Well, it has vastly changed in my adult years. When I was an undergraduate, long before Vatican II, the official governed the informal almost totally. For my part I had difficulty recognizing the marks of a Christian Church in Roman Catholicism, and the distrust was mutual. A godly Roman Catholic with whom I shared seminars took me to hear the Jesuit Joseph Christie give a mission address – and Anglicans came off pretty badly in it. I could not reciprocate, as my friend could not attend worship in any non-Roman Church, and was forbidden even to say the Lord's Prayer with me. Anglicans were separated from Rome not only by the polarizing processes of the Reformation, nor only by the Reformation issue of the authority of the Bible over Church tradition (though that division remains basic). They were further sundered by Vatican I's pronouncement on papal infallibility, by the two Marian decrees that depended upon that infallibility, and by *Apostolicae Curae*, the encyclical by which in 1896 Pope Leo XIII had condemned Anglican orders. Yet Rome had, at first sight, all the claims – and could these vast numbers all be wrong? I was (and remain) convinced that they are wrong – and, if I were not still so convinced, I would be a Roman Catholic tomorrow.

Changes afoot

Given my prior experience of things Roman Catholic, when I heard in 1959 that Pope John XXIII had announced that he was calling a Council, I was genuinely surprised. I said to myself, 'That's odd – I thought the Vatican Council in 1870 had dispensed with the need for any more Councils.' But then, in my diaconate, I read in *Church Times* a review of Hans Küng's book *The Council and Reunion*.[1] The review amazed me. I sent for the book. I read it. And I fell off my chair in stunned incredulity. Here was a Roman Catholic teacher in good standing discussing how the Church should meet 'the valid demands of the Reformers' – a topic nearly unthinkable among my Anglo-Catholic friends, let alone in Rome. Indeed, soon after, at the BCC Faith and Order Conference at Nottingham in September 1964 (i.e. halfway through Vatican II), John Moorman, the Anglo-Catholic who was the Archbishop of Canterbury's observer at the Council, came to the platform, and said he was off to Rome the next day and had prepared a message of greetings to the Pope for us to adopt.* He read it aloud. Its main thrust was to express our repentance for the Reformation! The steering group of the Conference managed to steer it off the agenda, and Moorman left, and that was that – but what a paradoxical contrast between Küng, a Roman Catholic, urging his Church to take the 'demands' of the Reformers into their system, and an Anglican, John Moorman, hoping to repent of them and get them out of ours.

When the Second Vatican Council convened, it proved flexible in many unexpected ways, and the informal often anticipated the official. Officially, too, in my own field of liturgy no one could have foreseen in 1961 where the reform of the Roman liturgy would reach a few years later. But here in this chapter, for the purposes of General Synod's agenda, I simply discuss the content and impact upon the life of the Church of the agreed statements of the two successive Anglican–Roman Catholic International Commissions (ARCIC-1, 1969–82, and ARCIC-2, 1983–2005). This takes us from the first mind-blowing agreement on the Eucharist in 1971 to the latest (and mind-blowing for opposite reasons) statement on Mary in 2005.

The Eucharist

After Michael Ramsey visited Rome in early 1966, a plan for ARCIC developed. After an interim commission, the teams for the definitive commission were picked in 1969, with the Roman Catholics being English-speaking theologians (two notable ones were French by nationality). On the Anglican side, the team included Julian Charley, a colleague at LCD, so that I was able to 'shadow'

---

* Curiously, it was at this same Conference that I first found a Roman Catholic in a non-Roman service. I sat on a bus outing with Cuthbert Rand of Ushaw, sent as an observer. I mentioned the morning Eucharist to him, and, to my amazement, he had been at it. When I asked him whether his attendance was out of order, he said he had been sent to observe and couldn't do that if he was not there. A year later I had, for the last time, the opposite experience – an LCD student went to the Mission de France at Pontigny on a kind of placement, and when he returned to be ordained deacon in summer 1965, some of the Pontigny brothers came over to support him – only to be forbidden by Cardinal Heenan to attend the service. They snorted somewhat.

ARCIC's work. Julian was the lone evangelical in the Anglican team, but he became a firm friend of a remarkable French theologian, Jean Tillard, and they did much drafting together. ARCIC-1 announced in September 1971 that they had reached at Windsor a 'substantial agreement' on the Eucharist – to be published on 31 December. I pressed Julian that, as the only overt evangelical on the commission, if he were to be reported as agreed with Roman Catholic teaching on the Eucharist, he would be stretching his constituency's credulity to breaking point; thus he must explain himself in print on the day the statement was published. He did this in *The Anglican–Roman Catholic Agreement on the Eucharist*, which emerged as the only commentary in the world available with the text of the statement on the day of publication.* My own view at the time was that it was amazing that the statement dodged transubstantiation and so nuanced eucharistic sacrifice as to take most of the sting out it. I have since written that I thought that Cranmer could have signed it and those who burned him could not have.[2] On later reflection I have pondered the wisdom of ARCIC's making a statement which never referred to the shape, contents or wording of eucharistic liturgies – for those rites in both Communions constitute powerful and fairly authoritative statements of eucharistic doctrine.

Once released, the statement was not fed into General Synod for formal debate. However, it was cited almost immediately in Synod, when in July it became the basis of amending the wording in the eucharistic prayer, 'Hear us, O merciful Father, and grant that these your gifts of bread and wine may be to us the body and blood of Christ.' The statement said (what actually the historic rites of neither Church had said) that transformation (or, as Roman Catholic authors have sometimes put it, 'trans-signification') of the elements was the work of the Holy Spirit. Could we not say in our rite, 'by the power of your Holy Spirit'? Synod could and did, and our eucharistic prayers have said at least that ever since.

Ministry and ordination

More immediately, in December 1973 came the Statement on Ministry and Ordination. At Julian's suggestion, earlier that year I had published a document Jean had written for ARCIC as *What Priesthood Has the Ministry?*[3] Jean showed

---

* This was Grove Booklet on Ministry and Worship no. 1! It therefore launched (and by heavy sales sustained) the whole Grove Booklet enterprise. Pressing Julian Charley to get his apologia written in a busy autumn term and published in time for New Year's Eve, I reached a day when I looked him in the eye, and said, 'Julian, we have reached the point where unless I publish you myself, it will not get done'. I had been working on eucharistic agreement myself for both *Growing into Union* (see Ch. 8) and Series 3 communion (Ch. 6), and I gave him some headings. He duly wrote; and so came the first Grove Booklet, and it ran to four printings.

from Scripture that there is *no* priesthood which belongs distinctively to the ordained ministry and is conferred in ordination.[4] Those who, like me, had feared what ARCIC-1 would say about ordination, found ourselves breathing more easily. And, when the statement came, Julian and Jean Tillard had again left their mark on it, and it matches the eucharistic agreement in its irenic steering round historical trouble spots. It presents all functions of ministry and all kinds of ministers as within the context of the Church at large and of the apostolicity of the Church. It is very clear about, 'the fact that in the New Testament ministers are never called "priests"', and that, of such ministers, 'their ministry is not an extension of the common Christian priesthood but belongs to a another realm of the gifts of the Spirit.' The statement does say that eucharistic presidency belongs to the presbyterate and that ordination belongs to the episcopate; but these links are set out undefensively in the indicative – 'this is how we invariably do it' – rather than the mandatory or dogmatic 'this is how it must be'. The papal condemnation of Anglican orders is stated historically, then left aside.

Authority in the Church

The third statement, in December 1976, was on authority, and known as the Venice Statement. History has redubbed it, 'Authority in the Church I', as a second authority statement came up five years later. It differs greatly from the two earlier statements, not least because it is far more rooted in Roman Catholic history (and correspondingly less rooted in New Testament concepts) than the first two. It takes episcopacy and papacy virtually for granted, and discusses the balances of power, influence and responsibility as between these two sources of authority. It views benignly the notion of a supremo bishop of all the world, i.e. a papal primacy, records that Rome alone has claimed such a universal primacy, and concludes therefore, 'in any future union a universal primacy such as has been described should be held by that see.'[5] However, the final section on 'Problems and Prospects' does set out four major qualifiers, indicators that Anglicans have not accepted the total papal package. These reservations are:

1. The 'Petrine texts' (i.e. the New Testament references to Peter having some authority over the other apostles) have been overstated (but the Roman Catholics admit it!);

2. Vatican I used the language of 'divine right' – but they hope to get round that;

3. Infallibility remains a stumbling block, not least in practice, for popes have made two declarations about Mary which Anglicans doubt;

4.   Universal jurisdiction is also a potential source of danger – but again they think is checked and unlikely to be out of control.

So Authority I represents, at best, convergence, not 100 per cent agreement. There was more work to be done.

First responses by Synod

General Synod had preliminary debates on these statements, on the first two in November 1974, and on the third in February 1977. Each concluded by commending the statements for study within the Church of England. Then in August 1977, Bishop John Howe, the secretary-general of the Anglican Consultative Council (ACC), asked for responses from all provinces of the Anglican Communion for ACC-4, due to meet in April/May 1979. Was the Synod able to give:

(a)   an affirmation of the congruence of the three ARCIC agreed Statements with Anglican teaching . . .

(b)   an affirmation that the three ARCIC agreed Statements provide a sufficient basis for further official dialogue between the Roman Catholic Church and the Churches of the Anglican Communion with 'United not Absorbed' as its goal?[6]

The Standing Committee asked, via the BMU, whether FOAG could produce a report for February 1979. They provided *Response by the Church of England to the Agreed Statements by the Anglican–Roman Catholic International Commission* (GS 394). They quoted the 1978 Lambeth Conference that the statements are 'a solid achievement, one in which we can recognize the faith of our Church'. They also emphasized the importance of the unresolved issues in Authority in the Church I.* On universal primacy, they are acutely perceptive: 'ARCIC's argument at present only succeeds because there is latent in it a suppressed presupposition, i.e. that Papacy *is* the correct answer.' (How right they were! – would that ARCIC-2 had borne that in mind.) They were interested in intercommunion, never part of the ARCIC thinking. But they ended by saying 'yes' to John Howe's questions.

When Synod debated this in February 1979, there was a general mood of euphoria. In an elephantine resolution, the Synod endorsed the positive judgement of FOAG that theological dialogue could continue, but also

---

* One slightly comic problem they raised, one which never sullied ARCIC itself, was the implications for the Act of Supremacy of the recognition of a Universal Primate.

specifically asked the ACC to note the 'comments and requests for clarification contained in this Report'.

Elucidations of the first three statements

Before ACC-4 met in Canada in May 1979, ARCIC published elucidations of its first two statements. These arose from worldwide comment, including misunderstandings, about the statements. On the Eucharist a section now came on reservation, the retention of consecrated elements in a safe place when the liturgy is over. The elucidation noted a 'divergence' between those who reserved in order to adore the elements, and those who saw no basis for such adoration. On the ordained ministry there was both a recognition that the ordination of women had 'created for the Roman Catholic Church a new and grave obstacle', and an insistence that, despite the groundwork done, recognition of Anglican orders 'can only be achieved by decision of our authorities'. ACC-4 duly (though briefly) endorsed the continuance of the work and started an Anglican enquiry as to how best to respond ultimately to Rome.

The elucidation of Authority I followed in September 1981. It teetered a little further along their knife-edge about a universal primacy seated at Rome. It excused any lack of a responsible place for the laity in the leadership of the Church on the grounds that most difficulties arose about the ordained ministry! More importantly, there was published at the same time the new statement, 'Authority in the Church II'. This moved on from primacy to jurisdiction (i.e. the powers of a Primate to intervene in other dioceses) – and also to infallibility. The Anglicans were reported as not yet agreeing with all Roman Catholic dogmas, as:

> the dogmas of the Immaculate Conception and the Assumption raise a special problem for those Anglicans who do not consider that the precise definitions given by these dogmas are sufficiently supported by Scripture. For many Anglicans the teaching authority of the bishop of Rome, independent of a council, is not recommended by the fact that through it these Marian doctrines were proclaimed as dogmas binding on the faithful.[7]

One wonders how this crucial linkage of infallibility and the Marian doctrinal decrees escaped notice two decades later.

At that Windsor meeting, ARCIC-1 put together all its statements and provided the *Final Report.*[8]* How was the package to be evaluated by the two Churches?

General Synod responds

A set of agreements by two small teams of theologians is far from an agreement between two Churches or Communions. In Synod we debated the ARCIC material in July 1983 alongside the question about the Lima Statement, *Baptism – Eucharist – Ministry,*[9] regarding 'the extent to which your Church can recognize in this text the faith of the Church through the ages'. The Synod referred both documents to FOAG.[10] FOAG duly produced its major report, *Towards a Church of England response to BEM and ARCIC,* for Synod to debate twice in February 1985.[11] This, quite apart from Lima, provided a particularly careful toothcombing of the authority statements.

In the first debate, which was general in character, I pressed the question how we were to get a Vatican response to the ARCIC statements. In the second debate came the definitive motions. The first had three parts. Each of the first two parts, on the Eucharist and on ministry and ordination, recognized that the statement and elucidation concerned 'is consonant in substance with the faith of the Church of England'. The third part said that the authority statements 'record sufficient convergence on the nature of authority in the Church for our communions to explore together the structures of authority and the exercise of collegiality and primacy in the Church'. For myself, I accepted the first two parts. But I had very grave doubts about the authority material, not only because of the still disputed issues about infallibility, but also because the statements gave no active place to the laity in the Church. Thus the 'convergence' was about the relative powers of episcopate and papacy, and that, to me, posed and then answered the wrong question. Synodical authority had been simply ignored. Nothing about the history, rationale, or even shortcomings, of joining bishops, clergy and laity together in decision-taking synods stirred in these pages. There was nothing about the accountability of a bishop to his diocese. They took us in a wrong direction. In Synod the chairman gave a hint that we might divide the motion, so late on I asked on a point of order if we could vote on the three parts separately, and this was granted. The first two went through overwhelmingly. The vote on the third was 238–38.†

* Oh yes, and in 1982 the Pope came to see us, and the whole Synod went by train to Canterbury cathedral to meet him and hear him there – with a sense of total incredulity. Could this really be happening? Roy Williamson and I went down from Nottingham together, and found ourselves (by a sheer blind date) in a train foursome with Michael Ramsey, the last day I ever saw him. Robert Runcie stated later that it was in Canterbury that he arranged with the Pope for ARCIC-2.
† Curiously, the *Report of Proceedings* records here 25 abstaining. It is no part of the chairman's task to count those who did not vote.

I was one of the 38, and have retained scepticism about all ARCIC statements on authority then and since. Synod referred our findings to the dioceses for their judgement.

The diocesan findings were reported back for final voting in Synod in November 1986.* On the original motions, the results now were:

Motions	Bps	Clergy	Laity
Eucharist: 'consonant in substance with the faith of the Church of England'	33–0,	189–27,	141–65
Ministry and Ordination: 'consonant in substance with the faith of the Church of England'	33–0,	173–31,	133–68
Authority: 'record sufficient convergence on the nature of authority in the Church for our communions together to explore further the structures of authority and the exercise of collegiality and primacy in the Church'	38–5,	182–43,	124–89
The *Final Report*: 'offers a sufficient basis for taking the next concrete steps towards the reconciliation of our Churches'	43–0,	200–8,	157–43

Clearly, there was a minority which grew as the Synod worked through the three specific topics, which was not easily satisfied, but was not convinced the process needed to be abandoned, and so the final motion had larger support. A following motion from Colin Craston asked that 'particular attention be given to the place and role of the laity ... in the exercise of authority', and this was carried without even a speech. A more searching motion came from a stalwart and very able Anglo-Catholic layman, Oswald Clark, who had carried it through his deanery and Southwark diocesan synods:

That this Synod

(a) welcomes the recognition [in documents before it] that in carrying further the ARCIC discussion on authority 'there are a number of points on which work is needed';

* A wonderful misprint (from an editorial scribble?) occurs in the list of contents in the edition of *Report of Proceedings*: 'Widows Statement' on inspection proves to be 'Windsor Statement'.

(b)   records its own conviction that for 'the next concrete steps towards the reconciliation of our churches' [from the resolution quoted above] to make real progress they must include as a matter of priority:

   (i)   a proper recognition of the place of the laity in the decision-making processes and ministry[12] of the whole body of the church;

   (ii)   a more adequate treatment of the Roman Catholic Marian and Infallibility dogmas; and

   (iii)   further attention to the case for a universal primacy necessarily based at Rome, including the official Roman Catholic claim that the Pope is the Vicar of Christ on earth, and accordingly

(c)   directs that this resolution be conveyed [with the others] to the World Council of Churches and the Anglican Consultative Council.

This resolution was adopted overwhelmingly, and put down (with Colin Craston's motion) strong markers that (a) the laity had been omitted from the ARCIC statements, and (b) (as the authority statements themselves had chalked up) Anglicans were bound to link Marian and infallibility issues.

The Lambeth Conference 1988

The last stages of the Anglican response to the *Final Report* came at the 1988 Lambeth Conference, where reports from the provinces were received by the section on ecumenical relationships. Resolution 8 duly affirmed that the statements on the Eucharist and on ministry and ordination were 'consonant in substance' with the faith of Anglicans. The statements on authority in the Church were to be welcomed 'as a firm basis for the direction and agenda of the continuing dialogue on authority'. I opposed this, emphasizing that the balancing of collegiality of bishops with the authority of a universal Primate completely excluded consideration of the laity and therefore took us in the wrong direction. I got nowhere; and the Lambeth 1988 resolution became the consolidated response of the Anglican Communion to the *Final Report*. On the Roman Catholic side, while there had been a cautious affirmation from the Bishops' Conference of England and Wales, the Vatican answer was still awaited.

ARCIC-2, 1983–98, Papal comments and *Clarifications*

Before the debates on the *Final Report* were completed in 1983, a new ARCIC had been appointed, the Anglican chairman being Mark Santer, then Bishop of Kensington and initially not a member of our House of Bishops. They had many issues to tackle, and produced as their first statement *Salvation and the Church* (1987). This took agreement on justification a long way forward. It was debated in General Synod in January 1989, and was sent to the dioceses for comment. The comments received were collated in a document *The Response of the Dioceses to Salvation and the Church* (GS Misc 400) in 1992. The main hesitations the dioceses expressed related to purgatory, prayer for the departed, penance and indulgences, more with a sense that difficult issues had been dodged or obscured, rather than that error had been clearly stated. But their response was never debated in Synod.

The next two reports, again relatively uncontroversial, received no synodical discussion at all. They were *Church as Communion* (1991) and *Life in Christ: Morals, Communion and the Church* (1994). But an odd, even pernicious, situation was developing in relation to the ARCIC-1 *Final Report*, and ARCIC-2, rightly or wrongly, decided to address it. In 1991 the Pope had finally pronounced on the ARCIC-1 statements as follows:

> Despite these very consoling areas of agreement or convergence on questions that are of great importance for the faith of the Catholic Church, it seems clear that there are still other areas that are essential to Catholic doctrine on which complete agreement or even at times convergence has eluded the Anglican–Roman Catholic Commission.[13]

The official comments indicated where the trouble lay concerning both Eucharist and ministry and ordination – the Pope mistrusted ARCIC-1's non-traditional terminology, and wanted to see the language of Trent.

In September 1993 ARCIC-2 therefore wrote, specifically for the Pope to meet the points he had raised, 'clarifications' of its first two statements. This document was published in 1994 (alongside *Life in Christ*) as *Clarifications on Eucharist and Ministry*,[14] and the booklet included the reply of Cardinal Cassidy, the president of the Vatican Council for Promoting Christian Unity, to it. He stated that the clarifications 'have indeed thrown new light' and 'no further study would seem to be required at this stage'. The Pope, we conclude, was happy now.

But *Clarifications* is for Anglicans appalling. About the Eucharist they move on from 'making effective in the present an event in the past' to 'the making present ... of the unique historic sacrifice of Christ'. The Eucharist has a 'propitiatory dimension' (which certainly echoes Trent). Then, when, in 1662, we pray that 'we and all thy whole church may obtain remission of our sins', we are, astonishingly, offering petition for the departed (who must still need remission of their sins?). No expositor of 1662 has seriously presented this case – it is artificial and perverse. But, even more amazingly, *Clarifications* states that, when we see in 1662 that consecrated elements are 'treated with reverence' we can tell how devoutly Anglicans accept both reservation and adoration of the consecrated elements. Yet 1662 was prescribing their *consumption*, precluding any possible reservation at all; and ARCIC-2 so far twisted it for their own purposes that the misuse shrieks out. The clarifications on ministry and ordination do not disturb the original statement as much, though, even so, they push the concept of apostolic succession to the very limits of a Romeward understanding.

This communication to the Pope was pernicious. It was wrong in principle – no commission in ARCIC's position should be conducting unilateral 'explanations' to one Communion without addressing the other; yet ARCIC-2 had sent its glosses on ARCIC-1 statements to Rome without the rest of us knowing. When those glosses were published in *Clarifications*, we learned that the Vatican was now satisfied 'no further study would seem to be required'. So the overall position was that the 1988 Lambeth Conference had said, on behalf of all of us Anglicans, that the first two statements were 'consonant in substance with the faith of Anglicans'. ARCIC-2 had then glossed the statements and the Pope had liked the glosses. So the two Communions had actually approved different documents from each other. If this subterfuge were to continue, then ARCIC-2 would not want Anglicans to start denouncing *Clarifications* (as I did unofficially in *News of Liturgy* in 1995). We on CCU were informed of it; and a Private Member's Motion rejecting it was tabled for the 1995–2000 quinquennium. As *Clarifications* was not circulated to members of Synod, insufficient people signed to debate the Private Member's Motion. There was, however, enough criticism to persuade ARCIC members in July 1998 to run an informal fringe lunch-time meeting about it, and they emerged looking fairly red-faced. Yet, somehow, CCU itself never properly focused the report, and, when I enquired, we got the standard answer that FOAG was considering it. John Hind, the chairman of FOAG, told us in February 1998 '*Clarifications* needs to be considered within a review of all the work of ARCIC' and '[after 2000] a report on all the work of ARCIC, including *Clarifications*, will be brought to this Synod ...' More extraordinarily still, the 1998 Lambeth Conference Section 4 report revisited the 1988 resolutions about the ARCIC-1 statements and said they ought to be better known. It then welcomed ARCIC-2's three relatively uncontroversial statements. A major resolution (IV.23) of the whole Conference repeated these major points. But *no one anywhere even mentioned the existence* of *Clarifications*. Was it forgotten, ignored or suppressed?* Yet that same year in England the Roman Catholic Bishops' Conference, in their teaching document *One Bread One Body*, unapologetically quoted from *Clarifications* as from an agreed document. We are left with the impossible analysis that either the two Communions have not agreed with each other (though each thinks it has), or they have only agreed with each other by 'agreeing' differing documents.†

And no overall report on ARCIC such as FOAG had promised ever came to General Synod.

ARCIC-2, 1999–2005, Papal authority and the Virgin Mary

In 1999 came *The Gift of Authority: Authority in the Church III.*[15] That which ARCIC-1 had left unresolved in 1982, ARCIC-2 now resolved. The Bishop of Rome should have a universal jurisdiction over the Churches, and, by God's gift, is preserved from error when he speaks on behalf of the whole Church. The Marian decrees, the expression (and acid test) of the preservation of the popes from error, were not mentioned. The laity were still hardly mentioned, as para. 40 which begins, 'In the Roman Catholic Church the tradition of synodality has not ceased' is almost entirely about bishops. It ends with the limp (and not very credible) sentence, 'a growth in synodality at the local level is promoting the active participation of lay persons in the life and mission of the local church.' I am unaware of these locally constituted synods, but they are all the evidence adduced.[16] I attacked the statement in *News of Liturgy*, and was asked to review it in the *Church of England Newspaper* in July 1999. I did so, suggesting that the Anglicans in ARCIC-2 had been hijacked, facing for so long the same pressing question about the Pope, that (like hijacked plane passengers) they had lost touch with their own realities and were seeing things through the eyes of their hijackers. I pointed out that ARCIC-2 ascribes to the Bishop of Rome *who now is* all the powers and infallibility of the universal Primate. Michael Nazir-Ali, the Bishop of Rochester and a member of ARCIC-2, replied denying the hijacking, and saying the ascription of powers and roles to the Pope was prospective, with a view to conditions that might one day apply. I responded, pointing out that all the verbs are in the historic or present indicative, and declare what has been and what is, not what might be. But suppose we go with Michael Nazir-Ali's interpretation – there is then something very odd in God's workings, if it is only

---

* Yes, I was there, and did not ask questions in the plenary, as perhaps I should have done – largely because I was up to my ears in another battle (see pages 260–1).
† The cover of the statement on Mary in 2005 (see below) says it is the 5th Statement of ARCIC-2. So *Clarifications* was not in that count, as it was not a 'statement'. On the other hand, it was not only published alongside *Life in Christ*, but in identical format to it. But what is the Pope to think if it is being quietly forgotten?

at some unknown date in the future, when some unspecified ecumenical advance has been made, that the Bishop of Rome of the day will then *and only then* become infallible. Martin Davie, in the later semi-official reactions, *Unpacking the Gift*, went as far as to say of Michael Nazir-Ali's understanding that 'the language that is used in this section . . . simply does not permit such an interpretation'[17] – and added in a footnote 'Bishop Buchanan's interpretation does seem to represent the most straightforward reading of the text itself.'[18] I was already concluding that, if I believed what *The Gift* says, I would no longer know why I was not a Roman Catholic.

An oddity in the set-up was that we could not get on with debating *The Gift of Authority* in Synod. I was on CCU when it first came out, and pressed for a debate. We even discussed whether it would come better in July 2000 (at the end of a quinquennium) or in November 2000 (which would enable a new Synod to have a wide and searching debate on a matter of great substance, without necessarily having to come to a conclusion on the first occasion). But then the usual delaying tactics somehow went to work, with even a muttering about our having to hear from the ACC before we would know when and how to handle it. Delays encourage the idea that the two Communions have agreed with each other, which somehow grows into a fact, simply on the basis of around 20 to 24 persons having agreed a statement. Finally, the debate was scheduled for February 2004.

As consideration of it came nearer, I was asked to write up my opposition in a one-off Grove Booklet. I wrote a 36-page booklet under the title, *Is Papal Authority a Gift to Us?* This was primarily for distribution (by some generous donor) to members of Synod, which occurred in July 2003. I would claim that the case it mounts against the ARCIC report is trenchant and difficult to refute – and, obviously, I cannot repeat it all here, though I would urge readers to get a copy and take it to heart.[19] That autumn CCU was seeking a fairly supportive motion on *The Gift of Authority,* and so commissioned Martin Davie, their theologian, to refute my booklet. Never have I seen such weak nit-picking forms of argument from such an able and admirable practitioner – he must have been instructed to 'see Colin Buchanan off', and therefore cobbled up arguments out of thin air. Refuting his critique was easy indeed – but in fact it had not been circulated, but was merely advertised to members of Synod as available to anyone who wanted it – and no one did.[20] I submit that my critique of *The Gift* stands unaffected.

Before February 2004 CCU blew hot and cold in crafting its own motion for debate.[21] Finally, Ian Cundy came with a covering report from CCU (GS 1532), and an elephantine motion with seven parts, some of which were faintly warm towards *The Gift*, others gently critical. Michael Nazir-Ali got in an eighth part which recognized the linguistic task ARCIC had set itself. The omission of the place of the laity and of the Marian decrees from *The Gift* was not even noticed; and CCU was emulating ARCIC itself in ducking central questions, bare-facedly disregarding the agenda set in the 1986 debates. I therefore tabled my own amendment to add:

> [That this Synod] recalling that ARCIC-1 so linked the teaching authority of the Bishop of Rome with the papal decrees on the Immaculate Conception and the Bodily Assumption of the Blessed Virgin Mary as to identify this particular linkage as the point where Anglicans would need to be satisfied before accepting papal pronouncements as the 'wholly reliable teaching of the whole Church' (para 43), regret that *The Gift of Authority* omits, without explanation, all reference to those Marian decrees, and believe any judgment on the report impossible for the Synod to reach in the absence of a treatment of such linkage.

Well, Ian Cundy opposed that linkage. A separate treatment of Mary was coming, and we should wait for it. He also went nit-picking about my word 'impossible', calling it a proposal to halt all debate. I could have wished that, if he thought the word 'impossible' too strong, yet thought the linkage of Mary and infallibility was worth handling, then he could have tried to agree a recasting of my amendment to say *something* about the omission of Mary which he could accept. As it was, he finished his brush-off thus: 'of course the Marian dogmas do continue to pose problems for Anglicans, *particularly in the area of authority.*' These are my italics – but, amazingly, his words were employed not to accept my amendment but to ask Synod to reject it. The debate then revealed that Anglo-Catholics on Synod, ignorant perhaps that it was Oswald Clark who had pushed the linkage of the two matters in 1986, wanted Mary kept out of sight, and rallied to oppose my amendment. It went down: 4–23; 51–105; 85–92. The platform proposal, now in eight parts, went through overwhelmingly. Like the idols of Babylon it will do neither harm nor good.

The Mary report

Then, a year later, just after Cardinal Ratzinger became Pope, the Mary report at last came among us, *Mary: Grace and Hope in Christ.*[22] It was advertised as the fifth statement of ARCIC-2, which 'brings to completion the mandate the Commission was given'. And here was another unanimous report where the Anglicans had come, presumably by slow steps and hard arguing, to embrace a position unrecognizable as Anglican to most parts of the Anglican Communion. While the worst excesses of Mariolatry are avoided, it is a Roman Catholic position which is reached. The report has not, of course, at the time of writing been brought to the Synod, but it surely must be, and, presumably, the definitive

Anglican response to both *The Gift of Authority* and *Mary: Hope and Grace in Christ* will be given at the 2008 Lambeth Conference.

To a Church which states that its doctrines must be visible in Scripture or have been seen by ancient authors as 'agreeable' to Scripture (Canon A 5), the Marian decrees have been an enormous stumbling block. Yet in ARCIC-2 the Roman Catholic doctrines were apparently placed on the table for the Anglicans to adjust themselves to them – and thus the report was bound to come out with the 'right' answers. At first encounter, I am left with profound questions, to which I would want answers if I were to be debating this extraordinary report myself.

Firstly, the nearest sign of a crack between the approach of the two sides is the discussion of the basis of believing in the decrees. Do Anglicans have to accept them because the Pope defined them? If so, a one-line report would have done! Well, no, paragraphs 62-3 make out that Roman Catholics already believed them before the Pope defined them (so, I suppose, why should not we?). Yet, if we are to reach the point of affirming the Immaculate Conception and the Bodily Assumption by sheer reasoning from Scripture, then the agreement runs the risk of not achieving what it hopes: firstly, because many of us will find (as I show below) that normal reasoning will not get us there; secondly, because, if we do get there, we shall have bypassed papal authority; and thirdly, because, if we do get there, such beliefs will still rank with us neither as fundamental to the faith, nor as more than a personal opinion.

Those things noted, once belief on the basis of a papal teaching authority is gently left aside, the major part of the report is inductive reasoning. It works from agreed data to discover where the proper organizing of those data might lead (though, I add *sotto voce*, we already know where it had to lead them). But the process at least provides a level playing field for others, less convinced of a necessary outcome, to challenge the processes they employ.

Mary – what does Scripture actually say?

So we next address Scripture. It is paradoxical that Anglicans at intervals have to handle doubts among themselves about the virginal conception and birth of Jesus – and not only from an extreme modernist wing. David Jenkins explicitly denied it. My own episcopal mentor, Hugh Montefiore, was very doubtful.[23] These denials and doubts have arisen despite the clear testimony of both Matthew and Luke (apparently reporting Joseph's and Mary's stories separately). To believe the Scripture (however unlikely or extraordinary its account) is one thing; but to be driven to believe even more unlikely and extraordinary accounts *of which there is no hint in Scripture or other early literature* – that is an amazing move indeed.

Mary has but a small place in Scripture, and almost all of it is concentrated on the birth stories. While John mentions her presence at the cross (partly in relation to himself), and Luke in Acts 1 mentions her presence with the other disciples after the Ascension, she does not figure at any point in any of the accounts of the life of the infant Church thereafter. She is neither visible in her person, nor cited by name in doctrinal or other teaching. Even at the point where the letters of John are most keen to oppose Gnosticism they only say, 'Jesus Christ has come in the flesh', and his human mother is not mentioned. The letters of Ignatius of Antioch, a decade or two later, with exactly the same purpose of refuting Gnosticism by emphasizing that Jesus Christ has come in the flesh, do no more than say, 'born of Mary' or 'born of a virgin'. That was their credal fixed point. Early baptismal confessions are the same. Sections 32–3 of the report give away the place of Mary in the first four centuries – for there is no quotation there from any author of those centuries which touches on either her conception and birth, or the ending of her earthly life, or the role she plays in intercession for us. We can be certain that any such hint in any author would have been seized upon and developed to the limit by ARCIC – if it could be found. Even the reference to Mary as the antitype of Eve, of which two instances are noted, is only an illustrative contrast of the disobedience of one woman and the obedience of the other. Of the doctrines in this report there is nothing. And the development of a cult of Mary begins, as far we can see, with the use by the Council of Ephesus in 431 of the term *Theotokos* ('bearer of God' or 'giving birth to God'). This, as far as I can tell, was in the context of defending the deity of Christ, and had no eye to magnifying Mary. But history has redubbed her Mother of God, and much has flowed from that.

The report pushes its luck to maximize her place in Scripture. The Magi are virtually said to be kneeling in worship before both the infant and his mother (though Matthew has 'him' only there – did they take their eye off the text?). And we all know that gifts for infants are given to parents! She is excepted from 'All have sinned and come short of the glory of God' and similar teaching. The wonderful phrase is that the Marian decrees are 'consonant' with Scripture (para. 60). So they are, in the sense that they do not connect anywhere with the sparse accounts of Mary that we have – and one is tempted to say that the depth of the Pacific Ocean is totally 'consonant' with there being no water on the moon. Such consonance is risible. The miracles of Scripture are *thaumata* – you see them, and gasp. In the case of the virgin conception and birth of Christ, only Mary and Joseph could know the miracle and gasp – and they did, and we are told of it. But the Immaculate Conception of Mary and her Bodily Assumption are without a contemporary gasp, without witnesses, without early mention, without credibility – and are at odds with the regularly attested universality of sin in the human race. The New Testament excepts only Christ himself from this condition, an exception which, without other witness, we must assume was a feature of his own miraculous conception, and not a genetic gift from his mother.

The Scripture gives no basis whatsoever for invoking the saints, and such practices were rightly abolished from Anglicanism at the Reformation (see Article XXII). And the Hail Mary, which the report tells us became a request for her prayers 'now and at the hour of our death' only in the fifteenth century (para. 67), is, I suggest, even without that, highly misleading. For the angel came, on God's behalf, to bestow a favour (she was *receiving* grace) and a responsibility upon her, a creature and a servant of God. But the Roman Catholic use of it is of us, as lowly and dependent beings, depending on her as 'full of grace' – which in that context so easily sounds as though she *dispenses* grace. The fifteenth-century addition takes it much further from Scripture also.

Finally

The Anglican signatories of this report are three from England, two each from the USA and Australia, one Canadian and one Brazilian. Have they really represented our Communion? The report calls our embracing the Marian beliefs a 're-reception' of that which we had lost. Without in any sense diminishing the role of Mary which we see in the New Testament, Anglicans would be wise to ask whether those medieval and latterday Roman Catholic beliefs are true, whether they actually mesh with the rest of our beliefs, whether they were rejected for good reason, whether they are in any sense necessary. (If they were lost for good reason, they should not be re-received.) There is also the issue of consistency. Is there anything like this report on Mary in our Porvoo, Meissen, Reuilly, or Anglican–Methodist Conversations? A note to the Synod members (GS Misc 785) tells us that the Inter-Anglican Standing Commission on Ecumenical Relations (IASCER) will be considering it – and it is certainly their task to keep all ecumenical dialogues in step with each other. Will they fudge the issue too, or deliver a verdict of 'inconsistent'? Synod will apparently get its chance after FOAG have considered it.

And I am left saying, as I did about the papal authority statement, that if I believed about Mary what this report is affirming, then I would become a Roman Catholic tomorrow. Rome makes amazing claims, so one can be an Anglican only if those claims are seen as incredible. If they are credible, we have neither need nor excuse to be Anglicans at all.

10

Multi-ethnic Anglicanism

He ... has broken down the dividing wall, that is, the hostility
between us.

(Ephesians 2.14)

*From the coming of the first Caribbean immigrants to England in 1948 to
having a Ugandan Archbishop of York in 2005 is a long pilgrimage – and
there is still a long way to go.*

A personal journey

I was born white into a white society, fairly confident of its destined place in the
world. We were enlightened imperialists. The notion was there in my bones.

South Africa ranked large in shifting my opinion. It started with the Malan
victory for the Nationalists in 1948. I shared the shock at the ruthless new
regime, but also slowly learned that the British held much responsibility. Then I
read, *Cry, the Beloved Country* – and I was convinced. When, during National
Service, I was asked at an Officer Selection Board how I would use six weeks
anywhere on earth with expenses paid, I answered, 'I would go to South Africa,
as the politicians there are soldering down a boiling pot.' Then, in my second
year as an undergraduate, Trevor Huddleston, coming from Sophiatown, spoke
in the Oxford Union, in white habit, with crew-cut hair and flashing eyes, the
nearest resemblance to John the Baptist I have ever seen. He expounded the
laws of the Union, particularly the Nationalist regime's Group Areas Act and
Bantu Education Act. Heckled by brawny white Rhodes Scholars in the front
row, he ran intellectual rings round them. They had never visited an African
township, and had no idea of the content, let alone the effect, of their own
laws.*

---

* Trevor Huddleston also encouraged sporting and artistic sanctions – naming Johnny Dankworth's
orchestra, which had declined to play in South Africa. The gesture had penetrated the tough racist
exterior of the white minority and had registered within the apartheid regime. In the Athletic Club
the invitation to South Africa we were expecting in 1957 did not come (and I might not have been
picked anyway), but I recall steeling myself to say 'no'.

While still at school, I belonged to Herne Hill Harriers as a track athlete and in 1951–3 trained with Clay Gibbs, a Trinidad international in his late twenties. He had come over during the war to join the RAF and had married a white Englishwoman. One day he said, 'I will not bring up children in this country – this is no place for a mixed-race child.' He then added, 'I hate this country' and went on, 'You don't know what the English have done to my country.' My childish persuasion that the British Empire was God's gift to the world died in that moment – I owe much to training with Clay.* In sharing our training, we were sharing our humanity.

My 21 years in theological teaching fully confirmed that Christian believers were one in Christ, internationalists before nationalists. Students, often already ordained, came from round the world – memorably in 1964–5 Janani Luwum, who became Archbishop of Uganda in 1974, and was assassinated by Amin in 1977. I first assisted at a presbyter's ordination when Leslie Brown ordained Horace Etemesi (now Bishop of Butere, Kenya) in our chapel. I first visited Uganda in the last days of Obote in 1984, attending their provincial assembly, meeting their bishops, and travelling north by ordinary bus to Lira and Gulu. I visited Namugongo, where in 1886 the Christian pageboys who refused Mwanga's homosexual advances were martyred – and a week later people I had met were themselves assassinated. Real partnership in Christ left little room for paternalism.†

Yet there was a contrasting lack of black candidates for the Church of England's ministry in those Nottingham days, when we had the largest college in the Church of England. The ground-breaking BCC publication, *The New Black Presence in England*, in the mid-1970s revealed how the black independent Churches were thriving, while the Church of England was losing out. General Synod debated this report in July 1977 (the meeting which I missed), following the passing of the Race Relations Act 1976 and the creation of the Commission for Racial Equality (CRE). Synod voted for a Special Church of England Fund 'to finance educational, self-help, and community projects among members of the Black and Asian communities'. But the Board for Social Responsibility (BSR) instead simply commended the Projects Fund of the Community and Race Relations Unit (CRRU) of the BCC, and thus distanced Synod from establishing

* A great near-contemporary was Arthur Wint, Jamaican Olympic gold-medallist. I never ran in the same race with him, but I once lent him my starting-blocks, a near approach to secondhand glory! Some 35 years later in Birmingham I confirmed a 15-year-old wheelchair-bound Jamaican lad with cerebral palsy – called Derek Wint. On enquiry, to my amazement he was a great-nephew of Arthur Wint – I wrote to Derek to say that, even though he could not run, he had great treasure in Christ. He died about 18 months later.
† I said to Henry Orombi – ex-St John's college, and now Archbishop of Uganda – 'Henry, I guess people like me blunder in, and behave in ways that embarrass you – do I embarrass you?' He smiled a near-compliment, 'Colin, believe me, you are less embarrassing to me than most visitors.'

its own fund – and made no donation to the CRRU Fund either. Black Christians were out of sight – and nearly out of mind.

My own life changed on becoming Bishop of Aston in 1985. Our home in Handsworth Wood bordered a most ethnically mixed area, in Handsworth, Soho, Lozells and Aston. I was to be consecrated alongside Wilfred Wood, who had come from Barbados in 1961 to minister here, and had been pioneering a role for black Anglicans in a Church widely believed to be racist, very ready to cold-shoulder them.* The consecration of the first black bishop for the Church of England now took us across an amazing watershed – and I was there! I said to Wilfred in our first phone conversation, 'It is Birmingham which needs a black bishop, not Croydon.' He replied, 'Do not give up your ambitions – perhaps one day you can be a black bishop' – but that has continued to elude me. In a great cosmopolitan event, bishops from around the world shared in consecrating Wilfred, and I, with what amounted to a small 'walk-on' part, incidentally got the benefit. Wilfred himself became a friend, also to my great benefit, and I am duly grateful.

We moved to Handsworth Wood in August 1985. I was to be installed on 9 October, and on Monday 9 September I was away at a conference. Hugh Montefiore, my diocesan, was in Israel. Driving home, I heard on the car radio at 10 p.m. news of riots and fires in Lozells. When I got in, the fires were visible on the television. I wrestled with myself – but reckoned a figure blundering around in the dark, saying 'I'm the new Bishop of Aston' was not going to help, and I went to bed – with a bad conscience.

The phone rang before 7 a.m. David Horn, vicar of St James, Aston, said. 'You'll want to know where this happened,' virtually telling me to get there. First checking the street map at St Silas' vicarage, I went to the local police station, where a member of the Police Authority took me in charge. We passed angry knots of people, went through police cordons, and reached the burnt-out Post Office in time to see the bodies of its Asian owners brought out. By midday Douglas Hurd, the Home Secretary, had arrived, and we met him at Police headquarters and accompanied him as he visited local community groups that afternoon. I went back on foot that evening to an unnaturally quiet area. I was not yet officially unwrapped, but my first day as a working bishop had launched me into the tensions, conflicts and fears of inner Birmingham. Church leaders formed an Aston and Handsworth Churches Forum, a truly multi-ethnic Christian forum – I was a member. It was knowledge of Aston and Handsworth

---

* The classic instance, duplicated a thousandfold, is where Anglicans, immigrating from Jamaica, Antigua or Nevis, attended their local parish church, and sidesmen told them, 'Oh, no, this is not your church; you'll find it down the road there', directing them to a West Indian Pentecostalist Church. I have heard such stories at first hand, and it is no exaggerated cartoon.

that led me to suggest Desmond Tutu for the Citywide Christian Celebration in 1989.

In Birmingham, of course, I discovered black Anglicans. Hugh Montefiore was striving to raise their profile in diocesan life, and in his last weeks launched an Adviser on Black Ministries, Rajinder Daniel. It was not membership we were lacking, but ministers, leaders and full participation. Hence Hugh's actions. Thus far the story is personal to me, relevant (and agonizing) for the city and Diocese of Birmingham, but not directly related to the General Synod. The synodical story, the subject of the rest of this chapter, arises from *Faith in the City (FITC)*.

Faith in the City and CBAC

Robert Runcie deserves much credit for *FITC*, published in December 1985. It was probably his outstanding achievement, and we should inhabit a different Church of England today without it, and without the ways in which it has been followed up.[1] From ministering in two highly deprived parts – inner Birmingham and south-east London – I know the benefits. The key lay in the extraordinarily far-sighted picking of the team (for which a special gathering of urban bishops was convened in 1982 – the forerunner of today's Urban Bishops' Panel). The commission had 18 members, four of them from ethnic minorities: Wilfred Wood (then Archdeacon of Southwark), Linbert Spencer (chief executive, Project Fullemploy), Mano Rumalshah (later a bishop in Pakistan), and Barry Thorley (vicar of Birchfield). These four were highly influential in the report.

So what profile have ethnic minorities in *FITC*? Pages 95–100 sketch out a story of marginalization in the Church of England. Later chapters describe effects, in employment and other areas of life, of institutionalized discrimination in English society. But for the Church, the commission recommended: 'The establishment of a wide-ranging Standing Commission on Black Anglican Concerns . . . for an initial period (perhaps five years).' Such a commission would follow up issues of employment ratios, vocations to ordination, ideology of Church schools, and a general enabling of black Anglicans to punch their weight in the kingdom of God.

FITC made 38 recommendations to the Church of England, and 23 to the government and nation. Wilfred Wood wrote to me:

> The Commission made 61 Recommendations and . . . Standing Committee . . . decided to recommend 60 of them for acceptance by General Synod. The lone exception was . . . a Commission for Black Anglican Concerns. When the matter [i.e. the omission] was debated in Synod, there was such consternation that, although Synod

accepted the Standing Committee's recommendations, Standing Committee was asked to look at the matter again. There was some very fast footwork by Derek Pattinson, David Sheppard, and Archbishop Runcie, and an emergency meeting of the Commission and others was held at Lambeth Palace. I reluctantly agreed to attend a meeting of the Standing Committee ... and I told them there that I was not there to accept on behalf of the black community any crumbs that they had to offer. I just wanted to see the faces of people who could be so insensitive as to make such a recommendation ... here was a group without a single black person on it who knew better what was good for the black community than a Commission that was so brilliant in its recommendations that all but one were accepted ... the one rejected was one relating to black people when there were four black people on the group that made the recommendation! All this was happening at the time that Cherry Groce, a black woman, had been shot in her Brixton home by the Metropolitan Police, and another black woman on Broadwater Farm had died when the Metropolitan Police invaded her home.

Standing Committee then recommended the establishment of a sub-committee of the Standing Committee called Committee for Black Anglican Concerns with a representative from each of Synod's Boards. I was appointed Chairman of that Committee, and I remember that Mark Birchall was one of its members ... such was their experience and education in matters relating to multi-ethnic Britain that these white members virtually went native. By a stroke of good fortune, Glynne Gordon-Carter had just arrived in Britain, and we were able to secure her services as our Officer.[2]

The hurt still comes through after nearly 20 years.

A tortuous synodical story

Behind that hurt, the record, as far as I can reconstruct it, went like this:

(a)   In February 1986, after Synod first debated *FITC*, Standing Committee proposed various actions, including establishing the Church Urban Fund, but omitting that Standing Commission on Black Anglican Concerns. Ivor Smith-Cameron moved as an amendment to the composite proposal:

> [This Synod] asks the Standing Committee, in consultation with the Board for Social Responsibility and ACCM, to bring forward in July

fully worked out proposals for the establishing of a Commission of Black Anglican Concerns as suggested in . . . *Faith in the City*.

Hugh Montefiore backed this, the only speech against was from Standing Committee ('not yet' ready), and Synod rejected it, 197–207. This was hurtful – Ivor Smith-Cameron later spoke of 'a wave of bewilderment, distress, frustration and horror through black constituencies'.

(b)   In November 1986 Standing Committee proposed a Committee on Black Anglican Concerns (CBAC), with direct access to Standing Committee. This passed 360–39.

(c)   CBAC was set up immediately and first met in April 1987. Wilfred Wood was appointed chairman, and other synodical bodies had representatives on it. Very happily, in an autumn by-election Wilfred joined the House of Bishops and General Synod, and could lead from the front.[3] In December Glynne Gordon-Carter, herself from Jamaica, became secretary to the Committee and served it for 15 years.

(d)   A major task for CBAC was to bring black people onto Synod. *FITC* recommendation 5.74 became a charter for CBAC's work:

> We . . . recommend that the new Synod [i.e. that elected in 1985] should consider how a more appropriate system of representation which pays due regard to minority interests can be implemented for the General Synod elections of 1990.[4]

(e)   CBAC proposed to Standing Committee a special provision of co-options for this purpose. Standing Committee said there should be some 'electoral content' to seating such persons. So CBAC proposed to Synod in November 1988 that 24 minority ethnic persons should join Synod through the electoral process. If fewer than 24 were elected, then the quota would be completed from the losers who had done best in the poll. In the proposal Wilfred drew a careful distinction between 'representation' and 'participation' – making his case for participation. John Habgood told Synod the Laity opposed increasing co-options, so precluding that route to participation.[5] But Peter Dawes, Bishop of Derby, moved an amendment to reconsider co-options, and lost 112– 169. Another similar amendment was withdrawn. The main motion, seeking Regulations, and even a Measure, to provide the quota of 24, was passed 214–74. Perhaps some bewilderment and distress would now be assuaged.

(f)   A draft Measure to amend the Synodical Government Measure was brought to Synod in February 1989 to incorporate the quota system.[6] The debate went wrong. The humanity of the autumn was missing (no speeches by Wilfred Wood, John Sentamu or Ivor Smith-Cameron) and the desiccation of the lawyers came uppermost. The Synod on a count by Houses voted 17–3; 103–62; 80–96. The laywoman who called for this count ranks low among Wilfred's favourites. The Laity had defeated CBAC's hopes.

'Distress' and 'bewilderment' were understatements. Wilfred very nearly called for a complete secession of black Anglicans from the Church of England. The sense of rebuff, the sense that, if not actually racist, the Synod was wholly uncomprehending, and had led this whole constituency irresponsibly up a garden path in November, only to disclose it was a *cul de sac* in February – these impressions, however subjective, were appalling. The original rejection of a commission was as nothing compared with this. The analysis that *they* would always slap down the struggling minority community was all too tempting to believe, and that perception bid fair to create, if not that wholesale walk-out, yet enormous suspicion and consequent confrontation.

I found this episode very difficult to evaluate. I was torn between a longing that black Anglicans should play a developing – and guaranteed – role in the Synod, and yet a contrary sense that the proffered route was grievously misconceived. Proposing protected constituencies within STV elections is perverse. If voting in such a twisted system, I would have used high preferences for white candidates, as the protected 24 black ones would not *need* any preferences (being in anyway); so I could better deploy mine in relation, say, to views on the ordination of women.[7] If other voters had reasoned similarly – and surely they would have? – the 24 might have appeared in Synod through a derisory vote, much lower than if they had been standard candidates. This woeful way of pretending people had been elected was a rotten borough.[8] Possibly, also, white or near-white persons would have labelled themselves 'black' for an easy (if scandalous) route into Synod. Being wise afterwards (though I warned Wilfred in advance), I believe a pressure for co-options (say, four Canterbury clergy and laity, and two York, for not more than two quinqennia) apart from those elected would have provided a straightforward and unimpeachable result. As it was, many expectations perished at the end of the *cul de sac*.

CBAC after 1990

In my life, in April 1989 I hosted Desmond Tutu in Birmingham.* It ended in my own humiliation.[9] I went into exile in Rochester Diocese – and was elected to the House of Bishops. In March 1991 I was appointed to CCU. The CCU then nominated me to represent them on CBAC, now chaired by John Sentamu. I brought my Birmingham experience, and shared in a fast-learning situation with leading black Anglicans – several from Southwark. The 1988–9 rebuff in Synod, widely remembered in that community as racist and treacherous, was still an open wound. Uphill healing work was to be done. But more black Anglicans had been elected to Synod in 1990, and on CBAC they would think through their responsibilities.

The CBAC prioritized visits to the dioceses, to vet their racial awareness and encourage rigorous rethinking. There was thorough preparation, probing encounter, and reflective reporting afterwards. No diocese was spared – we wanted to alert Hereford farmers and Lake District landladies to a contemporary multi-ethnic England, including fully multi-ethnic participation in the Church of England. I was not part of these teams – but was often the only white person present at CBAC meetings, where I told John Sentamu that I was becoming an oppressed ethnic minority. He replied that some more oppression might be good for me.

I also took seriously on CBAC that I represented CCU. The members were busy establishing a place in the Church of England for their constituency, and that I honoured and have laboured to achieve. But I reminded them at intervals about holding out hands to the burgeoning black-led or black-majority Churches, whom I had known in Birmingham – and where many erstwhile Anglicans are to be found.[10] I am unsure what would have counted as progress on this front; but these Churches, reported as showing the most substantial growth in the 1980s, hardly figured on Synod's agenda. The CCU themselves appointed me in the early 1990s as observer at the quarterly meeting of the International Ministerial Council of Great Britain, which provided a validation for independent black ministries, and helped over immigration and similar issues. It kept me alive to these Churches.

---

* I record one little gem from Desmond. In Coventry he spoke 'politically' on South Africa. He was asked, 'Surely religion and politics should be kept separate from each other?' Desmond usually replied to this FAQ, 'You must be reading a different Bible from mine,' but that day he replied, 'You must be rich – no poor person has ever asked me that question.' The day he left, the Birmingham *Post & Mail* headlined: 'Now we know politics and religion are inextricably linked'.

The Black Anglican Celebration 1994

The CBAC planned a major Black Anglican Celebration at York University in July 1994. One part I had was to urge including some sport – and hence played football at 60! But more seriously I urged the Committee to prepare a public statement. There was initial reluctance – 'We don't want to sit up half Saturday night.' I responded unrelentingly – 'Here is a once-in-a-decade opportunity to blaze something into the press and into hearts and minds, and you cannot stay a couple of hours out of bed to do it.' It happened – a trumpet call for the plenary session to adopt, and for *Roots and Wings*, the 1994 report of the Celebration, to publish. The text highlighted

the Black Anglicans, with the support of all others at the Celebration, issue this trumpet call:

To the Church of England and its leaders:

Black people are people. Black Christians are Christians. Black Anglicans are Anglicans. Our ethnic origins may lie in Asia, Africa or the Americas, and a few of us are visitors from those lands, but mostly we ourselves are English, a large proportion of us born in England, and glad to be Anglicans here in partnership with white Christians. We belong to this land and to every corner of it. Make us more visible within the life and leadership of our Church. Racism has no place in Christ; so let all discrimination against us, knowing or ignorant, cease. Let us reach our own fulness in Christ as ourselves. Let our gifts and calling be recognized and affirmed, our partnership in the life of the Church of England be evident and welcome. We seek to walk confidently in Christ, one in him with all of every race who name his name. Let the whole Church of England by deliberate will live this doctrine in practical love. Without it there is no gospel message of God's love for us to spread.

To our English society we say:

Black people are people. Black English are English. But there is as yet no true equality in jobs or housing or opportunity or the media and their message. True justice is too frequently missing from police methods and administration of the law. Institutional racism is deeply rooted, and we fear for our children if it is not rooted out.[11] We are here; we are English; we are part of the community. Give us justice.

To our God we say:

> We have sounded our trumpet call to redress wrongs done to us: yet we are humble before your love and are only seeking your glory. Let your trumpet-call now guide our feet, your judgement and justice cry out to the skies. We meet in your love to do your will. We place our cause in your hands. Do your will in us that your world may be transformed.

Within the Celebration proper, I toured the groups and workshops and reported encouragingly to the final plenary. My report was included in *Roots and Wings*. The CBAC gave a presentation about the Celebration to the November 1994 Synod.

1995 and beyond

The 1995 elections loomed next. I had earlier done a strategy document for CBAC (including seeking co-options); and now I wrote coaching notes for possible election candidates (each diocese had a search going). *FITC*'s original recommendations meant CBAC had always overtly worked to increase black representation on General Synod. I was in no danger myself, as Wilfred would not contest the suffragans' constituency, but instead nominated me. My draft notes included: 'you are safest with first preferences. So you are better off with 25% who really want you, and 75% who loathe your guts, than you are with 75% who vaguely wish you well, and 25% who vaguely give you a low preference.'

The electoral history was that back in 1985 seven black candidates had been elected (and Wilfred Wood plus five others arrived through by-elections). Then in 1990, 14 (plus Wilfred) had been elected, and another one or two through later by-elections. Now in 1995, again 14 were elected, and others came in by-elections (and the Bishops, without Wilfred, gained Michael Nazir-Ali, Bishop of Rochester).

John Sentamu continued as chairman when the Committee was reconstituted in early 1996. I had recommended that the Bishops should have their own representative – and they nominated me, so I was still there. The name became the Committee for Minority Ethnic Anglican Concerns (CMEAC). Then in 1996 I became Bishop of Woolwich. The Woolwich Area in its multi-ethnic composition paralleled Handsworth and Aston, and my CMEAC role now cohered with my daily experience in Southwark, Lewisham and Greenwich. In those boroughs unrest still seethed about the failure to convict the persons accused of Stephen Lawrence's murder in 1994. Vigils and anniversaries and a plaque on the South Circular kept the memories of injustice alive; and in 1998 the MacPherson Inquiry was held with John Sentamu as assessor. The report heavily emphasized institutional racism – and my new bishop, Tom Butler, asked the CRE to enquire into Southwark Diocese, to identify and defeat institutional racism within our structures and *mores*.[12]

I never spoke in Synod specifically on racist matters or on behalf of CMEAC, though *Seeds of Hope* was debated in November 1991 and its sequel, *The Passing Winter*, in November 1996. I had many fish to fry, and strong ethnic minority voices were being heard in Synod without my help. My part was to further the anti-racist and full-participation agenda by encouraging individuals, and helping drafting and publicizing of information and policy. I believe I held the confidence of CBAC's members, and remain thankful to God for delivering me into this unlikely role.

In the late 1990s, John Sentamu, by then Bishop of Stepney, and not on Synod,[13] vacated the chair. Rose Hudson-Wilkin, then representing Lichfield clergy, but moving to a London parish, succeeded him – a brilliant appointment. She was not elected in London in autumn 2000, but kept the chair, and duly succeeded at a by-election.

Ethnicity, census returns and electoral rolls

In my final years an issue of identifying ethnic origins of people generally, and church people in particular, came into prominence. The government decided in advance to include in the 2001 national census a question on ethnic identity. There were 16 categories listed for people to classify themselves. My recollections (solely impressionistic) are that some fears came from ethnic minorities, perhaps haunted by memories of pass laws in apartheid South Africa; but more antipathy came from that white thinking which unreflectively asserts, 'I don't see colour, I just see people.'[14] Elsewhere in the world ethnic minorities have sometimes been protected to save them from being deculturated by a swamping majority. In New Zealand in 1992 the Anglicans created three *tikanga* – perhaps loosely translated as 'cultural strands' – Maori, Pakeha (European) and Polynesian – for this purpose. That would not do for us: the Church of England is clearly called to live multi-ethnically, but to do so fairly must actually *know* how it is composed. The investigating started with a CBAC survey in 1992–3, published as *How We Stand: A Report on Black Anglican Membership of the Church of England in the 1990s*, and launched just before the Black Anglican Celebration in July 1994. It charted around 16,000 adult black Anglicans worshipping on an average Sunday. Southwark Diocese, mindful that that report rested on inadequate statistics, and noting the national census due in 2001, wanted a mandatory count. The diocesan synod started this in November 1997, and the intrepid Vasantha Gnanadoss finally moved it in General Synod in November 1999. She concluded it would be 'an important symbolic act that strengthens feelings of inclusion and a general sense of community and trust'. The motion, including an amendment she accepted, passed overwhelmingly thus:

That this Synod

(a)   recognize the advantages of showing that the Church of England is a multi-ethnic Church with multi-ethnic leadership at all levels;

(b)   call upon the Archbishops' Council to organize the collection of statistics at the time of the next general revision of church electoral rolls (2002) on the ethnic origin of members on electoral rolls, members of church councils, churchwardens, deanery synod representatives and clergy throughout all the dioceses of the Church of England; and

(c)   call further upon the Archbishops' Council to arrange the collection of the statistics by the procedure suggested in the background paper from the Diocese of Southwark.

It happened in March and April 2002. In all 75 per cent of dioceses participated, and in those dioceses taken together 54 per cent of parishes participated. Within participating parishes a high level of completed returns came in – 84 per cent overall. By July 2003 the 2001 national census results were available, so that the distribution of ethnic minorities in the Church of England could be compared with the proportions in society. But we could also see whether the proportions on electoral rolls were replicated in membership of PCCs and at other levels of synodical decision-taking. At the July 2003 Synod, Lynda Barley from the Research and Statistics Department of the Archbishops' Council, made a presentation of the statistics. She carefully pointed out the shortcomings of returns – those who had not made returns were possibly not random, but somewhat self-selecting. The proportion of ordained clergy from the ethnic minorities was demonstrably low – and the census showed that the ethnic distribution on the ground mirrored the indices of deprivation.

At this stage, I suspect that, in proportional terms, the minority ethnic community has recently been reasonably well represented in Synod – though, as the book goes to press, I am grieved to see the defeat of two valuable members from Southwark Diocese in the autumn 2005 elections. I would have wanted to be far beyond the co-opting stages by now anyway; and in the electoral maelstrom it is vital that candidates should not be seen as single-issue advocates, but have a coherent set of Christian policies to present. I think the constituency is well capable of providing such candidates, but it will more and more mean that ethnic identity will be weighed by the electors alongside views on the ordination of women as bishops, or the reform of theological colleges, or abortion, or whatever. And none of this passing assessment of mine affects the issue which was then coming to Synod.

In Synod on that day Rose Hudson-Wilkin then introduced the actual debate on the report, *Called to Act Justly* (GS 1512). She said, among other telling points: '*Called to Act Justly* suggests that a "colour blind" approach to dealing with racism is inadequate, in that it fosters or permits unquestioned racist attitudes and practices to prevail.' Vasantha Gnanadoss reported that Southwark parishes provided a 94 per cent return – submitting that the percentage of returns in each diocese reflected the kind of lead given in each. She also urged – an important point – that the exercise should be repeated when the rolls are made up anew in 2008.

Rose responded: 'What we have seen in the dioceses that failed to participate is that, frankly, they did not care enough about this subject'. She moved the substantive motion, which, after constructive amending, came out thus:

That this Synod

(a)   affirm its commitment to continue tackling the challenge of institutional racism within the Church of England and providing a prophetic voice in addressing the issues of racial injustice;

(b)   commend the report *Called to Act Justly* and invite bishops and their dioceses to consider its implications for their ministry, witness and work for racial justice;

(c)   endorse the recommendations in section VII of *Called to Act Justly* and ask the Archbishops' Council to report on progress in implementation within the next three years; and

(d)   recommend that bishops, in consultation with the Ministry Division, introduce valuing cultural diversity and racism awareness training as a standard requirement for all clergy, accredited ministers, and diocesan officers and staff.

The motion passed overwhelmingly. It put down a tremendously valuable marker. But the business concerned – integral to the nature of the kingdom of God – is not only unfinished: it has perhaps only just begun.

11

Colleges and courses

What you have heard from me through many witnesses entrust to
faithful people who will be able to teach others as well.

(2 Timothy 2.2)

Training clergy is vital to the Church of England's health – but overseeing
and coordinating the training causes considerable scratching of synodical
heads.

Theological colleges and courses come before General Synod intermittently,
and yet often somewhat emotively, as I shall show. The colleges were and are
independent foundations, not owned by the central authorities of the Church
of England, and free to take policy decisions in the light of their own charters
and the wishes of their own councils. Answerability to the Church of England
has come through the bishops 'recognizing' them as providing adequate
training – and recognition has been dependent upon regular five-year
inspections, and close monitoring of the courses offered and of the fees
charged. The colleges have traditionally been of a 'party' flavour, and I, having
attended one such, and taught for 21 years at another, have a ready apologia
for that apparently sectionalist interest. The courses by contrast are regional,
are meant to be comprehensive, and are often ecumenical. The central
authorities are always wrestling, as will be seen, with the relative
independence of the training institutions on the one hand – and of 44 dioceses
on the other.

In the 1960s the two evangelical colleges in Bristol got into big trouble,
originating, no doubt, in weaknesses of human nature, but escalating through
the lack of accountability of their councils to the wider Church. Robert Runcie
did an investigative round of the colleges in 1970–71, and saw no way the two
could unite or face the future together or apart. However, in the Synod debate
of February 1971 it was reported that Oliver Tomkins, Bishop of Bristol, was
chairing meetings to bring them together, and Synod, while endorsing other
decisions of the Bishops, gave Bristol a breathing space. The numbers of places
the Bishops would seek to secure in their continued recognition of colleges

were to be limited to 850.* There was an open-ended commitment to finance candidates and this made accountability the more urgent. Larger (and therefore fewer) colleges was the aim – with a better range of staff abilities as a result. Yet by 1971 numbers being recommended for training were declining year by year. The Bristol merger occurred, and confidence recovered. Elsewhere there were both mergers and closures.

In spring 1977 further financial alarm bells rang re training costs. A preliminary report by a working party suggested cutting all residential training by one year. The Bishops bought this projection in June 1977, and it came in the budget presentation to Synod in July 1977. The gloom led one member, a Dr Semple, to propose an amendment to reduce the training budget further from over £1 million to £837,000. However, Philip Lovegrove counter-proposed that the CBF 'reconsider the vote with a view to making further provision for the training of ordination candidates'. He accused the CBF of deliberately collecting gloomy returns from the dioceses; and he pointed out (as the colleges had already highlighted) that reducing the length of training does not save money overall, as stipends start a year earlier(!). Then he left a permanent mark on history with this unforgettable diatribe:

> Last night . . . I had a dream, in which I saw a lovely green sward. On it, huddled together in a tight-knit circle, was a bunch of paralysed purple rabbits. Dancing around the circle were a stoat and a couple of weasels, wearing that ubiquitous modern top-dress, the T-shirt, bearing mysterious hieroglyphs like 'ACCM', 'CBF', and 'Dismal Semple'. I awoke from the dream because the postman had arrived and delivered [the report].

Never were bishops so stung. The 'paralysed purple rabbits' characterization ran for years after. Synod swept away Semple, and bought Lovegrove. Training cuts were restored; Donald Coggan issued his call to every parish for more ordinands; people responded; costs were met; and some confidence in the future returned.

---

* 'Places' sounds credible, but in fact in the 1970s no one knew what a 'place' at a college was – nor is the present day different; and people do not know that they do not know, so use the term as though it were univocal. In 1971 the general presupposition was that 'places' were study-bedrooms; but other meanings were in contention, as, e.g., the ceiling number of ordinands the Bishops would approve, the numbers who could be accommodated for teaching and feeding (different from study-bedrooms as marrieds live out), the number calculated on a ratio of ten students to one staff member, the number (including non-ordinands, a feature of evangelical colleges) that gave best value for money to the institution and the students, and a host of others. In November 1976, I stated in debate, 'We have 75 single rooms, a ceiling of 80, and 113 students in residence.' Since then part-time and mixed-mode candidates have appeared at colleges. If 'places' is a fluid concept, then 'empty places' (right through to the Hind Report) beg virtually all questions of definition.

A pattern of accountability

Accountability finally found expression in the Guildford Report, *Theological Training: A Policy for the Future* (GS Misc 57) in early 1977. This overtook the previous report, and gave shape to the projected 'centres' – now to be 'institutes' governed by 'regional councils'. In the colleges 'a proportion (say, one-third) of members of their governing bodies should be elected by the General Synod or by Regional Councils [sic].' The outcome in practice was two General Synod representatives and a member of ACCM staff at least attending the council meetings, and, if possible, as full members of them. This was sent to the colleges during 1978, with time to discuss it on their councils and respond. But it came to pass. The centres did not.

Slow change in the 1980s

In 1979 John Tiller became chief secretary of ACCM, and was soon commissioned to write a major policy report on the Church of England's ministry. His task, which led to *A Strategy for the Church's Ministry*,[1] postponed further debate in these areas, certainly as affecting colleges, until he was done. The debates in Synod of November 1983 and February 1984 affirmed the mobilization of the whole *laos* on the one hand, and underwrote 'collaborative ministry' on the other, but effected little more than to flavour the atmosphere. The colleges went on as before, though more and more candidates were training on courses, and Local Ordained Ministry projects were also gathering force. There was a slow decline in numbers at the middle-of-the-road and Anglo-Catholic colleges throughout the 1980s, though the ordination of women as deacons gave increased encouragement to women. By 1990 further rationalization of colleges and courses was clearly inevitable.

Closures in the 1990s

In 1991 Bob Hardy, Bishop of Lincoln, was asked by the Bishops to conduct a survey of the colleges and courses, with a view to rationalization. His working party produced *Theological Colleges: The Way Ahead,* and this was circulated in strict confidentiality to the Bishops for their meeting in London in early October 1992. It had odd things to say about Midlands courses, wishing to unite the East Midlands and West Midlands ones in Birmingham. But horror erupted at the naming for closure of Mirfield, Salisbury/Wells and Oak Hill. Anglo-Catholics predictably rallied in defence of Mirfield (making it likely that, when the music stopped, Chichester would be left out). There was a heated defence of Oak Hill, which appeared to have been named, not because of inherent weaknesses but more through some *odium theologicum*, along perhaps with a cosmetic need to name one high college, one low and one central. Salisbury/Wells evoked less defence among the Bishops, though its relationship to the Southern course (SDMTS) had not been properly reported.[2] But a problem lay not only in the report's ill-considered contents, but also in its publishing process. The Bishops discussed it on a Wednesday morning, having been asked not necessarily to endorse it, but nevertheless to publish it. The college and course principals had been summoned to a meeting at 4 p.m. for the report to be released to them. In the morning the House agreed to publish it – by a majority on a show of hands. Over lunch, I found David Hope, Bishop of London, extremely unhappy, and after lunch we asked for an actual count. This was allowed, and was 32–13, and I was among the righteous 13. The report was delivered to the principals. It was now in the public arena.

One predictable effect occurred immediately. The DDOs and others ceased to recommend Salisbury/Wells to candidates. Naming the college was a blighting of it – and it went out of business. Oak Hill and Mirfield certainly had to fight (neither was going to fall on its sword), but they had good prospects of surviving, and DDOs and other advisers rather expected them to. The report came to General Synod on Thursday 12 November 1992 (the day after the debate on the ordination of women as presbyters). It was attacked from all sides, not least by David Hope. Philip Crowe, the principal of Salisbury/Wells, deplored the process by which he had been informed, and stated sadly that irresponsible publication of the report had prejudiced the college's future. The Synod declined even to 'take note' of the report, and the ball went back to the Bishops. They in January 1993 asked John Oliver, Bishop of Hereford, to do a fast job to restore a policy, and he, zooming around the country, recommended the retention of Oak Hill, the closure of Salisbury/Wells (which was by now, however, unjustly, clearly non-viable) and the substitution of Chichester for Mirfield. The Bishops acted and the colleges closed.

The other college to close in the 1990s was Lincoln, which had escaped previous rounds, but was clearly weak in numbers. The college held conversations with the University of Sheffield in 1993–4 and developed a confidential plan to move to Sheffield. There was, however, a snag – one I knew well from helping move LCD to Nottingham in 1967–70. Very few married students, who already have to move house once to go to college, are willing to move again *within* their training period – so they choose unmoving colleges. Thus announcing that a college will move might well be its own death sentence through fast decline of applications. I often reckoned that we in Nottingham would prove to be the last college which ever moved cities successfully. Lincoln from a weak base had grasped these implications of moving, and they therefore wrote to the Bishops in September 1994, with a tight timetable in view to avert any fall-off in applications. The college wanted that autumn term to begin with the new students already in place before being told of the move; but they also wanted the Bishops in early October publicly to endorse the projected move to Sheffield, so that recruiting for the following autumn on that open basis could start immediately. The Bishops were reluctant to act so fast, as though with a gun at our heads. I, who was simply an incumbent, had no close involvement with ordinands, so in the House of Bishops I said that I would have to oppose the move unless numbers of bishops would encourage candidates to go to Sheffield next autumn. Not a bishop responded positively. So I concluded, 'We cannot encourage Lincoln to invest in a project likely to have a promising prospectus and no candidates.' The decision was postponed to January. Lincoln then submitted that, unless they could announce the move after that January meeting, not only was the Sheffield venture finished, but the college had no future where it was. So in January, the House of Bishops, unable to back the move, accepted Lincoln's own submission and, by an admittedly slender majority, withdrew recognition. There was much uncomprehending criticism of the Bishops for this, and I wrote a long apologia for public consumption, quoting Lincoln's submission, to *Church Times*, which published it on 27 January 1995. Lincoln themselves produced a report entitled *A Lost Opportunity* (which, of course, maximized the pros, and played the cons fairly lightly); and the House of Bishops brought their own report to the July Synod, where the merits and demerits of the decision were tossed back and forward. There was reference to a concept of regional 'clusters', which Lincoln had ignored, but silence on the 'this or nothing' basis of Lincoln's second submission. I sat on my hands. The Synod took note.

The Bishops also closed the Aston (pre-theological training) Scheme in the mid-1990s. Having started with just a typewriter, it had more recently gone for a permanent office base, and costs per student had risen to rival the fees of residential colleges, far beyond those of the courses. I offered to open a half-price one-man show, but the Bishops did not take me seriously. Perhaps I had offered in too light-hearted a manner.

And then the Hind Report

The Archbishops' Council began in 1998, and exercised more responsibility as a central synodical agency than the previous Standing Committee had been doing. At an early stage they engaged with a continuing decline of numbers in residence at the colleges, and the financial implications of this. They appointed in 1999 a working party chaired by John Hind, previously principal of Chichester, and then Bishop in Europe, to consider the finances. Its wide-ranging membership, somewhat oddly, had only one member of a college staff, the principal of St Stephen's House, Oxford, which, with low numbers and the most pronounced Anglo-Catholicism, was very untypical. The six evangelical colleges, with over half the ordinands in residence of all the colleges put together, and long experienced in training non-ordinands alongside ordinands, were not represented. The working party was to consider the 'structure and funding of ordination training', but, taking the view that they faced a theological (not just a financial) question, their report set 'formation' in the forefront of its recommendations, and made other proposals to serve that purpose. After various stages of drafting, the final report, *Formation for Ministry within a Learning Church,*[3] was to come to General Synod in July 2003.

The overall plan was to provide a seamless pattern of formation for ordained ministers, leading through pre-ordination training, and on into lifelong development for each cleric. Each diocese would have some responsibility, but subject to central coordination and funding. The post-ordination provision (including residential periods in colleges) would incur central costs of around £1 million per annum. To find this money, each year 75 married ordinands who would have expected to train in residential colleges, would be switched to courses, thus saving up to 50 per cent of their fees, and family support costs also. I had planned to keep a neutral stance, as the timetable of decision taking stretched beyond my retirement, and the actual changes in practice years beyond that – but this proposal about marrieds pushed me into opposition. The fundamental principle I had known since 1957 was that candidates should have the appropriate training, even if this were not the cheapest to satisfy minimal criteria; and to divert candidates from that training – and do so on a quota basis and a marital basis – was a disastrous novelty. I reckoned it was also self-defeating on a different strategic canvas – for, if college numbers were already low (and there were colleges with less than 30 ordinands), then the diverting away of marrieds would cripple them further. The Hind answer, that they would be refilled with ordained clergy achieving their lifelong training (still at central expense), was totally incredible. Imagination boggles at the thought that, when a college's numbers went down, the requisite ordained persons would be directed there for six- or eight-week periods (or whatever) and would immediately (it would have to be immediately) arrive; and that, when they reached such declining colleges, they would find the resources and appropriate help to move them forward in their ministry – which would be needed to sustain confidence. Indeed, were such residential periods to be centrally directed, or would any element of personal choice remain? The question-begging in such a plan was astonishing.

Regional Training Partnerships

A core proposal of Hind was Regional Training Partnerships (RTPs), which would network the theological and training institutions of each region. Shades of the short-lived centres and institutes of the late 1970s and clusters of the mid-1990s! The RTPs would create a 'constitutional framework' and the 'legal entities ... and a Memorandum of Agreement' (6.35). But 'the model of co-operation ... could vary from region to region' (6.35). They would 'share administrative services and academic staff with a view to making savings' (7.13, proposal 7). There would be a 'governing body', and 'senior members of staffs ... would form a senior management team. This staffs group would report to the governing body' (7.12). Wonderfully, this total package – including, yes, a 'senior management team' and a 'governing body' – demonstrated that there would be *no* 'creation of another layer of management'. On my count it created *two* new layers! In the various regions, the institutions are not just a bike-ride away from each other; so 'sharing administrative services', if implemented, bid fair to stretch each institution's slender human administrative resources to breaking point – particularly if, when folk had travelled 50 or 100 miles to meetings, they had few substantial decisions to take on arrival. In the July 2003 debate I pitched in late on, and requested clarification of 'their composition, their powers, their accountability, their budget', and pressed the point that no one would use for their continuing ministerial education (CME) places at a wallowing under-resourced college, further sabotaged by the removal of married students. John Hind, in replying to the debate, did not address my questions. I was left in my scepticism.

To my astonishment, a marginal unclarity now assumed top priority. Hind had acknowledged problems about regional boundaries, and, after that 2003 debate, implementation was to begin with defining regions. Then I wondered whether I was dreaming – choosing boundaries was so high-profile, politically sensitive and far-reaching that one Sir Philip Mawer, Parliamentary Commissioner, had to be asked back to the Church of England to chair a working party to settle it. Sure that my own questions were the pressing ones, and that drawing boundaries, if not actually peanuts, would be easily solved within the various bodies concerned, I wrote to Philip Mawer to ask whether he was addressing other RTP matters, like powers, roles and membership. But no, he replied, he had just the one task.

Meantime other features of Hind were slipping into the sand. Synod resolved in July 2003 that ordinands would not be limited for training to institutions in their own region. This decision defended existing liberties and undercut some possible powers of RTPs. Synod rejected the proposed requirement of a degree for incumbents; and, in voting that the 75 marrieds should be restored to college training, asked that other sources for the £1 million should be explored.

Richard Turnbull (since appointed principal of Wycliffe Hall) ran a working party to find £1 million, and did a job which was efficient in itself, but did not convince the Bishops. Instead the House favoured not switching that original £1 million from training ordinands to CME. In June 2004 I opined to the House that the £1 million short should simply be put on the budget; but I added that the Archbishops' Council was giving other money away to dioceses for additional mission projects – and was apparently strapped in what absolutely *had* to be done and paradoxically generous in an extra which did not *have* to be done. The House reported to Synod in July 2004, and, in effect, left the CME proposals to be worked out and funded within dioceses, as at present. There were several voices in Synod to say that extra money could well be found.[4] There was still no light on my questions about RTPs.

In February 2005 the Synod had more fun. John Gladwin, the chair of the Ministry Division, brought a motion that specifically remitted responsibility for CME to the dioceses, while pursuing 'expected learning outcomes nationally'. Mike Parsons moved a near-wrecking amendment, stating that the Gladwin motion 'removes a major plank from the Hind proposals', and inviting the Archbishops' Council 'to take stock of the Hind process, to consider whether any major goal or goals can still be achieved'. This was defeated by 98–102, and the debate was adjourned in alarm till July 2005. Then in that July debate came a 'Reviewing Progress, June 2005' document (GS 1574), which harmlessly recognized 'scope for variety and flexibility' in training, but was able positively to welcome a detailed and efficient-looking set of Agreed Learning Outcomes which the Bishops had approved.

In 2005 RTPs were apparently taking on a bumbling cautious existence. The Mawer boundaries were in place, and GS 1574 recorded purposeful meetings in some regions, though the constitutions and powers of RTPs seemed to be still somewhat in the distance. While privately owned institutions remain, and residential training is still valued, and a relatively free choice for the ordinand of where to train remains, and central funding of ordination training remains, and CME is still funded (and therefore controlled) by dioceses, it is difficult to see what benign and cost-effective revolution those RTPs are supposed to usher in.

But the numbers . . .

The major newsworthy feature of GS 1574 was the lowish numbers in residence at the colleges in the year past – 501 ordinands spread between 12 colleges (with another 180+ non-ordinands).[5] In autumn 2005 the numbers had risen to 532 (with another 250 of ordinands from elsewhere and non-ordinands), which probably reflects the low numbers ordained in summer 2005, itself probably an outcome of low intake to colleges in 2002–3. The situation can never be determined by a mere head-count, as distribution of two-year and three-year periods in residence, and the flow over a period of years gives a much better picture. But the perilously low figures do show how cutting 75 marrieds from the colleges in order to save funds would have driven colleges towards bankruptcy (or sky-high fees). Small colleges are still there, and are identifiable as still at risk, and further closures do seem likely. It is grievous to see longstanding institutions go under, but the idea of large colleges, originally outlined in the De Bunsen Report of 1967, should not be lightly abandoned. I write from experience of both large and small.

12

The ordination of women

Whether, then, it was I or they, so we proclaim and so you have come
to believe.

(1 Corinthians 15.11)

*Can women be ordained? Can they be bishops? And how do we hold on to
those who believe this disobeys God and dissipates the Church's heritage?*

One of the most far-reaching of all synodical decisions of my time was the vote
in November 1992 to enable women to be ordained as presbyters. In theology I
confine myself here to my own (slowly reached) conclusion. While some verses
in the New Testament would relegate women to dependent roles, and to silent
acquiescence in whatever they were taught by their menfolk, the whole picture
is much more complex than that. I have concluded (and written up elsewhere[1])
that issues of ministerial orders are secondary in doctrinal importance, and
varieties of ministries are neither credal nor of the *esse* of the Church. I cannot
stop here on others' arguments as to why ordination issues are primary issues. I
simply presuppose that the revealed word of God is primary, and ministries, of
whatever sort, are provided to be servants of the word and of God's people. If by
any chance we misread Scripture when we ordain women, it is a mistake of a
secondary character, and the life of the Church should not be fundamentally
imperilled by it. And, I quickly add, I do not think we have made a mistake –
though, I confess, in student and curacy days I would have had, and did have,
vast difficulty in getting my mind round such a possibility.[2]

The 1970s

As far as I know the history, the first official writings on the subject in the
Church of England came when Gerald Ellison, then Bishop of Chester, chaired an
Archbishop's Commission which in 1966 published *Women and Holy Orders*.
This report saw little theological difficulty but considerable practical obstacles
to such ordinations, and the matter then rested for some years, before gathering
force in the 1970s. Hong Kong first opened the door for Anglicans – they asked
the support of the ACC for such ordinations at ACC's first meeting in Limuru,

Kenya, in April 1971. The ACC supported them – by 24–22. The Bishop of Hong Kong then ordained two women deacons as presbyters at Advent that year. The ACC asked all provinces of the Communion to forward their views on the issue to ACC by July 1973. In England Standing Committee passed the question to ACCM (and the Council for Women's Ministry about to join ACCM), and asked for a report. Under pressure of time the united council of ACCM asked Christian Howard, a distinguished member of the House of Laity, to write a 'consultative document'. She did so, at some length and depth – *The Ordination of Women to the Priesthood* (GS 104). Synod first considered this in November 1972, in a massive 'take note' debate. Then in July 1973, after some separate Convocation consideration, Standing Committee led Synod into consulting the dioceses before replying to ACC. The dioceses were asked to consider whether or not there were 'fundamental objections' to the ordination of women.

The dioceses duly replied; 30 of the 43 had passed 'no fundamental objections' in all three Houses. Synod addressed the responses in July 1975 in two separate motions.

First Kenneth Woolcombe, Bishop of Oxford, moved: 'That this Synod considers that there are no fundamental objections to the ordination of women to the priesthood.' Eric Kemp, already Bishop of Chichester, opposed. It passed 28–10; 110–96; 117–74.[3]

The debate about implementation was curiously presented as two motions in a curious sequence, the first not to proceed, and the second (if the first fell) to proceed. Once 'no fundamental objections' had been approved, the outcome was easy to foresee – the 'not proceeding' motion was lost in one House (19–14; 127–74; 80–96). So the motion to proceed came on – and, predictably, also went down (15–15; 78–108; 101–64). Synod then referred it to the House of Bishops to bring forward proposals when they saw fit, asking also that other Churches be consulted. A final motion about examining practical implications was defeated (112–128). The debates were slightly haunted by issues of marriage and families for women clergy (viewed by some as a handicap or even a disqualification for them); this reads today as sexist, dated, and so theologically irrelevant as to make us wonder how people dared air the matter.

Proponents of women's ordination thereafter nailed 'no fundamental objections' to their banners – often misremembered as 'no theological objections' (which may or may not mean the same). The banners were waved vigorously. As a fence-sitter I was under-impressed – firstly, because opponents were bound to say, and did say, 'Of course there *are* fundamental objections – and we can list them, and it is contemptuous to vote that we do not have them!' My further hesitations were that it had passed only narrowly, and, more importantly, that it recorded the opinion of a particular Synod when the clock stopped on it briefly at that Synod's last meeting before dissolution. The newly elected Synod of autumn 1975 might well have thought differently. Both the moral and the lasting force of the motion evaporated within minutes of its being passed, and, although I was becoming in my own person a supporter, I got weary of the chanted reliance on this depreciating currency.

The House of Bishops had plenty on which to cogitate. Canada ordained women in 1976, the United States and New Zealand in 1977. There was considerable derivative twitchiness about it all in England.[4] The House waited till after the 1978 Lambeth Conference, and then in November 1978 charged Hugh Montefiore to propose a motion to remove all legislation which would prevent the ordination of women as presbyters or bishops (backed by a Supplement by Christian Howard to her report – *The Ordination of Women: A Supplement to the Consultative Document GS 104* (GS Misc 88)). I have virtually no recollection of the debate (save that, for the last time, I abstained); but I have a very live recollection of a meeting 'off the field of play'.[5] A charismatic prayer meeting was running in the wings of Synod.[6] In London we met in Church House around 8.30 a.m., and that day (8 November 1978) was one where people of two strongly opposed convictions prayed aloud with each other extemporaneously, articulating to God both their desire and hope that their own view would prevail, and their desperate concern knowing they would be hurting others with whom they were praying. This memory influenced a small action of my own in 1992.[7]

Some nuancing amendments were rejected, and the vote was 32–17; 94–149; 120–106 (a 94 per cent turnout). This was the occasion on which Una Kroll shouted from the gallery, 'We asked for bread, and you gave us a stone', and hurled 30 pieces of silver onto our heads. I got one and kept it for years afterwards, though without, I think, being swayed in my opinions by it. Meanwhile the conflict was not going to go away. Maurice Chandler, an Anglo-Catholic layman, immediately tabled a Private Member's Motion asking the presidents to 'initiate discussions with the Roman Catholic Church, the Orthodox Churches, and such other episcopally ordered Churches as may be appropriate, on the subjects of the Ordination of Women and the Ministry of Women'.

Before this was reached, in July 1979 Standing Committee brought forward, from a group set up following the Lambeth Conference, a set of options as to how we should receive existing women presbyters from other parts of the Communion. From these options Paul Welsby, commissioned by Standing Committee but acting in his person, proposed the lightest possible recognition of such women presbyters, i.e. that they could preside at communion as visitors for a limited period, but not take up office in the Church of England. The motion was rejected (26–10; 87–113; 110–65). The issue went to the back-burner.

Maurice Chandler's Private Member's Motion was clearly intended to reinforce the case against women's ordination, but was crafted so that few would oppose it. In July 1980 it was carried without a count. Almost immediately after it came a first debate on the report of the Churches' Council for Covenanting. Three Church of England representatives had dissented from this, not least because the proposals would let in women ministers of other Churches 'by the back door'. The motion was simply to 'take note' – but the opponents, zealous to register their views, sought a vote by Houses, and Synod 'took note' by 35–2; 113–70; 138–45.[8]

The 1980s

After the General Synod elections in 1980, everything happened at once. Four policy questions bearing upon the ordination of women started to overlap with each other. Sorting them out retrospectively is intricate. I have done it thematically, rather than chronologically, but the overlap is important, as people addressing one theme always had in mind one or more of the other concurrent themes.

The Covenant issue ran on from that July 1980 debate, but the first theme in point of time for the new Synod was a Private Member's Motion by Tom Dye, a York layman, in July 1981. His overt theme was the diaconate, but his motion asked the House of Bishops to consider whether it should not be open to both men and women. The Bishops revealed they were already considering the matter, as a result of earlier prompting, also traceable to the 1978 Lambeth Conference. The debate made clear that a true diaconate would admit women to holy orders, to the third order of the historic threefold ministry. The Synod passed the motion.

The House of Bishops brought their report in November 1981, pointing out that it fitted well with the Dye motion, but was not due to it. The debate concentrated on the anomaly of the 'deaconess' order, which appeared to be an order – yet not holy orders but a *tertium quid,* which left its occupants still technically lay.* Ronald Gordon, Bishop of Portsmouth (and chairman of ACCM), moved that the Standing Committee should prepare legislation to enable women, including existing deaconesses, to be ordained deacons. He repelled delaying amendments and carried the motion.

When Standing Committee brought it back to Synod a year later, the same issues predominated. Some Anglo-Catholics, not least David Silk, then

---

* I recall that, once the ASB ordination rites were in currency, bishops often ordained male deacons and made female deaconesses at the same service, and with virtually the same prayers; I have even heard a bishop slip into 'deacon' *at the laying of hands* when a woman knelt before him to become a deaconess. I suppose God could sort out an uncanonical slip of the tongue.

archdeacon of Leicester and prolocutor of the Lower House of Canterbury, supported women becoming deacons, even though opposed to their becoming presbyters. Considerable heat was expended, not upon the principle at all, but rather upon what, theologically, was needed to turn existing deaconesses into deacons (conditional ordination was tossed back and forward). There was some call for delay to conduct a radical re-examination of the diaconate (possibly an alliance of genuine concern by some, with hope for infinite delay by others). But the motion for legislation went through (35–1; 120–63; 127–53).

The legislation came for General Approval in July 1983. This time I spoke up myself, as David Silk, at the request of the Standing Committee, asked Synod to 'instruct' the Revision Committee to replace conditional ordination with 'supplemental ordination' for existing deaconesses.[9] The precedents invoked either were irrelevant or were of the topping-up type for which North India was cited as a model. I saw ecumenical and other dangers arising if we gave any expression to a supplemental principle;[10] and we were rescued by an amendment which omitted 'supplemental ordination', but allowed us to retouch the liturgical forms. Deft drafting could acknowledge the past ministry of deaconesses, without imperilling the actual ordination of them as deacons. Synod gave General Approval (28–0; 118–33; 111–33).

The Revision Stage came in February 1984. By now, we knew that women would not be ordained deacon in time to vote (or stand as candidates) as clergy in the September 1985 elections to General Synod. There was therefore a provision that, after women were ordained as deacons, there should be a special constituency in the Synod (until 1990 only) by which women deacons would elect representatives on a provincial basis. The main question was then referred to the dioceses.

The dioceses' response and the decision on Final Approval came to the last meeting of the 1980–85 Synod in July 1985. Diocesan support had been very strong. Anglo-Catholic opposition to women presbyters only spilled over to some opposing women deacons. Evangelicals had no problem with women as deacons. Final Approval came 36–0; 147–49; 137–43. It now had to go to Parliament.

The second theme was the possibility of women ministers of other Churches being received as fully ordained presbyters under the interchangeability of ministers which would be ushered in by the Covenant. In July 1982, this probably determined the failure of the Covenant to reach its requisite two-thirds majority in the Clergy.[11] That locked the back-door, and Anglican advocates would have to return to the front-door.

Or would they? Amazingly, the third theme, the recognition of women ordained abroad, came up the very next day, with a Private Member's Motion from Diana McClatchey. She only proposed a lightweight recognition of such women presbyters for 'temporary visits', but emphasized that eucharistic celebrations under the illegal presidency of women presbyters had been growing in England as women presbyters from overseas had visiting increasingly. She mocked Anglo-Catholics who registered horror at these illegalities, pointing out how little respect they had ever had for liturgical laws, and, indeed, how by breaking laws they had effected change. She, however, would like a good legal basis. She carried her motion 24–4; 106–68; 103–60 – proportions not unlike those on the Covenant the day before (but Diana did not yet need a two-thirds majority). And perhaps there had been a real change in the balance of the Clergy since the 1975–80 Synod.

The next stage came with draft legislation about temporary visits in November 1983. The legal eagles had designated it Article 8 business, which had to be referred to diocesan synods before Final Approval, and to have the support of more than half of them. This designation itself caused unhappiness. In the debate some Anglo-Catholics insisted that, whatever happened in Canada or the USA, women were not actually being ordained, as they were incapable of receiving holy orders (an interruption typically cited – though misquoting – 'no serious theological objections' from 1975, two quinquennia earlier). General Approval came by 24–9; 112–73; 130–71. Two-thirds in each House looked a long way off.

The Revision Stage came in July 1984, and raised few new points, save that the provision was now for a seven-year period only, and no woman could be permitted to officiate in one parish for more than two weeks. The Measure went to the dioceses, which took time. A new Synod was in place (and I was not there) before, in February 1986, Synod debated the diocesan returns. These were broadly favourable, but not reaching two-thirds across the board. The Measure went to the House of Bishops. It came back in July 1986, and met its forecast end (28–12; 128–95; 147–88) – no two-thirds support in either Clergy or Laity.

Meanwhile the fourth and decisive theme, the ordination of women as presbyters, had emerged. Southwark had a diocesan motion awaiting its turn from 1982 onwards. By November 1984, when its debate came, Ronnie Bowlby, Bishop of Southwark, could point to similar motions from eight other dioceses. He moved:

> That this Synod asks the Standing Committee to bring forward legislation to permit the ordination of Women to the Priesthood in the Provinces of Canterbury and York.

The debate sticks in my mind, I fear, for the almost irrelevant attempt by Hugh

Montefiore to provide by amendment that this should be a 20-year 'experiment' only. Hugh, with total conviction, convinced exactly nobody, and voted on his own for his amendment, looking astonished that not one hand was raised in a packed Synod for such obvious sense! However, my reading of the debate over 20 years later is that opponents of women's ordination, while citing the need to stay in line with Rome, did not denounce the project as *ultra vires*, but debated it on its demerits, as they saw it. It was in the 1980s that all the argument that 'the priest at the altar is the *imago Christi*' burgeoned. Opponents were still fairly secure in their one-third blocking vote in the Clergy. In the event, after other amendments, partly about conscience clauses, had been defeated, the Southwark motion succeeded by 41–6; 131–98; 135–79 – still needing mountains more votes for two-thirds in each House. The issue was bound to affect the Synod elections in autumn 1985.

From 1985 to the ordination of women in 1994

In September 1985, the ordination of women as deacons was almost accomplished.[12] The Covenant was long dead. The minimal recognition of women ordained elsewhere was limping towards expiry. The one policy step which would outbid all the rest was the newly restarted proposal that women should be ordained as presbyters. Standing Committee determined to think through every aspect and secure ground as surely as possible on the way to the final vote. I summarize by numbers the stages to November 1992:

1.   Standing Committee appointed a group to address the issues – and included notable opponents of the ordination of women in it (not least George Austin, Brian Brindley, Oswald Clark and David Hope). The composition of the group produced a memorable denunciation in Synod by Michael O'Connor:

> It is as though the Home Office intended to build a new prison and handed over the design to a group composed mainly, or at least half, of prisoners. It would be one thing to have one or two, to give the prisoners' points of view; but to give them a majority and then be surprised when they come back with plans containing tunnels, ladders, secret passages.

The group's report was *The Ordination of Women to the Priesthood: The Scope of the Legislation* (GS 738). It said that, while in theory a 'one-line Measure' could be introduced, in fact 'safeguards' (the term used) were needed for those unable through conviction to receive the ministry of women presbyters. The report gave the first inkling of specific bishops, who had not themselves ordained women, being available for parishes wanting 'safeguards'. But it also aired other far-reaching structural separations as possibilities. There were financial issues too – was any kind of relief to be paid to clergy who reckoned themselves to be forced into resignation by profound ecclesiological changes in the Church of England?

2.   The report was debated in July 1986. Many who had not anticipated such provision for opponents expressed horror – Sister Carol in the first speech said it was 'compromise situation ... to receive a report that I would much prefer to consign to the wastepaper bin ... I was first of all dismayed and offended and then, frankly, incredulous.' Later, John Arnold said, 'I looked in vain for quotation marks and a footnote, giving the author's name as Lewis Carroll, because I felt I had gone through a looking glass to a world where values were turned upside down, perspectives reversed and a sense of proportion vanished.'

Horror was also expressed by the House of Bishops – horror in part that Synod was debating this report at all. It had not been ready when they had met in June, so they had had no chance to determine together courses of action which so deeply concerned them. At the actual Synod meeting, they drew up a Memorandum of their own (GS Misc 246). This became the rationale for an amendment moved for them in the debate, to delay decisions on preparing legislation until the Bishops had had opportunity to study the report as a House. The Synod easily accepted the amendment, with simply some worries about the timetable – for the issue was now going to run beyond the quinquennium.

3.   The Bishops produced for the February 1987 Synod, *The Ordination of Women to the Priesthood: A Report by the House of Bishops* (GS 764). Some issues were slowly clarifying: where possible, difficulties would be handled by a Code of Practice (though some legislation about 'safeguards' for minorities would be needed); a separate Measure would be a helpful way of handling financial factors; and a final decision could not be expected within that quinquennium. There were also hints that some bishops thought that no Anglican decision-taking body of any sort 'possesses the authority to make such a decision'.

4.   The main motion debated in February 1987 was to proceed with legislation. Various attempts to delay it came in amendments, which were all rejected. After more than six hours of debate the voting was 32–8; 135–70; 150–67. But the voting figures in the House of Clergy carried their own warning of struggles ahead.

5.   The next round came in July 1988. The Bishops presented a massive report, *The Ordination of Women to the Priesthood: A Second Report by the House of Bishops of the General Synod of the Church of England* (GS 829). The debate on this (a 'take note' one) helped the theological factors to be kept in view in the Synod. It was memorably characterized by John Sentamu as 'unanimous disagreement'. The draft Measure, which came the next day, was not far distant from the ultimate legislation under which the Church of England presently operates. When David McLean moved the approval, the selected opposing speaker, Colin James, Bishop of Winchester, recalled that Mark Santer, co-chairman of ARCIC-2, had the previous day indicated that ARCIC-2 was considering the issue (though would not be pronouncing for a long time[13]) – so how wise we would be, said Colin James, to wait. The draft Measure was approved by 28–21; 137–102; 134–93. The statistics were pored over long. And a following motion asked, uniquely, that the Revision Committee should be elected (rather than appointed as usual) – but that was turned down. The Financial Provisions Measure and the relevant Canons started their progress also.

6.   For the Revision Stage in Synod in November 1989, the Revision Committee proposed only minimal changes in the basic features of the Measure. Lengthy debating on the day made little impact on the text. The Measure provided for bishops to decline to ordain women, and for parishes to pass either or both of Resolution A (prohibiting any woman from presiding at communion there) or Resolution B (preventing a woman ever becoming incumbent or being licensed for that parish). The Measure, being Article 8 business, was automatically referred next to the dioceses. The Financial Provisions Measure was not handled until February, but it too was little altered.

7.   To assist diocesan understanding, the Bishops prepared their proposed Code of Practice and it was included in the document referring the draft Measure to the dioceses (GS Misc 336). It went out in April 1990 and responses were needed by the end of November 1991. That was going to take the whole business into another quinquennium, after another synodical election.

8.   The 1990 election itself was overshadowed by this issue, and the outcome changed the balances. The coming of women deacons on the one hand, and clear positions taken up by the clergy candidates in their manifestos on the other (and possibly a changeover from elderly Anglo-Catholic archdeacons to a newer breed) now gave the Clergy every likelihood of a two-thirds majority in favour. But the Laity had swung the

other way – raising a question as to whether candidates had revealed their views during the election, and whether the electorate might have been naive.

9. The question came to the dioceses after the General Synod elections. They had to vote for or against the draft Measure and Canons by Houses in each diocese, and report by 30 November 1991. At this point, the opponents employed a tactic both tempting and subtly deplorable, which was not well identified at the time. They pressed the point that ordaining women was bound to be divisive, and therefore even folk in favour of it in their own persons were being urged to vote against – in order to save the Church of England from disruption. This is an entirely right policy *at Final Approval*. But it could be desperately misleading at earlier stages. Thus, if, say, 10 per cent of the diocesan voters were opposed, but another 25 per cent could be persuaded it was divisive, then 35 per cent would vote against, and that statistic would then 'demonstrate' to General Synod how large was the opposition, how certain the divisiveness. But the true extent of opposition would not be known, and a cumulative argument about divisiveness would be taking legs far beyond the actualities. Consultation needs people to vote with their own convictions *at every point until the last*, and then and only then, with statistics displaying as far as possible the true state of convictions across the dioceses, General Synod must take a final decision in which members ask not only what they individually want, but what the effects of different decisions might be.

10. The statistical returns (in a complex GS 996) were debated in February 1992, solely in a 'take note' way. Elizabeth Paver (Sheffield) told us, as no mere male would have dared, 'Statistics are like a bikini: what they reveal is interesting; what they conceal is vital.' The supporters of the ordination of women generally viewed the 65–70 per cent voting in favour by 32,000 people in deanery synods and nearly 7,000 in diocesan synods as a fair charter. My own view is that, if this reported personal conviction, it was touch-and-go whether that was a sufficient basis – but if merely 10 per cent had been affected by the campaign I describe above, then the truth might well have been 10 per cent more in favour (and correspondingly fewer against). For surely, 78 per cent looks very different from 68 per cent. But I write this hypothetically, as I know I do not know (and no one knows) what the effect of the campaign was. Members said their bit; we took note; and we went on to a final drafting stage for the legislation. Virtually all of this was technical, and there were no surprises.

11. Hardly surprisingly, there was then, before Final Approval in Synod, a 'special reference'. When the Synod met in York in July 1992, the separate voting of the five Houses produced the following result:

	Ayes	Nos
Canterbury Upper House	21	7
York Upper House	10	6
Canterbury Lower House	114	48
York Lower House	50	26
House of Laity	148	93

Any one House could by simple majority have stopped the legislation then. However, no one expected that, and iff-ish support among York Bishops and Clergy was obviously going to be bolstered by over 70 per cent in the larger Houses of Canterbury. But, as forecast, the House of Laity figures looked daunting. If 241 had voted, those absent were a mere handful. How could 148–93 become (as it would need to, with the same persons voting) 161–80? Answer: 13 opponents would have to change their minds. And my impression is that every ounce of energy that could be mustered anywhere went into looking for the wobbliest 13 among the 93.

12. And so we came to 11 November. Proponents and opponents alike expected it to go down, though neither ceased praying on that account. I, with memories of 1978,[14] asked the neighbouring clergy in Gillingham if we could join together in a Eucharist around 6.30 a.m. (before I went off to Synod), as it might be the last time we could share communion together. We did so, and there was a profound sense of a storm (of some sort) looming. In the event the vicar of the next parish to mine departed to Rome shortly after the vote.

There were those who thought they had the likely vote of every member of the House of Laity taped. One of those supposed to be in favour, Carol Watson (Bath and Wells), died just before the Synod met. She had actually sent in her name to speak. More midnight oil was burned. Could two-thirds yet be achieved? How astonishing if her absence made the difference.

The whole day was given to the debate. There was a weighing of the diocesan statistics, and a genuine reflection on the likely divisiveness (and a report that estimates of clergy resigning and seeking financial relief varied between 3,000 and 50 – and could we afford the financial cost?). There was little or no reference to any expressed intentions of the bishops to provide 'extended episcopal care'. And there was a marked half-suppressed sense that far-reaching issues were at stake, and lives – indeed the life of the whole Church of England – bound up in the result.

There was little reference to the alleged lack of authority to take the decision at all. David Silk, the nominated principal opposition speaker, did mention 'another novelty for which there is no warrant in Scripture, provincial autonomy'. I go back to this 13 years later, because we have heard a colossal amount since 1992 about how the Church of England had no authority to address this issue. It is my own belief that, if this had been the main objection prior to the vote, then each time it came up, there should have been people to ask to pass to next business as handling the ordination of women was *ultra vires*. Indeed, if, when so asked, the Synod had persisted, then, arguably, those who took this stand should have walked out and declined to address the business. The difficulty for them was twofold – first, that not all opponents shared that view, so the walk-out might have been unimpressive; and, secondly, that it looked from 1975 to 1992 as though the opponents could raise a one-third majority in one or other of the Houses to block the final decision, *providing they were all present and voting*. So a small walk-out would probably have been ineffective in undermining the confidence of the Synod in its own processes, and yet highly effective as losing the blocking minority when it came to a vote. I reckon that their principle that this was *ultra vires* has been heard much more loudly since November 1992, than it was before it.

In the last half-hour of debate, one House of Laity member, Michael Hughes (Salisbury) said, 'I have talked against this for a long time ... honestly I now do not know which way to vote.' Less than 30 minutes to go – was it going to hang on such tension in perhaps two or three individuals? And then came the count: 39–13; 176–74; 169–82. Ten more in total had voted in the House of Laity than in July, and, even if they all had voted in favour (quite an assumption), still 11 more who had voted against in July had now voted in favour. If just two of those in favour had voted against, there would have been no Final Approval. And, like the open communion change I record in Chapter 2 above, the Church of England became a different institution through that cliffhanging decision of 11 November 1992.

The run-on is less emotive history. There was nit-picking in the Ecclesiastical Committee of Parliament before it was deemed 'expedient' to go to Lords and

Commons. There was no great problem in the Lords. There was a ludicrous (and typically less-than-Christian) debate in the Commons – with a large turnout and a heavy majority, many, as I see it, voting on secularist presuppositions.[15] There was Royal Assent on 5 November 1993, and the Synod met for one day only on 22 February 1994 to promulge the Canon and let the ordinations begin.

Which they did.

Aftermath

We need, however, to go back in time. After the Synod vote there was serious need to follow up some hypothetical thinking which had preceded it. In January 1993 the House of Bishops, meeting in Manchester, issued a statement about how they intended to assist those who in conscience had opposed the Measure. This was circulated to the February 1993 Synod for information, and was formalized in June 1993 into actual proposals in the document *Bonds of Peace*, attached to a covering report, *Ordination of Women to the Priesthood: Pastoral Arrangements* (GS 1074). A draft Episcopal Ministry Act of Synod was an appendix to it. The document had an unstated further purpose – it was intended, and apparently just succeeded, in getting the (fairly suspicious) Ecclesiastical Committee of Parliament, which met during the summer, to understand that the handling of a deep division in the Church of England would be done equitably, and not by steamrollering. It was commended initially by George Carey in his presidential address to the July Synod, and was then introduced for debate by John Habgood on the last morning. No legal change and no legal rights were to be conferred – but parishes which wished to distance themselves from their diocesan's sacramental ministrations would petition him for 'extended episcopal care'. This petitioning quickly became known as Resolution C (and could only be taken by those who had passed Resolutions A and B). The bishop was to provide such episcopal care from within the diocese, or by arrangement with a neighbouring diocese, or, as a fallback, by a Provincial Episcopal Visitor (PEV). So the Act anticipated three new suffragans, up to two for Canterbury, one for York, to provide such extended episcopal care. The Act (GS 1085) was debated in Synod in November 1993, all amendments were defeated, and John Habgood carried it to an overwhelming approval (39–0; 175–12; 194–14).[16] The process for creating the requisite suffragan sees was also started (but following motions to seat all three PEVs, or at least two, in the House of Bishops were thoroughly defeated). The Act of Synod was then proclaimed at the one-day meeting of Synod on 22 February 1994 immediately after the Canon about women presbyters was promulged. The actual ordinations as presbyter of existing women deacons started almost within hours.

The run-on from 1994

The decision of 11 November 1992 has brought a total change in the ministerial landscape. In the 12 years since ordinations began, women have moved from assistant posts into incumbencies, and have then become canons residentiary, archdeacons and deans. They fit into the landscape, in a way it had been difficult to imagine beforehand.

The pain has moved from the women to the opponents. The future now looks bright for the women, but opaque for the opponents. The effect of the Measure has been that the Church of England has officially and canonically opened the presbyterate to women; and so an opponent might well take the view that it has so damaged the Church of England's ecclesiology as to make the Church incredible. Rather over 400 clergy are reckoned to have taken this view and to have departed with some element of financial relief.[17] But the Act of Synod, while in no way diminishing that change in the ecclesial structure of the Church of England, has given some room to breathe to those who believe the ordination of women to be wrong. It sufficiently defends their position, and their right to say they believe the change to be wrong, as to allow them formally to hope for a rescinding of the legislation. Numerically, there now seems no hope of such a reversal; rather, they have had a scarcity of ordinands, and no indication of significant change in this. This has a downward spiral effect, for (apart from masochists) ordinands usually appear where there is hope for the future, and the lack of them breeds a further loss of hope. The ghetto effect has become very visible, as the Forward in Faith (FiF) folk (sometimes a self-appointed clergy 'chapter' in a diocese) find their courage from each other, and tend to denounce the rest of the Church from long distance (as in *New Directions*).

I suspect that mere prejudice or cultural mindset about the place of women now represents only a tiny proportion of the opponents, and, to that extent, there has been a growing visibility of those with irreducible theological objections or at least doubts.* My slightly cynical analysis says that (on their own view) the Church of England was a splinter of the Western Church. The Anglo-Catholic part of the Church of England has been a splinter from that splinter. And the FiF portion of the Anglo-Catholics is now defending a further splinter, a 'catholicism' which is in communion with hardly anybody else. And, though this is subjective, I have heard much more of the *ultra vires* verdict on the 1992 decision since it happened than I ever heard before. It is, of course, a prudent way of opposing – for it lessens the need to think through other theological issues, and, of course, it leaves open the door to change one's mind

---

* Alan Chesters, the last Bishop of Blackburn and an opponent, once said to me, 'I have always known theological reasons why women cannot be ordained, but when I came to Blackburn I discovered there were *Lancashire* reasons.' (italics mine)

if the Pope ever changes his. But I gladly acknowledge that there are also both wavering doubters and doughty 'impossibilists' to be found.

One inconsistency in the FiF position is that bishops providing 'extended episcopal care' are bound to be compromised. They are consecrated as suffragans of metropolitans who themselves accept the ordination of women. They receive communion from the archbishop at consecration, and are supposed to do so when the House of Bishops meets (archbishops tell us we are all in communion with each other there). Perhaps then they model that which they exist to oppose. But in larger theory the integrity of each diocese is retained, the conscience of the FiF people is respected, and the Church of England is divided but not disrupted. The Act and its workings were reviewed in Synod in July 2000 without any changes being initiated.

But can it all last? GRAS (Group for Rescinding the Act of Synod) has one answer. But if rescinding were (absurdly) to happen, bishops would still (less formally) have to make similar arrangements. Individual clergy, and often their senior laity, will not lightly change their consciences. I have opposed its rescinding. But it will be overtaken by the impending ordination of women as bishops. That step would make the Act history; and it threatens the FiF constituency far more deeply.

The ordination of women as bishops outside the Church of England

Once women were presbyters, it was inevitable that some would become bishops. In some countries the door to both orders opened simultaneously; in others, as in England, only one door at a time. American women were being nominated as episcopal candidates before Lambeth 1988, though none had been elected. The expectation that one would soon be elected overshadowed the Conference, and led to the Eames Commission. Barbara Harris was elected as suffragan bishop of Massachusetts within weeks of the Conference, and further elections and consecrations followed in America, New Zealand and Canada in quick succession. This precipitated a new problem for us, rather like the earlier Women Ordained Abroad issue. What validity or efficacy was to be attributed to their episcopal acts? Robert Runcie, in a presidential address to Synod in November 1988, declined to accept as ordained those ordained by a woman bishop, though he acknowledged that those 'ready and desirous' of being confirmed were still admissible to communion. But, in treating those confirmed by a woman bishop as being in some sense 'ready and desirous of being confirmed', he was, *au fond*, saying that such persons *were not actually confirmed*.

I chased this recognition issue myself. In July 1995, I asked whether Robert

Runcie's assertion left any legal problem for someone confirmed by a woman bishop to become a candidate for ordination (i.e. lest he or she be deemed by authority not actually to be confirmed), and the secretary-general appeared to assure me there would be no problem. I had a second cousin in New Zealand, ordained by Penny Jamieson, Bishop of Dunedin. So in February 1998 I asked:

> Has any committee of the General Synod given consideration recently to the question as to how a presbyter (male or female) ordained by a woman bishop could receive authority to minister word and sacraments within the Church of England (e.g. whether by licensing or by ordination *ab initio* or by ordination *sub conditione*) or whether such a person is neither lay nor ordained in the eyes of the Church of England?

The secretariat had reworked my question, thus letting the secretary-general give the factual answer 'no'. I asked my supplementary: 'I have a cousin ordained in the Diocese of Dunedin . . . To whom should she go, if she comes to this country, to find out how to minister?' The only reply acknowledged a 'difficult situation'.

So I did some homework on the Overseas and Other Clergy (Ministry and Ordination) Measure 1967. This states that, in deciding whether particular ministers have been episcopally ordained, the judgement of the two archbishops re the bishops who ordained them shall suffice, and their 'decision shall be conclusive'. In February 2000 I asked when the two archbishops planned to use their judgement on women bishops. The secretary-general answered that it was all dealt with in the presidential address back in 1988. I pressed that the present archbishops might address the question. Finally, in July 2000 I referred back to Philip Mawer's July 1995 answer, and pressed: 'did his reply imply either that such confirmations are legally recognized as confirmations in the Church of England, or, alternatively, that there is no need to be confirmed in order to become an ordinand in the Church of England?' Philip Mawer ducked and twisted again, and, after my supplementary, pressing that he had given no answer, said, 'I cannot go further on the matter.' Five years of questioning produced – nothing.

I gave it a rest. But at my last Synod, in July 2004, someone else blew it open, getting an unexpected answer:

> *Hugh Atherstone (to the chairman of the Legal Advisory Commission)*: Has the Legal Advisory Commission considered whether it is possible for a priest who has been ordained by a female bishop in another province of the Anglican Communion to obtain authority to serve as a priest in the Church of England?

Professor David McLean: A priest ordained in an Anglican province outside the British Isles . . . needs the permission of the Archbishop of Canterbury or York under the Overseas and Other Clergy (Ministry and Ordination) Measure 1967 . . . The Commission's Opinion is that, *contrary to the view taken by Archbishop Runcie in 1988*, as a matter of law permission may be given under the 1967 Measure [italics mine].

COB [supplementary]: Is this a statement that in fact the Church of England recognizes the episcopal acts of women bishops in other parts of the Anglican Communion?

Chairman: I think that question is out of order.

I don't think my question was out of order. The Church of England's theological position *is* its legal position. I asked David McLean afterwards why I had had five years of hitting the secretary-general's brick wall, labelled '1988', when he, the legal eagle, was sitting on the opposite answer. He simply said he had not been asked. I conclude that the secretariat answered my questions without asking him, and he heard their answers without correcting them. It takes an awful lot to move brick walls in Synod. But a crack had appeared, and a slightly thicker wedge went into it in February 2005. David McLean answered one question by reference to his July 2004 answer above, but emphasized that this applied only to those ordained 'outside the British Isles'. The next question probed the recognition of episcopal acts of a woman bishop *within* the British Isles. David McLean stated that such a woman bishop could not exercise episcopal ministry in the Church of England, but went on: 'A person ordained by an Anglican bishop in Scotland or Ireland could be invited to officiate in England [under relevant legislation] . . . less clear-cut in the case of Wales.' This seems unconditional – Scottish and Irish bishops, even if women, *are* true catholic bishops when they ordain. Welsh ones are less clear-cut.

. . . and in the Church of England

The question had to come in England. There is an inner logic which says that making women presbyters involves the expectation that the episcopate is open to them also. One of my friends in FiF at intervals sheds crocodile tears on behalf of women clergy who, unable to be made bishop, are subject to discrimination! The logic of history is that, sometime between 10 and 15 years from women being ordained presbyter, there will be women presbyters who appear eligible to be considered for the episcopate. So within a few years of ordaining women to the presbyterate the pressure was building up. Some people in the 1995–2000 quinquennium wanted a direct vote on bringing in legislation, but rushing fences was going to be self-defeating. Judith Rose, the first woman archdeacon in the Church of England, set a different kind of pace with a Private Member's Motion she moved in July 2000:

> That this Synod ask the House of Bishops to initiate further theological study on the episcopate, focusing on the issues that need to be addressed in preparation for a debate on women in the episcopate in the Church of England, and to make a progress report on this study to Synod within the next two years.

This was timely, and good sense, and the two-year requirement would sustain a sense of momentum. Judith saw off diversionary amendments, and succeeded by 36–1; 154–39; 165–49.

The Rochester Working Party was set up. It included those opposed to the ordination of women (evangelical and Anglo-Catholic[18]). It worked hard, and it heard every point of view expressed. It addressed questions of whether women could or should be bishops, but also the implications for those who could not recognize or accept a woman's episcopal ministry. Keeping to time, it reported in July 2002. Its report, a slender *Working Party on Women in the Episcopate: A Progress Report from the House of Bishops* (GS 1457), was a progress report, as it was in part simply identifying issues – though there was quite moving description of the pain experienced in the expressed polarization of standpoints. It was handled in Synod under a Standing Order that permitted a kind of seminar, without motions, without voting, and with the participation of working party people who were not Synod members. The mood was very constructive, and even appreciative.

The working party concluded its work in early 2004, and published its report in the autumn as *Women Bishops in the Church of England? A Report of the House of Bishops' Working Party on Women in the Episcopate* (GS 1557). This is a very substantial and well-researched document – and, at its practical end, it displays a series of options as to how women could be made bishops in the Church of England. This includes provision for opponents, whether by the Third Province radical solution, or by restricting in some way the scope or roles of women bishops.

The report was debated in February 2005, and a motion carried:

> That this Synod welcome the report ... and invite the Business Committee to make sufficient time available at the July group of sessions for Synod to determine whether it wishes to set in train the process for removing the legal obstacles to the ordination of women to the episcopate.

And so it came to July 2005. The official motion now would set in train the preparation of legislation, and thus would give a strong steer to the next Synod. The opponents, led by two diocesan bishops, urged instead that the Rochester Report be sent to the Church of England at large, without legislative process starting until that had been done and wide reflecting and debating had ensued. The Synod refused this, but did include a substantial amendment (the second half of (b) below) to ensure proper consideration was given to those who could not in conscience accept women as bishops. The amended motion, looking towards February 2006, was:

That this Synod

(a)   consider that the process for removing the legal obstacles to the ordination of women to the episcopate should now be set in train;

(b)   invite the House of Bishops, in consultation with the Archbishops' Council, to complete by January 2006, and report to the Synod, the assessment which it is making of the various options for achieving the removal of the legal obstacles to the ordination of women to the episcopate; and ask that it give specific attention to the issue of canonical obedience and the universal validity of orders throughout the Church of England as it would affect clergy and laity who cannot accept the ordination of women to the episcopate on theological grounds;

(c)   instruct the Business Committee to make sufficient time available in the February 2006 group of sessions to debate the report, and in the light of the outcome determine on what basis it wants the necessary legislation prepared and establish the necessary drafting group.

The vote was 41–6; 167–46; 159–75. Much now depends upon how the 2005–10 Synod turns out. But, I opine, the Bishops are sufficiently keen not to split the Church of England further, for the opponents to have some real clout in the policy making. But I cannot visualize that clout being sufficient to secure the mirage of the Third Province. At the time of this book going to press, General Synod, at its February 2006 group of sessions, has just asked for legislation to be drafted to provide for Transferred Episcopal Arrangements (TEA) – a kind of middle way providing a provincial episcopal ministry for parishes which have, in certain sacramental and pastoral oversight respects, been 'transferred' to the care of the Archbishop of the province. The legislation will not insist that archbishops themselves must be male, but apparently all concerned expect them to be for some time ahead. Without attempting to discern what is theologically right in this situation, I do detect that the opponents are over a barrel – if they make positive noises about TEA, then they may well get just that; but if they start to denounce TEA as unacceptable, then there are many in Synod who will be urging a return to a 'one-line' Measure and a virtual exclusion of the 'traditionalists'.

13

Lay presidency

On the first day of the week, when we met to break bread.

(Acts 20.7)

Do you have to be ordained to preside at Communion? There is a sufficient division about the answer to the question to have brought it into a Synod which would often rather not know.

Who is to preside at Communion? Can a lay person? The question has emerged among Anglicans in the twentieth and twenty-first centuries as, step by step, lay people have undertaken more and more roles that were once confined to the clergy – and have fulfilled them well, until presiding at the Eucharist has seemed the only door still closed to them, a door which pastoral need has often suggested should be opened.

The Scriptures do not prescribe who presides. But, amid the somewhat misty origins of the Church, from the earliest times it was the authorized ministers of the Church, initially the bishops, who did so preside. This responsibility was in principle a pastoral one, but it had strong ecclesiological implications. From early centuries also the presidency of the Eucharist was delegated from bishops to presbyters, but it never went further. By the dawning of the middle ages, the presbyter was seen as a 'priest' who alone had the power to consecrate the elements; and the elements were transubstantiated by the priest's consecration. Furthermore, the ordination rite commissioned him 'to offer sacrifice for the living and the dead'. That anyone else should fulfil this dual role was unthinkable.

The Reformers returned to a pastoral and teaching model of the ordained ministry, and their ordinals (unlike the medieval ones) made presidency of the Eucharist almost incidental to the presbyter's task. However, any suggestion of lay presidency would have been rare as an idea, on the one hand, and would have counted as incipient bare-faced schism and defiance of authority, on the other.[1] The Reformers had a high doctrine of ministerial office, even with a low doctrine of the sacrament.[2] Finally the 1662 Act of Uniformity imposed a fine of £100 on those not episcopally ordained who presumed after 24 August 1662 to 'consecrate and administer the holy sacrament of the Lord's Supper'. This clearly excluded lay presidency, though its purpose was to eject ministers who had been presbyterally or otherwise ordained during the Commonwealth and were still in post in Church of England parishes. In that it succeeded.

The nineteenth-century Anglo-Catholic revival drew totally on this 1662 rule. But Anglo-Catholics advocated more than was in 1662 – a return to medieval theologies about ordination. Thus, right through to my own lifetime, a wide swathe of Anglicans has believed that ordination was substantially *defined* as empowering the new presbyters (and ontologically remaking them) to become presiders at Communion. This been so widespread that talk of lay presidency (or celebration) has tended to run into a linguistic brick wall – 'lay' and 'presidency', one learns, cannot be said in juxtaposition; they produce an oxymoron, as odd and meaningless as 'married bachelors' or 'legless sprinters'. After receiving such a hint, an Anglican of any sort who persists in talking with such meaningless concepts is obviously gauche and insensitive – not inhabiting the real world of Anglican social proprieties. Finally, if one continues with the gauche concept, the answer comes back, 'If you *are* able somehow to authorize lay persons to preside at Communion, then by that very process you *are* ordaining them.' This, if taken seriously, would entail that ordination could come by means *other* than the laying on of hands with prayer, but the response is meant to demonstrate that the implication is an impossibility, and thus ensure that a brick wall is experienced *as* a brick wall. If it is a contradiction in terms we cannot debate it; even opposing it would give it substance and meaning; and so opponents have regularly proposed procedurally to pass to next business.

But what's this? Hans Küng recounts a private conversation with Karl Rahner in May 1962 (i.e. just before Vatican II):

> On the basis of the results of New Testament research I have ventured to claim that just as according to the New Testament any Christian may baptize, so in principle any Christian may celebrate the eucharist ... By its nature the eucharist should always be a community celebration. But if the priest who should normally preside at the eucharist isn't there, the community can celebrate the eucharist without celibate ordained priests ... just as according to 1 Corinthians, in the absence of the apostle Paul the community of Corinth had celebrated the eucharist completely without ordained ministers ... never been reflected on even by progressive theologians.[3]

Küng was defending his earlier writing in *Structures of the Church*; and he pressed the Corinth point again strongly in *The Church*.[4] He asserted both that there is no such tie-up of ordination and Eucharist in the Scriptures as his

Church had insisted on for centuries, and also that the Bible has authority over the traditions of the Church.

Nevertheless, post-Tractarian Anglicanism has not presented it that way. The 1956–72 Anglican–Methodist Conversations (see Ch. 8 above) treated lay presidency as a Methodist indiscretion to be quickly swept under the carpet.[5] Evangelical Anglicans until the 1960s were often non-sacramentalist and not bothered – and had their own tendency to clericalism in leading worship, even when equipping lay people for responsible witness outside of the liturgy. When I was ordained in 1961, I might have made a theoretical case for lay presidency (as, e.g. in a prisoner-of-war camp) – but I had no great instinct to press it within Anglican structures. For the 1967 Keele Congress, I drafted the Worship section report, and the amended final text said: 'Authorized lay people, in addition to Readers, should assist by reading the lessons, by leading the intercessions, by preaching, and by administering both elements.'[6]

This pushed the agenda ahead of the official position for lay people in 1967, but that ground had to be possessed before lay presidency could emerge as an issue. Keele also identified a weekly celebration of the Eucharist as the main Sunday service, and informal Eucharists were beginning to arise also. So the question of a pastoral provision of lay presidency grew – and evangelicals knew no doctrinal objections; the most they would concede was a congruity, a mere appropriateness (far from a divine command), of the restricting of presidency to presbyters.

The 1970s

These signs in the 1960s suggested that (leaving aside Anglican–Methodist factors) the issue might well arise as one internal to Anglicanism in the 1970s. It duly did, though the evangelicals were slightly overtaken in point of time by others. A pioneer in 1975, who was by no means evangelical, was Anthony Harvey, warden of St Augustine's College, Canterbury. He raised the analogy of the chairman of a board, who presides at board meetings; but, if he is ill, the board does not adjourn but seats a vice-chairman or other substitute. This genuinely ordered, but basically functional, view of ministry he applied to eucharistic presidency, and the logic is obvious.[7]

In 1975, also, FOAG produced *The Theology of Ordination* (GS 281). It arose initially from debates about the Church of South India, and was referred to FOAG by Standing Committee.[8] FOAG was following up with further work a 1974 interim report, *The Theology of Ordination and the Integration of Ministries*. FOAG now, perhaps surprisingly, named lay presidency and discussed it – and found against it; but the naming and opposing were unlike most previous and later practice. The 'take note' debate in February 1976 included passing comments on lay presidency, not least one which welcomed it as being a subject at all. Yet, if it *was* a subject, it was still everywhere spoken against and light years from being put into practice.

An evangelical goal?

Evangelicals were just becoming articulate on the subject. One thrust was at the Islington Conference in 1975. Another was at St John's College, Nottingham, in 1976. Then in March 1977 Trevor Lloyd edited Grove Liturgical Study 9, a symposium on *Lay Presidency at the Eucharist?* This lifted the subject on to a level playing field, where the pro-lay presidency team had the better of the conflict.[9] I did more to level the field than to try to score on it, and that has been my overall reaction – not minding terribly if lay presidency does not happen, but passionately wanting it treated as a true subject to be debated fairly, and to be implemented if it prevails. However, Trevor Lloyd himself then led a section on local church at NEAC-2 in Nottingham, and the statement of his section said: 'F1: General: (d) We urge that such leaders, duly authorized by the bishop and accountable to the Parochial Church Council, should be able to preside at Communion services where there is no ordained person present.'[10]

Lambeth 1978

The issue was gnawing away elsewhere in the Communion also. The 1978 Lambeth Conference apparently had no advance preparation of themes or draft statements, and each section's written report reads as a kind of afterthought. But something blew up in the Ministry and the People of God section which meant that they created a new Lay Presidency of the Eucharist subgroup from within themselves, and moved bishops from their existing groups into it. It was no homogeneous cluster of evangelicals.[11] The section reported thus about its subcommittee's work:

> In their report they held that where it is not possible to provide a president the bishop is still responsible for making the sacrament of Holy Communion available, and they believed there might be circumstances in which it would be justifiable for him to authorize a lay member to preside in his name providing that such a person had the support of the local congregation. They recommended that where there was need, particular members of local congregations should be authorized to preside at the Eucharist under certain specified conditions.

When the report was presented to the section it was decided that the subject should not be further discussed.[12]

The 'should not be further discussed' may signify that the section's agenda was in practice dominated by the ordination of women. Whether or not that was so, the group's apparent unanimity is astonishing, while the section's judgement 'should not be further discussed' is totally unsurprising. But how did it originate? Was it from the four diocesan bishops from South America (where it was a live issue) who were in that section?[13] Or did David Gitari of Mount Kenya East raise it? (I have correspondence from him indicating both that Kenyan deacons were authorized in 1979 to preside at the Eucharist, where a bishop saw fit, and that he knew of the 1978 Lambeth discussion.)

The 1980s

By 1980 lay presidency was just surfacing as a fit topic for Anglican conversation. General Synod got its first possibility of that conversation in February 1983 in a Private Member's Motion of John Williams of Chelmsford:

That this Synod requests the House of Bishops to set up a small representative group to consider in what circumstances lay people should be permitted to celebrate Holy Communion in the Church of England and report to the Synod.

He might helpfully have put 'if any' after 'circumstances', and he was pleading that even opponents could vote for the enquiry – but his advocacy showed his own hand. He provoked two responses.

First came a wonderfully shocked maiden speech by Mrs Ffinch; the Synod would hear her 'cry in traditional maidenly manner, "No, no, a thousand times no." and I hope and pray that most of the Synod will feel with me that they would rather die than say "yes" to this incredible motion.' The other response was the one the reader is expecting. George Austin moved: 'That the question be not now put'. He argued, interestingly, that the defeat of the Reconciliation of a Penitent the previous day meant that getting priesthood right was the higher priority.[14] John Williams resisted the guillotine, but lost (119–134). Synod was not going to have to divide on this one yet.

Another rippling of calm came in October 1986 when John Austin Baker, Bishop of Salisbury from 1982, and chair of the Doctrine Commission, said in passing in a Selwyn Lecture in Lichfield: 'I see no reason why any group of Christians should not invite one of their number to preside . . .The exclusive link between presidency and ordination is wrong.'[15] But, as far as I know, he never pressed the case in the House of Bishops or the General Synod, and the ripples died down and the issue went back under the carpet.

There were, however, bigger ripples in South America. The Province of the Southern Cone was formed in 1983, and lay presidency was quickly laid before a Primates' Meeting (which did not want to know), and then brought to their own provincial synod in May 1986. The motion was to permit the Diocese of Chile (where North to South distances are vast) to authorize lay presidency under controlled conditions. The story is told sardonically by a member present, that observers from, yes, the Episcopal Church (USA) leant heavily on the synodspeople to consider the consciences of other Anglican provinces and not take boat-rocking unilateral action.[16] This embryonic provincial synod, with one bishop, one clergyman and one lay person from the five dioceses, then defeated the motion 7–8! It was a near thing.

The Chileans still smarted when the 1988 Lambeth Conference met. I was secretary to the group working on worship.[17] South American bishops from our Mission and Ministry section urged me at least to air lay presidency as one remedy for a lack of communion where congregations are scattered at enormous distances and an indigenous ordained ministry is only slowly being developed. I drafted 'airing' texts, but, while the group was willing, the section vetoed it.[18] The outcome was:

PRESIDENCY AT THE EUCHARIST

205. We note the received tradition that the president at the eucharist should be a bishop or presbyter. We also note that in dioceses which are geographically large, or offer grave hindrances to travel, the ready availability of an ordained presbyter may not match the proper sacramental hopes or expectations of some or all of the congregations. Two practices have found acceptance in some parts of the Communion:

(i)   The ordination of local persons – who are acknowledged leaders ... but who may lack some of the traditional requirements for ordination ...

(ii)   The 'extending' of communion through space and time by the hands of specially authorized lay persons (or deacons) who take the elements from a normal celebration ... to needy individuals and congregations.[19]

The keen-eyed will spot that our problem was tackled in one of two ways in 'some parts'. But at the Conference a remnant reckoned both these practices were unsatisfactory – the first as giving a lifetime ordained role to a not-well-qualified person, to cover a eucharistic gap which might be merely temporary; the second because it diminished the normal and normative character of eucharistic celebration. But the third possible practice dared not state its name.*

The 1990s

In the first half of the 1990s Sydney Diocese made great synodical moves to permit deacons and lay people to preside at Communion.[20] More surprisingly, a working party in Cape Town Diocese reported in 1993, not exactly recommending lay presidency, but saying they wanted to do so, and then so marshalling arguments for and against as to make it self-evident that lay presidency was needed. The international dimensions were always there in the background.

In the Church of England a previously unreported groundswell in evangelical parishes became far more visible when in 1993 the Church of England Evangelical Council asked every diocesan evangelical union (or its equivalent) to discuss lay presidency. There was a widespread response to this, but a General Synod debate in November 1993 on meeting pastoral need with extended communion triggered people (as in South America) into raising the lay presidency issue in Synod as the way to address the problem. I was asked how the issue could best be pursued in Synod, and I then advised Tim Royle, who was putting down a Private Member's Motion, about its form. He then framed it thus:

> That this Synod, recognizing the desire of the Church for an effective shared ministry, request the House of Bishops to report on what, if any, theological grounds exist for reserving the Presidency of the Eucharist to Bishops and Presbyters.

It was tabled early in the week. At the end of the week, so many members had signed it, it was top of the list.[21] The beauty of it was that those in favour of lay presidency, but equally those opposed, could sign up together to have it debated. And the House of Bishops, if they wanted to oppose the motion, would appear to be blocking it because they did not have a good answer to the question.

The Royle debate came in July 1994. The Bishops were indeed reluctant to be driven into voting either for or against the motion, and equally would not have risked moving that the question should not be put. Instead there was an amendment, moved by Stephen Sykes, then Bishop of Ely, to rewrite the motion thus:

> That this Synod, whilst accepting that lay presidency at the Eucharist

---

* Does that phrase ring a bell from another context? It was meant to.

is incompatible with Anglican tradition, would welcome a statement from the House of Bishops about the theology of the Eucharist and about the respective roles of clergy and laity within it.

Synod bought the amendment and passed the motion. Its text now did mention lay presidency, but its title became more neutrally 'Eucharistic Presidency'. I got into correspondence with Alec Graham, then Bishop of Newcastle and chairman of the Doctrine Commission, about the meaning of 'incompatible with Anglican tradition'. Clearly some thought that they had blocked off lay presidency from any report by using this formula. I pointed out to Alec Graham one could have written, right up to November 1992, that 'the ordination of women as presbyters is incompatible with Anglican tradition'. Yet the women had just been ordained in the then very recent months of February to June 1994. 'Incompatible', when read carefully, was merely saying 'we have not done this before'.[22]

The House of Bishops took the motion very seriously, and determined to produce a substantial report. Their Standing Committee, via Stephen Sykes, gave the drafting task to Jeremy Begbie, vice-principal of Ridley Hall, with various persons to be consulted and various stages for criticizing drafts. The resultant report, *Eucharistic Presidency: A Theological Statement by the House of Bishops of the General Synod*, is clear that it is addressing lay presidency; it names it, looks it in the face, sets out some history of the debate, and quite fairly states the strength of the case for it.[23] It then finds against lay presidency on the grounds that restricting presidency to bishops and presbyters is most strongly congruous with our theology of the Church. Congruity, however, falls short of divine imperative and, in effect, classifies Anglican tradition as provisional and open to further investigation and debate.

General Synod discussed it in July 1997, but not in a debate on actual motions. Instead we suspended standing orders and had a kind of seminar. The report was criticized, in its treatment of priesthood at para. 3.24, for relying on *The Priesthood of the Ordained Ministry*.[24] The overall mood was interesting, for, as a speaker late on commented, the thesis was presented defensively. No strong Anglo-Catholic statement about God's tying presidency to presbyteral orders emerged.[25] The dynamics of the debate were becoming a 'Why not?' And Christina Baxter raised the question, 'Why are some aspects of oversight ministry capable of delegation and not others?' She said the report did not tackle that question – neither did the speakers who replied to her.

The discussion ended. There were no motions, so no decisions. It just stopped, and all went home saying they had had a good debate. I have been surprised that no one in the nine years since then seems to have asked for a decision-taking debate. For lay presidency was left *sub judice*, unfinished business without a decision.

14

The charismatic movement

When the day of Pentecost had come.

(Acts 2.1)

Can the work of the Spirit be reduced to speeches and writing? Well, I worked hard to bring the question into Synod and it is a broadly happy story.

I see myself as a pre-charismatic. It is not that I came before Pentecostalism, for that is conventionally traced back either to an amazing night in Topeka, Kansas, on 31 December 1900 (the eve of the new century, correctly counting), or to an even more amazing one in Azusa Street, Los Angeles, on 7 October 1906. From these starting points sprang a form of fervent experiential Christianity, identified particularly by outbreaks of 'speaking in tongues', attributed to a single swamping event, the baptism in the Holy Spirit. The very experiential basis of Pentecostalism regularly drove those thus baptized out from their somewhat sedater brothers and sisters in Christ, into forming new denominations. In England the traditional networks were the Pentecostalist Church, the Assemblies of God and the Elim Foursquare Churches. When I was an undergraduate not only were there no Pentecostalists in the university Christian Union, but there never had been any – though rumours reported a man a few years back who had treated himself as the sole Christian at Oxford, and had run his own one-man mission to the university. The general (if cartoon) image of Pentecostalists was of people without the grey matter to have obtained A levels.* Yet, as I discovered at theological college, Lesslie Newbigin, in his Kerr lectures in 1952, had identified three strands of world Christianity – a body strand (Roman Catholicism), a word strand (Protestantism), and a Spirit strand (Pentecostalism).[1] This was prophetic indeed. Yet Lesslie told me in later

---

* Once when doing National Service, I hovered near a preacher at Speakers' Corner in Hyde Park on a Sunday afternoon. When he finished, and people melted away, I was still there. 'Have you been born again?' he asked. 'Yes,' I managed to reply. 'Ah, but has the Holy Spirit overflowed through your mouth?' he continued. I mumbled, and went my way – and lost sleep for three nights. I think (but this is a long time ago) I then took comfort from St Paul saying one person has one gift, another another – still the simplest answer to questions posed as this man posed his question to me.

life that, when he propounded this thesis, he had never actually met a Pentecostalist.[2]

When I went to Bristol as a theological student in 1959, there were some hints of an Anglican Pentecostalism in the atmosphere, but they amounted to very little.[3] The traceable history of a new Pentecostalist strand of Anglicanism began in 1959 in Los Angeles, in the person of Dennis Bennett, an Anglo-Catholic priest. His newly dynamized ministry was too much for his affluent and respectable congregation in Van Nuys, Los Angeles, and in 1960 he moved to St Luke's, Seattle. This was a very different kind of parish, indeed a bankrupt one, where his message was received with joy. Thus a thriving Pentecostalism was to be found by 1962 in an Episcopal Church parish. Christians in England were receiving news and visits over those years, and by 1962 instances – perhaps outbursts – of the distinctive Pentecostalist phenomena were reported in the Church of England. A difference was that here the phenomena were occurring among convinced evangelicals, and were bringing growth, even revival, to evangelical parishes – but also division.[4] One of the first 'renewed' parishes was St Mark's, Gillingham, in Kent (where I was vicar later), where John Collins (previously curate at All Souls, Langham Place) was vicar, and David Watson and David MacInnes came as curates.[5] It was at All Souls itself that public division occurred – and led to some counter-pamphleteering about the baptism and gifts of the Spirit. The charismatic movement was new to Anglicans in England in 1962. That casts me, ordained in 1961, as pre-charismatic.

The key figure at All Souls was Michael Harper. He resigned his curacy in 1964 to found the Fountain Trust, an agency to promote charismatic renewal – interdenominational but very influential among Anglicans. Through the 1960s the movement grew in the Church of England, largely among evangelicals, but in a semi-underground way.[6] In 1965 Dennis Bennett came and spoke at LCD. Charismatic ordinands appeared – some even became charismatics while at college, and LCD was not alone in witnessing this. But parishes and colleges may still seem at a great distance from the business of Synod.

1970 onwards

The year of the inauguration of General Synod, and of LCD's migration to Nottingham, 1970 was also a pivotal year in the charismatic movement. Curiously it is academic *opposition* to the movement which marks it in my memory. Jimmy Dunn, a young tutor at Nottingham University, produced a major book, *Baptism in the Holy Spirit*,[7] which exegetically left the most determined 'two-stagers' virtually no biblical ground on which to stand. It might seem odd to treat such a demolition job as illustrating a hinge time, but that is what it was – it was the first time that the movement had ever been

191

taken seriously enough for some of its distinctive features to need scholarly refutation. From then on it was above ground.

The years from 1970 onwards also saw prominent charismatics emerge from non-evangelical circles, including John Gunstone, Colin Urquhart and Richard Hare, Bishop of Pontefract (Wakefield Diocese) from 1971 onwards.* These gave a broader look to the charismatic constituency, but theologically the movement still looked like a variant within evangelicalism. So, during the 1970s, at St John's College, Nottingham, we found ourselves slowly coming to be trusted by leading charismatics, and they recommended ordinands to come to us for training. Our staff included persons in various ways identified with the movement – George Carey, Graham Dow and David Gillett all became bishops – and, from the evangelical stream of Anglicanism, two significant strategic moves were taken in the mid-1970s. The first was the setting up of a pan-evangelical working party to look at theological issues – and this led to a joint agreed statement, *Gospel and Spirit*. The second was the readiness of the Fountain Trust, which ran big spring residential conferences, to omit such a conference from their 1977 programme, and instead to encourage their constituency to attend the second National Evangelical Anglican Congress (NEAC-2) at Nottingham in April 1977. This latter had 2,000 participants, and saw a reuniting of charismatic and non-charismatic evangelicals in ways which have proved to be pretty durable since.

I was on the *Gospel and Spirit* working party, and I had a hand in the planning of NEAC-2. Alongside this, the Grove Booklets authors' group, which was soon to be the Group for Renewal of Worship (GROW), held an overnight conference in 1975 in order to engage with charismatics. This led to Tom Walker joining the group and writing *Open to God*; and I wrote a Grove Booklet myself entitled *Encountering Charismatic Worship*.[8]†

---

* Richard Hare told charismatics in prayer groups in Wakefield Diocese: 'Revival needs two components – the wind of God, and the dry bones. I have come to contribute the dry bones.' He did just that – and received the wind of God.

† I wrote in the Introduction: 'I am not technically a charismatic (or at least not a card-carrying one!).' The students of St John's College at lunch the following day solemnly presented me with a 'card' – a Mountain Dust Official Membership Card which licensed me to

> 'feel free' to
> raise hands in public services
> use such words as 'beautiful', 'gentleness' etc.
> give charismatic hugs
> sing 'woozy' choruses
> dance in the Spirit.

The card I still have, though it was too big to be carried at all times, as it itself required, so I became an honorary card-carrier.

But what about General Synod? The 1975 elections delivered to Synod a clutch of charismatics. Would their spiritual energies find any useful channel for exercise in the worldly and sometimes legalistic agenda of Synod? Interestingly, a group of us found ourselves running charismatic prayer meetings to a pattern – early morning in London, late night in residence at York.[9] But what could be done within Synod? Did 'charismatic' have such a sufficiently clear connotation as to mean we would have the right people debating the right subject matter in a debate? I had in mind a Private Member's Motion but wanted it to be so worded as to give the best possible debate – or, ideally, two debates, as I go on to show.

I got one pointer from a Private Member's Motion which got in before me. Reg Priestnall of Peterborough Diocese tabled in November 1975 one which called upon the whole Church of England, 'to pray for the renewal of the whole church in our country by the power of the Holy Spirit'. This was very far-reaching in its most searching meaning, *but* it was too easy for the Synod to support; and in February 1977 we had a brief motherhood and apple pie kind of debate, where a poorly attended chamber all voted in favour; and, as far as those on earth can tell, absolutely nothing followed from it. Perhaps I should actually name the charismatic movement in my Private Member's Motion.

I learned a lesson in procedure as well as content from that motion. What was needed was a substantial report, *brought before the Synod because the Synod had asked for it.* So in July 1976, I tabled the following Private Member's Motion:

> That this Synod, noting the rise in recent years of the Charismatic Movement within the Church of England and being concerned to conserve the new life it has brought into many parishes, asks the Standing Committee to bring before the Synod a report which will explore the reasons for this upsurge, pinpoint the particular distinctive features of spirituality and ethos which the movement presents, and indicate both the points of tension which exist with traditional Anglicanism and also how the riches of the movement may be conserved for the good of the Church.

I reckoned this would bring out the troops, and ensure an ongoing interest. It gathered its signatures, rose to the top, and was due in July 1977. But a problem arose. This was the one occasion in all my time on Synod when I was to be away – I was due in New Zealand that July. I had anticipated that, when the motion came, Richard Hare, the wonderfully 'renewed' Bishop of Pontefract, would move it. However, he too had to be absent. I would not risk having anyone else move it, so I withdrew it, and tabled it again in November. It attracted signatures again, and was running second for the Synod in July 1978. There were just 30 minutes allocated late on the first Saturday night for those first two such motions, and mine looked extremely unlikely to be called. But the first one summoned the government to give better financial help to families with children; and, although substantial, it was, synodically speaking, completely uncontroversial, and went through 315–1 almost without debate. So my motion had ten minutes left – and, of course, once moved, it was bound to get decent debating time in November. I was called, and I set out eight features of the movement suggesting why we needed to know what was happening among us:

1. An emphasis upon spiritual experience;

2. A release of inhibitions – in witness, personal relationships, etc.

3. A new expectation that God will work powerfully;

4. A surge of creativity;

5. An emphasis on 'every-member ministry';

6. An inarticulate doctrine of creation;

7. A radical concept of discipleship, including sacrificial giving;

8. A great flow of ordinands.

I urged that, after 15 years or so, the movement needed monitoring and evaluating, and it would be grievous if future generations concluded that this had been happening among us, and Synod had gone its way without even noticing.

The debate and the report

Well, the debate was duly adjourned. And it was duly resumed in November, kicked off, at my request, by Richard Hare. He made reference to 'an arm-waving, hand-clapping, exorcizing, tongue-speaking, alleluia-shouting, liturgical whoopee, with a stack of Anglican bishops dancing round the altar in Canterbury cathedral thrown in for good measure'.[10] The Bishop of Middleton, Ted Wickham, raised some warnings, including 'every few weeks ... some new sectarian exotic religious group', and 'a flight from rationality', and even mention of astrology and studying entrails! But various charismatics and fellow-travellers gave testimony, very much as I had hoped they would. The Standing Committee had an amendment, moved by Margaret Hewitt, which would simply have commended some books for study, and would not have led to a report. This, I judged, was finance-driven, saving the Standing Committee expenditure, though Margaret Hewitt had not mentioned costs. I resisted it, and, lo and behold, the Synod defeated her (94–117). I also pointed out that, if the task were given to the already existent Doctrine Commission, no extra expense would be involved. So how would my motion be turned into action? For the Standing Committee now, however reluctantly, had to 'bring before the Synod a report'.[11]

The upshot from the Standing Committee was both responsible and, in one outcome affecting me personally, very surprising. Derek Pattinson thoughtfully consulted me about a process (not involving the Doctrine Commission). Then in October 1979 the Standing Committee convened an overnight consultation in Ely of around 30 persons, both charismatic and non-charismatic, including about 20 members of Synod, senior staff of Synod, and experienced ecumenical guests.[12] The consultation recommended that a small working party should now write the desired report; and the Policy Subcommittee of the Standing Committee invited seven persons, of whom I was one, to form the working party. Two Synod staff members were on it: Derek Pattinson himself (a model of uncharismatic outward orderliness), and David Gregg of the Board of Mission and Unity (anarchically charismatic). We discussed the sort of report needed, and who should write it – and the other six looked at me. 'No,' I protested, 'I elicited this report – it is meant to be a report *to* me, not one *from* me. I am the archetypal person to be enlightened by the report.' My protests were overruled. I drafted the report. The others decided my style was so idiosyncratic (and therefore recognizable) that they might as well come clean, and acknowledge in the text that I had drafted it. Drafting tested me as to whether I could (as I kid myself I can) distinguish between squaring the ropes for two opposite views to contest, and entering the ring as one of those two opposed contestants. The last stages of drafting were rushed, to catch General Synod in July 1981, and the report was published by the CIO around June 1981 as *The Charismatic Movement in the Church of England*.

Debating the report

The Standing Committee was 'to bring before the Synod' the report. They did so, not in July but in November, with a brief covering note (GS 507), and it was introduced by Colin Craston.[13] But it ran into trouble. Various speakers spoke of excesses. Sister Carol CHN put up a happy positive word (including 'I do dance in the Spirit, which is great fun – and I do it really rather well'*). Then, as the

---

* Carol's dancing was ultimately seen all round the world, when, as a chaplain at the 1998 Lambeth Conference, she spontaneously danced to the music at the final Eucharist in the Conference Centre, and *Church Times* reported, 'It is not all over till the thin nun dances' – and, true to her earlier word, she did it rather well.

allocated time ran out, Ted Wickham, now in his last hours in Synod, returned to the attack, incensed by the supposed charismatic flight from rationality. Off he went:

> 'Moonies', the 'Children of God', the 'Family of Love', the Unification Church, Scientology, the Hare Krishna and the Bhagwan Rajneesh movements, Transcendental Meditation ... there are lots of them. We might even include Uri Geller and his spoon-bending and von Daniken and his astronauts ... I see the Charismatic Movement in a sense as a very tame, Anglican, English equivalent.

Whew! We were being hit by a great wave of super-charged irrationality – but it was sidetracking the Synod from an astonishing spiritual movement. As time ran out, Hugh Montefiore rescued us by asking: rather than conclude, could we not simply adjourn? 'If we were having a debate on the evangelical revival, would we really have thought that the speeches we have heard today would be adequate to the seriousness of the subject which we were debating?' Colin Craston from the platform welcomed the proposal, and Synod carried the procedural motion.

We met again in February 1982. And what a difference. Hugh Montefiore kicked off for the second half – very appreciative of a strand of spiritual life in his diocese. Others contributed positively. Critics were urging further theological work rather than being dismissive. And so Synod 'took note', and moved to Colin Craston's second motion:

> That the Report of the Working Group be commended to the dioceses
> and parishes for study in the wider context of spirituality as a whole.

I moved an amendment (possibly by collusion with Colin Craston – I cannot remember). Certainly he accepted it warmly and the Synod bought it, so the motion passed as follows:

> That this Synod (a) commends the Report of the Working Group to the dioceses and parishes for study in the wider context of spirituality as a whole and (b) requests the House of Bishops to refer it to the Doctrine Commission for a report on the doctrinal issues involved.

The Good Wine and *We Believe in the Holy Spirit*

There were two run-on effects from this debate and from the amended motion passed. On the one hand, the BMU were to follow up issues of spirituality which had been raised. This task, recommended at the Ely consultation, was recorded in the report, and was almost in view in the slightly-less-than-transparent phrase, 'in the wider context of spirituality as a whole'. The BMU commissioned Josephine Bax to do a year's research and write a book on 'Spiritual Renewal in the Church of England'. She got the message, took the year, and wrote *The Good Wine*. It was never debated in Synod, and perhaps may have finished in thin air. But it was a thorough bit of work, including the results from a questionnaire sent in 1984 to every diocesan missioner 'asking for information about the extent and forms of renewal taking place in their dioceses, and about lay participation, training and ministry'.[14] It reads as almost criminal that only one-third replied, though the replies received hinted that few people expected much change of any sort in rural parishes anyway, and that may mean it was largely rural dioceses which failed to reply. Those who did reply reported positive trends: greater active participation of the laity, more people on programmes of education and training, one-off initiatives, conferences and study days.

The Good Wine is, from one point of view, a *tour de force*. It encompasses an amazing array of authors, testimony and phenomena: Mother Julian, the Cursillo Movement, Donald Allchin, John Gunstone, Peter Mullen, John Gladwin, Pat Harris, David Wasdell, Catholic Renewal, Eastern Orthodoxy, Jung, Jürgen Moltmann, John Wimber, desert spirituality, the decline of the confessional, Taizé, Anglican Renewal Ministries, Jean Vanier, Graham Pulkingham, Post Green, and on and on. It reads like a telescope on a hilltop sweeping fast through 360 degrees to show the appearance of the surrounding landscape, with vastly different scenes coming and going before the eye. John Collins, in the blurb on the back cover, says, 'Her reflections cry out for action.' My problem was that it had exactly the opposite effect on me. I glimpsed this panorama without seeing any particular focus, and could not know where I wanted the sweeping telescope to stop. I have heard little of the book since.

There was, however, another part of the 1982 motion. Long after I had first suggested it, the Doctrine Commission was to address a theology of the Spirit. In 1981–6, chaired by John Austin Baker, Bishop of Salisbury, the Commission produced the 'God report' – i.e. *We Believe in God*. Then, when the next quinquennium began, I found myself (to my surprise) among the Commission's members. And the task was – what? Why, the doctrine of the Holy Spirit. So we laboured for our five years (John Austin Baker being soon replaced by Alec Graham, Bishop of Newcastle) and published *We Believe in the Holy Spirit*.[15] Its tightly written Introduction concludes: 'We were asked to reflect on the charismatic movements; therefore we have gone there first and done some fieldwork, on which we have done some theological reflection.'

The first chapter is consequently advertised as experiential – a distillation of interviews Sarah Coakley conducted in Lancaster with charismatics about their prayer lives. The chapter is called 'Charismatic Experience: Praying "In the Spirit".' It includes not only freshness and joy in prayer, but also 'aridity and failure'. It is well worth a revisit.

The next chapter ('Is this that?') has an element of my input into it. Can the distinctive phenomena which have marked the charismatic movement be identified with, and named as, those similar-sounding phenomena recorded in the New Testament, specifically (a) baptism in the Holy Spirit, (b) gifts of the Spirit, (c) tongues and prophecy, (d) healings, and (e) the word of knowledge?[16] The Doctrine Commission was taking a focused view of the distinctive phenomena here, before addressing a great range of other relevant questions about the Holy Spirit, particularly in relation to the present age.

The report was completed as the Commission's quinquennium finished in early 1991, and it was to be debated in General Synod in July. The debate was allocated rather less than the two hours I had predicted, and the motion was simply to 'take note', without even commending it for study.[17] So it bid fair to pass into the pigeonholes of history, an impression strengthened by a thin attendance. Alec Graham showed how the charismatic movement had been a theme in the report. Others followed, mostly giving the Commission good marks, and with a word of praise for the Holy Spirit also.[18] The Synod did take note; and the charismatic movement has continued.

A further outcome

The Board of Mission in 1996 published a brief assessment of *The Toronto Experience*; and then, through its Mission, Evangelism and Renewal in England Committee (MERE), commissioned a more comprehensive book, *The Way of Renewal*, which was edited by Michael Mitton, previously director of Anglican Renewal Ministries, then deputy director of the Acorn Healing Trust.[19] This presented 27 different testimonies varying from the experience of Alpha courses, through Celtic sprituality and pilgrimages to Walsingham, to participation in the worship of the WCC, all lovingly stitched together (in nine chapters of three testimonies each) by the editor. A Foreword by Nigel McCulloch, the chairman of MERE, expressed the confidence that had developed among General Synod bodies in the work of such renewal agencies as Michael Mitton represented. There was no direct linking to the previous synodical work, but the central authorities of the Church of England were maintaining their responsibility not only to monitor, but also to encourage, spiritual renewal in its widest range of expression.

But, in the last analysis, while Synod no doubt always needs spiritual renewal, it is only at rare intervals that charismatic renewal has any need of Synod.

15

Homosexual issues and *Issues in Human Sexuality*

This is the will of God . . . that each one of you knows how to control your own body in holiness and honour.

(1 Thessalonians 4.3–4)

No one could pretend this is other than a major presenting issue in the Church of England today.

When Michael Ramsey reflected on the report of the Wolfenden Committee, in the run-up to the 1967 Sexual Offences Act, which legitimated homosexual relationships between 'consenting adults', he drew his famous distinction between sin and crime. He was ready to see decriminalized that sexual activity which he took for granted, among Christians, to be still sin. So said the Bible: so said Christian history.

When I went to London Diocese in 1964, perhaps because of the prohibition in law (and thus possibilities of blackmail, etc.), the clergy revealed nothing of which I was aware about homosexual relationships. However, I slowly learned that a number had their, quietly concealed, homosexual private lives; but, as with, say, befriending the bottle, these were kept private. Among Anglo-Catholics celibacy was still highly valued; and two men could share a house without anyone jumping to conclusions. From the standpoint of the angels, surreptitious ways cannot have been very satisfactory, but the public front of the Church of England and the visible modelling of the Christian life by its clergy was relatively conformable to the scriptural standard. I was unaware, both as a theological student and in my early years on a college staff, of men in my own vicinity who either sought or found a male sexual partner.

It was Mervyn Stockwood who gave me a different angle. In an expansive mood on the Liturgical Commission in the latter part of the 1960s, he confided to me: 'I say to the young men, "Don't do anything which I would not like to know about – but, if you must do it, do it North of the Thames."' This, it seems to me, opened an official connivance which contained the sparks of a revolution. In the early 1970s it was stoked into flame by the sexual anarchy reported at St Stephen's House in Oxford. The then principal apparently presided over a college which did not just turn a blind eye to homosexual relationships (in the context of a camp subculture of what in those days would be called foppishness and pansied behaviour), but actually encouraged them. Rob Marshall writes about the college at the point that David Hope inherited the principalship, i.e. September 1974: 'St Stephen's was in crisis . . . suffering from a culture of moral degeneracy . . . [and specifically in respect of homosexual behaviour].'[1]

According to Marshall, David Hope himself rather confirms this account, though, to be fair, St Stephen's House was not necessarily totally out on its own among colleges. My own memory confirms that there was an awareness around the country that something was badly wrong.* Marshall quotes an anonymous source which asserted years later, 'David Hope introduced a Draconian regime . . . Prospective students were told all sexual activity unhallowed by the bonds of matrimony was forbidden.'[2]

A quest for decision

However, a more corporate reaction came from the conference of college principals. I was present myself (standing in for Michael Green) at the meeting of principals in January 1974, when St Stephen's House was still under its previous regime. An awareness of inconsistency between colleges, as well as a fear in some of a slippery slope and in others of being viewed as the Church's freestanding moral arbiters, led the conference to ask the central authorities for guidance on the homosexual issue, especially in relation to ordinands. The task went to the BSR in February, and it set up a weighty working party, chaired by John Yates, Bishop of Gloucester. The working party report said they had met 27 times in the next four years, three times residentially (a staggering total). The report acknowledged that Old and New Testaments condemn homosexual practices – but then marginally qualified the authority of the Bible in its relation to today's ways of life: for those 'who genuinely cannot achieve this ideal [monogamous marriage] with members of the opposite sex . . . is there a place for them in the divine order wherein they may fulfil the sexuality which is theirs?'[3] The report handled this question very carefully, but its answer was 'yes – and the Church must recognize and respect that place'. Its further question about clergy (which, granted the origin of the question in the colleges, was needed) produced a less indulgent answer:

---

* A very cool witness to this comes from an unexpected quarter. Michael Ramsey retired to Cuddesdon in Autumn 1974, and, after the union of the College with Ripon Hall in 1975, found himself consulted more than he would have wished about the propriety of homosexual relations in ordinands and clergy. This was a contributory factor, we are told, in the Ramseys moving to Durham in 1977 (see Owen Chadwick, *Michael Ramsey: A Life* (OUP, 1999) p.385).

> A homosexual priest who has 'come out' and openly acknowledges he is living in a sexual union with another man should not expect the Church to accept him on the same conditions as if he were married.

> What then should a priest in this situation do? ... In the end we came to the conclusion that a priest in this position should offer his resignation to the bishop of the diocese ...

> We realize that the obligation to offer his resignation would be a moral one. It would not be enforceable.[4]

The working party completed its unanimous and thorough report in July 1978. However, it ran into immediate trouble with its own Board. After the synodical elections in 1975, more conservative members had been elected or appointed to the Board – among them the appointed chairman, Graham Leonard, Bishop of Truro. In September 1978 the Board looked at this Gloucester Report and concluded that it was too liberal. It was unsurprising that a unanimous 'liberal' report arose from a broadly 'liberal' working party, which (culpably?) had no visible evangelical member of any sort. The Board included not only Graham Leonard, a very toughly traditionalist Anglo-Catholic, but also R. J. Berry, Gervase Duffield and David Holloway, equally toughly scriptural evangelicals. The Board discussed for ten months whether to publish the report at all, and, if so, with what kind of endorsement (or disclaimer) to qualify it. Finally they published it without endorsing it (calling that Part I), and added seven and a half pages of 'Critical Observations of the Board' (calling them Part II). The chairman's Foreword, dated July 1979, stated that 'it is Parts I and II together that we submit to the Synod as a contribution to its discussions'.

The debate moves on

Events had not stood still in the meantime. I had myself, as proprietor of Grove Books, published in 1976, as Grove Booklet on Ethics no. 9, David Field's *The Homosexual Way – A Christian Option?** In November 1977, Sister Marion Eva successfully moved an amendment to a BSR motion, which led to the BSR

---

* The Booklet's answer to its own question, sensitively investigated and handled, was, 'No, it is not a Christian option.' The title, however, nearly landed me in great trouble. The printers delivered me 400 bound copies in the early evening of a day when I was due to take the bulk of them to London for distribution early the next morning. The title was printed in black on a cream cover – *and the question mark from the end of the title was missing on the front cover.* Two of us sat up late that night inking on to the cover in manuscript the missing question mark for the 400 copies, so as to enable the distribution to happen without delay – or misapprehension. Of all the coincidences, when a reprint was needed, the same mistaken cover came from the printers again, and the same emergency action was taken all over again in my home that night!

asking Basil and Rachel Moss (a formidable pair) to write fairly fast a statement on *Humanity and Sexuality*. Synod debated this in July 1978, in the very month when the Bishop of Gloucester was signing his working party's report – but the debate involved no mention of same-sex relationships. A following motion, to commend that report for further study, was narrowly defeated in Synod.

The 1978 Lambeth Conference came the next month, and, although, by some accounts, the bishops did not assemble prepared to make statements or pass resolutions, homosexual relationships were clearly coming onto the agenda. They passed Resolution 10, where para. 3 read:

> While we re-affirm heterosexuality as the scriptural norm, we recognize the need for deep and dispassionate study of the question of homosexuality, which would take seriously both the teaching of Scripture and the results of scientific and medical research. The Church, recognizing the need for pastoral concern for those who are homosexual, encourages dialogue with them.
>
> (We note with satisfaction that such studies are now proceeding in some member Churches of the Anglican Communion.)

Did they know about the Gloucester Report and the hiccups it would cause? Certainly, the 1978 Lambeth Report gave few hints as to the rumpus this issue was to create through the Communion in the next quarter of a century.

The debate on the Gloucester Report

The Gloucester Report was finally published (i.e. Parts I and II) in October 1979. At the November 1979 Synod there was a forest of questions about it, directed to Graham Leonard as chairman of the Board. Somewhere around the ninth supplementary I slipped in this:

> In view of the origin of this report in a request from the principals of the theological colleges, is this report the reply to the principals of the theological colleges or do we look for something else?

That elicited this reply from Graham Leonard: 'I think it is for the theological college principals to tell us what they think.' So, nearly six years on from the request, with an actual (if ambivalent) report in front of us, we were being told we might as well have made up our own minds in the first place.

Synod expressed demands to debate the report urgently, including a Private Member's Motion which had attracted 109 signatures by February 1980. But the BSR was itself not wanting the debate till February 1981 (in the life of a new Synod), and it stuck to its guns, so that the report was not debated until two and a half years after its original presentation to the Board, seven years after the request of the college principals. The debate, technically on a brief covering report by the chairman of the Board, ranged over the whole issue – and beyond it, as Sister Carol spoke warmly about celibacy. Robert Runcie set out a concept ('to which I incline myself') of homosexual orientation as a 'handicap'. To me, the memorable contribution was by Bob Lewis, previously chaplain to Stuart Blanch. He included this comment:

> The Synod needs to hear . . . from people who know this subject from the inside, and here is one . . . So, generosity first towards Gloucester, and generosity towards gays . . . they really do want to be accepted . . . not legislation, not sermons, not reclamation. If anyone wants to reclaim me, I shall run the other way rather quickly . . .

> I have this against the gay movement, that it communicates . . . that here are two states, hetero and homo . . . the one is as good as the other. How in a way I wish I could attain to that doctrine, but I cannot . . . I cannot ditch the weight of Scripture and tradition . . . homosexuality . . . is a disability. It is part of the fault of things. Homosexuality is a cheat.

The debate ran its course. The Synod 'took note' of the covering report, and then following motions came on. Bill Persson wanted Synod to state that it 'does not associate itself with the conclusions of the Working Party'. But Synod voted to pass to next business (191–125). Douglas Rhymes tried to 'commend' the Gloucester Report to dioceses and deaneries, but Synod decided, in the light of its previous decision, 'that the question be not now put'. So the Gloucester exercise ended in thin air without even a pointer or direction, let alone a decision. And in the next five years all I can discover is my own question of July 1984:

> *COB*: Has the House of Bishops plans to issue guidance for the theological colleges and courses . . . as to the acceptability of practising homosexuals for ordination or comparable lay ministry?

> *Robert Runcie*: The House is aware of the concerns . . . We believe, however, that guidance is best given in particular cases and that it is best provided by consultation . . .

This, being interpreted, meant a vacuum of corporate guidance or even concern – it was back unhelpfully to the colleges.

The Osborne Report and the Higton motion

In early 1986, the House of Bishops decided to seek some expert resourcing. The Standing Committee of the House asked the BSR to set up a working party. Its terms of reference were:

1. To review current thinking about the nature and practice of homosexuality and lesbianism and how the Churches have responded to these matters.

2. To consider the method and content of Christian theology and ethics as they relate to these issues.

3. To advise the House of Bishops how to handle homosexuality matters in the Church of England.

These terms were not quite asking for straight judgements on homosexual practice, though the questions run close to this. The seven members, led by June Osborne, were not brought together until early 1987. Meanwhile a newly elected evangelical member of Synod, Tony Higton, tabled this Private Member's Motion:

That this Synod reaffirms the biblical standard, given for the well-being of society:

(i) that sexual intercourse should only take place between a man and a woman who are married to each other;

(ii) that fornication, adultery and homosexual acts are sinful in all circumstances;

(iii) that Christian leaders are called to be exemplary in all spheres of morality, including sexual morality, as a condition of being appointed to or remaining in office;

and calls upon the Church to show Christ-like compassion to those who have fallen into sexual sin, encouraging them to repent and receive absolution, and offering the ministry of healing to all who suffer physically or emotionally as a result of such sin.

The Osborne working party timetable ran independently of this Higton motion, though, perhaps because of Higton, the group was asked to work with speed. Their work was supposed to be anonymous and private, though their existence and terms of reference were aired in Synod the night before the Higton motion was debated in November 1987. This was in a debate on the annual report of

ACCM, where a speaker alleged both that men in homosexual relationships were being recommended for ordination training, and that in at least one theological college 'sexual immorality was rife'. The *Sunday Times* had raised these things with a sensational touch, and they emerged in flaming colours in the debate. The chairman of ACCM, Bishop Barry Rogerson, replied, casting responsibility not on the selectors ('the Church as a whole has not yet come to an agreed mind on some of these issues'), but on sponsoring dioceses. This virtual admission that the allegation had substance (and that there was a vacuum of policy) was cited accusingly in the next day's Higton debate.

The Higton debate reads fairly coolly to someone like me who was not there. But it was experienced as generating as much heat as light. Malcolm Johnson, now known to have been in the Osborne working party, moved a bland (but wrecking) amendment calling for encouragement of 'commitment and permanence in all human relationships'. Tony Higton replied that Malcolm Johnson's church hosted the Lesbian and Gay Christian Movement, and added that the LGCM literature, including material written by Johnson himself, displayed no insistence on commitment in gay relationships anyway. The amendment lost by 46–325. A substantial amendment, formulated after consultation in the Bishops, came then from Michael Baughen, Bishop of Chester:

That this Synod affirms that the biblical and traditional teaching on chastity and fidelity in personal relationships is a response to, and expression of, God's love for each one of us, and in particular affirms:

(1)   that sexual intercourse is an act of total commitment which belongs properly within a permanent married relationship,

(2)   that fornication and adultery are sins against this ideal, and are to be met by a call to repentance and the exercise of compassion,

(3)   that homosexual genital acts also fall short of this ideal *and are likewise to be met by a call to repentance and the exercise of compassion,*

(4)   that all Christians are called to be exemplary in all spheres of morality, including sexual morality, and that holiness of life is particularly required of Christian leaders.

The words in italic in (3) were not in the Baughen amendment, but were an addition from Peter Forster, then representing Durham and Newcastle Universities. Various speakers had said the Baughen amendment would need this addition to get their support, and Peter Forster duly advocated them,

205

drafted as an exact replica of the second half of (2). Point (3) was duly strengthened, and the Baughen amendment then passed 388–19. Synod swept away other amendments, and passed the amended motion 403–8 (with 15 abstentions recorded). The total voting numbers were high; the 98+ per cent in favour was astonishing. Many have muttered since – not least within the Bishops – about the character and outcome of the 'Higton debate'; but that overwhelming vote remains the last recorded findings of Synod on the subject. If it was precipitated by a private member, then a likely reason is that, as shown above, *nearly 14 years* after the request of the principals' conference, amid a growing concern in the Church, there had been a total lacuna of public guidance from ACCM, BSR, Synod or Bishops. And, if the motion passed was tough, the nuancing provided by both the Baughen amendment and the Forster amendment to it meant that Synod had really had the chance to think carefully about the form of words recorded, and had overwhelmingly wanted what they got. At the same time the anonymous Osborne working party members, whether in the Synod or the gallery, were unable to bring their own role into the debate. Their report later expressed their frustration that the debate had intervened at the particular stage in their thinking together, and had done so in ignorance of their more sophisticated task.

The working party finished its report around the time of the 1988 Lambeth Conference (the findings of which barely addressed the issue), and delivered it in confidence to the Bishops. It was intended solely for the Bishops' Meeting (an annual meeting of all working bishops, where it was considered in both 1988 and 1989) and for the BSR, but in fact many people have read it. Because the working party was not charged with delivering a moral verdict on homosexual relationships, its report has often, from whatever motives, been read as supportive of such relationships. But the working party members themselves would say they were doing groundwork for the Bishops, and expected the Bishops to take responsibility for any public declarations or actions with a doctrinal, moral or disciplinary edge to them.

Issues in Human Sexuality and beyond

The House of Bishops discovered during this same period they could write their own doctrinal and policy statements, which they did initially in relation to David Jenkins, and his denials of the bodily resurrection of Christ.[5] The options of work done by the Doctrine Commission, or by FOAG, or by an ad hoc working party (such as Osborne), were extended by this possibility of the Bishops doing it themselves. So a drafting team was appointed, and drafts were brought to the House in early 1991 (which was in my own time as a member). After comment and criticism the report was finished and published as *Issues in Human*

Sexuality. It was a thorough bit of work, though George Carey's commendatory Preface included the pregnant words: 'this Statement – which we do not pretend to be the last word on the subject'.

Issues was open about the Osborne Report (and the name of its chair); and, without in any sense neglecting foundational doctrinal, moral and psychological questions, it focused more closely on the matter of policy for the House of Bishops. The crucial chapter 5 begins with a differentiated evaluation of two outlooks: 'Heterosexuality and homosexuality are not equally congruous with the observed order of creation or with the insights of revelation as the Church engages with these in the light of her pastoral ministry.'[6] This differentiation stood very close to the mind of the bishops in 1991. But the chapter then gave slightly different treatment to homophile lay people and clergy. For lay couples, *Issues* said:

> While . . . unable to commend the way of life just described [faithful and lifelong homophile bonding] as in itself as faithful a reflection of God's purposes as the heterophile we do not reject those who sincerely believe it is God's call to them.

Such non-rejection did relate solely to exclusively faithful couples – *Issues* gave no ground where other patterns of sexual relationships were found. For clergy the message was tougher: 'We have . . . to say that in our considered judgment the clergy cannot claim the liberty to enter into sexually active homophile relationships.'

Perhaps in 1991 the principals were getting an answer to the question of 1974, but it was becoming ever clearer that the bishops would have to take the responsibility themselves – though *Issues* also reveals the bishops hesitant 'to interrogate individuals on their sexual lives, unless there are strong reasons for doing so'.[7]

This 'two-tier discipline' has been frequently attacked, and not from one quarter only. Yet it is not difficult to defend – for instance, in many congregations cohabiting couples regularly worship without being excommunicated, but cohabitant worshippers would not be considered for church warden or reader. Because we do not excommunicate readily, but leave matters with people's consciences, the House of Bishops' findings about lay coupling seem to me to have a consistency – and, equally, to expect the clergy to have fairly rigorous standards of personal behaviour and modelling of leadership is also consistent. We function with two tiers all the time.

Issues became a way of stating a reasonably common approach by bishops to ordination questions. It was not laid before Synod, but it existed as a backdrop throughout the 1990s. If anyone asked what Synod's own position was, well, the Higton debate and its 403–8 result were on record. George Carey is believed to have asked all new bishops (at least in the Southern province) to exercise their respective episcopates in conformity with *Issues.* The report provided a good holding of the line – if the line was to be held. The Bishops simultaneously appointed a small group with a standing brief to attend gay Christian meetings and retain contact with their representative leaders.

Growing tension

In fact the line was being challenged in all sorts of ways. In 1994 Peter Tatchell's Outrage! attempted to embarrass the leadership by 'outing' allegedly gay bishops. This threatened real damage until, marvellously, David Hope rounded on Outrage!. How he saw them off in early 1995 is well described in the Rob Marshall book.[8] Within the Church of England there was more and more coming out occurring. 'Coming out' means of course that it is otiose to complain about bishops or others thrusting cameras into bedrooms – for then it is the individuals who are inviting the cameras in. In autumn 1996 I went to Southwark Diocese not only with occasional clergy (including at least two who have gained national publicity) notifying me in advance of their same-sex sexual relationships, but with the famous LGCM service having been held in Southwark cathedral a fortnight before I started. Some at that point thought that, simply by fostering what had become a well-charged atmosphere, they had established a 'diocesan policy'. The appointment of Tom Butler as diocesan bishop in 1998 was interpreted as pressure from the CAC (including the Southwark representatives) to bring in someone to confront that 'atmosphere'.

Synod in 1997

In General Synod, a Southwark archdeacon, David Gerrard, seeing that the House of Bishops was not bringing *Issues* to the Synod, tabled early in 1995–2000 this Private Member's Motion:

That this Synod

(a)   commend for discussion in dioceses the House of Bishops' report *Issues in Human Sexuality* and acknowledge it is not the last word on the subject;

(b)   in particular, urge deanery synods, clergy chapters and congregations to find time for prayerful study and reflection on the issues addressed by the report.

Its debate came in July 1997, a debate more memorable for its procedural oddities than for its content.

A procedural conundrum confronted the House of Bishops as this debate came up. Suppose nuancing amendments got moved, ones that might visibly divide the House, what publicity would follow? So the Bishops, accepting the neutrality of 'prayerful study', etc., decided to protect the Gerrard wording, by forcing a vote by Houses on all amendments and then as a House killing off each amendment. Nevertheless, during ten years since the Higton debate, Synod had expressed no mind, so was this the moment? Two amendments were tabled, both of which would have weighted the motion against homosexual partnerships. The House of Bishops followed their plan and slew them both. They were in fact lost in both other Houses also, though very narrowly in the House of Laity.

I was myself seized by a synodical non-event. Outside the Synod stood Richard Kirker of the LGCM, with his standard placards 'Ordain gays now'. But inside there was no such amendment tabled. Here was the once-in-a-decade opportunity to affect public policy; here indeed was a mover of the main motion who was probably sympathetic to gays; and, even if the House of Bishops resisted an amendment, for gays to put their aspiration into the arena, and perhaps even carry it in two Houses, was surely their right tactic? But no such amendment was moved. The debate conveyed an asymmetrical picture, that conservative amendments had been defeated, while gays had been left untouched. I tackled Richard Kirker after the debate and asked him why there was not attempted inside the chamber that which he so deafeningly pursued outside it. He replied that there was no hope of getting an amendment through. As a connoisseur of unsuccessful amendments, I put it to him that, where there is deep conviction, you go for it anyway, whatever the chances. He shrugged.

I put this on a larger canvas. General Synod deliberated and took decisions in 1989–90 about the terms on which those who had been divorced and married again might be ordained. Synod likewise decided in 1992 on the ordination of women as presbyters. No bishop in England, however sympathetic to a particular candidate or to the principle of such candidature, ever jumped the gun. So I submit that it is entirely reasonable to expect that, when a further new category of persons previously debarred, those in homosexual relationships, is to be eligible for ordination, then Synod must first affirm (and legislate) the principle behind the admission of the category. Furthermore, as such couplings have had no institutional identity, any decision would have to include the conditions for a couple to be recognized as in a permanent coupling. Kirker sought to cut all these corners, and alongside the shouting of slogans, work for the silent intrusion of active homosexuals into the ordained ministry. The lack of any attempt to amend the Gerrard motion in Synod demonstrated that non-synodical methods had pride of place in the movement.

So I analysed the debate. But I missed a trick. Richard Kirker had a letter in *Church Times* the following week, *thanking the Synod for its promotion of the LGCM cause!* Then I wondered whether, if a pro-gay amendment had been tabled, that would have delineated the neutrality of the original wording, whereas LGCM had all along reckoned to treat the original wording as their liberal charter? I responded myself in *Church Times*, emphasizing the neutrality of the motion the House of Bishops had defended and Synod had passed – and suggesting the Kirker spin was not just wrong, but was deliberately perverse, twisting the meaning in the interests of his own ends.

The motion was one to promote study, suspended upon the report's own words, quoted in the motion, that *Issues* was 'not the last word' on the subject. Christina Baxter, chair of the House of Laity, had risen in the debate to say that further study might mean that 'the Church makes a more severe resolution than even the 1987 one' (as well as offering the possibility of a more liberal one). So, she said, we had to vote strictly on the meaning of the text, and not on the basis of partisan advocacy of it. Perhaps Kirker had not been listening. The motion was passed 44–0; 186–38; 150–88 – over 500 voted, exceeding all other counts save on the ordination of women.

Lambeth 1998

If the ordination of women as bishops caught the headlines at Lambeth 1988, homosexual relationships did so in 1998.[9] Bishops from the conservative South feared in advance that the Americans would arrive with a liberal agenda and an enormous block vote to endorse it. This may have increased the confrontation before the Conference even convened. The mood was not helped by Jack Spong's much-publicized advance denunciations of African attitudes as emanating from ignorance, superstition and their inhabiting a pre-Copernican world. Section 1, 'Called to full humanity', included in its report a relatively brief treatment of 'human sexuality'. The section members acknowledged they were of different minds, but they were overtaken by a powerful groundswell in the Conference that wished more trenchantly to oppose homosexual unions. So the Conference plenary carried by 526–70 (with 45 recorded abstentions) the famous resolution (I.10):

This Conference:

(a)   commends to the Church the subsection report on human sexuality;

(b)   in view of the teaching of Scripture, upholds faithfulness in marriage between a man and a woman in lifelong union, and believes that abstinence is right for those not called to marriage;

(c)   recognizes that there are among us persons who experience themselves as having a homosexual orientation. Many of these are members of the Church and are seeking pastoral care, moral direction of the Church, and God's transforming power for the living of their lives and the ordering of relationships. We commit ourselves to listen to the experience of homosexual persons and we wish to assure them that they are loved by God and that all baptized, believing and faithful persons, regardless of sexual orientation, are full members of the Body of Christ;

(d)   while rejecting homosexual practice as incompatible with Scripture, calls on all our people to minister pastorally and sensitively to all irrespective of sexual orientation and to condemn irrational fear of homosexuals, violence within marriage and any trivialization and commercialization of sex;

(e)   cannot advise the legitimizing or blessing of same sex unions nor ordaining those involved in same gender unions;

(f)   requests the Primates and the ACC to establish a means of monitoring the work done on the subject of human sexuality in the Communion and to share the statements and resources among us;

(g)   notes the significance of the Kuala Lumpur Statement on Human Sexuality and the concerns expressed in resolutions IV.26, V.1, V.10, V.23 and V.35 on the authority of Scripture in matters of marriage and sexuality and asks the Primates and the ACC to include them in their monitoring.

This has become an important backdrop to all discussions since.[10] I voted for it, and have endeavoured both to uphold its standard and to do the listening undertaken in paragraph (c). As with the 1987 Synod motion, so at Lambeth the majority was overwhelming, and, I think, a surprise even to the proponents. I wonder too how the 70 opponents were comprised – my guess is no more than 40 Americans and around 30 from the rest of the world. If that is so, then the 131 American bishops present had a fairly strong weighting *in favour of the resolution* even amongst themselves. They were no clone.

What has struck me as extraordinary is the later assertion that 150 or so of those who voted for the resolution later regretted their action. A bishop goes to Lambeth knowing that serious matters touching the life of the Anglican Churches throughout the globe are being tackled. He goes as a man used to synods and assemblies (almost inevitable in a bishop!). He goes to use his mind, his convictions and his experience. He goes knowing findings may get worldwide publicity and run for many years ahead. He goes knowing his own diocese and especially his clergy. In that plenary a clear minority is ready to vote against the resolution, and he will not be on his own if he does so. Yet we are told hordes of bishops were then swept along into endorsing a resolution contrary to their convictions and conscience. Can 30 per cent of those 526 be retrospectively deemed to have wanted to vote the other way, but somehow did not manage to?

An archbishop, Reading and *Some Issues in Human Sexuality*

Then we come to Rowan Williams. The press named him for Canterbury just before the July 2002 Synod, and it was officially announced from Downing Street immediately after. Concerning homosexual relationships he was an equivocal figure following the unequivocal George Carey. He had been closely associated with Affirming Catholicism, for whom Jeffrey John was a leading theologian and author; he had written about the (conservative) St Andrew's Day Statement, at least opening the door to a more liberal application of it in practice; he was said to have ordained in Wales at least one person known to be in a homosexually active relationship; and he was thought to have voted among the 70 at Lambeth (in fact he had abstained).[11] Reform and Church Society thundered against him, and the organizers of NEAC-4, scheduled for Blackpool in September 2003, stated that for him to address the Congress would dissuade hundreds of people from coming.

But Rowan Williams' theology included an element both quickly evident and yet widely ignored. He might have his own convictions – indeed he had. He might have spoken as still engaged in exploration – and indeed he was. But he did not view the archbishopric as simply a platform for his own views and practice, for he had a doctrine of the Church, and of the bishop in the Church, which took the Lambeth Resolution I.10 (quoted above) very seriously. He thus wrote to every Primate in the Communion, on the day of the announcement that he was to be Archbishop of Canterbury, to say precisely that he viewed the Lambeth resolution as highly significant in the Communion, a stance to which he wished to be loyal. In the light of later events in 2003, he could not have made it more clear that he took the mind of the church as having *prima facie* authority in his public dealings with the Communion.[12] In his first encounters with the Bishops in the Church of England, he put his exploratory openness into the discussion – he would ponder deeply on contrary ideas as well as the frontier-pushing work which he had already undertaken.

The test in England came all too soon, in June 2003. Richard Harries, Bishop of Oxford, nominated Jeffrey John to be Bishop of Reading, an Oxford suffragan. Jeffrey John, canon-residentiary of Southwark, had been an incumbent in the Woolwich Area when I first arrived. A very able theologian, he was on most doctrinal issues to be found among the traditionalists.[13] He advocated homosexual relationships only where they are 'permanent, faithful, stable' – and thus he was more conservative than many in LGCM, whose stance he found uncomfortable. He openly acknowledged that he had had a homosexual lover for over 20 years, since his residence at St Stephen's House in the mid-1970s.[14] He stated that he had had his principal's approval of the relationship. However, with this known background, he was now reported as not in any sexual relationship with his lover, and thus technically 'abstinent' and appointable. On those grounds, i.e. the defensibility of his present position, he had the support of our diocesan, Tom Butler.

But that bare outline leaves vast questions unanswered. The particularly pressing one was how far distanced he was from his own past. I had certainly been asked about my own past when nominated as a suffragan bishop. Had this weighed with the archbishop's adviser on appointments, who had forwarded his name for Bishop Richard Harries' shortlist?

Richard Harries, once he had accepted the name into his shortlist, and had arranged interviews of the shortlisted persons, was almost bound to accept the person who emerged as best qualified – and that was clearly Jeffrey John. But the nomination does not seem to have had such widespread support among the diocesan clergy, and a significant number in Reading Area itself were affronted and quickly expressed their opposition. The announcement came also at a point in Rowan Williams' archiepiscopate where, because of evangelical voices raised against him, gaining public confidence around the Church of England was vital. Why, people asked, had he consented to Richard Harries' choice? The answer, now of only historic interest, must lie somewhere between the bishop and archbishop concerned.

The unrest finally boiled over in a letter from nine diocesan bishops to the Church press on 17 June 2003, including the following:

> We are glad at the reassurances from the Bishop of Oxford that Jeffrey John's life is now celibate. But it is the history of the relationship, as well as Dr. John's severe criticism of orthodox teaching, which gives concern.

More widely, the appointment appears to prejudice the outcome of the Church's reflection on these matters. We have been repeatedly assured that the House of Bishops' position stated in *Issues in Human Sexuality* has not changed. A major study guide to this document is to be published towards the end of this year. It does not, we are assured, seek to change the Church's mind on the matter. Yet, in view of his previous teaching, Dr. John's statement that he now stands by *Issues* has to be received somewhat cautiously.

We must therefore express our concern because of the Church's constant teaching, in the light of Scripture and because of the basic ordering of men and women in creation. We must also express our concern because of our responsibility for the Church's unity, both in this country and throughout the world.

Yours sincerely

Seven suffragans added their names. The cat was among the pigeons. It was less now a matter of Oxford Diocese or Reading Area, more an ideological struggle for the future of the Church of England. Jeffrey John, for all his personal shyness, had become iconic. Christians all round England, Anglicans all round the world, the press in all its irresponsibility, were asking, would the Church of England cross a hitherto uncrossed line, would it move into new territory, if Jeffrey John were consecrated as a bishop in the Church of God? Would Jeffrey John be simply a slightly exceptional newcomer to an unimpaired episcopate, or would he, with his personal history, become the thin end of a wedge in an episcopate which, thus pierced, could never regain its integrity again? Rowan Williams took the letter very seriously, weighed the risk about the wedge's thin end, and, however reluctantly, asked Jeffrey John to withdraw. After a morning of pain, the man at the centre of it all did so. There were, understandably, both hurt and fury in many places – but there were also gratitude and relief; and arguably the Church of England was preserved relatively intact in the Anglican Communion by that withdrawal, and Rowan Williams' role as convenor of the Primates was also unimpaired as, within days, it needed to be.[15] England and the Anglican Communion were being overtaken by the Gene Robinson affair, reported in my Chapter 19.

In reflection on the 1998 Lambeth Conference (and on the 1997 Synod debate on *Issues*) the Bishops in 2000 commissioned a follow-up to *Issues*, conceived as 'a guide to the debate'. The four diocesan bishops of the Working Group on *Issues in Human Sexuality* planned a fairly massive publication, and this, after being vetted in draft by the House as a whole, was published in November 2003 as *Some Issues in Human Sexuality: A Guide to the Debate*. It was carefully drafted not to allow any claims that the bishops had shifted their position (in any direction) since *Issues*. It is not only massive (seven times the length of *Issues*), but magisterial. Like *Issues* itself it ranges over the whole field of sexuality, and it includes a very substantial bibliography. It is accompanied by a slimmer volume: Joanna Cox and Martin Davie's *A Companion to Some Issues in Human Sexuality*.[16]

Synod debated *Some Issues* in February 2004 to 'take note' and then to commend it for study. The debate was marked, and, I think, remembered for a very 'out' speech by a gay member of the House of Clergy (from Southwark) who spoke about his 'partner', and of being, at 40, 'five years into a relationship of lifelong commitment to my partner'. There were repercussions from this, not least a letter of 75 members of Synod to the Archbishop of Canterbury, pressing him to clarify the position, one which had been compromised by the introductory speech by the Bishop of Oxford, of which the text given to the press implied rather more relaxing of the discipline of the Church of England than the actual speech he delivered to Synod – and, of course, the press had used the text given without checking against delivery in Synod. That had led to reports such as, 'the mood of the Church had taken a sudden swing in the liberal direction', true neither to *Some Issues* nor to Richard Harries' actual speech nor to the text of the motions under debate.

More recent debate

The context in the country has moved on since I retired. The parliamentary legislation that provides for (same-sex) 'civil partnerships' has presented the House of Bishops with a painful dilemma. The underlying presupposition of the legislation is, as with matrimony, that of sexual union. However, that is not explicit, and, as I understand it, non-consummation would not be grounds for severance. The Bishops have, therefore, had to face the question of how to interpret any such partnership entered by a licensed cleric, and their public statement says that they will expect clergy entering such a partnership first to give an undertaking of sexual abstinence. There are questions whether they can stand together or stand long by this statement.

A reflection

I have done my utmost in my ministry both to stick with the Bible and to be open to the actual experience and testimony of gay Christians. I conclude by reflecting (*not* advocating) how in theory the Church of England could openly reach the unemotive recognition of gay clergy which they seek. This is all hypothetical; it is, I repeat, not advocacy. It is close to the argument I used in debate with Gene Robinson in the Oxford Union in November 2005.

First, there would be needed a recognition of the institution of gay coupling. It is amazing that questions of 'blessing' same-sex unions seem to have come *after* questions of accepting clergy already in them. But the Church of England would have to know how such unions were effected, how binding they were in any analogy with marriage, what would count as being unfaithful, and under what conditions a union could be dissolved (including questions about innocence and guilt). What line should be drawn between acceptable relationships and unacceptable ones – for lay Christians, even before we approach clergy questions?

Next, with the institutional character of unions established, the Church of England could look at the conditions under which persons in such unions could be ordained. We once had it with the illegitimate. We have had it since those days with those divorced and remarried, who are viewed as in a different kind of marital institution from those where neither party has been previously divorced. When the barrier was lifted, a difficult 'faculty' route was required, quite separately from the testing of vocation itself. We have also had it with the ordination of women – the institutional condition of being a woman was historically a bar to ordination, then it ceased to be a bar to being a deacon in 1987, and to being a presbyter in 1994.

These precedents are very important. No one tried to smuggle barred categories past bishops before there was synodical (and parliamentary!) authority. No bishop in England (unlike America), however sympathetic, ordained a woman before the relevant Measure was passed. That is how the ordination of persons in gay unions should be handled. Unless and until such a procedure is followed, 'acceptance' allows even dissolute forms of sexual behaviour amongst gay clergy, even while strict monogamy is still expected of heterosexuals. Any serious recognition would have to define the institution, then provide guidelines to a disciplined – indeed exemplary – life among gay clergy, and then synodically (and possibly under strict conditions) accept the candidature of those in the institution. Only then would bishops be able (as with marriage) to know what would count as in breach of it.

But this is not advocacy.

If a non-synodical, arguably immoral or at least improper, movement from the ground reckons it must be recognized because it has slipped through a badly maintained fence and is 'here', then parity of reasoning might lead to all sorts of other movements.

Suppose, for instance, the advocates of lay presidency adopted a similar course?

16

Church and State

Give to the emperor the things that are the emperor's, and to God the things that are God's.

(Luke 20.25)

Can the ownership of the Church of England by the State still be defended in the twenty-first century?

We regularly hear about the advantages (occasionally the disadvantages) of being 'the established Church'. The lovers of establishment claim it gives the Church of England extra clout and extra opportunities in the country. But what can those claims mean? And what exactly does it mean to be the 'established Church'? As I have written, spoken, and moved motions, about disestablishment, we had better be clear at the outset what establishment is.

It was in Henry VIII's and Elizabeth I's days a statement that the Church of England, being by law the same people as the citizens of England, was governed by the same instrument, the monarch in Parliament. State law and Church law were identical, and the doctrine and organization of the Church of England were governed by Parliament.

And so it continued right into the twentieth century. But the identification of the English people with the English Church has come unstuck on both sides, and the present establishment is a limping relic of that original pattern. On the Church side, the Church of England has an identity in its worshipping members, who are quite distinct from the citizenry at large, and it has organs of self-government in PCCs, diocesan synods and General Synod. These share a common explicit Christianity which is not mirrored – and is not expected or required to be mirrored – in Parliament. On the State's side, Church of England business started to gum up parliamentary agendas in the nineteenth century, and to embarrass unbelieving MPs in the twentieth. It became a relief from 1919 onwards to delegate many powers to the Church Assembly and, from 1970, to the General Synod. Yet that relic remained that the Church of England was in the last analysis still governed from Parliament.

217

A moment of definition came after the defeat in Parliament of the 1927 and 1928 'Deposited' Prayer Books. A proportion of the Commons debate had been genuinely theological. But the Bishops subsequently stated:

> the Church – that is, the Bishops together with the Clergy and the Laity – must in the last resort ... retain its inalienable right ... to formulate its Faith ... and to arrange the expression of that holy Faith in its forms of worship.

This crossed a watershed. Parliament was one entity, and it had powers over the Church – but the Church was a different entity, differently composed and differently counted, and now it was denying the State the right to rule over it, and was defining itself over against the State. Parliament is sovereign, but, apart from seating 26 bishops in the Lords, it has no religious test for membership, and is strictly godless in its procedures. So no establishmentarian can nowadays pretend that Parliament is somehow *a way by which the Church of England governs itself.* No, there are two separate chalk-and-cheese entities, and today's establishmentarian has the odd task of promoting *on Christian grounds* the rule of a secular State over a Christian Church. Traditionally this has been dubbed Erastianism, which Anglicans have generally been ready to recognize as a heresy, *except in their own case.*

Despite the formal godlessness of Parliament, the Church of England has regularly claimed English society as somehow its own. When I was young, I think most people knew in which parish they lived.[1] In 1950 67 per cent of live births in England led to infant baptism in the Church of England within 12 months. When in 1954–5, as a National Service subaltern, I was receiving recruits from civvy street, the sergeant would tell the newcomers how to complete their forms, but (unless they knew they were something else) 'Let's have no nonsense – if you were born south of the border you put "C/E" against "Religion" on your forms.' This atmosphere, that the default position of the nation is 'C/E', has led the Church of England to count its members in tens of millions, to appoint its parish clergy to the cure of thousands of souls, and to retain the appointment of its churchwardens by a meeting of all parishioners regardless of faith or attendance.[2] It is, of course, a supreme megalomaniac fantasy. It has knock-on ill-effects also – the figures usually trotted out for the whole Anglican Communion, somewhere under 100 million, include around 30 million from England. Thus *The Lambeth Conference 1978: Preparatory Information* listed 30 million.[3] I asked in February 1993 when the Church of England would cease producing such ludicrous figures, and was told by the secretary-general, Philip Mower, that all such calculations had ceased in 1979. Yet an American wrote in 1999: 'As late as 1978 a majority of the world's Anglican population lived in Britain ... [twenty years later] By contrast the Church of England estimates its present membership at 26 million...'[4]

Sure enough, despite the answer I received in 1993, the 2006 *Yearbook* has 26 million on page 357 as the 'baptized membership'. I doubt whether there are 26 million baptized English citizens of any sort in 2006, let alone 26 million baptized members of the Church of England. The world of 1950 – let alone that of 1550 – has disappeared round us with little trace, but the Church of England marches on in its world of fantasy. I try to avoid fantasy; but have I lost the Anglican plot, or have those who go on counting 26 million[5]?

The 1970s

So what structural steps has the Church of England taken since 1970 towards becoming a 'free' Church? At the very beginning of Synod, there was the major Chadwick Report, *Church and State 1970*. It came in the first mailing I received, and became a dominant element in those early years of Synod. For Michael Ramsey it was a congenial theme (matching his enthronement sermon of 1961) to mark his last four years.

This Chadwick Report was the fourth Church and State report of the twentieth century.[6] It usefully defined 'establishment' as the relationship springing from those laws of the land which govern the Church of England only. The classic instance, still partly in force in 1970, was the 1662 Act of Uniformity. But the Church of England Assembly (Powers) Act 1919 had created a new category of Church laws, ones devised, drafted, amended and approved in the Church Assembly. These laws, entitled Measures, become parliamentary law by a single reading, with a yea or nay vote, in both Houses of Parliament. (By convention Parliament would not thereafter employ its undoubted sovereign powers to control the Church of England by its own naked Acts, generated and passed solely within the Palace of Westminster without the participation or assent of the Church.)

This post-1920 relationship was tested to the limit by the rejection of the 1927–8 Prayer Books.[7] That precipitated the quest for ways in which the Church might authorize liturgical forms without Parliament's involvement. The quest led, through the wearisomeness of Canon Law revision, to the Prayer Book (Alternative and Other Services) Measure 1965, which came into force on 1 May 1966 – 38 years after the crisis which led to it. It was only a first taste of liturgical freedom, for its charter would expire around 1980, and longer-term provision was urgently needed. The subscription and assent of the clergy, which were tightly bound in with liturgical freedom, needed close scrutiny also. The Alternative Services Measure did a kind of holding job by defining the weasel phrase in the clerical undertaking, '[to use the Prayer Book and no other liturgical forms] *except so far as may be ordered by lawful authority*' (my italics). The Doctrine Commission had since recommended a new Declaration of

Assent, which was refined in Synod and proved to be unitive and has been so in the Church at large since.[8] So the Chadwick Report set in train major legislation in the Worship and Doctrine Measure. A more slippery issue, which Church authorities hoped to handle without legislation, was the appointment of bishops, treated in Chapter 18.

In Synod, we had the odd experience, when this Measure was being devised in 1970–74, that the major question to debate was actually nothing to do with new services or subscription. It was this: would Synod seek power to abolish 1662 or not? Without that power 1662 would remain entrenched by Parliament, and we might one day have to submit another Measure to loosen it from the politicians' grip; but, if we sought that power now, we might raise alarms in Parliament that we intended to use it, and then find they vetoed the Measure entire. It went to the dioceses, and all but London wanted the Measure (London asked for disestablishment instead!), and a majority asked for the wider power. But Standing Committee trod delicately, seeking only the narrower power. When Synod debated the principles in November 1972, Gerald Ellison, Bishop of Chester, ('a dangerous left-wing radical', Peter Cornwell dubbed him), moved the wider power proposal as an amendment. Paul Welsby spoke splendidly:

> I ask: does there never come a point when the Church of England ceases to look over its shoulder at the Crown lawyers and on matters where it believes principle is involved goes ahead in doing what it believes to be right and accepts what consequences may ensue?

How often I have asked that question myself! The broadly accurate answer is 'no'. That day it was equally wondrously countered by George Goyder: 'I much regret to tell the Bishop of Chester that if he has his way, disestablishment inevitably follows.' That would certainly have brought Gerald Ellison, the establishmentarian *par excellence*, to heel – had he believed it. Others too feared Parliament would disapprove. Amid those fears, the amendment was lost (11–19; 66–134; 43–128). Gerald Ellison reappeared two days later to move the Measure containing the narrower power ('I do try to be a good Synod man'). After General Approval it was revised in Committee, and had its Revision Stage in Synod in July 1973. But further fears were raised about how to resolve disputes about liturgy between incumbents and PCCs. So another Revision Stage in November 1973 eliminated any adjudicating role for bishops – partly, it seems, because the members in charge feared Parliament would doubt whether bishops could be trusted to defend 1662! Final Approval came in Synod in February 1974. Michael Ramsey piloted it through the Lords in November 1974 on his last day in office, and the Commons produced a large vote to pass it 145–45.

Analysing establishment

It was by Measure that Synod had acquired its own constitution and powers. Since then, in the years 1970–2005, further Measures, devised in Synod, have regularly delegated powers from Parliament to Synod. Among these are the various Pastoral Measures (actually beginning in 1969, in Church Assembly days), the Worship and Doctrine Measure (described above), the Dioceses Measure, and the Benefices Measure. Each of these has given more freedom to the Church of England to organize its life without reference to Parliament. The process invites the illustration that the Church of England is like a goat which was tethered on a very tight chain in Henry VIII's day, but a chain which has been lengthened and lengthened over the centuries since. The upshot is that the goat can now browse unrestrictedly over almost the whole field, and in the process can even deceive itself into thinking it is free. But at intervals it pulls towards a corner of the field where the chain will still not reach – and then it is brought up short. It cannot ultimately control much of its own legislation nor choose its own bishops (and churchwardens); it *is* chained.

Supporters of the establishment fall into two categories. One sort likes the *sound* of 'established Church' and simply wants to be regularly reassured that the chain exists and that the goat is firmly attached to it. These persons will gladly believe the establishment is safe, even if the chain is lengthened till it provides no restriction at all. The other, more hard-nosed, group believes that establishment consists in keeping the chain precisely the same length as it is at the moment, and that lengthening it might be fatal. No amount of past changes affect this judgement – they are irrelevant; such changes may even have been beneficial; but, whatever happened *then*, nothing more must happen *now*.[9] The trouble with the first sort is that there are actually few State-and-Church principles to which they adhere – they simply want to hear the word 'established' at intervals. The trouble with the second sort is not only the inconsistency between their approaches to the past and to the future, but also that they can frighten the first sort into thinking that any change proposed means the goat will slip its chain.

A short synodical March

Well, Worship and Doctrine became law, though it piled up some parliamentary trouble for the future. There was a brief flurry about establishment, when the Earl of March in July 1977 moved a motion which included:

> That this Synod [wanting to save time] requests the Standing Committee to bring forward proposals to reduce the need to seek

> Parliamentary approval when changes in the life and work of the
> Church of England are desired.

This of course was the most pragmatic and undoctrinal basis for change. It was simply trying to save Synod wasted labours by its officers and increasing mountains of synodical paper. He succeeded by 106–100.

Standing Committee reported (GS 400) in February 1980 that the Earl had got it wrong – Gerald Ellison said: 'only a small part of our work has been occupied with Measures which have to fulfil Parliamentary requirements.' No change was needed. The Earl himself confessed surprise that his item was labelled 'Church and State' rather than 'Simplification of Legislative Procedures'. He asked the Synod for a commission to seek simplification, without now mentioning the State. The motion was defeated. The March up the *cul de sac* was finished.

The 1980s and 1990s

The 1980s began with a Partners in Mission (PiM) consultation for the Church of England in Summer 1981.[10] The external partners, when meeting by themselves, could not swallow the establishment, and viewed the English as blind to their own problem. They initially drafted:

> We propose that it [the Church of England] try a slow separation –
> step-by-step of Church and State ... The establishment of the
> Church is a hindrance to the mission of the Church and the Church is
> unable to perform its prophetic ministry freely.

However, the internal (i.e. Church of England) partners joined them, and, lo and behold, all the discerned 'hindrance' and inability 'to perform its prophetic ministry' melted away. The trouble was not the establishment itself: no, no, it was the unconscious superior attitude of the Church of England, and it was *that* which must be changed – 'So we do not propose any effort to restructure the Establishment.' There was, however, a Postscript at the end of the report which included, 'In fact substantial changes are needed in [several things] ... in state relations.' But what did that mean?

The PiM report, *To a Rebellious House?*, had a seminar-type presentation at the July Synod that year. Stuart Blanch, Archbishop of York, preaching earlier in the Minster, began his sermon with 'The question of disestablishment is not on the agenda'. And it more or less wasn't – the seminar style delivered the Synod from hard questions. There was a 'take note' debate about PiM in the February following, but mission, communication, and even God were dominant, and that last-gasp mention of changes 'in state relations' never arose.

In fact, the 1980–85 quinquennium contained more reminders than any period since 1927–8 of the existing absolute sovereignty of Parliament over the Church of England – and of Parliament's theological incompetence to exercise it. There were two different eloquent instances of this, one in the Lords and one in the Commons.

On 8 April 1981 Lord Sudeley brought the Prayer Book Protection Bill into the House of Lords, and got it passed by 24–12. Amazingly, Viscount Cranborne's similar bill before the Commons succeeded there at an initial stage by 152–130. It was to provide that, if any 20 persons on the electoral roll so petitioned an incumbent, he was to provide a Prayer Book service at the 'principal Sunday morning service' at least once a month. The Bill came five months after the ASB was published, and was staked upon the perception that the wicked clergy had used the cover of the Worship and Doctrine Measure to discard the BCP. Parliamentarians display two characteristics rarely combined in other worshippers – that is, they may attend Church at rare intervals (as do many others), but they also have a platform to complain that the liturgy has moved on when they were not looking (as do few others). The Lords manifested these tendencies.

Lord Sudeley got no further in 1981, but returned with the same Bill in April 1984, and this time I listened in the gallery – and it was appalling.[11] The upshot for both liturgy and legislation is irrelevant (in fact Lord Hailsham so ruthlessly dismembered it, from the Woolsack, that Sudeley withdrew it). The critical point is Parliament's action in both 1981 and 1984 to begin unilaterally to amend the Church's legislation, the Worship and Doctrine Measure. The agreed conventions of 1919 were being ignored – and always can be.[12]

In July 1984 the Commons defeated a Measure to abolish the medieval ceremonies in the appointing of bishops, and this is reported (and evaluated) in Chapter 18 below. Synod had voted overwhelmingly in favour, and the Commons vote against was 17–32 (with 600 MPs absent). The determinative element was the opposition of Enoch Powell and Ian Paisley, both from Northern Ireland constituencies (another wonderful oddity of parliamentary control of the Church *of England*), and apparently venting wrath upon the Church of England for the views of the new Bishop of Durham, David Jenkins. They sprang an ambush after midnight, and that was that.[13]

Could Synod begin it?

Criticisms of establishment from PiM external partners and malign exercise of powers by Lords and Commons had this in common – both sets of criticisms impacted (or threatened to impact) the Synod from outside. Synod itself rarely tried to get Parliament off our backs, or get the establishment otherwise reduced or abolished.[14] Even a Private Member's Motion by Robert Dell, archdeacon of Derby, in November 1982 to enable clergy to stand for Parliament only passed 181–147 – and was ignored by Parliament until after 2000. The goat grazed on, feeling free most of the time; it hit the limit of its chain not only in the arbitrary use by Mrs Thatcher of her powers in appointing bishops, but also when the Commons in July 1989 defeated the Clergy (Ordination) Measure, to allow the ordination of men and women who had been divorced and married again (or whose marital partners had been), by 45–51. The Synod tightened the Measure and it went through in 1990.

So, when the goat reached the limit of its chain, it did not seem to mind! It perhaps thought that was inherent in the life of being a goat – and by moving slightly it got what it wanted. Clearly a greater crisis than MPs blocking the ordination of the divorced and remarried was needed to provoke a change. So suppose Parliament in 1993 had turned down the ordination of women. As it was, it held the process up by 12 months; but hypothetically (yet not impossibly) it could have taken much longer, if John Major had been leading a minority government in a hung Parliament after the June 1992 election, and another election had come within 12 months. In the end, the ordination of women passed by 215–21. But a defeat that day might have provoked a Greenham Common in Westminster (an engaging prospect), would certainly have demonstrated that powers were totally wrongly located – and would have produced the elusive crisis.

Well, I tried to help. In early 1992 I tabled a Private Member's Motion:

> That this Synod request the Standing Committee to bring forward proposals for the lifting of direct State control upon:
>
> (a)   the appointment of diocesan bishops; and
>
> (b)   the authorization of legislation coming from this Synod.

I was also during 1993 at work on the most substantial book written against the establishment in the post-war years, *Cut the Connection: Disestablishment and the Church of England.* Then by November my motion, as above, was running second in the waiting list.[15] The one-day meeting due in February 1994 (to promulge the Canon about the ordination of women and the Episcopal Ministry Act of Synod) was not going to have PMMs. So I came on in July 1994, only days after the publication of my book. As I was only proposing two specific changes (though admittedly the most prominent), I denied that this was a proposal for disestablishment. I hoped for synodical establishmentarians of the 'so long as there is a chain, it does not matter how long it is' sort, who might look at the proposals as unthreatening. But the others, who say establishment is, and must be defended as, keeping the chain exactly where it is, surfaced strongly. The debate was enlivened (though hardly enlightened) by an ascent into a private stratosphere by Michael Alison, the Second Estates Commissioner (i.e. leader of the Church of England in the Commons, appointed by the Prime Minister). Off he went:

> [If a Measure of this sort came to the Commons] The vote in the end would be decided ... by the out-turn between the forces and benefits of prayer and dirty tricks ... whichever way the vote went ... following a rowdy, scurrilous and unsavoury debate, the Church of England would emerge tarnished, damaged and divided from the great debate. A big detonation can always attract attention, but at a price. When a well-functioning but discreetly located central heating boiler suddenly blows up in a house, everybody quickly discovers where that central heating boiler is and how important it is; but meanwhile the hot water, in a great network of hidden pipes and radiators, turns cold.

So now we knew. Not only was Parliament keeping us warm, but we could provoke a ('scurrilous') explosion there. It was hardly calculated to make us love our dependence on it. John Habgood came to the rescue: 'I am not totally convinced by the apocalyptic scenario ... by Michael Alison.' No, indeed – he was embarrassed by it. The debate actually had many good features. There was a wonderful mocking speech from Elaine Storkey:

> I have been struck by the sudden stream of prophecy ... Five prophecies have struck me particularly. One, that English people will lose their sense of belonging to the Church; two, that the ship of state will somehow come unloosed; three, that the ballot box will become God; four, that central heating boilers will start to explode everywhere; and five, that Britain will move into a new ice age. What ... brings on this cataclysmic effect? Well, the cause of this unexpected trauma is that the Prime Minister will no longer appoint bishops. I had no idea that John Major was exercising such charismatic leadership.

We had a vote at the end, and I lost 110–273. John Bullimore, who had chaired it, commented to me, 'You won the argument and lost the vote.' I still think that true – institutional irrationality and purblindness affect the Synod when the word 'establishment' gets thrown into the argument.

My last direct intervention in such matters came when the first proposals for the new National Instruments came to a new Synod from the Turnbull

Commission in November 1995. While the public front of the whole exercise was a 'unified administrative structure', it left the Church Commissioners in being, albeit belonging slightly more to the Church of England than before. David McLean's motion was to turn the recommendations into actual proposals for the next meeting of Synod. My amendment said: 'including the complete assimilation of the Church Commissioners and all their existing functions into the projected unified structure'.

I asked that David McLean should not reply, 'it might even be timely and consistent, but of course Parliament would not like it.' Well, he avoided the actual words, but his reply was exactly that. There was no comment on the benefits of so unifying the structure, only on 'sensitive soundings', etc., with Parliament – and, he said, 'If we are going to look at these deep constitutional issues, let us do it straight on and not on a side wind...' Well, I thought my motion in July 1994 had been 'straight on'. But I had had no support then from David McLean, and I suspect he had voted against me.

An ecumenical discussion

Most of my other efforts have been challenging the scandalous retention of powers by Prime Ministers over the appointment of bishops, reported in Chapter 18. But the Churches Together in England (CTE) Forum in 1998 requested an ecumenical exploration of establishment 'in the context of the search for visible unity'. A Consultation on the subject followed on 30 November that year. I was not part of it – perhaps unsurprisingly. I assume the Church of England representatives were chosen to keep a common front – harbouring disestablishmentarians is as ecumenically embarrassing as is harbouring favourers of lay presidency. Such un-Anglican manifestations need to be concealed. Philip Mawer, the secretary-general, reported the Consultation to Synod members in a memorandum (SecGen(99)1). He was silent on who had represented us, but wonderfully reassuring with:

> The thrust of these [recent newspaper articles] is wrong – the Church is not moving, secretly or otherwise, towards disestablishment.

> The object was to try to clarify the facts surrounding both the reality and perception of the Church of England's established status.

> While views both critical and supportive ... were certainly expressed, the Consultation did not explore disestablishment, nor ways of loosening ... ties with the Crown and the State.

> The [Archbishops'] Council discussed the recent press coverage ... and wishes to make it clear that:

(1)   no significant proposal for change ... could emerge ... without wide consultation which would include the Synod;

(2)   neither Government nor Synod ... has called for such a change. Indeed ... Synod voted firmly against change;

(3)   service to the nation is at the forefront of the Church's mission.

Synod members, unable to sleep through fear of being sold into being a sect by their leaders, could now sleep happily in their beds again.

The 2000s

In the new Synod of 2000, the appointment of bishops was already coming before General Synod from both Southwark and the Perry Commission, so I put down a simple Private Member's Motion:

That this Synod desire that the Church of England should be free of Parliamentary control by Measure, and should only live under the law of the land as other religious bodies do, and to this end ask the Archbishops' Council to initiate the steps requisite to obtain that freedom.

It got nowhere, lapsing through lack of signatures after 12 months. But, like my 1994 proposal, it enshrined a principle which is almost as important to me as disestablishment itself – that is, that all such proposals should come *from us*. Self-respecting colonies in the days between 1946 and 1966 *negotiated their own freedom*, and were not simply cast loose. The very procedure of legislation by Measures devised in Synod gives us, the colonized, the opportunity to set the process in hand; and we would then find ourselves in negotiation with Parliament before the legislation went into unchangeable form – and we dared them to say 'no' to it! But it would be grim simply to be cast loose by a Tony Benn kind of move or by a Liberal Democrat deal with another party in a coalition. We have to make a start ourselves.

A most extraordinary feature of my time has been the ever-growing complacency. In 1970, three members of the Chadwick Commission dissented in favour of full disestablishment. Would they even get put on such a Commission today? The two most recent defenders of the establishment – John Moses in *A Broad and Living Way*, and Paul Avis in *Church, State and Establishment* – totally disregard any contrary arguments.[16] Reading them, we might conclude there is no case against; they serenely roll out a one-sided commendation of

227

that which has been, is, and presumably ever shall be.[17] A new Commission seems a desperately remote hypothesis – until 1970 Church and State Commissions came at average intervals of 18 years, but twice that time has elapsed since 1970 without official proposals. Whatever happens in Church or nation, all rolls on undisturbed in an establishment which, on examination, is not only archaic but incredible, and, as Erastian, arguably heretical. But examining it is just what we do not do.

17

Political structures and the
Single Transferable Vote

The law of the Medes and the Persians, which cannot be revoked.
(Daniel 6.8,12,15)

Does our concern for God's righteousness have any bearing on our confronting the political structures of today?

In the Introduction I tell how I came across STV in Church elections, tested it and embraced it. I marched in this learning process with Peter Dawes, and we wrote a booklet to promote the case.[1] Our central thesis, obvious in itself but appallingly incomprehensible in a first-past-the-post atmosphere, was 'You cannot "split" a transferable vote.' Candidates of similar views can stand in an STV election without fearing they will split the vote and let in someone with the opposite views – and thus pressure upon people not to run 'lest you split the vote' is marvellously lifted.

It is very simple. A voter who can arrange ten preferences in order, numbering them '1' to '10', is clearly making an exact statement. It contrasts with the crudity of a vote in parliamentary elections, where I am simply 'for' this one and 'against' all others *equally* – even if the one I am 'for' has no chance. It is obvious at sight (see all United Kingdom general election results, most recently those declared five days before I write) that being 'for' one and 'against' all others simply vitiates the votes of all who plumped for a loser. If my vote goes to a no-hoper, I cannot influence the actual result – so I am under enormous pressure not to 'waste' my vote on the vegetarian or the Kilroy-Silk candidate, but to use it to help decide what purports to be a straight conflict between Tory and Labour. It is amazing that, in this climate of 'don't waste your vote', the Liberal Democrats, a third party, have scrambled up the vertical rock face, and have not only won 62 seats in the 2005 general election, but have become the credible contenders, running second, in dozens more constituencies, where they can themselves tell Tory or Labour supporters 'not to waste your vote'. In Scotland and Wales, where nationalist parties also win seats, four-way contests occur, and seats may be won with less than 30 per cent of the votes and, by almost random chance, *be won by the candidate most disliked by the electorate overall*. 'Tactical' voting in a three-way contest gives a fraudulent message, revealing the system not as giving true representation, but as one which, if accurately second-guessed, may permit damage limitation.[2] In a four-way contest it requires an accurate crystal ball (which, as a Christian, I do not expect to see) – hence the occasional success of the BNP in local elections. Fair voting needs a system which enables voters to express their preferences truly; and this implies multi-member constituencies, so that parties and persons are returned in accord with the true wishes expressed – and no one tries to beat the system, for it cannot be beaten.[3] A system which presses people not to run for election, and tells voters to favour some person or cause they do not want in order to 'keep this or that party out', is not only random and unrepresentative in its results, but has a deeper flaw still. It runs near the apostle's condemnation that we should not be 'doing evil that good may come'.

The Church of England was practising STV in electing the Church Assembly for 50 years before Synod was formed. Synod is elected by STV, and has slowly entrenched it for elections made by Synod to Boards and Councils, and for representation at WCC assemblies and other outside bodies. Apart from elections of prolocutors of the Convocations or chair of the House of Laity, the structures usually present multi-member constituencies, where representation can be properly proportionate – and where multiple *X*s (or, say, first-four-past-the-post) would multiply injustice. General Synod has also enforced it for certain purposes within diocesan synods.[4] So did we have a message for the politicians? In 1975 Peter Dawes tabled a Private Member's Motion:

> That this Synod believes that the time has come for a change in the present parliamentary voting system and urges all political parties to adopt a preferential system of proportional representation.

It was debated in February 1976. Everyone pulled the same end of the rope, not least Mervyn Stockwood, Bishop of Southwark, who graciously visited Synod, commented that it was good to discuss elections on St Matthias' Day,[5] and wonderfully, without any sense of self-contradiction, advocated *both* that the nation should adopt proportional representation *and* that Labour should gain power by it.[6] The motion was adopted overwhelmingly and the political parties were duly exhorted. But parties which have hoped, even through long periods in opposition, to gain or retain an overall majority in Parliament through the random inequitabilities of first-past-the-post voting have been slow to address the issue of fair means of representation.

The 1983 general election was extraordinary, though nearly matched by others since. Michael Foot provided the 'longest suicide note in history', and Margaret Thatcher glowed in the wake of her Falklands triumph. The upshot was ludicrous – Tories 42 per cent of the vote and 375 seats, Labour 27 per cent and 200, the Liberal–SDP alliance 25 per cent and 23. Quite apart from whether people had voted for their first preferences (see the discussion above re tactical voting), Margaret Thatcher vastly increased the Tories' seats simply because the opposition was split – and she gained 60 more seats with 600,000 less votes than in 1979. Labour had nine times as many seats as the Alliance because their votes were concentrated in winnable constituencies, and the Alliance voters were spread across the country. Never was a case for electoral reform made more eloquently (no, not even in 2005).[7] Peter Dawes, now an archdeacon, tabled another Private Member's Motion:

> That this Synod reaffirms the motion passed overwhelmingly in February 1976 'That this Synod believes that the time has come for a change in the present parliamentary voting system and urges all political parties to adopt a preferential system of proportional representation as a policy commitment for future public elections.'

The November 1983 debate repays reading verbatim. The Tory MP, Sir William van Straubenzee, opposed with a substantial speech, which played into the hands of the motion's supporters (and, following him, I deployed his material against him immediately). Peter Dawes made the best of a very good case. Synod duly endorsed it by 251–61.

Leaving aside my church, ministry and sacraments agenda, my major endeavours on behalf of a just society have been focused (along with my concern for the Church of England to be truly multi-ethnic) in promoting proportional representation by STV.[8] My concern for disestablishment has also inevitably had me wrestling with structures of government, and, when Tony Blair was elected in 1997 with a manifesto that undertook to review electoral systems and to reform the House of Lords, I regularly besought the BSR to make the constitution a major theme to bring before Synod. To such a question in November 1997 I received the reply that I could try a Private Member's Motion. In July 1999 I asked in Synod:

> At what point will the Archbishops' Council initiate for this Synod a debate on the reform of the House of Lords and other issues of current constitutional concern, including the implications for England of devolution to Scotland and Wales, the establishment of a London Assembly and regional instruments, and issues of justice in forms of representation?

I might well have added voting in European elections and the (appalling) party list system. I was answered that there were no such plans, but I could table a Private Member's Motion. In November 1999 I asked a similar question and was again told I could table a Private Member's Motion. In February 2000 I abandoned questions and spoke in the debate on the agenda. We now had an outline of future business and were promised a debate on the constitution in July. I explained why I still rejected the Private Member's Motion idea: first, because in an established Church the lead in such things should come from the leadership of the Church, and, secondly, because we needed a serious and authoritative document brought before us (and I could now add in references to the Wakeham Report also[9]). But perhaps, with the promise of a debate in July, we would now get such a document? Pete Broadbent, running the business, promised: 'The document will be a composite one . . . It does need all of us to be involved in generating our response to the major issues of constitutional change in our society.' But no such document appeared, and all we had was, in July 2001 (a year later), the Private Member's Motion on bishops in the Lords, which I discuss in the next chapter. Not only was this narrow in its constitutional concern, but its narrowness looked simply like a defence of Church of England vested interests. We were light-years from serious consideration of the constitution by the BSR. Meanwhile the Jenkins Report on electoral reform had come and gone, and we, the established Church, with our own fingers in our practice deep into forms of fair representation, had not even noticed it synodically.[10] In that debate on bishops in the Lords, I stated we were having the wrong debate; and Michael Perham, chair of the Business Committee, responded. He said that after each call like mine 'there has been applause . . . It seems likely therefore that we shall come back with a proposal before too long for a general debate' – not exactly a promise, but very near one.

The BSR finally produced in November 2002 a bland toothless resolution supporting democracy and urging citizens to take a responsible part in it. It contained no critique or proposal for change of anything in the constitution (apart from condemning 'party list' elections). The BSR simply wanted us 'to have a good debate'. The debate stuttered that November, and was adjourned till February 2003. Edmund Marshall of Wakefield moved an amendment to call upon the parties to adopt proportional representation. I moved an amendment to his (one which he resisted) to specify that it was by STV that proportional representation should be sought, and the Synod carried it – against the tepidity of the chairman of the Board, my diocesan, Tom Butler, moving the main motion. We then passed by 226–6 (including the amendment, shown here in italics):

> That this Synod, concerned at the fall in voter turnout at elections and at the perceived marginalization of Parliament in the nation's political processes,

(a)   recognize the role of the print and broadcast media in shaping public attitudes to political discourse, and urge the media to exercise responsibility in the performance of their function;

(b)   call upon Her Majesty's Government and leaders of the main political parties

    (i)   to work together to enhance the effectiveness of our parliamentary institutions;

    (ii)   to encourage and enable, by legislative and administrative action, *and especially by introducing proportional representation by the single transferable vote for elections to Parliament,* all members of our society to play a full part in our democracy;

    (iii)   to abandon the use of the closed party list election system; and

(c)   to affirm the value of public service as an important part of Christian witness, commend such service as a Christian vocation, and call upon dioceses, deaneries, parishes and our ecumenical partners to support that vocation with prayer and practical action.

I called it 'toothless' in the form in which it came from the BSR. I simply cannot comprehend why political structures had been treated as such a low priority (in breach of the promise reported above). But the floor of the Synod had now inserted real teeth. One can only hope that our Church leaders are now properly pushing this almost unanimous call for justice in representation upon our political leaders.

Since the 2005 election the case has been reinforced. While one cannot be sure, because electors may vote 'tactically', that all votes cast expressed people's first preferences, yet the actual distribution of votes had no resemblance to the outcome in seats – and the media and the public know it, and have been vocal in exposing the injustice done to the electorate by the crudities of the system. There is a proper Christian call for justice in representation, which the Church of England, being ourselves both leading practitioners of STV and guardians of a conscience for justice, must press hard into the future.

18

The appointment of diocesan bishops

Lord . . . show us which one of these two you have chosen.

(Acts 1.24)

Should Downing Street and the Crown have any say in the appointment of our leaders?

How should a Christian Church appoint its own leaders? Or, to narrow the focus to the Church of England, is there a case that a Christian Church should appoint its own leaders? It seems extraordinary to say that these questions do not matter, yet that appears to be the stance of most of the Church of England most of the time; and bishops themselves are rarely in the vanguard of reform. Is it possible that, as with much of the Labour and Tory approaches to electoral reform ('there cannot be much wrong with a system which elected me'), so our bishops have largely concluded that a system which made them bishops must itself be right. This, of course, would be justifying the means by results, which is both perilous (indeed immoral[1]) as a procedure – and also depends upon taking the results as good without further scrutiny.

So how does the Church of England get its diocesan bishops? I restrict myself to diocesans, noting that suffragans are chosen by diocesans who then delegate powers and roles to them.[2] And from Henry VIII's Ecclesiastical Appointments Act of 1534, still largely in force, these are the legal steps followed:

1. A vacancy occurs, and the monarch names and announces the new bishop.

2. The monarch commands the Greater Chapter (changed in very recent years to the College of Canons) of the cathedral of the vacant diocese to 'elect' her named candidate. They meet and do so.

3. Following the election, the legal officers of the province hold a 'confirmation', at which the bishop-elect appears in person, and, being confirmed, actually becomes legally the bishop of the diocese.

4.   The new bishop, if he has not already been consecrated, is consecrated by the archbishop of the province, acting on a royal mandate.

5.   The new bishop pays homage, swearing he receives the 'spiritualities' as well as the 'temporalities' solely from the monarch.

6.   The archbishop issues a mandate for enthroning the bishop in his cathedral, and the enthronement (it may have another name) duly takes place.

Granted that Henry's law is still in force (with minor changes), a series of preceding conventions has been added to produce a name to be submitted to the monarch for her to nominate. In the eighteenth century Prime Ministers started to advise the monarch. In the twentieth century, the Prime Minister's appointments secretary started to keep files and enable the name to 'emerge' (though it was conventional to consult with archbishops). Then, after the Howick Report in 1964, each vacant diocese had a vacancy-in-see committee appointed, to draw up a description of the diocese and, up to a point, a profile of the kind of bishop it needed, and the Prime Minister's appointments secretary would consult with leading persons in the diocese. At Stage 1 in the order above, the name of the man 'chosen' by the monarch has for many years been announced (as it still is) from 10 Downing Street. The role of the Prime Minister is not only overt – it is one which has never abashed the occupant. As things stood in 1970, only one name was ever heard, that is, the name of the one man to be appointed bishop. This name was undisputed, no other names were known – with a little imagination it could even be taken to be the choice of God. On the other hand, the one man was sent to his diocese by royal command, and, apart from the mockery of the police-state kind of 'election', the incoming bishop would have received no positive indication that anyone in the diocese actually wanted him. And the Prime Minister, who was personally advising the monarch, did not have to be a Church of England member, or Christian at all, to qualify for selecting bishops: to be the leader of the majority party in the Commons was sufficient. Some did not even represent English constituencies.[3]

So how can we reform the system?

The Chadwick Report, *Church and State 1970*, addressed this Tudor anachronism with a wonderful and rare anti-establishment analysis:

> Previous Commissions suggested that disquiet [*sc* in other Churches] was the result in some measure of ignorance of the extent to which the Church is consulted under the present system. But ... the impression we form today is that those who are disquieted and

uneasy are usually aware of the main features ... and that more detailed information often tends not to diminish but to increase their disquiet.[4]

It had two different proposals for reform.

Proposal A, favoured by the more cautious half of the Commission, was for the creation of a Church Advisory Committee. This half was prepared to defend the procedure they inherited, as 'the Prime Minister is not a free agent in this matter.'[5] No, he was subject to six important safeguards. They then listed five (had they lost one at proof?) – and all were totally jejune: public opinion is against the misuse of patronage; the candidate must already be a priest; the archbishop approves a small list first; the dean and chapter have to elect the candidate; and other bishops have to share in consecrating him. As safeguards these hardly amount to a row of beans, yet the eight proponents conclude: 'it is difficult to understand how ... the exercise of the present system can be regarded as other than a choice by the Church.' Nevertheless, they girded themselves to improve it, and their Committee was to have the two archbishops, six other members of General Synod (one bishop, two clergy and three lay people), and five from the vacant diocese – the dean or provost ex officio and then four (two clergy, two laity) appointed by the vacancy-in-see committee. This Committee would 'propose two or more names for submission to the Prime Minister'. The proposal then went on:

> As the State came to have confidence in the representative organs of the Church, it might become customary, as it has become customary in the case of suffragan bishops, for Prime Ministers to submit the first of a number of names submitted to them.[6]

After names had been sent to the Prime Minister, he would submit one to the monarch and the Tudor legislation would then be followed.

Proposal B, favoured by the five more adventurous members of the Commission plus (if driven to the choice) the three who dissented from the whole report in favour of total disestablishment, wanted a direct Church election, without any participation by the Prime Minister. They concluded that a diocesan electoral body would be too narrow in membership, and a provincial one too impracticable to implement, though it was 'in theory the system which ... gives most apt expression to the desire of Church people to participate in responsibility for choice of their chief pastors'. So they proposed an electoral board, almost identical in membership to the Church Advisory Committee outlined under Proposal A. But the powers were to be quite different – in effect this board would *appoint*, not just shortlist. This adventurous five cheerfully wrote:[7]

> We find it difficult to believe that nowadays the State, in the person of the Prime Minister . . . has any great interest, as a matter of public concern, in appointments to diocesan bishoprics, *even though the bishop in question may in due course take his place in the House of Lords.**

They were ready to keep the monarch in the loop, and, acknowledging that constitutional procedure would not allow names to come to the monarch except from the Prime Minister, yet proposed to change that ('the British constitution has proved remarkably adaptable'). It was fundamental that the Prime Minister must be excised from the process for the following reasons:

(1) It is inappropriate in the context of modern England.

(2) It offends some members of the Church.

(3) It helps to identify the Church with the (colloquial) 'establishment'.

(4) Reunion with anyone is impossible unless it ceases.

(5) We see no reason to think that other systems would not work well.

That, we might remind ourselves, came from half the Commission, over 35 years ago.

Chadwick in Synod – and with the politicians

Synod came to this one slowly. Worship and Doctrine came before it. But there were two major debates on the appointment of bishops. The first came in February 1973, and Eric Kemp, then Dean of Worcester, moved that Standing Committee should bring forward proposals 'to secure for the Church a more effective share' in appointing bishops. The role of the Prime Minister was criticized very strongly by eminent speakers – both on principle and with hints about results.[8] The Earl of March, one of the Proposal B righteous five, strengthened it with an amendment that the proposals should be such as 'to enable the Synod to decide whether or not . . . the final choice should in its view rest with the Church'. The amended motion was passed.

At the final debate in July 1974, Norman Anderson moved on behalf of Standing Committee:

* The italics are, of course, mine. Note the point and keep reading.

That the General Synod

(i) affirms the principle that the decisive voice in the appointment of diocesan bishops should be that of the Church;

(ii) believes that, in arrangements to effect this, it would be desirable that a small body, representative of the vacant diocese and of the wider Church, should choose a suitable person for appointment to that diocese and for the name to be submitted to the Sovereign;

(iii) instructs the Standing Committee to arrange for further consideration of these matters ... and to report the results to Synod in due course.

The words 'the decisive voice' were a good marker put down. Various reactionary amendments were seen off, and Norman Anderson rode home in triumph by 270–70.

What was sought was a convention, not legislation. So the incoming Archbishop of Canterbury, Donald Coggan, was asked by Standing Committee to accompany Norman Anderson to Downing Street and seek Harold Wilson's agreement. Wilson brought in Margaret Thatcher (by 1975 leader of the Opposition) and Jeremy Thorpe, leader of the Liberals. By the time an answer came in 1976, Jim Callaghan was Prime Minister. The answer revealed that in essence the politicians had beaten down our two suppliants (who may have yielded too quickly). Jim Callaghan answered a contrived parliamentary question from Margaret Thatcher on 8 June 1976, and we learned it as parliamentary business:

There are ... cogent reasons why the State cannot divest itself from a concern with these appointments of an established Church. The Sovereign must be able to look for advice on a matter of this kind and that must mean, for a constitutional Sovereign, advice from Ministers. The archbishops and some of the bishops sit by right in the House of Lords, and their nomination must therefore remain a matter for the Prime Minister's concern. [But we can have some changes, with the Church having a greater say.]

So the monarch's role was undisturbed, the Prime Minister's right and duty to advise her was entrenched, and, because some bishops were going to the Lords, the Prime Minister's discretion was non-negotiable. But, he (and the other political leaders) would settle for a Church commission, like the Chadwick proposals, which would forward two names to him (and he could return them and ask for more).

Norman Anderson reported this deeply compromised answer of Jim Callaghan to Synod in July. He insisted it was not 'half a loaf', and said, 'I myself have not gone back on the somewhat radical position which I took up in this building just two years ago.' He reported that ideas of bypassing Downing Street to get a name direct to the Crown were self-deceiving (William van Straubenzee still hoped archbishops would pass names to the queen at Privy Council meetings). Dismayed speeches recalled 'the decisive voice', which had clearly been sidelined. Amendments tried to view the Callaghan solution as temporary and up for renegotiation in the future – and Brian Brindley wanted to get the bishops out of the Lords and undercut the Callaghan argument – but Norman Anderson saw them off, and won 390–29. Rejecting his motion would have left us without even half a loaf. Passing it, we got exactly that.

Bishops in the Lords

Was Brian Brindley on to something? Do we have to fight to have bishops in the Lords? The defenders of the 26 Lords Spiritual (including many bishops) have reckoned their presence spoke symbolically, even when they themselves spoke neither a wise word, nor even any word. In fact they do better than that; and a side-benefit sometimes aired is that they, alone in the House, belong to an actual geographical area from which they can speak. (Do life peers, if they wish to take part in the Lords, start to gravitate towards London, leaving great tracts without a life peer of any sort?). However, the 26 bishops are there in a quite random geographical way, so this year there may be nobody from the South-west, in two years' time nobody from East Anglia and so on (and, of course, permanently no one from beyond Offa's Dyke). So, if the presence of the 26 has been highly valued by many apologists, is there a downside? I offer the following:

1. The queue to enter the Lords shortens the stay once there – Hugh Montefiore had but two years; while Peter Dawes never arrived (though Margaret Thatcher's nomination of him was grounded upon his future elevation).[9]

2. The business of the House is fixed only a short way ahead, while bishops have dates in their diaries a year or more ahead. This means that usually one bishop is on duty, and two or three more (mostly from round London) are summoned if needed. How many bishops does it take to change a regulation? Is it not an overkill to entrench 26 to ensure that one is always present?

3. The presence of bishops has precluded other Anglican persons from

sitting – regius professors, canons of Westminster, women, authors and theologians, distinguished persons of all sorts. What Anglican other than a bishop has ever gone to the Lords because of what his or her theological contribution might be?

4.   In any case, why should not bishops have been treated as dynastic peers rather than as life peers? Their presence in the Lords goes back to the days of the dynastics only, is a fixed corporate number, and far antedates the life peers arrangement. Prime Ministers do not pick dynasties.

5.   Or, suppose our negotiators had said to the politicians of 1975–6: 'Of course you can choose 26 bishops – just let us choose bishops originally, and you then choose to elevate whichever 26 you wish to the Lords, and pass over any you do not want.' This would have been comparable to the leader of the Opposition submitting a list of candidates for peerages, from which the PM would choose at his or her discretion.

See the end of this chapter for some thoughts on the reform of the Lords.

Appointing bishops, 1977–93

The system in use today then took shape. In November 1976 the composition of the Crown Appointments Commission (CAC) was agreed, and in February 1977 standing orders to elect to CAC three representatives of the Clergy and Laity were also agreed. One proposed standing order would have entrenched one place in each House for York province, and flawed the use of the STV. Michael Hodge, long-standing guardian of pure STV, tabled an amendment to eliminate the flaw. I said that, as a Northerner (two miles from the provincial border), under this standing order, I would give my higher preferences to Southern candidates, as a Northerner would get in anyway – however derisory his or her support.[10] Christian Howard (of York itself) dismissed me as a 'midlander' (sic), but Michael Hodge prevailed (159–128), and CAC was to be elected by unsullied STV.

So, CAC had to send two names to Downing Street, with a note of its votes for the first and second. For its first vacancy, Birmingham, it nominated Hugh Montefiore, who ought to have been a diocesan years before. Insofar as the system can be tested by results, it got off to a flying start. Jim Callaghan, having retained his 'discretion', never exercised it against the CAC's first choice. Perhaps the two names for diocesans were being treated just as the two names for suffragans were – viz. that an unbreakable convention meant number one would always be chosen. But that was not what the discretion entailed; and when Margaret Thatcher came in, she used her powers as she saw fit.[11]

From Synod's point of view we jump to February 1982. The workings of the CAC system were reviewed (but not the results of their work, the quality of bishops appointed); and David McLean, on behalf of Standing Committee, proposed the abolition of both the election by the dean and chapter and the confirmation ceremony (stages 2 and 3 in the order on pages 234–5). In a long-remembered phrase, he labelled them 'an expensive farrago of legal gobblydegook' – wherein the 'moment' of becoming bishop of one's diocese happens virtually behind closed doors. He proposed a single 'ceremony of record'; the archbishop of the province would preside, receive the monarch's nomination, and thereupon publicly make the candidate the bishop of his diocese.

I moved an amendment to keep the election by dean and chapter (which would have left the ceremony of record to replace the confirmation nonsense). My thesis was: 'The whole system of appointment of bishops ... is incredible, theologically without defence, and up for abolition and change ... and we do not do ourselves any good turn by trying to make it marginally credible.' I compared the proposals to digging up the *Mary Rose* from Portsmouth harbour (then recent), and putting an outboard motor on it to make it go. The Synod enjoyed the illustration, but, of course, turned down the amendment (perhaps over one-third supported me). Other amendments were lost, and the historical nonsenses of 'election' and 'confirmation' were apparently doomed.

In November 1982 David McLean moved The Appointment and Resignation of Bishops Measure.[12] I had another go. I quoted Douglas Brown in *Church Times*: 'the end of one of the most blasphemous relics of the Henrician Establishment, the flummery of the "final" election.' I deployed another analogy – suppose hanging (actually abolished two decades before) was a blasphemy, and we dealt with it by abolishing the Black Cap? That was the kind of proposal before us – the 'blasphemy' lay in Margaret Thatcher's 'discretion':

> The real issue ... is not whether the nakedness of monarchical appointment ought to be faintly concealed behind the marionette show of election by dean and chapter, or ought to be thoroughly revealed by the abolition of the dean and chapter. The real issue ... is whether appointment by the monarch, and thus by the Prime Minister, ought to be tolerated at all.

I also asked whether, in a Measure with 'Appointment of Bishops' in its title, I could move an amendment to alter radically how the appointment was made. David McLean replied that that would be *ultra vires* for the Synod. General Approval was granted.

I picketed Standing Committee about this bizarre response that addressing the method of appointing bishops was *ultra vires* in a Measure about the appointment of bishops. They conceded that it was not *ultra vires*, and so, at the Revision Stage in February 1983, I moved the addition of an enabling clause: 'It shall be lawful for the General Synod to provide by Canon for the appointment of diocesan bishops.'

This was arguably a total revolution – for the power the Church of England did not have (and does not have) is to make rules about appointing its bishops. No such Canons exist. Yet it was not precipitate, for Synod could work at any speed at the kind of Canon it would like. It was chewed up by David McLean, not on principle, but with the words: 'It is frankly naive to suppose that Parliament would ever give us carte blanche in that form' – in other words, we are captive and *must not even seek to be free.* (No one then knew what Parliament was going to do to *his* clauses.) A motion that my question should not be put was passed. The Measure proceeded, and in July 1983 triumphed at Final Approval (22–0; 101–5; 110–3). I was among those five clergy.

But then it went pear-shaped. After the 1983 election Margaret Thatcher took a little while to appoint an Ecclesiastical Committee. They had to meet, declare the Measure expedient, and find time for it in the Lords and Commons. It ultimately went to the Commons on 16 July 1984 – and it was defeated there around midnight 17–32 (with around 600 absentees). The speeches against rather suggested there were MPs irate about the appointment of David Jenkins to Durham, though he had been 'elected' by the dean and chapter of Durham on Her Majesty's nomination, and retaining such elections was unlikely to block unwanted appointments. So elections and confirmations would continue – the result I sought, provided by a means I deplored, though fostering a provocation that I welcomed.

In November 1984 I questioned the secretary-general whether votes in the Commons could be secured for Measures sent from Synod. As I anticipated, he replied 'no'. So when, in February 1985, Standing Committee asked us to resubmit the Measure, I pointed out that I had never wanted the Measure, that (as in 1927–8) Parliament might take offence at it being sent to them a second time unchanged, and that, if we counted our troops (as in the Bible), we might decide not to go back. Standing Committee's motion was lost 16–16; 66–114; 99–84. The *congé d'élire* and the confirmation remain to this day – unchanged witnesses to the absolute powers of the monarch (and, er, of the Prime Minister).

Experience in practice

At this point my practical experience of making appointments began – and reinforced my objections of principle. From early 1985, I experienced, as a senior member, vacancies in four successive dioceses in 14 years.* I was three times on vacancy-in-see committees, though never on CAC. I have briefed CAC members, and debriefed their leaks; and I have had interviews with the two appointments secretaries doing their rounds (in Birmingham I lined up the great and the good to meet them†) – and have evaluated what I experienced. I remain deeply unconvinced; supposed confidentiality has been breached; CAC has nominated people it has not met; and totally inadequate references have been provided. Four diocesan representatives have been insufficient to be representative. And in Birmingham, when Margaret Thatcher refused in 1987 to nominate Jim Thompson, placed number one on the list almost unanimously by the CAC, she displayed a shameless and unaccountable use of her Erastian powers.[13] The situation was exposed by great breaches of confidentiality (which I as suffragan had to avow in public were unthinkable), and by further claims that various people both on and off the CAC had had private access to Margaret Thatcher to influence her choice. My opposition to Downing Street's powers was a principle which far anteceded my experience, but the actual experience was hardly calculated to soften my adherence to the principle. It was a paradoxical further factor in that Birmingham mêlée that the man on whom her choice fell was probably the only suffragan in the land who had been in print opposing both that very power she was exercising and our spineless connivance with it.

Still I lived with the system; and in those, for me, recurrent vacancies I developed my personal responses:

1. During each vacancy I moved a motion in the diocesan synod to remove Downing Street and the Crown from the process. During a vacancy this could not refer to any actual bishop – but simply opposed the system. In Southwell (1985), Birmingham (1987) and Rochester (1994) the motion was debated as I requested, and I lost each by around 40–48. In the fourth, Southwark (1998), it came out differently, and I report it below.

2. I attended three of the four *congés d'élire* to which I was summoned. I

* I chalk up that, living through 4 vacancies, I had 8 different diocesan bishops in those 14 years: Denis Wakeling and Michael Whinney (Southwell), Hugh Montefiore and Mark Santer (Birmingham), Michael Turnbull and Michael Nazir-Ali (Rochester), and Roy Williamson and Tom Butler (Southwark). Is this a record?
† Michael Kinchin Smith, who was then the Archbishop's adviser, told me that, when the two secretaries met a cluster of Birmingham city councillors whom I had lined up, they asked what the councillors would look for in a new Bishop of Birmingham. 'Why, a born-again Christian, of course,' came back from a (West Indian) woman Pentecostalist – one wonders how often the secretaries were so answered. Later, when they met black Anglicans, the group they were meeting started by asking if they were going to open with prayer – and Michael gently evened the score by saying firmly at the end, 'Now we will all hold hands and say the grace together.' I wonder how many of his successors have ventured anything similar.

first attempted to get the chapters to adjourn without voting. Having failed in this, I then voted against Her Majesty's nominee (even if a friend of mine) – and twice got just one other voter to join me. Votes in favour (being coerced by Her Majesty the Queen) could hardly be viewed as supportive, but as merely legally compliant, so votes against could hardly be viewed as hostile to the nominee, but only as treasonable resistance to Her Majesty to defy her powers.

3. When the new bishop's name had been announced, I moved a motion of welcome in the diocesan synod – an invented synodical step which the system had not contemplated, one in which, as the mover, I could publicly express personal support.

There is reason to think John Major also on occasion chose number two on the CAC's list, while Tony Blair in respect of Liverpool in 1996–7 exercised a reserve power and sent both names back and asked for more.

Synodical flurries, 1990–99

Brian McHenry attempted a Private Member's Motion in the early 1990s to reform the election and confirmation ceremonies, rather hoping this could be done without legislation. Vain hope – the attempt ran gently into the sand, and the ceremonies continue little affected to the present day. And, as I have already made clear, I am in favour of keeping the Tudor package entire until it can be superseded entire, and I do not want to see it made intelligible, viable, or even just credible at all.

I asked Robert Runcie in January 1991, at his last Synod as Archbishop of Canterbury (and only two days before his retirement), whether he would advise his successor to reopen the nature of the convention with the political leaders, following the departure of Margaret Thatcher. There were now none of the three party leaders who had agreed the original convention in 1976 still leading their parties, and it was therefore the right time to go again and attempt to negotiate 'the decisive voice'. Robert Runcie replied that the politicians concerned had not negotiated as individuals but 'by virtue of their offices'. He therefore declined to advise his successor. For my part I think a convention can always be revisited (or it becomes hidebound), and this one was in any case far more the outcome of individual negotiators than Robert Runcie was allowing.[14]

In February 1993 Synod debated the report *Senior Church Appointments*. This did not relate to diocesan bishops, but to other senior appointments. However, it did invoke the Calcutt Opinion. Sir David Calcutt, QC, offered as an opinion that Crown appointments could be made without names going through Downing

Street – by the theoretical expedient of passing names to the Queen at Privy Council meetings. It was not irrelevant that the Commission, which took seven years over its report, was chaired by one Sir William van Straubenzee.[15] The Calcutt Opinion was seen off smartly by John Habgood, who recalled that Prime Ministers have no discretion in appointing suffragan bishops anyway, so he suspected within the airing of the unnecessary Calcutt Opinion there must be some hidden agenda. As head of state, the monarch must receive advice from her constitutional adviser alone, 'and I therefore urge the Synod to stop wandering around in this particular minefield and concentrate instead on some of the helpful remarks made elsewhere in the report.'

I had already tabled my Private Member's Motion, reported in Chapter 16, and I urged in this debate that diocesan bishops should not be handled separately from others. (I also enjoyed the rare occasion of agreeing with John Habgood.) In November 1993, I started writing *Cut the Connection*; my Private Member's Motion stood near the top of the list; and I also slipped in a logical point in the debate on the Episcopal Ministry Act of Synod, about the clause guaranteeing no discrimination in respect of views on the ordination of women in appointment to senior office:

> I find it very odd that the Act attempts to bind the Prime Minister who makes a lot of these senior appointments ... I do not see the force of it if we do not bind him, and I do not see how we can bind him if we do want to bind him.

The point was lost on thin air. No one attempted to answer it.

So we came to the July 1994 debate on my two-pronged Private Member's Motion to reduce the powers still adhering to the political institutions. My book was published just before the debate. I was given a reasonable crack. And the forces of reaction or indifference prevailed again (see Ch. 16). How could the matter be restarted?

It came about in an extraordinary way. The historian Tim Yates, summoned as an honorary canon to the *congé d'élire* to elect the new Bishop of Derby in 1996, found himself in a ceremony which stretched his, perhaps innocent, credulity to breaking point. He sought the backing of the chapter and brought a Private Member's Motion to Synod to seek a reform. His initial form of words would have transferred the election to the CAC, but he learned that this would take the process round in a circle (for the CAC's part comes before the constitutional part, and the election is near the end of it), so instead he proposed:

> That this Synod request the Standing Committee to introduce

amending legislation to end the present cathedral chapter elections of bishops as a Tudor anachronism which has become offensive to democratic and Christian conscience; and to initiate a new method of consultation with chapters within the existing procedures represented by the Crown Appointments Commission and the vacancy-in-see processes.

While his motion awaited its turn, in February 1998 I asked a question of George Carey about reforming the apppointment of bishops. He replied he was open to a review 'so long as it took place within the framework agreed . . . in 1976'. Then came:

Supplementary Question: Why is the Archbishop so content with the 1976 framework?

Ans: In short, we are the Established Church . . .

George Carey was here saying: (a) being established of itself is the warrant for doing things the way we do; (b) we do not therefore need to consider any other merits or demerits of a particular process; and (c) it is impossible to consider better ways. Establishment to him meant keeping the chain at exactly its present length. He has since said in his memoirs, that way back in 1990, before accepting the appointment as Archbishop of Canterbury, he himself asked Robin Catford, the Downing Street appointments secretary, for assurance that he was number one on the CAC list.[16] This action, honourable before God and his Church, actually betrays deep distrust of the Erastian system (and/or of Margaret Thatcher – making her last appointment). He was not only, in his own person, showing distrust of the 1976 agreement; he was also taking an action which, if imitated by everyone who was offered a diocesan bishopric, would demolish the system. Robin Catford should surely have declined to tell him. Or is it that, although he answered George Carey, he would have refused all others?[17] But I wish now that I had had George Carey on the record to this effect when I asked my supplementary in February 1998.

Tim Yates's motion was debated in July 1998. It was deflected by a substantive amendment from Standing Committee, moved by a smooth establishmentarian, Sir Timothy Hoare. Synod, he argued, should forget reform by legislation, but simply provide a comprehensive review of the existing procedures. I sought to supplement his amendment, with the review to include consideration

of the repeal of Henry VIII's legislation of 1533, substituting therefor power of this Synod to make Canons providing for the appointment of diocesan bishops by a Church process which does not involve the Crown, the Prime Minister or any other features of the state apparatus.

I think I made a good speech. I ended with my illustration of 14 years before (a fairly safe interval in Synod):

> Canon Yates has come to urge us to abolish the Black Cap. That is entirely understandable, though I do not agree with him while hanging persists. Sir Timothy Hoare invites us to inspect the Black Cap. I propose to abolish hanging.

I was duly seen off ('This not the moment . . . the Church in time will gain much of what Bishop Colin is seeking'). Sir Timothy's amendment was carried; and Bishop Mark Santer then intervened, urging of all things that the *Church* factor – i.e. the farcical *congé d'élire* – should be strengthened. This was the motion passed:

> that this Synod . . . request the Standing Committee to institute a review of the constitution and methods of operation of the Commission, the review to include consideration of the operation of the Vacancy in See Committees Regulation [and Timothy Yates's concerns].

Standing Committee established a weighty working party under Baroness Pauline Perry.

The Perry Report and Southwark, 1999–2002

I picketed this working party, and finally appeared before it. I urged them to break their terms of reference and revert to Synod's affirmation of '*the* decisive voice' in 1974, which had never been honoured. However, I also sent a detailed memorandum about what could be done within their terms of reference. But meanwhile my motion originally intended for Southwark diocesan synod in March 1998 (see page 243) had been delayed by the Bishop's Council until July 2000 (which gave me the slight embarrassment of moving it in front of my own bishop, Tom Butler, who had then been in office for two years!). It ran:

> that this Synod seek a reform in the method of appointing diocesan bishops in the Church of England so as to detach the process from any involvement with Downing Street and the monarchy, and to provide for a more participatory and open Church procedure than is currently possible.

This passed by 66–30 (though Provost – now Dean – Colin Slee opposed it), and was forwarded to General Synod.

The Perry Report, *Working with the Spirit: Choosing Diocesan Bishops*, was published in early 2001, and was debated in July 2001.[18]

On procedures of the CAC (and subsidiary functions, such as the keeping of records and the processes of vacancy-in-see committees), it contained much obvious sense, including that proper references should be required, notifying people that they were shortlisted, and asking for statements from them. It even included debriefing of those shortlisted but not appointed.[19]

On election and confirmation ceremonies, it included an extraordinary – indeed mind-blowing – attempt to take them seriously as part of a responsible and even theologically appropriate process. The Howick Commission in 1964 had reckoned they were a farce; the Chadwick Commission in 1970 had thought them a farce (but abolishing them not within their projected reform); the Synod had voted in 1983 almost unanimously for their abolition as a farce (save for COB, for reasons stated on page 242); Brian McHenry had campaigned against confirmation as a farce; Tim Yates had wished to abolish the election as a farce; and, out of the blue, Perry and co. were saying, with brilliant special pleading, that these ceremonies made theological sense and should be maximized. Even Michael Nazir-Ali's theological appendix says, in effect, 'The participation of four from the vacant diocese in CAC is insufficient; and the election by the College of Canons bolsters the diocesan involvement.' To emphasize their point they wanted CAC renamed the Crown Nominations Commission – perhaps leaving room for the fantasy notion that the College of Canons does the appointing. I opposed the change.

Was the Southwark motion now to be an amendment to Perry motions? This would have brought together all debate on the appointment of bishops, but would have been complicated within too little time, and (from my point of view) I would not be able to reply to the debate. So Perry came on in July 2001, and the debate endorsed much of the thrust of the report, and asked the Archbishops' Council to bring forward recommendations for actual change. Southwark waited in the wings.

In November 2001, Synod's scheduled business one morning suddenly evaporated and brought on the Southwark motion. I had been warned, and was prepared, but Synod generally was not. It started well, not least because David McLean, after about 30 years of magisterial caution, finally championed the change. George Carey, responding off the cuff, was slightly wrong-footed. I had drawn attention to Michael Nazir-Ali's 4,000-word theological appendix to Perry, which contained only one passing mention of the Prime Minister (it simply said 'he chooses' without justifying it). 'Theological principles' which he was discussing did not, and could not, relate to Prime Ministerial roles! Michael Nazir-Ali himself then spoke, re-emphasizing his theological points, *and did not mention the Prime Minister or the Crown at all.* But Synod's unease at not being ready led to an adjournment to July 2002.

In July 2002 it went wrong. We left the world of theology and reason and entered an Anglican cloud-cuckoo-land of romance and sentiment – with several, not least Michael Turnbull, insisting that lengthening the chain in any way at all would bring about disestablishment. Christopher Herbert, Bishop of St Albans, denounced the motion as 'smoke and mirrors' – an amazing metaphor, as the arcane operations of monarchical appointments are much smokier and involve distorting mirrors. Most vocal of all was Colin Slee: 'This is the Golden Jubilee of Her Majesty the Queen. By rejecting this motion, Synod has a golden opportunity of showing its loyalty far more potently than any unanimous vote for a Humble Address might do.' That is the cloud-cuckoo-land – retaining the Prime Minister's discretion pays tribute to a fine monarch. I have passed by here the role of monarchy in the establishment, but, I suppose, an occasion when the monarchy was not riding as high as in the Golden Jubilee euphoria might reverse this ludicrous argument. In reply I did poorly on the day in dismissing all these absurdities, the mood had swung, and I predictably lost the vote.

So we had to pick up the crumbs from Perry. In November 2002 we voted that the CAC should have eight diocesan members, should have proper references taken (at last), should notify persons they were being considered, and, on an amendment that went beyond Perry, should actually interview candidates. Some extraordinary, even Machiavellian, revisiting of the decision to have eight diocesan members in February and July 2003 brought the diocesan representatives down from eight to six. However, even the provision of six now provides a better range of diocesan opinion.[20] I have not had the opportunity to enquire whether the new figure was negotiated with the party leaders, or they were simply told that six would now roll up – or had Downing Street breathed somewhere that winter that if it were eight the deal was off, but six would be acceptable? David Hope, Archbishop of York, stated in Synod in July 2003 that the CAC was postponing introducing interviews. I wrote to him to protest that Synod's decision was being ignored, but got little change. Standing orders were amended, including the change of name to Crown Nominations Commission (CNC) – which I unsuccessfully opposed.

Confidentiality

Apart from the sheer Erastian powers exercised by Downing Street, a secondary issue has been that of confidentiality. The public never knows who nearly got a peerage, or who was runner-up in the New Year's Honours.[21] The appointment of bishops has the parallel fiction that one name emerges loud and clear and uncontroversial (the man of God's sole choice?). This was sustained into the CAC processes, and CAC members have all vowed not to reveal anything during their lifetime (though I have nevertheless picked up quite a bit).

The Perry factors sustain the myth of confidentiality while further weakening its credibility. If people are told they are being considered for a diocesan bishopric, will they be able to forget it – or will their view of themselves have been irretrievably altered? Will they mention it when approached about other posts? In writing references, how many people will know that this or that presbyter is being considered for a diocesan bishopric? How frequently will the references be updated? Will they never go any further? With six diocesan representatives, will they all keep mum in all circumstances? And, if they ever do interview candidates, will there never be anyone commenting on the propriety or fairness of his interview? These outcomes from the Perry process run a not insignificant risk of sowing the seeds of the system's destruction.

In the interests of their own recommendations, the Perry Report's authors commented adversely on open elections elsewhere in the Anglican Communion, and speeches on the Southwark motion cited some allegedly bad overseas examples. But bad must be compared with bad (and our system has plenty) and good with good, and a good (and open) system could well be found. Note the view of half the Chadwick Commission on page 236 (and I put forward an outline of a possible process in *Cut the Connection*). Should not the people of God participate widely and openly – and Downing Street not at all – in the choice of their leaders?

The reform of the House of Lords (and the place of bishops in it)

The Labour manifesto in 1997 promised a reform of the House of Lords. It was arguable before then that the Tories liked it as it was, as the dynastic peers gave them a built-in majority; and that Labour liked it as it was, because it had such weak actual powers. But New Labour was going to do something about it. The dynastics were quickly reduced to 92, elected among themselves (bizarrely, there is a by-election now when a dynastic peer dies and dynastics provide the only elected members of the House). So Tony Blair got to first base and stopped. He had, however, appointed the Wakeham Commission.

The Wakeham Commission, including Richard Harries, the Bishop of Oxford, reported in 2000, recommending the retention of 16 bishops (who might possibly not be bishops) and adding token numbers from other Christian denominations and non-Christian religions.[22] Presumably all other religious representatives would be appointed by their own bodies. But if the Anglicans

250

were not, or not all, bishops, how were they to be chosen? And if they were bishops, would not 16 in the queue mean few would exceed two-year stints? The result would be ludicrous for the Second Chamber, but it all, without mention, deeply undercut the Callaghan rationale for retaining the appointment at 10 Downing Street.

The General Synod Press Office issued a press release in the name of the Church of England (*tout simple*) with a response far different from mine. So I issued my own, questioning the figure of 25 million Anglicans and putting Wakeham alongside that Callaghan rationale (see page 238):

> under the Wakeham recommendations, every feature of that Parliamentary answer of Jim Callaghan would be negated:
>
> 1. No appointment to the Second Chamber would be political;
>
> 2. No appointment to the Second Chamber would be done by the Prime Minister [Wakeham had an independent Appointments Commission];
>
> 3. The Prime Minister, in accepting the recommendations [of Wakeham], must relinquish all such powers of patronage;
>
> 4. No bishop would be appointed to the Second Chamber simply as an automatic consequence of being a diocesan bishop, but the Church of England would make its own separate appointments to that Chamber.

In June 2000, the secretary-general, Philip Mawer, circulated a document, *Reform of the House of Lords* (GS 1385). This reviewed the position, declared the presence of bishops in the Lords (seeking 20 of them) to be almost non-negotiable, and stated that, 'The agenda for the July Group of Sessions includes provision for a debate on a take note motion about the report of the Royal Commission on the Reform of the House of Lords.' Yet no such debate came in the July 2000 Synod, nor any apology for its omission. The promises of debating the constitution were again honoured in the breach.

The government clearly disliked the Wakeham Report, and delayed action until after the June 2001 general election. Curiously, in July 2001 David Houlding moved a Private Member's Motion, calling upon the government to sustain the 26 bishops in the Lords. It was first business, due at 8.30 p.m. on the Friday night. I arrived at 4.30 p.m. and submitted an amendment to set aside any mere sectional interest in keeping bishops there, and instead to seek a far more representative Second Chamber. The secretariat said that four hours was not enough time and declined to duplicate the amendment, so I became a somewhat helpless participant in the wrong debate (though I got a cheer for saying it was the wrong debate). It was amended and passed 372–25:

> That this Synod call upon Her Majesty's Government, in the reform of the House of Lords, to ensure that provision fully adequate to enable bishops of the Church of England to contribute effectively to a reformed House be retained, and that members drawn from other Christian Churches and other faiths also be added to the composition of a new second chamber in our parliamentary democracy.

The 'drawn from' left questions open. In November 2001 came the government White Paper *The House of Lords – Completing the Reform*, and they marginally adapted the Wakeham recommendation and proposed a 20 per cent elected House, and sought responses to such a solution. In May 2002 came the joint Committee of Lords and Commons, assessing the responses. They proposed in December 2002 seven options for the composition of a reformed House, and recommended that Lords and Commons should each vote on each in turn. With seven options taken one at a time – oh for a transferable vote – none survived in the Commons in February 2003 (but the proposal for an 80 per cent elected House lost only by three votes). The Lords wanted no change! Far from completing the reform, the government seemed to have got stuck. They published a White Paper in September 2003, but these proposals would have consolidated the all-appointed character of the House, which evoked heavy opposition. In March 2004 the government called off the attempt. In 2006 there were rumours, but no more, that Tony Blair was coming round to an interest in a largely elected house.

I greatly prefer a largely elected House, but if faith constituencies are to have a reserved place, then the Church of England's representatives should be chosen by us – and episcopal membership and Prime Ministerial political patronage should be totally sundered from each other.

19

The Anglican Communion

Go therefore and make disciples of all nations.

(Matthew 28.19)

While the Church of England still has a pivotal role in international Anglicanism, how can we best serve that worldwide Communion?

Why should a General Synod buff – or the General Synod itself – care about a world beyond our borders? Well, being an Anglican Christian is the reverse of being a nationalist – we are by our calling internationalists. In my own life it has worked out in a dozen ways. Athletics with West Indians in the 1950s opened my eyes. Seeing a Pakistani Muslim converted at Oxford, and then a white Southern Rhodesian converted a year later, and within a fortnight sharing a room on a weekend houseparty with the Pakistani – that was the gospel passing into life. Hearing Trevor Huddleston as an undergrad, and then Martin Niemöller and Guy Clutton-Brock (deported from Southern Rhodesia for his anti-racist activities) in theological training, added to the picture. Being at college with overseas missionaries on furlough confirmed my internationalism. Being curate to an incumbent who had been a missionary in Israel also broadened my horizons (though I had to reject his premillennialism). Then, when I joined LCD staff in 1964, we had fine ordained men from East and West Africa doing further studies with us – not least Janani Luwum. By autumn 1966 I had a project to publish eucharistic liturgies of a single decade from the whole Anglican Communion (and the 1958 Lambeth Conference report was my bedtime reading – and people all around the world were becoming penfriends).[1]

Yet I was almost 40 when I first went overseas to minister (though I had been to Eire and Guernsey).* But since 1974 I have ministered in one way or another on all the continents and in 16 Anglican provinces (plus Sri Lanka) and in the Mar Thoma, Old Catholic and Porvoo Lutheran Churches. I was one of two Church of England participants in the 1984 Hartford, Connecticut, bicentenary of Seabury's consecration as the first overseas Anglican bishop.[2] During the 1990s

* I did a holiday *locum* in Guernsey in 1969–73 – and once met an ordinand there who had been advised at Selection Conference to 'get overseas experience'! So perhaps I was also overseas?

I wrote a fortnightly column in *Church Scene*, the Anglican weekly tabloid in Australia (now, sadly, defunct). During my exile (1989–91) I was approached about being nominated for election as bishop in three other Churches of the Anglican Communion – and was also approached about theological college principalships in two. I was a founder-member of the International Anglican Liturgical Consultations in 1985, have been at each Consultation since, and served on the IALC Steering Group from 1995 to 2001. In Africa, I have been at both the CAPA consultations on liturgy. I took part in the Lambeth Conferences of 1988 and 1998, and so shared in small groups with bishops from around the world. In 1988 I wrote up the work of a group on liturgy, and in 1998 I prepared the liturgical texts from round the world for the Conference worship. Old students of mine have reappeared as bishops at these Conferences also. In my 21 years with St John's College there were close links with Uganda, many arising from our engagement with Janani Luwum and our response to his martyrdom. In Birmingham we were twinned with Malawi (and I brought Desmond Tutu to us), in Rochester we were twinned with Harare (a link now sadly but inevitably ruptured), in Southwark my Area was twinned with Manicaland in Eastern Zimbabwe (I took a party of 20 there in 2001), and in Bradford we are twinned with northern dioceses in Sudan. In 1993 I applied to be secretary-general of the ACC; and over my last seven years as a stipendiary bishop I compiled a *Historical Dictionary of Anglicanism*, which the Scarecrow Press in the USA had commissioned, and have now published while this book has been in the press.[3]

The nature of the Anglican Communion is under severe investigation as I write, for the benefits of autonomous decision taking on a province-by-province basis, which I have lauded at the end of Chapter 1 in respect of the Church of England, have limitations. There are Christian bonds of interdependence, raising a question of how far one province can differ from another without disrupting the Communion, and what duty there is of mutual consultation as potential differences come into view. All that exploded into the public arena when Gene Robinson was consecrated as a bishop in the United States and the blessing of same-sex coupling was approved in Canada.

Over the years there have developed four agencies (often called 'instruments') of cooperation and unity, all of which, as agencies, have a servant and facilitatory role in the Communion, and none of which has actual powers over the provinces. In the order of chronological origins, they are:

1. The Archbishop of Canterbury

The pre-eminence in England of the Archbishop of Canterbury led naturally to Samuel Seabury requesting consecration from Archbishop Moore in 1783. Similarly the Canadian bishops looked to Archbishop Longley in 1865 to convene a conference of all Anglican bishops. New dioceses around the world have been set up under the Archbishop of Canterbury's metropolitical authority, and the position of the Archbishop has therefore been more and more deeply entrenched.* The Communion has been generally defined as 'Churches in communion with the see of Canterbury'. Thus the Archbishop of Canterbury is expected to convene Lambeth Conferences and Primates' meetings, technically at his own discretion, and is *ex officio* president of the ACC. All this would fall apart without him, yet he has few powers beyond England.

So need the Archbishop be British? The Australians pressed this strongly at Lambeth 1988, but I believe they were on to the wrong issue. It is obviously ludicrous that diocesan bishops in England have to have a British passport (as they are going to the House of Lords), and the occasional exception to that requirement ought to be possible (but of course is not), yet to internationalize the office of Archbishop of Canterbury would raise very serious problems. Firstly, it is doubtful whether it would be good for the Church of England, for there is quite a dose of inculturation needed to exercise leadership in England, let alone as Primate of all England. Who – apart from a certain Welshman – could step into that?[4] But, secondly, if the appointment were open to, say, the Archbishop of Uganda, then the message would be that he was assuming international powers – and the occupant would not only have great difficulties in his ministry in England, but would also elsewhere have impossible expectations heaped upon him. The Australians' attempts in 1988 in relation to Resolution 18 failed; how much better it would have been if they had called for the end of the role of the Prime Minister in the appointment of an Archbishop of Canterbury! The Archbishop comes into an office which has a strategic role internationally and he needs to be seen around the world as the true choice of the Church of England itself for that post, and not as that of the leader of the Tory or any other party in the Commons.[5] But that is my own angle.

Archbishops may occasionally have wished they had constitutional powers to prevent provinces elsewhere getting out of line with the rest of the Communion. However, it is not clear to me either how such powers could be defined, entrenched and exercised in common as between the different provinces, or whether in fact any Archbishop of Canterbury would want such powers, or would know when and how to exercise them anyway. The present Archbishop has made it very clear he does not desire them.[6]

---

* The Archbishop of Canterbury is still metropolitan to Bermuda, two dioceses in Sri Lanka, the Lusitanian and Spanish Reformed Churches in Portugal and Spain respectively, and both diocesan and metropolitan to the one (cathedral) parish in the Falkland Islands.

2. The Lambeth Conferences

Lambeth Conferences started in 1867 in response to the call of the Canadians for a coming together of Anglican bishops to adjudicate on the situation in South Africa, where Colenso, the Bishop of Natal, had been deprived for heresy, had appealed to the Judicial Committee of the Privy Council in London, and had been legally reinstated by them. Archbishop Longley convened a Conference; but he made a clear provision that it was only a 'conference', of bishops taking counsel with each other, and had no legislative or constitutional powers as an assembly (and, in his intentions, was to avoid discussing Natal!). Lambeth Conferences have continued on that principle ever since, that every ten years or so the Archbishop of Canterbury at his own discretion personally invites bishops of the Communion to join in conference with him. It is arguable that, until the ACC was formed in 1971, the only *definition* of the Anglican Communion was that it was a fellowship of dioceses whose diocesan bishops were invited by Archbishops of Canterbury to the Lambeth Conferences. This left the slippery notion of membership entirely to the Archbishop's discretion.[7]

Archbishops have exercised a more positive discretion about the character of Lambeth Conferences in different ways. Thus in 1968 Michael Ramsey invited theological consultants to the Conference (and they have been coming ever since). In 1978 Donald Coggan invented a parallel (and sleeping apart!) Wives' Conference (this continues, with more appropriate marital arrangements). In 1988 Robert Runcie invited the ACC (and they came again in 1998). And in 1998 George Carey included all the working suffragan and assistant bishops, of whom only an invited third had attended previously.

In 1988 that third of the Church of England's suffragan bishops amounted to 21 in all. In first place came the nine elected to the House of Bishops. Robert Runcie nominated me as one of the next twelve, and I was allocated to Section 3, Ecumenical Relations. However, I discovered that Section 1, Mission and Ministry, included liturgy. I wrote to John Habgood, who was leading the Church of England bishops, and asked to be put in the liturgy group – and he organized a transfer for me. So what was I to expect? The 1987 Blackheath Consultation of 45 planners (bishops, consultants and secretaries) produced around 25 pages of A4 for each of the four Sections. Just over one page treated Liturgical Renewal. In essence this said:

(a)   Worship is important;

(b)   The influence of the old BCP 'is waning';[8]

(c)   We must be ready for newer forms;

(d)   The centrality of the Eucharist leaves us with issues about 'word' services;

(e)   'We commend the appointment of a new International Anglican Liturgical Commission';[9]

(f)   There should be sharing of information between provinces, and production of guidelines for new writing of texts.

The section finished with three questions:

1.   Is the revival of 'passing the peace' in new liturgies an important symbol of what liturgical renewal is all about? How and why?

2.   The 1662 BCP and its derivatives in other provinces were once regarded as an essential ingredient of Anglican unity. What is its status in your Province today? What aspects of Anglican worship in your Province are signs of Anglican identity? How are the signs of transcultural unity related to the distinctive local flavour of worship?

3.   What is the nature and extent of non-eucharistic worship in your Province?

For a group to tackle liturgy, the above seemed thin preparation. Early in 1988 I wrote to Colin James, Bishop of Winchester and chairman of the Church of England Commission, asking whether we could or should do some drafting ourselves in preparation. He replied that this would be jumping the gun – we all had to start level (and, he almost hinted, with equally blank minds). At Lambeth, we did indeed start from scratch. We were well chaired by the youthful Roger Herft, a 37-year-old Sri Lankan who was a bishop in New Zealand, and has since been in Newcastle, NSW, and is now Archbishop of Perth. I became group secretary because, having come by car, I had my computer and printer with me and could therefore do the work. A growing fear I had had before the Conference now started to come true. Here were 600 bishops solving the world's problems without their office back-up, their chaplains, assistants or advisers, without books, resources, or access to libraries, many of them struggling with the language, the climate, the culture and dynamics of the Conference. They came naked – my word-processor represented a fig leaf.

After about two days of group discussion, I offered to run up something reasonably substantial overnight to start our thinking. They accepted this, and so our statement took shape. We remarked about 1662: 'But if we do not dwell on its strengths today it is because we judge its era is slipping irretrievably into

257

the past ... The presuppositions ... were of a static "Christendom" England.'[10] The word got around, a heavyweight Church of England consultant visited our group pretty quickly, obviously alarmed on behalf of 1662, and, I think, suspecting that I was manipulating the group. In reply, I looked across the table at Dinis Sengulane, Bishop of Lebombo in strife-torn, desperately poor, Mozambique, and said, 'Dinis, do you stand by this?' And he said, 'Yes'. It stood.

Within the Section, our secretary, Pat Harris, about to become Bishop of Southwell, could not get photocopying facilities when our group needed them, first for ourselves, and latterly for distribution among the Section. Without my computer, either we would have been struggling with each other's handwriting, or Pat himself would have been trying to get our drafts typed before they were photocopied. Our statement on Worship was far more substantial than most of the Section's drafting, largely, I think, for these logistical reasons.[11] We did not solve all the problems; and one or two, particularly lay presidency of the Eucharist, we could not even name, but we laid out useful ground, and politely called in question the projected International Anglican Liturgical Commission. We provided one Resolution, no. 47 on Liturgical Freedom, adopted by the Conference unanimously. This became a starting text for the IALC-3 statement in 1989 on inculturation in worship.[12]

In the plenaries in the final week, much of the action centred on the divisive effects of the ordination of women, particularly with the prospect of women bishops. A restive plenary of the 600 discussed this, trying to handle amendments under no standing orders and dependent simply upon the personal strength of the chairman. It was ghastly.

Without going further into my diary (which I published in *News of Liturgy* at the time), I quote from a letter I wrote to Derek Pattinson in answer to a query in January 1990. In relation to this Lambeth Conference, I wrote of

> the appalling inability to handle its own agenda when it does meet. I mention the following points:
>
> (a) very poor preparation ...
>
> (b) very poor servicing ...
>
> (c) very poor personal resourcing of bishops ...
>
> (d) very inadequate procedures ...
>
> (e) very chaotic plenaries ...
>
> Thus the bishops' *experience* of catholic fellowship may have been good – indeed it and so many other things were very good – but the

competence of the gathering to mark out the way ahead, or the approach, say, to world governments, must be profoundly questioned. Bishops may be the right people to speak with authority, but there is no automatic *mana* in their utterances, and the less so when you see how their utterances were produced on this occasion ... no-one ought to run conferences on the basis that the oomph of a large number of bishops put together will corporately surmount the very poor procedures to which they are subject. (And I now read earlier Lambeth Conference reports with different eyes ...).

I stand by that as comment on Lambeth 1988.

I came into the 1998 Conference by an unexpected route. A problem about worship at the Conference dated back to 1978, the first Conference in residence in Canterbury. The oral tradition was that the worship arrangements were that, for the plenary worship, provinces would take responsibility in turn, and each one could bring its own liturgy, or follow whichever pattern it wished. The American bishops then brought to Canterbury hundreds of hardback copies of their new *Book of Common Prayer*, and distributed them to everyone. This so outbid all other provinces, that they were reluctant to produce something duplicated and lightweight, and possibly (when put in English) not far distant from English or American forms anyway, and the American book scooped the pool. The story continued that the Primates then, in the light of this experience, asked Robert Runcie to lay on for 1988 a single core liturgical programme, even if provinces still had scope to vary it. Robert Runcie asked Alastair Haggart, ex-Primus of the Scottish Episcopal Church, to be senior chaplain to the 1988 Conference and to provide the services. Alastair actually wrote to me in 1987 and asked if anything in his drafts would be a problem to evangelicals. My recollection is that what he sent was mostly psalmody, so I could hardly object! He added in the Scottish Eucharistic Prayer – which itself provides various problems. But the main problem was not doctrine, but the unchanging diet of old English culture. This was buttressed when in 1988 *Hymns A & M* repeated the American process of 1978 – giving us all a free copy of their hardback music copy of *Hymns Ancient and Modern New Revised*. Bishops from overseas were landed with Alastair's liturgical texts and this English hymnbook, and were yet told on arrival, 'you can vary it if you like'. Halfway through the Conference the West Indians discovered 'Give me oil in my lamp, keep it burning' at the back of the hymnbook – and we sang that with some embarrassed clapping. In the third week the officiants were bolder. I had myself raised the question of multicultural worship at the Section meeting on the first Monday morning – and I was shouted down by a well-known reactionary English diocesan.

However, the point registered somewhere. George Carey, in planning for 1998, asked me in 1994 to assist Roger Herft, especially in relation to texts, in his own overall role of leading the chaplaincy team.* I recommended we bring in Geoff Weaver as director of music – he had already edited *World Praise*. We forbade any freebies from liturgy or music publishers. And so we were able to work through the run-up years, to provide indigenous worship at every plenary event. We began with the new Kenyan rite in Canterbury cathedral, and ended with the new Australian rite back in the cathedral to conclude. Lambeth it was – but with much multilingual, multicultural, worship, taking us to all ends of the earth to share the worship of, for example, Melanesia (we had a pidgin rite!), Tanzania and Brazil. There was joy in seeing the worship events take place, and experiencing the participants catching the mood (usually of joy and devotion) of each.

But what of the Conference agenda? Now the technological world had moved on. This time half the bishops would have laptops, with access to the Web, and email to contact anyone with expertise. This half would be far from naked – but the other half could still arrive never having seen a computer, as naked as in 1988, but actually worse off compared with the other half. There was serious preparation in some spheres (e.g. with the major Virginia Report on the meaning and nature of communion provided in advance for us), but none at all in others. We did adopt some Standing Orders to guide us in controversial plenaries (homosexual relationships would dominate this time); and we had nothing like the 1988 bottleneck at the photocopier.

But this time, while revelling in the worship, I had a daunting experience in my group. The time available was frittered away by the Section chairman, who for two days exhorted us with an unbroken and unmemorable monologue. Then five of us became a group considering worship, chaired by a transatlantic bishop without expertise or goals in the worship area, and no idea what our agenda should be. However, on the second Monday, our Section chairman changed all the group chairmen round (simply to give more people a crack!). By this ill-judged turn of the wheel, the chair of the Liturgy Group slid under me. I promptly starting drafting against the clock. In five days we reached the point where the draft went through a subsection – and was then tried on other Sections. But Section 4 declared war. They labelled our draft unacceptable, and, as our chairman reported their opinion to us, neither told us what was wrong with it, nor how it could be retouched to make it acceptable. I have my suspicions the fuss was about communicating unconfirmed children.[13]

Our group had also drafted a resolution for the plenary sessions, commending the International Anglican Liturgical Consultations to the support and funding of the various provinces. Section 4 produced 50 signatures to declare that this

---

* My name is missing from the chaplaincy team listed in the report – not through modesty, but in error.

too was controversial, and needed debate in plenary, rather than being nodded through as unchallenged. It was a double whammy from their Section, without our even meeting identifiable persons. Our Section 3 chairman had this time told us to go off and spend a day reading other Sections' documents – so we ourselves could not be reconvened. Our statement was simply lost: Lambeth 1998 said nothing about liturgy.[14] One typical side-effect was that a French-speaking presbyter, an ACC representative from Burundi, who had asked to be in our group for one purpose, then went home with nothing. He sought a Lambeth cue that eucharistic elements did not have to be wheat-bread and grape-wine, but in vain. Then, when the allegedly controversial resolution on IALCs came to the plenary, no one from Section 4 spoke – the numbers who had signed the statement that it was controversial had simply walked away from their own signatures, and it went through without dissent. I later wrote at length to the chairman of Section 4 about the whole unhappy business, but he simply asked me not to picket him at such length again.

Was my experience uniquely bad? Most bishops' reflections have turned upon their view of the famous Resolution 1.10.[15] But I read a perceptive critique from Graham James, then Bishop of St Germans in Truro Diocese, now Bishop of Norwich, in *Anglican World* in 1999. He had been refreshed by the worship, but found the plenary sessions, especially the one on sexuality, 'uncomfortable'. On the processes he wrote:

> There was no review of the resolutions from the 1988 Lambeth Conference. The lack of attention to them reveals the modesty of the authority of those we passed this time. It was evident that few bishops seemed to have read any reports or resolutions of previous Lambeth Conferences at all. It was as if we were doing everything from scratch. In the sub-section on euthanasia of which I formed part we certainly were, and woefully under-resourced to do so. But rarely did any Lambeth document quote any previous Lambeth report or resolution. Vatican documents, by contrast, are a sort of patchwork quilt of previous papal utterances and encyclicals. Suddenly I found myself sympathetic to the Curia. Anglicans publish endless reports and documents, but seem to do little to connect them.

Many bishops will have been working at issues not central to their concerns, and not areas of their expertise or special interest. Graham James certainly suggests that was how a large proportion of his group on euthanasia were placed. My own summary is that, whereas in 1988 the group work was fairly congenial, but the plenary processes ghastly, in 1998 the Section and group processes were awful, but I had less problems about the plenaries than did many.

3. The Anglican Consultative Council (ACC)

The ACC began in 1971. It is the only one of the four instruments which provinces actually *join*. There is a constitution, seating a bishop, a presbyter and a lay person from each province, though with a slight reduction of that representation for smaller provinces. It meets as a Council roughly every two years (but not near to Lambeth Conferences), and, from the 15 meetings since 1971, it has regularly published reports and resolutions. Between meetings its tasks are sustained by the Anglican Communion Office (ACO), located in London with a small secretariat headed by the secretary-general. The ACO funds and services the work of international Commissions, and, at the request of the Archishop of Canterbury, provides the basic administrative back-up for Lambeth Conferences and Primates' Meetings as well as for the ACC itself. A development of the 1980s and 1990s has been the emergence of 'networks' – groups of Anglicans with focused interests from across a series of provinces in different parts of the world who get together (and stay in touch electronically) to promote their stated concern. A good instance arose from the efforts of Roger Sainsbury in 1998. The bishops in Resolution II.7 asked the ACC 'to give support to the formation of an Anglican Urban Network to share information and experience on urbanization and urban mission'. This was duly formed and has been coordinated by Andrew Davey from Church House, London. Similarly, the IALCs, of which I have been part since their origins in 1985, are in essence a network. Networks are monitored by the ACC and report to it, but are responsible for their own funding and constitutions.

One of the ACC's most extraordinary actions came at its first meeting in Limuru in 1971. Resolution 28 included:

> (b) . . . this Council advises the Bishop of Hong Kong, acting with the approval of his Synod, and any other Bishop of the Anglican Communion acting with the approval of his Province, that, if he decides to ordain women to the priesthood, his action will be acceptable to this Council; and that this Council will use its good offices to encourage all Provinces of the Anglican Communion to continue in communion with these dioceses.

Amazingly, this was carried 24–22, and became the permission for the Bishop of Hong Kong to ordain two women at Advent that year. No one knows what the outcome of a 22–24 vote the other way would have been – and there does seem a slight (if providential?) randomness to the vote, for most provinces did not choose their representatives with an eye to women's ordination. At any rate, when the ACC met in 1973, the Hong Kong ordinations had happened and other provinces were at various stages of preparing to follow. The ACC then voted nearly unanimously to recommend that the ordination of women in any province ought not to 'cause any break in communion in our Anglican family'. The Windsor Report cites those ACC discussions and resolutions as an established precedent for provinces consulting widely before taking unilateral steps which could be disruptive of communion between provinces.[16] The principle is surely right, but that 24–22 looks like a fairly weak link.

The Limuru voting was astonishingly paralleled at the Nottingham meeting in June 2005. Then the proposal that the American and Canadian representatives be asked to withdraw was also passed by two votes (30–28). The Americans, who operated on the basis that the two-vote majority in 1971 opened the door to women's ordination, could have no reason to complain if a split vote now went against them.[17]

4. The Primates and the Windsor Report

The formalizing and strengthening of Primates' Meetings has proceeded since Lambeth 1978, when Donald Coggan urged that they should become a regular feature of the Anglican Communion's life. The growing ease of international travel, and the relatively small numbers involved, have probably contributed to the role played by these meetings. On the other hand, though there have been press releases, there have not been published reports like those of Lambeth Conferences and ACC meetings. And, no doubt, the Primates themselves have to be cautious as to how far they are truly representative of their provinces and how far are simply speaking from personal conviction or inclination. Several provinces have less than 30,000 members, and others have many millions.[18] Financial resources and physical assets would give a different scale of evaluation. So the weight of the 38 current Primates is not evenly distributed when they meet.

At the time of writing, they have found a vital role, which no one else could have filled. When Gene Robinson's election to be Bishop of New Hampshire was confirmed at the ECUSA General Convention in August 2003, Rowan Williams convened an emergency meeting of the Primates for October 2003, just prior to Robinson's impending consecration. The Primates asked Rowan Williams to appoint a powerful and fast-working Lambeth Commission to address issues raised by that consecration and to make recommendations, reporting to him personally. They asked the provinces to avoid precipitate action during the twelve months while the Lambeth Commission was at work. And they planned to meet again in February 2005 to consider the Commission's report four months after its publication. The Windsor Commission, chaired by Robin Eames, Archbishop of Armagh, was duly appointed. By its terms of reference it was to handle, not the moral issues of same-sex relationships, but the consequential issues of broken and distrustful relationships between and among member Churches of the Communion. Primarily the Commission was to handle 'the canonical understandings of communion, impaired and broken communion, and the ways in which provinces of the Anglican Communion may relate to one another'.

The Windsor Report was published in October 2004, a very tightly argued piece of work, which itself urges that the Communion should not be dismembered. It was not to address homosexual relationships directly, though it inevitably put the Americans and Canadians into the dock for taking steps which were not only unprecedented and taken without consultation, but also morally questionable. The report recommended an advisory panel for the Archbishop of Canterbury (this has been appointed), and an Anglican Covenant, which would help define and sustain the identity and unity of the Communion. If this proves to have mileage it will itself become an 'instrument' of unity, and will, I assume, require trenchant endorsement – possibly by Canon – by our General Synod.

There were early signs that the report has stirred the Communion. The General Synod in Australia voted in October 2004: 'This General Synod does not condone the ordination of people in open committed same-sex relationships.' I stayed with a New Zealand bishop a month later and he told me their bishops (who have been fairly liberal) had agreed a moratorium on ordaining people in same-sex relationships. New Zealand had two members of the Lambeth Commission.

But the major question was how the Primates, meeting in late February 2005, would handle it; and in the meantime the report was brought to our own General Synod by our Bishops.

The Windsor Report in General Synod
General Synod gave a morning to the Windsor Report in February 2005, and I watched it on TV. The covering report from the Bishops (GS 1570) accepted the report's principles, so Tom Wright, Bishop of Durham and a member of the Lambeth Commission, was moving:

> That this Synod
>
> (a)   welcome the report from the House (GS 1570) accepting the principles set out in the Windsor report;
>
> (b)   urge the Anglican Communion to take action, in the light of the Windsor report's recommendations, to secure unity within the constraints of truth and charity and to seek reconciliation within the Communion; and
>
> (c)   assure the Archbishop of Canterbury of its prayerful support at the forthcoming Primates' meeting.

He began the opening speech: 'Sin, sex and skulduggery: that is what this report, and this debate is not about.' He went on to say that 'Windsor represents a worldwide Anglican consensus . . . the only way down the mountain'. The motion must have been rare in our synodical history in urging the Primates of other Churches to take action of any sort, let alone 'taking all steps necessary to seek to achieve reconciliation'.[19] The debate was of a high order. The only amendment to go to a vote was Paul Collier's proposed addition to urge listening to gay and lesbian people, creating 'a climate of safety' for them to speak of their experience 'without fear of reprisal', and allowing 'voices to be heard across national and provincial boundaries'. This was lost 140–209. Replying, Tom Wright said: 'the report is not an ultimate fudge. I know all about Anglican fudge: I have criticized it on other occasions; but . . . the Windsor report is something much more solid and substantial.' His motion was adopted unamended.

Back in the arena of the Anglican Communion

The Primates duly met in Ulster in February 2005. They asked the American and Canadian Churches to withdraw from the ACC until the next Lambeth Conference. The Americans stated they would abstain from ordaining any bishop at all until their General Convention in August 2006, but this did not, it seems, stir sufficient international applause. So they simply sent persons to the ACC in June 2005 to make an explanatory presentation about their pro-gay actions – and to take no other part.

The Windsor Report had a second theme, consequent upon the actions of the American and Canadian Anglican Churches – the existing and prospective practice of bishops crossing borders to other bishops' dioceses, in order to provide 'acceptable' ministrations and oversight to parishes which were polarized from their diocesan over the main substantial issue, such as the favouring of gay relationships. While the Windsor Report calls for restraint, yet the problem appears at the time of writing to be multiplying. An appalling disruption has occurred in the province of Brazil, where the Bishop of Recife confirmed candidates in an Episcopal Church (USA) parish which was at odds with its own bishop. He was then suspended by his Primate; and, when his clergy showed themselves in solidarity with him, 35 of them were sacked also.

The Anglican Communion, profoundly networked and interdependent, has thus far survived. Rowan Williams, coming to Canterbury in early 2003, has had a vastly difficult task of damage limitation. I doubt myself whether that would have been possible if Jeffrey John had become Bishop of Reading. Still, however chequered the Church of England's history may have been, and however vulnerable Rowan Williams' personal history may have been, others so far give us the benefit of the doubt to continue, even if under scrutiny, at the heart of the Communion.

Appendix A

A few personalities

Archbishops of Canterbury (with their dates as Archbishops)

Geoffrey Fisher (1945–61): Geoffrey Fisher was Churchill's choice when he would not have George Bell. He was regularly known as The Headmaster, not only from his past career, but from his contemporary style. His sermon on unity in 1946 started up much in Chapter 8, and his directing the Convocations and the Assembly to give priority to revising Canon Law gave a base for much recorded here. I never met him, but he wrote to me after retirement, when we were both (for vastly different reasons) opposing the Anglican–Methodist Scheme.

Michael Ramsey (1961–74): Michael Ramsey wrote *The Gospel and the Catholic Church* when he was just past 30, and became an outstanding theologian. After professorial chairs, he became Bishop of Durham in 1952, and Archbishop of York in 1956. One commentator tipped him for Canterbury on the grounds that he alone looked like St Augustine. Synod loved him – he was profound but simple, magisterial but engagingly humble, and with a great sense of humour. What he had not got was small-talk or an interest in administration. He often came to Synod more than filling the passenger seat of a Morris Minor.

Donald Coggan (1975–80): Donald Coggan had worked for the Inter-Varsity Fellowship before the war, and revived the London College of Divinity after it. He became Bishop of Bradford in 1956, then followed Michael Ramsey to York and to Canterbury. A learned Hebraist, he chaired the translators of the *New English Bible* and of *The Revised Psalter*. A renowned Bible expositor and preacher, he never bonded well with General Synod, but both by a national appeal encouraged vocations and, internationally, worked fruitfully to build up the Anglican Communion.

Robert Runcie (1980–91): I knew him as principal of Cuddesdon in the 1960s, and Synod was new to him in 1970. He never wrote anything theological (and he was castigated by Gary Bennett in that famous *Crockford's* Preface as liberal), but he had an easy touch, a delightful sense of humour, and Brian Brindley and I revelled in bantering with him at questions (and he enjoyed it too, in an indulgent way). He could bring a new approach to an issue, and use his charm to a maximum.

George Carey (1991–2002): Now we come to my own times – the Careys were near neighbours at Nottingham for five years and we took each other's kids to school. He and I ran against each other in the (biological) fathers' race at the primary school. He was the first Archbishop of Canterbury since Lang to have been an ordinary parish incumbent – and all still know exactly what they were doing when they heard he had been made Archbishop, so surprising was it. He (and Eileen) bent enormous energies to the Canterbury task. In the job, he was wildly, even naively, wrong about establishment, but did very well on almost everything else.

Rowan Williams (2002–): Now we come beyond my times. However, I published Rowan in 1981, shared with him in the Doctrine Commission in 1986–91, and raced dangerously across England to St Asaph to lay a hand on him in May 1992. He may be around until 2020, so it is early to assess – but he had a horrific task from his first day, and I would like to be counted a fan. He has an admirable theological wife.

Other key characters

Christina Baxter (oh, not ordained, but Dr and Canon and CBE): If I prove to have done nothing else of value in my life, the appointing of Christina Baxter to St John's College staff in 1979 should outweigh all the omissions. She was elected to Synod by Southwell Laity in 1985, and then elected by the House of Laity to Standing Committee before she had made a speech. She put in stalwart work, including the report on freemasonry and the rescue of Church House itself from a seriously misconceived plan to sell it off, and this, rightly enhanced, profile meant that she became vice-chair of the House of Laity in 1990, and chair in 1995, and has held the chair (brilliantly) since (while she has also become a very able principal of St John's College).

Stuart Blanch (Bishop of Liverpool 1965–75, Archbishop of York 1975–83): Stuart was a Bible scholar and Bible teacher right the way through his episcopal days. Humane and self-deprecating, he was impatient of administration, and not much addicted to Synod, but wedded to the establishment. He got *The Liturgical Psalter* through Synod in 1979 by offering to Donald Coggan to have one copy made, especially for FDC, in which the latter's beloved *Revised Psalter* would be bound in with the ASB rites, if the rest of us could have *The Liturgical Psalter* in ours.

Peter Dawes (Bishop of Derby 1988–95): Peter was an old friend, with whom I wrote on STV before General Synod started – and we both then benefited from fair voting and were elected, he for Chelmsford Diocese in 1970. In 1975, he pipped me for election to the Standing Committee (we almost certainly had the same persons backing us, but his preferences were ahead of mine in the STV), and that began to determine his life. In the 1980s he became chairman of the Business Subcommittee of Synod, and introduced a great element of fun into his reporting and replying – and no doubt his very attractive synodical profile brought his name to the fore to be made bishop.

Gerald Ellison (Bishop of Chester 1955–73, of London 1973–81): Gerald Ellison had been chaplain to Cyril Garbett and was said to model himself on Garbett. He certainly had a touch of the prince-bishop, and was profoundly establishmentarian. I think he was the last bishop I ever saw in gaiters. He also, as an old Blue, umpired the boat-race for some years. He ordained me, and was generous to me thereafter.

John Habgood (Bishop of Durham 1973–83, Archbishop of York 1983–95): Becoming a senior bishop at 45, he hit the synodical floor running, and never stopped for 22 years. He dealt me some hard knocks in Synod, but was quite trusting outside. He always achieved – and appeared more in Synod as a practical (strong-arm) achiever than as the scientist-cum-theologian that he was outside. When he chaired the House of Bishops we found we had made up our minds faster than with any of the other four Archbishops I knew in the chair.

Margaret Hewitt (grand lady of the House of Laity, 1970–91): Margaret Hewitt was an Anglo-Catholic lay woman to her fingertips, and, herself a professor of English, represented what in 1970 was one of the most solidly Anglo-Catholic dioceses, Exeter. She has been generally remembered for her wide range of broad-brimmed hats; but to a smaller number she was known as one of the Exeter Twins, as she and Roy Porter, professor of theology at Exeter, kept each other unamorous company, not least in the (to them unwelcome) liberal protestant atmosphere of the BCC, on which they represented us.

Graham Leonard (Bishop of Willesden 1964–73, of Truro 1973–81, of London 1981–91): Graham Leonard took theology (and himself) very seriously, and I appreciated him as my Area bishop in North London in the 1960s – and, as chronicled in this book, shared with him in writing on ecclesiology. He chaired the BSR for many years. His appointments looked idiosyncratic. A firm opponent of women's ordination, he became polarized from much of the Church of England in his latter years, and, after 1994, he went to Rome and was ordained by a Roman Catholic bishop, and, as I write, there are rumours he might be made a Monsignor.

Eric Mascall (professor of theology at King's, London, retired 1972): I owe Eric a mention here as, though he had nothing to do with General Synod, he was important in my life in the writing of *Growing into Union* (1970), and, entrenched and highly scholarly Anglo-Catholic of an earlier generation though he was, he worked with me as a peer, and engaged in theological discussion very Christianly. When accused by fellow Anglo-Catholics of changing his mind, he replied '*Accused?* Even an amoeba changes, and I count myself a higher form of life than an amoeba.' While actually a bachelor, he would have been a wonderful grandfather. His autobiography (*Saraband*) is the one of the kindest yet funniest examples of that genre of writing that I have ever met.

Hugh Montefiore (Bishop of Kingston 1970–77, Bishop of Birmingham 1977–87): I knew Hugh in four stages – firstly via his wife, Eliza, who was on the Liturgical Commission from 1962 to 1980; secondly, through opposing him (mostly successfully) on a whole series of secondary matters in General Synod from 1976 to 1985 (though also sitting in open-mouthed admiration for his speech on The Bomb in the famous debate in 1983); thirdly, through being invited to be his suffragan and then having 18 hectic and memorable months with him (at the end of which I edited a tribute to him); and fourthly for the next 18 years in which he was highly supportive, still theologically combative (and often magisterial), and, perhaps not quite as sweeping with his judgements as before, a mellowing friend. I count myself very privileged to have stood near to him.

David Say (Bishop of Rochester, 1961–88): David Say was the last bishop in post who had been consecrated by Fisher (and thus had a Lambeth DD from the morning after). Indeed he exercised the longest single post-war episcopate. He looked down on us all from a great height, and his shadow still fell across Rochester Diocese when I was in it.

David Silk (Rector of St George's, Beckenham 1975–80, Archdeacon of Leicester 1980–94, Bishop of Ballarat (Australia) 1994–2003): David Silk was invited onto the Liturgical Commission in 1972, and through the 1970s became the Anglo-Catholic end of an axis of which I was at the evangelical end. He was doctrinally and politically tough, but fair and a joy to work with. In 1980 he became prolocutor of the Canterbury Convocation, and emerged as a chosen synodical opponent of both the 1978–82 Covenant for Unity and the ordination of women to the presbyterate – and escaped the run-on from the latter synodical decision by being consecrated for an Australian (FiF!) see the day after the Canon was promulged in 1994. He had a propensity for debating by saying: 'Mrs Jones thinks this; and the Bishop of Chippenham thinks that; and others have offered their opinions; but *the truth of the matter is as follows . . .*'

Mervyn Stockwood (Bishop of Southwark, 1959–80): Mervyn was one of the most colourful characters on the Bench in the second half of the twentieth century. He was an amazing combination of the egalitarian socialist (his Anglo-Catholic peers called him Councillor Stockwood in Bristol) and the dressed-up flamboyant egocentric aristocrat. I met him on the Liturgical Commission in the 1960s (and I enjoyed contributing a story to Michael de la

Noy's biography of him). He made John Robinson a suffragan against Geoffrey Fisher's opposition; he made David Sheppard a suffragan when he was quite outside the structures of the Church of England; and he made Hugh Montefiore a suffragan at a time when Downing Street was declining to make him a diocesan. He had little patience with the rules, which were regularly bent to his purposes – and, as a showman having little patience with Synod and less attendance, he always hinted when he did come that he needed a round of applause for coming to Synod at all. And the memory of his near-omnipresence lingered on in Southwark Diocese decades afterwards.

Roy Williamson (Bishop of Bradford 1984–92, Bishop of Southwark 1992–98): Roy, from a strongly protestant Ulster family, was an incumbent in Nottingham who sponsored me for General Synod in 1970 (protesting he had no interest in it himself). He later became my incumbent in Bramcote, and then, as Archdeacon of Nottingham, chairman of St John's College Council when I was principal – and a very firm friend. He came to Synod simply as an archdeacon, and initially had little obvious heart for it: but I think a speech he made in a debate in the early 1980s on capital punishment, in which he set out a sober scenario of what this would mean in Northern Ireland, fixed his identity in people's minds and led to his nomination to be Bishop of Bradford. He was trusted by all in the House of Bishops as being, I think, the most guileless of men. He remained a stalwart friend – not least when my job in Birmingham disappeared underneath me – and in time, after proper process, as Bishop of Southwark he invited me to be Bishop of Woolwich. He chose his occasions to speak with care – and then he spoke with great weight (and an Irish joke or two).

Appendix B

Biographical timeline and index to sessions of General Synod

You are invited to use this table to pursue references and cross-references within this volume to specific events and sessions of General Synod. The numbers in the columns are chapter numbers within the book. Most of the chapters are arranged chronologically, so that the progress of a theme can be traced from the numbers in the columns. In some chapters, however, notably Chapter 7, the chapter goes back on its chronology to handle further discrete themes. When a theme arose simply by a question in Synod, that has usually been omitted here, unless the theme were on the agenda for that group of sessions anyway.

Year	COB	National Involvement	Convocations House of Laity
1934	Born in Croydon		
1944–53	School in Croydon		
1953–55	National Service in RA		
1955–59	Mods and Greats at Lincoln College, Oxon		
1956	Confirmed at Oxford		
1957	Selected for ordination training		
1958	Chair of Bp Jewel Soc. – run study groups		
1959	Graduated – 2nd class		
1959–61	Ordination training at Tyndale Hall, Bristol		
1960	'10 out of 10' in GOE Worship Apply for Stephenson Fellowship, Sheffield		3,4
1961	Founder-member Latimer House Liturgy Group (LHLG), later GROW Appointed to curacy in Cheadle		

Year	COB	National Involvement	Convocations House of Laity
1961–64	Cheadle, Chester Diocese		
1961	Deacon 24 September		
1962	Presbyter 23 September		
1963	Marriage	Write against Ang.–Meth. Scheme	
1964	Appointed to LCD staff		
1964–85	Staff of LCD (from 1970 St John's, Nottingham)		
1964		Appointed to Liturgical Commission	2
		Member BCC Faith & Order Conference	
		Run for election to Convocation	
1965	Take over college bookshop	Contr. to Packer (ed.), *All in Each Place*	8
1966		Dissent re Series 2 communion	2,3,4,6,7
		Write booklet re dissent	
1967	Drafting for NEAC–1 Keele re worship and ecumenism	Agree final form of S2 communion	4,6
	LCD decides to move to Nottingham in 1970	Run in Convocation by-election	
1968		Publish Christopher Byworth and Trevor Lloyd (eds), *Eucharist for the Seventies*	4
		Edit *Modern Anglican Liturgies 1958–1968* (OUP)	
1969	Shortlisted for principalship of St John's College, Durham	With two Anglo-Catholics and two evangelicals address letters to the Convocations re the Ang.–Meth. Scheme and begin with them to write a book on reunion	2,7,8
1970 (Jan–June)	Move house in March to have sabbatical in Nottingham	Co-author with Eric Mascall, Jim Packer, Bishop of Willesden (Graham Leonard) *Growing into Union: Proposals for Forming a United Church in England* (SPCK)	
	Licensed in Diocese of Southwell		

Year	COB	Synod		
		Jan/Feb/ Mar	*July*	*November*
1970–85	St John's College Nottingham years			
1970 (Jul–Dec)	Elected to Synod by Southwell Clergy	[No Synod]	[No Synod]	1,2,7,8
	Begin Grove Books			
1971	Elected by Synod to BCC Assembly	2,5,8,11	1,2,4,5,8	2,6
	Begin Grove Booklets			
1972	*The Job Prospects of the Anglican Clergy* (Grove)	6,7 [8May]8,18	2,6,7,8,9	6,7,12,16
1973		18	2,12,16	16
1974	First trip abroad – Canada	4,5,	4,18	9
1975	Appointed vice-principal		8,12	8
	News of Liturgy (monthly till Dec 2003)			
	Further Anglican Liturgies 1968–1975 (Grove)			
	Re-elected to Synod			
1976	Latimer House Liturgy Group becomes GROW	3,13,17	5,8,18	4,11,18
1977	Help organize NEAC-2	3,8,9,14,18	7,10,11,16	4,7
1978	Robin Nixon, principal of St John's, dies	3,7	6,7,8,14	4,12,14
1979	Appointed principal of St John's	4,6,9	6,7,12	3,6,15
1980	Re-elected to Synod	16	8,12	12
	Co-edit *Anglican Worship Today* (Collins)			
1981	Draft *The Charismatic Movement in C/E* (CIO)	7,8,15	7,12,16	12,14,16,18
	Canon of Southwell			
1982		14,16,18	7,8,12	7,12,16,18
1983	Consultation on Grove Books recommends forming a company	5,7,13,18	8,9,12,18	11,12,17
1984	First time visiting Africa – two weeks in Uganda	3,11,12	12,15	7,8,12,18
	Vacancy-in-see Southwell			
1985 (Jan–Jul)	Invited to become Bishop of Aston – say 'yes'	9,18	8,12	[New Synod – next page]
	Grove Books Ltd formed as company – COB as company secretary			

Year	COB	Synod		
		Jan/Feb/ Mar	*July*	*November*
1985–89	Bp of Aston, suffragan in Birmingham			COB off Synod
1985 (Jul–Dec)	25 July consecrated bishop (with Wilfred Wood, first black bishop in C/E) Founder-member of International Anglican Liturgical Consultation (IALC) (Boston, Mass.) First visit to South America Run for election as suffragan on House of Bps – defeated	[on previous page]	[on previous page]	5
1986	Not reappointed to Liturgical Commission, but to Doctrine Commission Hugh Montefiore announces retirement in March 1987 Chair vacancy-in-see committee Nominated by Robert Runcie as nominated suffragan for 1988 Lambeth Conference	10,12	12	8,9,10
1987	Explore Desmond Tutu availability for 1989 Mark Santer Bishop of Birmingham Contest suffragans' by-election – defeated	12	7,8	7,15
1988	Invitation to Desmond Tutu of 55 Christian leaders of Birmingham – chair executive committee of Celebration 1988 Lambeth Conference – group on liturgy, secretary	7	12	4,10,12
1989 (Jan–Jun)	First time in India: Mar Thoma Maramon Convention 18–23 April: Citywide Celebration with Desmond Tutu 10 May: Resign post, following loss of money in the Celebration	4,9,10		12
1989–91	**Exile in Rochester Diocese**			
1989 (Jul–Dec)	Move to Shipbourne Hon. Asst Bp in Rochester Begin itinerant teaching December, visit India to share in consecrating Mar Thoma bishops			
1990 (Jan–Jun)	Appointed CCBI Assembly Invited onto diocesan House of Bishops (toward election to GS House of Bishops)	6	3,8	[New Synod – next page]

Year	COB	Synod		
		Jan/Feb/ Mar	*July*	*November*
1990–96	Hon. Asst Bp in Rochester Diocese, and vicar, St Mark's, Gillingham			COB in H/B
1990 (Jul–Dec)	Elected CCBI Steering Group Offered incumbency St Mark's, Gillingham Elected to House of Bps Decline overseas approaches Accept St Mark's, Gillingham	[on previous page]	[on previous page]	5
1991	25 January, instituted at St Mark's Appointed to CCU Appointed by CCU to CBAC	12,16	4,5,14	5,6,10
1992		7,16,18	7,12	11,12
1993	Lambeth DD Cease as company secretary of Grove Books Consultation on inculturation by CAPA at Kanamai, Kenya *Infant Baptism and the Gospel* (DLT) Apply for secretary-general of ACC post – not shortlisted	7,18	12	12,13
1994	Asked by George Carey to assist in preparing worship at Lambeth 1998 *Cut the Connection* (DLT)	12	6,7,13,16, 18	6
1995	Michael Nazir-Ali Bishop of Rochester Join Eucharistic Prayers Revision Committee		4,6,11,12	[New Synod – next page]

Year	COB	Synod		
		Jan/Feb/ Mar	*July*	*November*
1995	Re-elected to House of Bps Elected by Synod to CCU Appointed by House of Bps to CMEAC	[on previous page]	[on previous page]	16

1996	Join Initiation Services Revision
	  Committee
	Invited by Roy Williamson to be
	  Bishop of Woolwich
	Short sabbatical writing book
		6	6	4,5,10

1996– 2004	**Bishop of Woolwich, Area Bishop in Southwark** 30 November, installed in cathedral			
1997	Vacancy-in-see committee in Southwark	[No Synod]	6,13,15	4,6,8
1998	*Is the Church of England Biblical?* (DLT) Lambeth Conference Tom Butler Bishop of Southwark	7,12,18	6,7,18	7
1999		[No Synod]	6,17	6,7,10,17
2000	Millennium year (and Dome chaplaincy) Re-elected to House of Bps Leave CCU and CMEAC	6,12,17	7,12	5
2001		[No Synod]	17,18	18
2002		[No Synod]	8,12,18	7,17,18
2003	Cease to edit *News of Liturgy*	10,17,18	8,11,18	[No Synod]
2004	**Retire after July Synod** Hon. Asst Bp in Bradford Diocese	7,9,15	7,11,12	[No Synod]
2005		7,11,12,19	5,7,8,11,12	[New Synod] *(Beyond this book)*

Appendix C

Bibliography of Colin Buchanan's writings as they relate to the chapters of this book

NB: Most of the writings listed were, as readers would expect, pressing a case. I have written more objectively about many of the subjects in various dictionaries. I have also just produced my own single-author dictionary, *Historical Dictionary of Anglicanism* (Scarecrow Press, Lanham, Maryland, USA, 2006) – and this handles each subject in the context of the worldwide Anglican Communion.

Introduction

Is the Church of England Biblical? Darton, Longman & Todd, 1998.

1. The Synod

'The authority of synods', *Churchman* 95.1, 1981.

2. Open communion

With Graham Leonard, 'Intercommunion: Some interim agreement', *Theology*, October 1969.

3. The Liturgical Commission and liturgy in Synod

'1928 and all that', in R. T. Beckwith (ed.), *Towards a Modern Prayer Book*, Marcham, 1966.

Recent Liturgical Revision in the Church of England, Ministry and Worship 14, Grove Books, 1973.

Supplement for 1973–74 to Recent Liturgical Revision in the Church of England, Ministry and Worship 14A, Grove Books, 1974.

Supplement for 1974–76 to Recent Liturgical Revision in the Church of England, Grove Booklet on Ministry and Worship 14B, Grove Books, 1976.

Supplement for 1976–78 to Recent Liturgical Revision in the Church of England, Ministry and Worship 14C, Grove Books, 1978.

Latest Liturgical Revision in the Church of England 1978–1984, Grove Liturgical Study 39, Grove Books, 1984.

News of Liturgy monthly from January 1975 to December 2003 – 348 issues.

'The Background to the Alternative Service Book', in *The Alternative Service Book 1980: A Commentary by the Liturgical Commission*, CIO, 1980, ch. 1.

'Liturgical Revision in the Church of England in Retrospect', in Kenneth Stevenson (ed.), *Liturgy Reshaped*, SPCK, 1982.

With Harold Miller and Trevor Lloyd (eds), *Anglican Worship Today: Collins' Illustrated Guide to the Alternative Service Book 1980*, Collins, 1980.

4. Baptism and Confirmation

Baptismal Discipline, Ministry and Worship 3, Grove Books, 1972.

A Case for Infant Baptism, Ministry and Worship 20, Grove Books, 1973.

One Baptism Once, Ministry and Worship 61, Grove Books, 1978.

Liturgy for Initiation, Ministry and Worship 65, Grove Books, 1979.

Adult Baptisms, Grove Worship 91, Grove Books, 1985.

Anglican Confirmation, Grove Liturgical Studies 48, Grove Books, 1986.

Policies for Infant Baptism, Grove Worship 98, Grove Books, 1987.

'Confirmation', in David Holeton (ed.), *Growing in Newness of Life*, ABC, Toronto, 1993.

Infant Baptism and the Gospel: The Church of England's Dilemma, Darton, Longman & Todd, 1993.

The Renewal of Baptismal Vows, Grove Worship 124, Grove Books, 1993.

Infant Baptism in Common Worship, Grove Worship 163, Grove Books, 2001.

With R. T. Beckwith and K. F. W. Prior, *Services of Baptism and Confirmation*, Latimer Monograph II, Marcham Manor, 1967.

With Michael Vasey, *The New Initiation Rites*, Grove Worship 145, Grove Books, 1998.

5. Children in communion

(Ed.), *Nurturing Children in Communion*, Grove Liturgical Study 44, Grove Books, 1985.

Children in Communion, Grove Worship 112, Grove Books, 1990.

New Introduction to Boston Statement in Ruth Meyers (ed.), *Children at the Table*, Church Hymnal, New York, 1992.

6. Eucharistic prayers

The New Communion Service – Reasons for Dissent, Church Book Room Press, 1966.

(Ed.), *Modern Anglican Liturgies 1958–1968*, Oxford University Press, 1968.

'Series 3 in the Context of the Anglican Communion', in R. C. D. Jasper (ed.), *The Eucharist Today: Essays on Series 3*, SPCK, 1974.

(Ed.), *Further Anglican Liturgies 1968–1975*, Grove Books, 1975.

What Did Cranmer Think He Was Doing? Grove Liturgical Study 7, Grove Books, 1976.

The End of the Offertory: An Anglican Study, Grove Liturgical Study 14, Grove Books, 1978.

(Ed.), *The Development of the New Eucharistic Prayers of the Church of England*, Grove Liturgical Study 20, Grove Books, 1979.

(Ed.) *Latest Anglican Liturgies 1976–1984*, Alcuin/SPCK, 1985.

Eucharistic Consecration, Grove Worship 148, 1998.

Eucharistic Prayer H – an Unauthorized Account (offprint from Ushaw Library Bulletin, available from COB).

With R. T. Beckwith, 'This bread and this cup: An evangelical rejoinder', in *Theology*, June 1967

With David Silk, 'Holy Communion: Rite A', in *The Alternative Service Book 1980: Commentary by the Liturgical Commission*, CIO, 1980, ch. 6.

With Trevor Lloyd (eds), *Six Eucharistic Prayers as Proposed in 1996*, Grove Worship 136, Grove Books, 1996.

With Charles Read, *The Eucharistic Prayers of Order One*, Grove Worship 158, 2000.

7. Six other liturgical issues

Petitions for the Departed

The New Communion Service – Reasons for Dissent, Church Book Room Press, 1966.

Absolutions

See *News of Liturgy* in 1981–3.

The Lord's Prayer

The Lord's Prayer in the Church of England, Grove Worship 131, Grove Books, 1995.

Ordinal

Ordination Rites in Common Worship, Grove Worship 186, Grove Books, 2006.

Reservation

Contributor to *Reservation and Communion of the Sick*, Ministry and Worship 4, Grove Books, 1972.

8. Anglicans and Methodists

'The Church of England and Apostolic Succession', *Churchman*, August 1961.

'The Church of England and the Church of South India', in J. I. Packer (ed.), *All in Each Place*, Marcham, 1965.

'Services of Reconciliation', in Packer (ed.), *All in Each Place*, Marcham, 1965.

'The Place of Ambiguity in Schemes of Reunion', *Churchman*, Vol. 81, 1967 no.3.

(Ed.), *Unity on the Ground*, SPCK, 1972.

'The Unity of the Church', in Ian Cundy (ed.), *Obeying Christ in a Changing World: 2 The People of God*, Collins, 1977.

Anglicans and Worship in LEPs, Grove Worship 101, 1987.

Is the Church of England Biblical? Darton Longman & Todd, 1998.

With E. L. Mascall, J. I. Packer and the Bishop of Willesden (Graham Leonard), *Growing into Union: Proposals for Forming a United Church in England*, SPCK, 1970.

9. Roman Catholic relationships

BEM and ARCIC on Baptism and Eucharist, Grove Worship 86, Grove Books, 1983.

Is Papal Authority a Gift to Us? Grove Booklet (no series), Grove Books, 2003.

10. Multi-ethnic Anglicanism

[No published writings]

11. Colleges and courses

'The Role and Calling of an Evangelical Theological College in the Eighties', *Churchman* 94.1.1980

12. The ordination of women

Is the Church of England Biblical? Darton, Longman & Todd, 1998.

13. Lay presidency

'Lay Presidency: Some Anglican Historical Perspectives', in Trevor Lloyd (ed.), *Lay Presidency at the Eucharist?* Grove Liturgical Study 9, Grove Books, 1977.

14. The charismatic movement

Encountering Charismatic Worship, Ministry and Worship 51, Grove Books, 1977.

'The Pentecostal Implications', in Kenneth Stevenson (ed.), *Authority and Freedom in the Liturgy*, Grove Liturgical Study 17, Grove Books, 1979.

The Charismatic Movement in the Church of England (drafted for General Synod Working Party), CIO, 1981.

15. Homosexual issues and *Issues in Human Sexuality*

[No published writings]

16. Church and State

'Mission and Establishment', in P. Turner and F. Sugeno (eds), *Crossroads Are for Meeting*, SPCK, USA, 1986.

Cut the Connection: The Church of England and Disestablishment, Darton, Longman & Todd, 1994.

'Surely We Should Disestablish?', *Anvil* Vol. 19, 2002 no. 4.

'Disestablishment – The Straightforward Case', in M. Mills-Powell (ed.), *Setting the Church of England Free*, John Hunt, 2003.

17. Political structures and the Single Transferable Vote

The Christian Conscience and Justice in Representation, Grove Ethics Booklet 53, Grove Books, 1983.

18. The appointment of diocesan bishops

See Chapter 16 bibliography above.

19. The Anglican Communion

Lambeth and Liturgy 1988, Grove Worship 106, Grove Books, 1989.

Historical Dictionary of Anglicanism, Scarecrow, USA, 2006.

Notes

Introduction

1. See Chapter 8.
2. See Philip Crowe (ed.), *Keele '67*, Falcon Books, 1967.
3. His death came at an extraordinary moment. I was being asked to put my hat in the ring for the principalship of Wycliffe Hall; I was in the throes of the 'steering' role for Rite A (see pages 75-77); I was chairing a college appeal for financing the new extension of our buildings, an appeal which was to come to a climax two and a half weeks later; and St. John's was scheduled to be inspected by the House of Bishops' Inspectors four weeks later; and then, to cap it all, immediately after Robin died I was asked to join the Churches' Council for Covenanting (see page 112). As the emergency acting Principal of a large bereaved college, yet with existing commitments to be in London an average of two days a week in that term, I had regretfully to decline this latter invitation.
4. This is no place to write an apologia. I am dealt with kindly by Lesslie Newbigin in his second edition of his autobiography (*Unfinished Agenda*, St Andrew Press, 1993, pp. 257-60), and in the recent centenary history of Birmingham diocese by Terry Slater (*A Century of Celebrating Christ*, Phillimore, 2005, pp. 102–104 and 177–80).
5. There is a thumbnail view of some of the names mentioned in the chapters, often simply in passing, in Appendix A.
6. See my rationale for Synod in Chapter 1.
7. Gavin Reid records in *To Canterbury with Love* (Kinsgway, 2002) that hearing this debate on the radio whetted his appetite to enter Synod.
8. See Chapters 10 and 17.
9. My footprints are there in my *Mission in South East London* and *Follow-Up in 2003 to Mission in South East London*, Southwark Diocese, 2002, 2003.
10. I asked questions during the 1990s as to the savings if stipend differentials were abolished, and in 1996 voted amid four righteous bishops when the Synod rejected a Carlisle diocesan motion to this end, and in 2004 voted to the same end, this time amid five bishops (including an archbishop) who supported a PMM to the same effect. I have endeavoured personally to take comparable steps in the various posts I have held.

1 The Synod

1. These were the longstanding gatherings of elected clergy representatives in the 'Lower Houses' of Canterbury and York, meeting with their diocesan bishops, who formed the 'Upper Houses'.
2. For a note on Michael Ramsey see Appendix A.
3. See Chapter 16 about the impropriety of a secular Parliament controlling the internal rules of a Christian Church.

4. This all happened remarkably quickly after the launch of the Life and Liberty Movement in 1917. There was an element of pretence about the whole event, as, for delicate church reasons, the authorities did not want it to look as though Parliament were *creating* the Church Assembly. So it was constituted without powers by the Convocations in May 1919 – which meant that the 'Enabling Act' later that year could be called the Church of England Assembly (Powers) Act, giving legislative *powers* to this (just) pre-existent church body. In reality it was the bestowal of the powers which 'made' the Assembly. And a whole infrastructure, including electoral rolls and parochial church councils, was part of the package which took shape then.

5. See page 71.

6. The origins of STV lie right back in the beginnings of the Church Assembly in 1920, and Synod inherited it. Getting internal elections – as, e.g., to Standing Committee – done by STV was a slower business, but was mostly secured by 1975.

7. The folly of being unbothered about the calendar is illustrated on pages 78–9.

8. See footnote on page 77.

9. This happened in relation to the representation of ethnic minorities in 1989. See page 146.

10. See page 44.

11. The contrast is worth making, because critics readily compare Synod to Parliament, and attribute the shortcomings of the latter (which are legion) to the former, and thus condemn it. A classic title betraying this aim is Peter Moore (ed.), *The Synod of Westminster: Do We Need It?* SPCK, 1986.

12. The cynic might say, 'You reported simply to get elected next time.' There is *some* truth in that, but (a) my synodical activities have so often been seen as partisan that my reports may not have attracted votes, and (b) I reported more in the years 2000–2004 (when I could not stand for election again) than in previous quinquennia (email helped). I conceive it a simple duty.

13. See page 209.

14. See page 80.

15. Gerald Ellison, once chaplain to Garbett, was Bishop of Chester, 1955–73, and of London, 1973–80. David Say was Bishop of Rochester 1961–88, the last bishop appointed when Geoffrey Fisher was Archbishop of Canterbury. See Appendix A for names.

16. My one intervention in the process was far from trying to trim its powers – it was an attempt to increase them. See page 226.

17. I suppose this was a precedent for reckoning certain kinds of business are *ultra vires*. At later stages I twice had to point out that liturgical drafting had produced '*Prayers to be used after death*' – also a sphere where Synod's writ does not run.

18. I believe the original case arose through the lack of guaranteed non-contributory pensions for continental chaplains, when the scheme began in England in the mid-1960s. A simple Measure would have provided the pensions, but no, we needed a diocese 'of' the Church of England. Robert Runcie was said to have said, when he heard this, 'That sounds like buying a bus company in order to get your kids to school.' Ironically, that pension scheme has gone, and

dioceses have to raise the pension contributions themselves anyway, so the rationale for incorporation into 'us' has completely gone – and a province on the continent might resemble, say, the Southern Cone of South America. A last twist was that the suffragan bishopric of Fulham was not eliminated in 1980, but seized by Graham Leonard a year or so later to increase effortlessly the number of working London bishops.

19. See Chapters 16 and 18.
20. An article I wrote on 'The Authority of Synods' in autumn 1980 (actually on the day of the count in the 1980 synodical elections) carries a high degree of credibility still – and I have drawn without hesitation upon it. See *Churchman* 1981–1, pp. 33–42.
21. Churches with bishops do not usually call themselves 'connexionalist', but that is the truth of them. See my *Is the Church of England Biblical? An Anglican Ecclesiology*, Darton, Longman & Todd, 1998.
22. 'Oversight/overseer' in English exactly matches the *episkopos* (i.e. 'bishop') stem in Greek and the 'superintendent' stem in Latin. I have investigated and written at some length about the origins of episcopacy in my *Is the Church of England Biblical? An Anglican Ecclesiology*. Needless to say, there is a great host of other authors also.
23. This was put with telling depth and clarity by John Henry Newman (in his Roman Catholic days) in his *On Consulting the Faithful in Matters of Doctrine*, originally published in a fairly eclectic journal, *The Rambler*, in July 1859, and republished in a critical edition, with an Introduction by John Coulson, by Geoffrey Chapman in 1961. Newman got into trouble in the Roman Catholic Church (for telling it the way it was!), and presented his material in a slightly less controversial form for an appendix to the third edition of his *The Arians of the Fourth Century* in 1871.
24. Article VIII of the Thirty-nine Articles. The Articles redefined the authority of Councils: 'And when they be gathered together . . . they may err, and sometimes have erred, even in things pertaining unto God' (Article XXI). Their findings had to be demonstrably scriptural to warrant their becoming credal.
25. For Europe, see pages 17–18.
26. And it is sadly impossible in Zimbabwe today, where it is greatly needed.
27. See Chapters 16 and 18.
28. See Chapter 19 for further discussion of this.

2 Open communion

1. Richard Baxter, himself confirmed before the Civil War, commended this practice gently to a new unconfirmed generation of dissenters.
2. See the essay by S. L. Ollard in *Confirmation; vol. 1 Historical and Doctrinal.* SPCK, 1924.
3. Randall T. Davidson and William Benham, *Life of Archibald Campbell Tait, Archbishop of Canterbury*, Macmillan, 1891, vol. 2, p. 71. Someone – Tait himself or the biographers – put 'rubric at the end of the Communion Service' instead of (what Carter's memorial had quoted verbatim) the 'confirmation rubric'.

4. Another *cause célèbre* arising, not mentioned in Tait's biography, (though he was involved), happened in 1873 in America. The interdenominational Evangelical Alliance held an international conference in New York. The Dean of Canterbury brought greetings from Tait, and assisted in a Communion service at a Presbyterian church and received communion from the pastor. The next Sunday George Cummins, the Assistant Bishop of Kentucky, acted similarly. Cummins was intemperately attacked – and seceded.

5. See, e.g., the 1920 Lambeth Conference Resolution 12; 1930 Lambeth Conference Resolution 42; and Church of England Convocation Resolutions of 1933. All assume that exclusion is the norm, though differing slightly in the emergency variations they permit. The 1920 Resolution includes, 'it should be regarded as the general rule of the Church that Anglican communicants should receive Holy Communion only at the hands of ministers of their own Church, or Churches in communion therewith.' No minority voting against this resolution is recorded – the novel ecclesiology of the 1870s had swept the board.

6. This included a counter-attacking element, as some, perhaps many, Anglo-Catholic parishes displayed a placard, 'Members of the Church of South India will not be administered communion in this church' – i.e. even if episcopally confirmed, they had apostatized. It was joked that such notices appeared in remote rural churches where in those days no Indian had ever yet come. But the Church Society notice stood in its own right, properly invoking a history suppressed by the post-1870 'norm'.

7. A *gravamen* is (typical) Convocation-speak for a corporate formal complaint; the *reformandum* is the correction desired. This *gravamen* (I suspect the last in history) is printed in Appendix IV of *Intercommunion Today: Being the Report of the Archbishops' Commission on Intercommunion*, CIO, 1968.

8. *The Canon Law of the Church of England: Being the Report of the Archbishops' Commission on Canon Law, together with Proposals for a Revised Body of Canons*, SPCK, 1947.

9. Section 3 provided for 'Regulations of the Convocation of the Province' allowing admission of others. But the Laity did not want such regulations, and in any case disapproved of their being written solely by the Convocations.

10. The Standing Committee of the Laity in autumn 1965 independently asked the Legal Board of the Church Assembly to interpret the 'present state of the law governing admission to the Holy Communion'. The Board opined that, whatever the 'historic practice' had been, the literal text of the confirmation rubric was 'the present state of the law'. It is endemic that lawyers make judgements of policy (unconsciously or consciously) when interpreting the law – surely the case with the Legal Board then? They had one case history behind them (in *re Perry Almshouses*: see *Intercommunion Today*, pp. 151–2), but I, and many others, would have gladly battled for the opposite opinion within that Legal Board.

11. See Chapter 8.

12. *Intercommunion Today: Being the Report of the Archbishops' Commission on Intercommunion*.

13. *Intercommunion Today*, p. 100.

14. *Intercommunion Today*, p. 162.

15. Measures are explained in Chapter 1, p. 8.
16. Of course, they were often the same bishops as ten years before. Falkner Allison, now Bishop of Winchester, was vice-chairman of the section (see footnote * to page 25). Honour where honour is due.
17. This, unlike 45, was subject to a vote, and passed 351–75.
18. See pp. 107–8.
19. Reprinted as an appendix in C. O. Buchanan, E. L. Mascall, J. I. Packer and the Bishop of Willesden, *Growing into Union: Proposals for Forming a United Church in England*, SPCK, 1970, pp. 176–85.
20. See the implications of this for the communion of unconfirmed children (pp. 54, 59–68), and for revision of initiation rites (pp. 41–51).
21. See Chapter 5.
22. The bishops did notably better, though (or perhaps because) Stretton Reeve, Bishop of Lichfield, said he had been in favour in February but was opposed now.
23. July 1972 was just two months after the burial of the tortuous Anglican–Methodist Unity Scheme – and the carefully defined mutual communion at the inauguration of Stage One was completely undercut by the Canon.
24. These were originally conceived at the BCC Faith and Order Conference at Nottingham in 1964, but often assisted by the Sharing of Church Buildings Act 1969.
25. *Report of the Commission on Reciprocal Intercommunion*, GS 155, CIO, no date, p. 25.
26. My mention above that Michael Ramsey received communion in the Kirk was of an individual exercising his own conscience. The Anglicans presented neither common line nor corporate decision. I doubt whether Roy Porter and Margaret Hewitt (the 'Exeter twins') received communion in Dunblane. But the crucial feature was the lack of prohibition of such practice.

3 The Liturgical Commission and liturgy in Synod

1. Ronald Jasper, writing in the 1980s, records, 'where liturgical revision was concerned the Archbishop was really out of his depth . . . Nor, frankly, could one expect a very great deal from our chairman.' See *The Development of Anglican Liturgy 1662–1980*, SPCK, 1989.
2. *Prayer Book Revision in the Church of England*, SPCK, 1957; *Baptism and Confirmation*, SPCK, 1959. This process is described in Chapter 4.
3. See Chapter 6.
4. *Alternative Services: First Series*, SPCK, 1965. The storm-centre of 1928 – reservation – did not appear. Page 94 was headed 'VIII. AN ORDER FOR THE COMMUNION OF THE SICK'. Under the heading, alone on a blank page, came '*A form of service and rubrics are under consideration.*' Well, maybe, but nothing appeared for 15 years.
5. See Jasper, *The Development of Anglican Liturgy 1662–1980*, p. 246.
6. See Chapter 4.
7. See Chapter 7.

8. Thus in early 1969 they declined even to discuss Series 2 burial sent from the Convocations, which had refused to follow a unitive course. See Chapter 7.
9. *Modern Liturgical Texts*, SPCK, 1968. The first positive task entrusted to me on the Commission was drafting part of the commentary. On the Lord's Prayer see Chapter 7.
10. Namely, the alternative confession, humble access and post-communion prayers – all three there in *Common Worship* today. The first two were savaged and excised in Synod in November 1971, and it was hard work restoring them in the ASB.
11. See Chapter 16.
12. In January 1975 I began the monthly *News of Liturgy*. This means that I have a month-by-month contemporary record of debates, synodical moves and matters like dates of publication of documents, which goes far beyond the synodical verbatim transcripts.
13. There was one exception in my case where I fought at the outset – see page 74.
14. ASB also gave 100 pages to the Tudor English Rite B. In July 1979 I narrowly lost an amendment to drop it (127–162). It was the great survivor (see Note * to page 33).
15. It was at that final approval stage that there were presented the petitions of 600 scholars and linguists (some of them unbelievers), calling upon us to protect and propagate the AV and the 1662 BCP. I think that until then they had thought the cult of modern language was a passing fashion and would soon go away. They now weighed in hard – but too late, and misjudging where worship had reached.
16. See Chapter 7.
17. One could hardly argue that imposing ashes on Ash Wednesday was an 'alternative' to the BCP Commination.
18. The Commission's work is chronicled by its then secretary in David Hebblethwaite, *Liturgical Revision in the Church of England 1984–2004: The Working of the Liturgical Commission*, Alcuin/GROW Joint Liturgical Study no. 57, Grove Books, 2004.
19. *The Liturgical Ministry of the Deacon*, CIO, 1987. To be scrupulously fair, Michael Vasey, new on the Commission then, might have done.
20. *Making Women Visible*, CIO, 1988.
21. *Faith in the City* fulminated: 'A Church ... which orders even its most contemporary forms of worship by reference to a closely printed book of over a thousand pages can never hope to bridge the gulf which separates it from ordinary people'. *Faith in the City*, CIO, 1985, pp. 66–7.
22. *Patterns for Worship*, CIO, 1989; *The Promise of His Glory*, CIO, 1990.
23. See the story in Chapter 6.
24. During the Revision Stage the lawyers enforced their ruling, that absolutions had to be officially authorized. The outline structure grew a vast appendix of absolutions. See Chapter 7.
25. See Chapter 7.

4 Baptism and Confirmation

1. *Baptism and Confirmation*, SPCK, 1959, p. ix, quoting the Lambeth 1958 report, which itself asserted as history a supposed policy of the Reformers which it is very doubtful that they had held, or at least held as an organizing principle.
2. *Baptism and Confirmation*, p. ix.
3. A related aspect about admission to communion is handled in Chapter 2.
4. The York rite has nearly disappeared from history. I believe it arose when the first draft of Canon Law revision (contained in the 1947 report of the Canon Law Commission) drafted a Canon that gave 'lawful authority' to texts approved in Canterbury or York Convocation, simply for their own province. The Convocation of York set up a group which produced this rite (a highly bowdlerized 1662), but Canon Law revision moved on and provincial uses had no mileage (or, to be precise, no more mileage than, say, the technically illegal 1928 rite). I once saw copies in a northern parish church in the early 1960s.
5. Some stylistic features also got attacked – not least the rubric (allegedly by Milner-White): '*The Font should be set in spacious and well-ordered surroundings*'. One speaker in York Convocation said the report 'enthroned liturgy, and made theology its eunuch'.
6. The Commission put Edward Ratcliff up to take apart the York rite on liturgical grounds, which he did in 'The York Revised Service for the Public Baptism of Infants – An Appraisement', *Theology* 63.485, 1960. And I don't think it has ever been heard of since.
7. I was myself confirmed in 1956 with the 1928 rite. But I recall talking to Willy Greer (Bishop of Manchester 1947–70) in the early 1960s, and he told me he had never used 1928.
8. In the mid-1960s I was addressing sacramental initiation in other places also. A joint drafting group of the Eclectics and LHLG which was writing a proposed modern baptismal service, published as R. T. Beckwith, C. O. Buchanan and K. F. W. Prior (eds), *Services of Baptism and Confirmation*, Latimer Monograph 2, Marcham Manor, 1967. It provided a ground-breaking unified adult-and-infant baptismal rite, claiming that missionary baptism is family baptism. In spring 1967 I was also drafting a statement on worship for the Keele NEAC. I drafted that confirmation is not needed after adult baptism, but at NEAC, which I was not at, the members were led into endorsing the Commission's patterns more than I myself wanted to, though the result reads self-contradictorily: '73. Christian initiation is sacramentally complete in baptism. The confirmation of those baptized as adults should be combined with their baptism, as proposed by the Liturgical Commission.'
9. See Chapter 6, page 71.
10. See Chapter 3 re this publication.
11. Geoffrey Lampe, *The Seal of the Spirit*, Longmans, 1951; James Dunn, *Baptism in the Holy Spirit*, SCM Press, 1970; Charles Whitaker, *Documents of the Baptismal Liturgy*, 2nd edn, SPCK, 1970. 'Integrated' was of course a kind of sleight of hand which loaded the reasoning process in favour of a 'two-staging' rite – for we subliminally interpret 'integrated' to be 'healthy' and

'disintegrated' to be 'unhealthy'. If we call biblical baptism 'simple' and later accretions 'complications', then the opposite subliminal message is given.

12. *Growing into Union: Proposals for Forming a United Church in England*, SPCK, 1970, p. 67. See Chapter 8 re this book.

13. The Ely Report (*Christian Initiation: Birth and Growth in the Christian Society*, CIO, 1971), recommendation 128, p. 43.

14. The processes are written up more fully in the next chapter.

15. The original Ely Report had simply stated 'sincere desire' by the parents as the qualification, but it came out this way from the Cornwell Report.

16. The Commission was drafting, and did publish, a derivative 'Series 3' infant baptism rite in 1975. I even published a Grove Booklet on it. It appeared twice on the General Synod agenda but was never debated and slowly slid from sight until a full Series 3 package came. I did, however, draw on it for my deanery and diocesan motion described lower down. The lead-in to the Decision and the baptismal affirmations now included (from the Latimer Monograph mentioned above), 'You must answer both for yourselves and for these children'.

17. It was Standing Committee's failure to report back that made me phrase my 'charismatic' motion to *require* them to bring a report *before the Synod*. See p. 193.

18. Christopher Byworth and John Simpson, *A Service of Thanksgiving and Blessing*, Grove Booklet on Ministry and Worship 5, Grove Books, 1972. In a complex history not only the Ely Commission, but also the Doctrine Commission, had recommended a dry run for infants (each apparently in ignorance of the other). The Doctrine Commission's report (*Baptism, Thanksgiving and Blessing*, GS56, CIO, 1971), debated in February 1972, had more readily called the service a 'blessing', a distinction just sufficient for the question to the dioceses to be a choice between 'thanksgiving' and 'blessing'.

19. See Note 16 above.

20. I had in fact launched in 1975 a new series of Grove Liturgical Studies with no. 1 being Charles Whitaker's *Sacramental Initiation Complete in Baptism*.

21. *Alternative Services Series 3: Initiation Services – A Report by the Liturgical Commission of the Church of England*, SPCK, 1977, pp. 6–7.

22. The prayer occupied a place comparable to that of exorcisms in the medieval rite, and the sign of the cross now reinforced the comparability, but the prayer is strictly 'apotropaic' – i.e. not so much expelling the evil one as defending the candidate against his future attacks. Geoffrey Lampe opposed the changed position just because the word 'exorcism' was used in the explanation.

23. Jim Roxburgh told the Committee that he had once given a name to a newborn child in danger of death – where the mother was haemorrhaging and the father was drowning his sorrows. After he had named the child, the father appeared roaring drunk, and, learning he had given a name to the child, threatened to kill him. I redrafted the rubric myself.

24. See page 49.

25. What was moral status of this issue? Was it one where we find ourselves wrestling with whether we can advise people on *how* to do that which we wish they wouldn't do at all (like prescribing the pill for 13-year-old girls, or providing clean needles for drug-takers)? Here we would look as though we

were saying that abortions could (or should) be done with prayer – and, if we did say that, would we be endorsing in liturgy that which we were denouncing elsewhere as an issue on its own? We were safer without it, but the wrestling with the complex moral matter remained.

26. I wrote both a Grove Booklet on the rites as authorized: *Liturgy for Initiation: The Series 3 Services*, Grove Booklet on Ministry and Worship 65, Grove Books, 1979; and a chapter on their ASB form in Colin Buchanan, Trevor Lloyd and Harold Miller (eds), *Anglican Worship Today: Collins' Illustrated Guide to the Alternative Service Book 1980*, Collins Liturgical, 1980.

27. It led to the foundation in 1986 of the Movement for the Reform of Infant Baptism (MORIB – now redubbed 'Baptismal Integrity'). I became president of the Movement in 1988 and retain that role today.

28. There was an amazing nonsense still going on behind this about incorporating the (1974 Cornwell) phrase 'willing and able to make the requisite promises' into the Canons. I have attempted to unravel this absurdity in my *Infant Baptism and the Gospel*, Darton, Longman & Todd, 1993, pp. 137–8.

29. Canons B 21 and B 22 do *not* charter indiscriminate baptism, but provide for delay for preparation, and an appeal to the bishop if this seems over-prolonged. See my *Infant Baptism in Common Worship*, Grove Worship Series 63, Grove Books, 2001, which devotes an appendix to this.

30. David Hebblethwaite reports it as though its title were *The Initiation Conundrum* (in his *Liturgical Revision in the Church of England 1984–2004*, p. 26).

31. See also Hebblethwaite, *Liturgical Revision in the Church of England 1984–2004*, p. 26 – his chapter is entitled 'The Cradle to the Grave'.

32. The original form said Synod believed that 'baptismal practices ... should be reviewed', and we were told a review would cost £37,000, but the proposer had said something less formal would do – and it is also worth noting that believing something should be done is a long way from requiring or even requesting it.

5 Children in communion

1. See Chapter 2.
2. The literal meaning of the 'confirmation rubric' undergirded both the doctrine and practice of Anglo-Catholics from 1870 onwards (see Chapter 2).
3. *Confirmation Today*, 1944, p. 42 footnote, cites recommendations of prior reports on Christian education in 1929 and 1938.
4. *Baptism and Confirmation Today*, 1954, Schedule, pp. 7–14. Two of the three, T. G. Jalland and J. D. C. Fisher, lived on into my time.
5. Troublesome? Yes; 'disintegration' is a pejorative and not a neutrally descriptive term – 'integrated' is good, 'disintegrated' bad. See Chapter 4.
6. This 'blessing' of non-communicants was a distinctly Anglican – and, I suspect, English – invention. Until the 1930s or 1940s non-communicants never went near a communion rail. But, if my analysis is right, then the first children to be so 'blessed' may still be alive today. My odd attempts to trace the origins of the practice have been fruitless.

7. Philip Crowe (ed.), *Keele '67*, Falcon Books, 1967, p. 35. The bit about 'baptismal discipline' was irrelevant (as lapsed families would not send their children to communion), but in the haste of the Congress it slipped in.

8. See page 2. I was not actually at Keele.

9. 'An Anglican Evangelical looks at Sacramental Initiation', *Faith and Unity*, May 1968, pp. 47–8.

10. The beginning of the New Zealand story is told in Brian Davis's book, *The Way Ahead: Anglican Change and Prospect in New Zealand*, Caxton Press, Christchurch, 1995, pp. 58–60.

11. In the mid-1970s I was rung by an Anglican missionary in Isfahan in Iran, who was passing through Nottingham and wanted to see me. I dropped everything and spent time with him. 'You must change the Church of England's rules,' he said. 'I agree,' I replied, 'but how come you in Iran are so determined about it?' 'Well,' he replied, 'our diocesan rules require expatriates to adhere to the canons of their home country – so American children receive communion, while British ones do not – a pastoral disaster.'

12. Ely Report (*Christian Initiation: Birth and Growth in the Christian Society*, GS 30, CIO, 1971), p. 48.

13. See the discussion of initiation rites on pages 42–4.

14. *Christian Initiation: A Working Paper by P. R. Cornwell*, GS 184, CIO, 1974.

15. We had some momentary diversion (though none laughed at the time), as the Bishop of Peterborough, one Douglas Feaver, moved an amendment to change 'April 1975' to 'January 1976' ('I believe it would be absolutely impossible for the dioceses to do this by April 1975 with any degree of decency or order'). The irony was that no member of Synod ever expected Douglas Feaver to encourage debate anywhere – or even to be present at General Synod, let alone to be moving an amendment. So arguably we had egg on our faces; but, for Feaver's reasons, we approved the change.

16. Only the diocesan bishop constituted the diocesan House of Bishops in those days – and thus Canterbury diocese voted in favour in both the other houses, but this was not recorded in the cumulated results because Donald Coggan was abroad when they met. (He might not have been in favour anyway . . .)

17. Oh yes, and Peterborough (see the reference in Note 15 above)? Well, the diocesan synod must have met, because it voted overwhelmingly (in a different category) against any service of 'blessing' of children not being presented for baptism. But on the three motions under examination here, no returns were received at all. Clearly the time Douglas Feaver gained for serious discussion had not been sufficient for his own diocese, which was alone in sending in no figures for these three motions.

18. Over the years this weighed heavily with me (see my later speech on p. 66). But I kept silent that day, as I had other initiation fish to fry, and had to avoid over-exposure.

19. The only practitioner known to me was Simon Barrington-Ward (Bishop of Coventry ten years later). Simon, with a strong charismatic (and romantic) approach to episcopal ministry, revelled in confirming seven-year-olds.

20. The first year of Grove Booklets (i.e. 1972) had three titles on Ely themes,

including no. 8, Christopher Byworth, *Communion, Confirmation, and Commitment.* Our group (see pages 1 and 3) was totally behind the communion of unconfirmed young children, and advocated it strongly. A second edition of no. 8 in 1974 addressed the questions sent to the dioceses. Later, nos 85, 112 and 149 in the series pressed the issue further. See also Ron Green's prospectus for London Diocese, *Confirmation Reform: Time for Decision,* 1972, and his parish experience in *Not in Front of the Children,* 1980.

21. These were broad diocesan initiatives; but there were plenty of parish ones, with or without episcopal connivance.
22. One such case, in which I was proud to be involved, was when the youthful Canadian, David Holeton, gave the Annual Alcuin Club lecture on 'Infant Communion – Then and Now' in 1980. This careful exposition of history was turned into Grove Liturgical Study no. 27 under the same title in 1981.
23. See the report, . . . *and do not hinder them,* WCC, 1982.
24. Paradoxically, their enthusiasm exceeded their synodical skills. They submitted no return on the principle, and on the first alternative this global figure combining clergy and lay voting in disregard for the instructions from General Synod, and it was consequently omitted from the national statistics.
25. The working party had on it both youth advisers and educationalists, and their respective concerns all pointed in the same direction. Another member was the American Dr John Frederick, who was then rector of Bletchingley in Southwark diocese, but had been ministering in the USA when the changes there began around 1970. A little later he produced a book, *The Future of Liturgical Reform* (Churchman Publishing, 1987), and, while he said little in it about liturgical text, he wrote forcefully (and at some theological depth) in favour of unconfirmed children being in communion.
26. This was published both as an 8-page pamphlet, *Children and Communion,* and, with supporting essays, in C. O. Buchanan (ed.), *Nurturing Children in Communion,* Grove Liturgical Study 44, Grove Books, 1985. Years later, I did a new Introduction to a different symposium on the Statement, Ruth Meyers (ed.), *Children at the Table,* Church Hymnal, New York, 1992.
27. See page 3.
28. *Children in the Way,* National Society/Church House Publishing, 1988, p. 52.
29. Brian Davis, now Archbishop of New Zealand, was in this section and inspired every positive mention of Boston and Knaresborough. The report cites 'the resolution of the 1968 Lambeth Conference concerning the admission to communion after appropriate instruction' (ACC-7, *Many Gifts, One Spirit,* ACC, 1987, p. 71). The actual 1968 resolution was much less specific than this, but Brian Davis tended to quote it in this form.
30. See my comments on this on page 256.
31. See page 256.
32. *The Truth Shall Make You Free: The Lambeth Conference 1988,* Church House Publishing for ACC, 1988, Mission and Ministry p. 70.
33. See Chapter 4, page 48.
34. *Christian Initiation and its Relation to Some Pastoral Offices,* GS Misc 366, CIO, 1991.
35. The Statement and recommendations are published in David Holeton (ed.),

Christian Initiation in the Anglican Communion, Grove Worship Series 118, Grove Books, 1991. A substantial volume of accompanying essays is in David Holeton (ed.), *Growing in Newness of Life*, Anglican Book Centre, Toronto, 1993.

36. On a separate but linked issue, the endorsing of the Boston recommendations (see pages 60–61), Mark Dalby dissented and Colin James abstained.

37. I asked questions in February and November 1993. Colin James spoke kindly about Toronto but hinted that I (because of Grove Books connections) had some pecuniary interest in selling the Statement! He said it would not be appropriate to have a debate just on Toronto (which no one had requested), adding, 'I am sure that they [the Toronto findings] will be referred to the dioceses in due course' – which of course never happened, nor ever looked likely.

38. I made a kind of side-effort when, in November 1991, Molly Dow brought a diocesan motion to Synod, asking for a eucharistic prayer to be 'suitable for use ... with children present'. I tried to use the (very mild) leverage of pointing out that it is a distorted discipline to write eucharistic liturgy for non-communicants, and I tried an amendment to end the motion with 'at services where children are likely to be communicating'. Of course it got nowhere. But can we pray for fruitful communion for a congregation of non-communicants?

39. The five are:

1. The acknowledgement of entry into adulthood;
2. The highlighting of individual faith;
3. The need to have a clear framework in which to follow up the results of a tradition of open infant baptism;
4. The importance of prayer and the charisms of the Holy Spirit in the initiation of the Christian;
5. Responsible commitment to the life and mission of a local church.

On the Way: Towards an Integrated Approach to Christian Initiation, GS Misc 444, Church House Publishing, 1995, pp. 105–106.

40. *Admission to Communion in Relation to Baptism and Confirmation: Report by the House of Bishops*, GS 1212, Church House Publishing, 1996, para. 15, p. 4.

41. See pages 55, 60 and 64.

42. She was Archdeacon Judith Rose, the first woman archdeacon, and previously in my own congregation in Gillingham.

43. See pages 259 and 261.

44. See *News of Liturgy* 285, September 1998, the only place where this 'disappeared' text is published.

6 Eucharistic prayers

1. This, as a living tradition of practice, is normally traced to W. H. Frere's *Some Principles of Liturgical Reform* (1911), though it had precedent in the seventeenth century, and actual contemporary models in a somewhat embellished form in Scotland and America.

2. My innocence was such that this struck me as an out-and-out 'catholic' takeover. What I did not realize till it was all over was that Couratin and Ratcliff

were fulfilling a scholarly dream to take Hippolytus' words (*ipsissima verba* of the second century, as they saw it) and bring them into actual use in the Church of England today. Couratin was 'teeing up' the prayer for the Sanctus to be transferred next time round to the climax of the prayer, where our two patristic scholars were hypothesizing Hippolytus had used it (though it is in fact absent from our texts of Hippolytus). Other Anglo-Catholics might have expressed the anamnesis with different wording, but our two were unshifting about it (Eric Mascall said to me later that he saw them as wholly hung up on actual words, rather than handling the text at the level of ideas).

3. At the time, it was called 'second series' (1928 services and the Interim Rite were 'first series'). In the early 1970s it was all reversed and became 'Series 1', 'Series 2', etc.

4. I also dissented over petitions for the departed. See Chapter 7 below.

5. I have passed by the history of Series 1 and its successors, except for brief coverage in Chapter 3.

6. See R. C. D. Jasper, *The Development of Anglican Liturgy 1662–1980*, SPCK, 1989, p. 310.

7. The actual progress of the complete eucharistic rites can be charted in my three international Anglican collections of eucharistic liturgies, the first two with an introductory essay to each text. Series 2 is in *Modern Anglican Liturgies 1958– 1968*, Oxford University Press, 1968; Series 3 in *Further Anglican Liturgies 1968–1975*, Grove Books, 1975; and Rite A in *Latest Anglican Liturgies 1976– 1984*, Alcuin/SPCK, 1985. There is a considerable treatment of the theological character of the rites in Christopher Cocksworth, *Evangelical Eucharistic Thought in the Church of England*, Cambridge University Press, 1993. Christopher borrowed my files of correspondence and Commission memoranda when doing his doctorate, of which the book is a re-edited version.

8. The Commission also produced a commentary on it, published the same day.

9. For the ARCIC-1 Statement see Chapter 9.

10. Further contemporary reflection came in R. C. D. Jasper (ed.), *The Eucharist Today: Studies on Series 3*, SPCK, 1974.

11. See Chapter 7.

12. See my *Latest Liturgical Revision in the Church of England 1978–84*, Grove Liturgical Study no. 39, Grove Books, 1984, p. 9, quoted in Jasper, *The Development of the Anglican Liturgy 1662–1980*, p. 351.

13. There was a text in R. T. Beckwith and J. E. Tiller, *The Service of Holy Communion*, Latimer Monograph 3, Marcham Manor, 1972, pp. 104–116.

14. 'For' had been a contribution he had made to Series 3. The debate was enlivened by not only nuances of logic and theology, but also a side-discussion as to which of 'who' and 'for' was the worse word for starting a sentence up with.

15. This had gained considerable international Anglican standing, not only because some parts of the Communion had followed something like it since the eighteenth century, but also because, at the IALC interim conference the previous year, Tom Talley had given a very compelling lecture on it, since published in David Holeton (ed.), *Revising the Eucharist: Groundwork for the Anglican Communion*, Alcuin/GROW Joint Liturgical Study 28, Grove Books, 1994.

16. Trevor Lloyd and I had been planning a Grove Worship Series Booklet (no. 136)

to give a commentary and guidance on the six prayers. As it was, we had quickly to revamp the plan, and produced in April 1996 *Six Eucharistic Prayers as Proposed in 1996* (a title echoing the 1928 Prayer Book). It includes not only the text of the six prayers with a theological and historical introduction, but also an essay by the Liturgical Commission – 'Eucharists when Children are Present: Pastoral Issues and Suggestions', which the Revision Committee had recommended should be published with the texts when authorized. This might therefore have perished if we had not incorporated it in this slightly piratical publication.

17. In the debate, one speaker said that 'make the memorial' is greatly valued by Anglo-Catholics. I see some signs this is true; but I see it in their persistent use of what is now Prayer B. Has this denting of Prayer A actually led to more use of it?

18. I wrote this up for the Ushaw Library Bulletin as *Eucharistic Prayer H: An Unauthorized Account*, and offprinted it by permission as a 14-page pamphlet, obtainable from me, which gives the whole story.

7 Six other liturgical issues

1. See my *The New Communion Service – Reasons for Dissent*, Church Book Room Press, 1966.
2. *Prayer and the Departed*, SPCK, 1970.
3. I wrote up this little battle in 'Some Loose Legal Cannons', *Ecclesiastical Law Journal* 20, January 1997.
4. Compare the treatment of the Southwell motion on infant baptism on page 44.
5. On p. 404 it says the material listed has been 'commended by the House of Bishops . . . pursuant to Canon B.2', but this, I understand, is a misprint, and new printings will simply indicate that the material is commended in order to be available for use under Canon B 5.
6. In my judgement the form remains theologically wobbly (or wrong), and, chairing the editorial board of the Joint Liturgical Studies, I longed for a more rigorous critique of it in no. 58, Trevor Lloyd and Phillip Tovey (eds), *A Celebration of Forgiveness: An Original Work of Michael Vasey*, 2005. Michael Vasey's material was the source for much in the Commission's new rites.
7. *The Lord's Prayer in the Church of England*, Grove Worship Series 131, Grove Books, 1995.
8. *Modern Liturgical Texts*, SPCK, 1968.
9. Rome-watchers know that in 2001, before any response came from the Vatican, the encyclical *Liturgiam Authenticam* abolished Roman Catholic involvement in ecumenical liturgiography, and gave priority to Latinate texts. This, if implemented, might salvage 'temptation' but restore 'trespasses'. The encyclical was not foreseen in 1999.
10. I write 'parishes can relax', but I have to qualify that immediately. A contrary view has been strongly urged against me – namely that, because vesture is covered by Canon B 8, and the provision for changes of no substantial

importance refers to services authorized under Canon B 2, there is no discretion re vesture. I originally stuck with my guns, because the conduct of services is all of a piece, and Canon B 8 lies behind and within the services authorized under B 2, not as a wholly separate category from them. But the lawyers advise that the contrary view is correct. My only fall back is that I believe that no one should go hard and fast on the boundaries of this discretion in B 5, unless or until there is a complaint to a bishop, and I once had to head off Robert Runcie during Questions in Synod from giving off-the-cuff opinions about what the 'discretion' covered and what it did not (he just blushed slightly and said he was trying to be helpful). I am convinced that vesture is a matter of 'no substantial importance', and we reinforce a cartoon view of Anglican priorities if we allow liberties with the text of services, but are inflexible about vesture. But the law has spoken. I say no more.

11. For the Scheme and its fate see page 107. For the relationship between CSI rites, the Anglican–Methodist Ordinal and ASB texts, see C. O. Buchanan (ed.), *Modern Anglican Ordination Rites*, Alcuin/GROW Joint Liturgical Study 3, Grove Books, 1987.

12. I cannot delay on the deacons' 'ministry'. But I emphasize that the Church of England knows no 'concelebration', and its eucharistic rites provide for a single presidency only. See John R. K. Fenwick, *Eucharistic Concelebration*, Grove Worship Series 82, Grove Books, 1982 – commenting on the Liturgical Commission's GS Misc 163, 1981.

13. Royal mandates and Declarations of Assent among others.

14. Particularly anointing, but also washing deacons' feet, and the whole fussed invention of 'the deacon of the rite'.

15. This account concentrates on my points of concern. For a more rounded account see my *Ordination Rites in Common Worship*, Grove Worship Series 186, Grove Books, February 2006.

16. R. T. Beckwith, J. I. Packer, C. O. Buchanan, *Reservation and Communion of the Sick*, Grove Booklet on Ministry and Worship 4, Grove Books, 1972.

8 Anglicans and Methodists

1. The exclusion of the unconfirmed from communion (see Chapter 2) also consolidated not just a separation but even an antipathy between the Church of England and the Free Churches.

2. See Chapter 9.

3. G. K. A. Bell (ed.), *Documents on Christian Unity: A Selection from the First and Second Series 1920–30*, Oxford University Press, 1955, p. 55.

4. The SIUC came from a union in 1909 of Presbyterian and Congregationalist Churches; see Bengt Sundkler, *The Church of South India: The Movement Towards Union, 1900–1947*, Lutterworth, 1954.

5. I am precise about this, not only because for decades I cited CSI as the model way to unite churches and their ministries, but also because the last surviving bishop consecrated on that day, Lesslie Newbigin, virtually became my bishop after I resigned in Birmingham. I had been powerfully moved, years before, by

his second edition of *The Reunion of the Church*, where his defence of the CSI method of union appears impregnable – as staked upon justification through faith. When I became Bishop of Woolwich in 1996, I inherited the same Lesslie Newbigin, now 87, as an honoured resident of my Area, and promoted a celebration of his 50 years as a bishop in Herne Hill on 27 September 1997. He died in January 1998. I pay tribute to his memory.

6. *Conversations between the Church of England and the Methodist Church: A Report*, CIO; Epworth Press, 1963. This prompted me into print (see pp. 1–2 above), and I write from here on from within the situation.

7. The principal literature was: J. I. Packer (ed.), *The Church of England and the Methodist Church*, Marcham, 1963; J. I. Packer (ed.), *All in Each Place*, Marcham, 1965; and J. I. Packer (ed.), *Fellowship in the Gospel*, Marcham, 1968. I wrote in each of these and elsewhere also. The Keele Congress Statement responded in April 1967 in paras 98–102, affirming a desire to unite with the Methodists, a request for the Methodist dissentients to be included, an appreciation of doctrinal improvements in the newly published interim report, *Towards Reconciliation*, and a precise criticism and conditional rejection of the Service of Reconciliation – 'at this stage few of the clergy among us would feel able to commit themselves to take part in [it].' Philip Crowe (ed.), *Keele '67*, Falcon Books, 1967, p. 40. An Open Letter of 52 evangelicals in June 1968, after the final Scheme was published, was similar.

8. References to 'the Scheme' from here on refer back to this 1968 Scheme.

9. Michael Green, just becoming my principal at LCD, was also partially involved.

10. The text of both these letters is contained in an appendix to *Growing into Union: Proposals for Forming a United Church in England*, SPCK, 1970.

11. Graham Leonard and I wrote on 'Intercommunion: Some Interim Agreement' (see page 27). Michael Green and Eric Mascall contributed 'Eucharistic Sacrifice: Some Interim Agreement'.

12. C. O. Buchanan, *The Clarified Scheme Examined*, Grove Books, 1971.

13. See pages 28–29, not least Michael Ramsey's own practice.

14. In November 1970 (i.e. as General Synod started) the church unions had gone ahead in North India and Pakistan – and General Synod (though not I) voted that the ambiguous unification rites there *had bestowed episcopal ordination on the non-episcopal ministers* who had undergone them.

15. I wrote about the Propositions for NEAC-2 at Nottingham in April 1977, in 'The Unity of the Church', in Ian Cundy (ed.), *Obeying Christ in a Changing World: 2. The People of God*, Fountain, 1977, pp. 114–41.

16. I was invited to be one of these, but regretfully had to decline – see page 3 and note 3 (Introduction) on page 283.

17. I was somewhat freer of other liturgical matters by winter 1979–80 when this liturgical work was done, and I took a full part in the subcommittee's task. However, I missed a trick, in that a Scottish Episcopal Church eucharistic prayer was slipped in by one drafting person, and, with my eyes on all the unique liturgical material, I missed this, and had to complain rather apologetically and out of time about it.

18. See Chapter 6.

19. In the interests of accuracy I ought to report that there was a brief further

infuriating look at CSI. In November 1982 I asked a question about it, referring the then Archbishop of Canterbury to the erstwhile initiative of an earlier Bishop of St Albans (see page 110). He did remember it, and, now that the Covenant had failed, he nudged the BMU to set up a working party of four, plus a BMU officer, to revisit our relationship to CSI. I was on the working party, and Geoffrey Paul, then Bishop of Bradford, chaired it. We met in February 1983 *during Synod time* (when I had to speak in the Chamber), and then worked by post. Geoffrey Paul died, and the work ceased. A brief report was cobbled together, recommending no change, but carrying my dissent, which sought true full communion with CSI – but Geoffrey Paul had not seen this when he died. As he had died, and as Horace Dammers also dissented, the Bishop of Chichester, Eric Kemp, remained alone as the 'majority'. Our report went to the House of Bishops in Autumn 1983. During 1984, the idea of 'full communion' without change in the rules obviously took over (Eric Kemp wanted that now). So in November 1984 Robert Runcie on behalf of the House of Bishops wished to declare the Church of England in full communion with CSI (which is exactly what Eric Kemp had declined to do in 1972: see page 110), and Peter Dawes carried the Synod for an amendment which said the Synod would like to enter into full communion with CSI on the basis of the definition in the 1958 Lambeth Conference report (i.e. with full interchangeability of ministers). But no further action occurred.

20. For myself, in 1985–90 I was off Synod. I was, however, a nominated participant in the Inter-Church Process ('Not Strangers but Pilgrims'), looking to bring new ecumenical instruments into place on 1 September 1990. I was present for the Swanwick Declaration of 4 September 1987. I claim a very small walk-on part in the Process. On the evening of 2 September 1987 there was an open forum at the final Swanwick Conference, and it was chaired by Derek Worlock, Roman Catholic Archbishop of Liverpool. At the very end of an evening of secondary matters, I rose in some frustration and said, 'Archbishop, what many of us here are waiting to know is whether the Roman Catholics – who have not been in the British Council of Churches but are taking an active part in this Process – are going to participate in these new ecumenical "instruments"?' Derek Worlock smiled gently and closed the meeting. At 11 a.m. the next day Cardinal Hume announced (to everyone's delight) that they would be fully participating. I am usually sceptical about *Post hoc ergo propter hoc*, but tempted by the old Adam this time to believe it.

21. *The Priesthood of the Ordained Ministry*, GS 694, Church House Publishing, 1986.

22. *The Priesthood of the Ordained Ministry*, ch. 13, paras 142, 148.

23. EKD is Evangelische Kirche in Deutschland, which in 1991 was forming a single federation (calling itself a 'Communion') of West and East Germany Churches, following political reunification.

24. *Commitment to Mission and Unity*, Church House Publishing/Methodist Publishing House, 1996.

25. I have some comments on this report (apart from the membership question):

   (a) 'Mission' in its title (let alone 'Commitment' to Mission) was eyewash. It did not address mission.

(b) On the integration of ordained ministries, the conversationalists, beyond their brief, outlined a mad proposal.

(c) The Foreword by the co-chairmen was interestingly defensive: 'In view of past experience we hope that the General Synod of the Church of England will declare its mind . . . before the Methodist Conference is asked to do so' (pp. 17–18).

(d) There was no real mention of the URC. I still hoped for trilateral approaches.

26. See Colin Podmore (ed.), *Visible Unity and the Ministry of Oversight: The Second Theological Conference Held under the Meissen Agreement between the Church of England and the Evangelical Church in Germany*, Church House Publishing, 1997.

27. Podmore, *Visible Unity*, p. 5.

28. *Called to be One* (1996) was an exercise of Churches Together in England (CTE) to discover what unity we enjoyed and to prompt further moves.

29. *Conversations on the Way to Unity 1999–2001*, United Reformed Church, 2001.

30. The Formal Conversations looked for the URC to be somewhere between observing and participating, and arguably did better here than our trilaterals. The URC Assembly seems itself to have let the matter run into the ground.

31. They also worried about the not-quite-explicit dissent of a hard line Anglican evangelical, Angus McLeay, on behalf of the Calvinism of the Church of England.

32. For 'previous experience', see note 25 above.

33. *In the Spirit of the Covenant*, Methodist Publishing House, 2005, p. 2.

34. Re the CCU's opposition, see page 121.

35. See pp. 110–111 of the report. It exactly matches the proposal of Cyril Bowles in July 1971 (see page 109), and is very close to what Geoffrey Fisher asked of the Free Churches in his November 1946 sermon.

9 Roman Catholic relationships

1. Hans Küng, *The Council and Reunion*, ET Sheed & Ward, 1961.

2. See C. O. Buchanan, *What Did Cranmer Think He Was Doing?* Grove Liturgical Study 7, Grove Books, 1976, p. 7 n. 1.

3. Jean Tillard, *What Priesthood Has the Ministry?* Grove Booklet on Ministry and Worship 13, Grove Books, February 1973.

4. This is wholly in line with what Bob Taft, the Roman Catholic (Eastern rites) liturgist, attested: 'I was made a priest at my baptism, and a presbyter at my ordination.' See also Hans Küng, *The Church*, ET, Search Press, 1968, pp. 364–7.

5. *Authority in the Church*, end of para. 23.

6. The quotation is from John Howe's letter as quoted in GS 394, p. 1. The 'United not Absorbed' quotation within it echoes the paper read by Dom Lambert Beauduin at the Malines Conversations in 1925, 'L'Eglise Anglicane unie non absorbée'.

7. *Authority in the Church II*, para. 30.

8. *Final Report*, SPCK/Catholic Truth Society, 1982.

9. *Baptism – Eucharist – Ministry*, WCC, 1982.
10. This led me to write a Grove Booklet, *ARCIC and Lima on Baptism and Eucharist*, Grove Worship Series 86, Grove Books, October 1983.
11. *Towards a Church of England Response to BEM and ARCIC*, CIO, 1985.
12. The words 'and ministry' were not in Oswald Clark's original motion, but came in by an amendment.
13. This quotes from para. 10 of the official response, a text published in Latin. The translation is in Christopher Hill and Edward Yarnold (eds), *Anglicans and Roman Catholics: The Search for Unity*, SPCK, 1994. This extract is from p. 158.
14. *Clarifications on Eucharist and Ministry*, Church House Publishing/Catholic Truth Society, 1994.
15. *The Gift of Authority: Authority in the Church III*, ABC Toronto/Church Publishing NY/Catholic Truth Society, 1999.
16. The overall impression is almost the reverse – that the laity are there to receive the faith from the hierarchy and believe it because it has been taught by authority.
17. Martin Davie '"Yes and No" – *The Gift of Authority*', in Peter Fisher (ed.), *Unpacking the Gift*, Church House Publishing, 2003, pp. 33–59 (55).
18. *Unpacking the Gift*, p. 112 n. 48.
19. I acknowledge three small errors in it: the prospective date of the Synod debate on page 3; a brief exposition of the doctrine of the Assumption which states that Roman Catholics do not believe Mary died before being assumed, when in fact the 1950 decree leaves open that question (p. 10); and the attribution to *Ut Omnes Unum Sint* of the citations from *Clarifications* which are in fact in *One Bread One Body* (p. 34 n. 2). Otherwise, my polemic stands.
20. Let anyone who doubts this ask CCU for both the critique and my point-by-point answer. But read the actual Grove Booklet first.
21. Michael Nazir-Ali, the only member of ARCIC-2 on General Synod, commented in his speech: 'I was very concerned to see the first draft of this motion which is now set before you. After discussion in the House of Bishops, it was toned down a little, but it has since somehow returned to a more negative form.' So its character had been fairly volatile. I of course thought it ought to be more 'negative'.
22. *Mary: Grace and Hope in Christ*, ACC/Pontifical Council for Christian Unity, 2005.
23. See his *The Womb and the Tomb*, HarperCollins, 1992, passim.

10 Multi-ethnic Anglicanism

1. Its origins are charted in the Introduction. See *Faith in the City*, Church House Publishing, 1985, pp. xiii–xiv. See also Adrian Hastings, *Robert Runcie*, Mowbray, 1991, pp. 90–93, and David Sheppard, *Steps along Hope Street*, Hodder & Stoughton, 2003, pp. 241ff. David Sheppard was vice-chairman of the Commission – much noted in the church papers on the Friday that I write this, for he died last Saturday, and today brings the obituaries.
2. Wilfred Wood, in a personal letter in answer to my enquiry in March 2005.
3. Once a by-election occurred, Wilfred needed to be elected. I tried again myself,

but reckoned he had a prior claim – and, when I was eliminated, my first preferences moved on to Wilfred (making us both happy).

4. *Faith in the City* 5.74, p. 100. But the surrounding argument about quotas for protected groups (and precedents for such protection) needed careful probing by experts in STV, and I don't think that was done.

5. Wilfred told me about this at the time, conveying the impression the Laity had recently been leant upon to co-opt some category of persons for some cause, where they reckoned they were being overborne – hence John Habgood's reporting a negative response about co-options. But I am not convinced that co-opting ethnic minority persons (CBAC's own initial proposal) would have been unwelcome to Synod.

6. I have mentioned further in Chapters 1 and 16 that Synod cannot amend its own constitution without going to Parliament. But here the identifying of a special representation of an ethnic group made legislation all the more important, lest Synod breach the Race Relations Act 1976.

7. The ordination of women was *the* presenting issue in the 1990 Synod election – I make no abstract point here.

8. I wrote thus to John Habgood after the November 1988 debate. In reply he rebuked me for encouraging such 'distorted' voting. I responded that the system promoted the distorting and I simply went with its grain. To Wilfred I wrote that, if we were again both in the same election, but with this system, I would say to the electors, 'If you put Wilfred above me, you will get him, but may not get me. If you put me above him, you will get me AND him.' If each candidate wrote similarly, then Wilfred would have appeared rejected by the electorate. *That* is the 'grain' of that system.

9. While the organizational (and financial) task stretched our team to the very limit (and I bear the major responsibility), yet we were also victims of crude yet skilled racist propaganda from the apartheid regime in South Africa, of hostility to Desmond in the Tory minority on the city council, and of opposition from the Royal Society of St George.

10. I assisted the New Testament Church of God in 1993, when, as company secretary of Grove Books, I published *From Scepticism to Hope*, a semi-autobiographical account by their chief bishop, Selwyn Arnold, of the origins and growth of the NTCG in Britain, and of their move from simple preaching of salvation to social concern and community relations.

11. The term 'institutional racism' was in use in 1994, not invented in 1998 by the MacPherson Enquiry. It was well known among the victims long before that.

12. The CRE was unready for this – its experience was of one party (e.g. employees) delating another party (e.g. their employers) for racist practices. No institution had put itself on the block before! The upshot, outlined in Glynne Gordon-Carter's *An Amazing Journey* (Church House Publishing, 2003), pp. 133–4, belongs to Southwark's history rather than General Synod's.

13. Sentamu (as he is now known) declined to stand for election in the suffragans' constituency both in by-elections and in the full election of 2000. In autumn 2002 he became Bishop of Birmingham (a wonderful appointment), and rejoined Synod ex officio. In 2005 he became Archbishop of York (is there no stopping him?) and thus a President of Synod.

14. Words of the Revd Lorraine Dixon (British born of Jamaican origin) in *An Amazing Journey* (p. 74), where she continues: 'However this notion of colour blindness is put forward, the result is the same "I am not seen".'

11 Colleges and courses

1. *A Strategy for the Church's Ministry*, CIO, 1983.
2. I had a slightly vested interest. Philip Crowe was an old friend, and I had taught worship courses there to stay alive during my time in exile in the winters 1989–90 and 1990–91 – and, having actually enjoyed the place, I may have had a higher opinion of it than many did.
3. *Formation for Ministry within a Learning Church*, Church House Publishing, 2003.
4. Each £1 million in central funds is only an average of £1 per head *per annum* by reasonably regular worshippers. For each diocese it is probably less than one clergy stipend – and annual variations in stipendiary numbers are much more substantial than that. But the discussion also touched on the need and the genuine possibility of better giving.
5. The figure '12' includes St Michael's, Llandaff, of the Church in Wales, with 3 Church of England candidates in residence.

12 The ordination of women

1. See C. O. Buchanan, *Is the Church of England Biblical? An Anglican Ecclesiology*, Darton, Longman & Todd, 1998, pp. 333–6.
2. In *Growing into Union* (see pages 107–8) in 1970 we were able to defer the question. If pressed, I suspect we would all then have opposed the ordination of women.
3. Unusually, abstentions were recorded – two Clergy and three Laity. I was one of the two.
4. An illustration of 'twitchiness' was the row on the Ripon College, Cuddesdon, Council around 1977, when it was reported an American woman ordinand was in training there.
5. I was not alone in my amnesia. Reading in the *Report of Proceedings* that Hugh Montefiore had introduced the debate, I wrote to him shortly before he died to ask him why and how he got the task. He could not place it in his memories, which were much more focused on his later attempt to have a 20-year experiment (see page 168). But his biography suggests that it was because he had just edited a book, *Yes to Women Priests* (Mowbray/Mayhew-McCrimmon, 1978); and his autobiography recalls Graham Leonard opposing, and the birth of MOW from the defeat.
6. See page 193 about this.
7. See page 172.
8. For a fuller account of the Covenant and related events see pages 111–3.
9. One of the oddities in the discussion was a proposal that deaconesses should hand in their existing New Testaments at an early point in the service, and then

have them returned, suitably endorsed by the ordaining bishop, at the usual point.

10. See the discussion in Chapter 8.

11. See pages 112–13.

12. It had some trouble at the final fence, as the Parliamentarians spotted that in the 1662 Ordinal new deacons are virtually promised that if they behave themselves they can come back a year later to become, er, priests? Few bishops were using 1662 for ordinations, but its text and rubrics were the lawful determinant and a way round this had to be found, and ultimately it was March 1987 before the first ordinations of women as deacons occurred.

13. Mark Santer said that ARCIC was considering how far differences of practice could be contained within a pattern of full communion – I am not aware that, even 18 years later, ARCIC has actually said anything that touches on the ordination of women in relation to this (*Church as Communion* in 1990 did not help), so Colin James would have secured a long wait.

14. See page 164.

15. I described this debate in detail in the chapter about Parliament in my *Cut the Connection*, Darton, Longman & Todd, 1994; see also Chapter 16 below.

16. My own contribution was to ask (as I had in the House of Bishops) how Synod could promise 'no discrimination' in senior appointments, when so many of them are made by the (unaccountable) Prime Minister. I received no answer (it is unanswerable), but I still voted for the Act. See also Chapter 18.

17. The categories of departures from stipendiary ministry are not simple; some had no financial entitlement (and some of course will have simply retired on their pensions); some have gone elsewhere; and some of them have returned.

18. FiF appointed their own parallel working party which in 2004 published *Consecrated Women? A Contribution to the Women Bishops Debate*, Norwich: Canterbury Press. It is serious, although we know the 'bottom line' before reading the first. It is the weightier for including a thought-through plan for a 'Third Province', though its chances of implementation are slim. It includes powers to make canons about appointing bishops (which our present Synod cannot do!). But a Province of Andrarchy would vitally need to choose its own bishops.

13 Lay presidency

1. This should not be confused with any theological notion that ministers not episcopally ordained *could* not preside. The readiness of Anglican leaders to receive communion in Lutheran and Reformed Churches on the continent from the Reformation time onwards makes that clear.

2. See my *What Did Cranmer Think He Was Doing?* Grove Liturgical Study 7, Grove Books, 1976.

3. Hans Küng, *My Struggle for Freedom*, Continuum, 2004, p. 250. Rightly or wrongly, he depends upon the lack of any mention of ordained ministers in 1 Corinthians in relation to worship or discipline or pastoring or with any other responsibility for implementing Paul's injunctions.

4. Hans Küng, *The Church*, Search Press, 1968, p. 403.
5. There are actually two sorts of lay presidency in Methodism – one a provision for meeting emergency pastoral need, whereby a licence is issued on an annual basis, and the other the general provision for probationers, prior to ordination, to preside in a regular way for that limited period.
6. Philip Crowe (ed.), *Keele '67*, Falcon Books, 1967, p. 36.
7. A. E. Harvey, *Priest or President?* SPCK, 1975, pp. 46–8.
8. See Chapter 8.
9. The Study included an attempted refutation by Douglas Davies, specifically commissioned for this purpose. Debating lay presidency in print has helped it become a theological issue, rather than a social indiscretion! There is a chapter against it by Paul Gibson in Thomas J. Talley (ed.), *A Kingdom of Priests: Liturgical Formation of the People of God*, Alcuin/GROW Joint Liturgical Study 5, Grove Books, 1988; and there are passing (weak) comments in the IALC 'Dublin Statement' – see David Holeton, *Renewing the Anglican Eucharist*, Grove Worship Series 135, Grove Books, 1996.
10. *The Nottingham Statement*, Falcon Books, 1977, pp. 22–3.
11. They included Cyril Bowles, David Brown, John Eastaugh (England), John Lewis, John Grindrod (Australia), Fred Crabb (Canada), Leonard Ashton (Cyprus), Jabeez Bryce (Polynesia) and two US bishops.
12. *The Report of the Lambeth Conference 1978*, CIO, 1978, p. 83.
13. Colin Bazley, Bishop of Chile and prime mover of this concern, was absent through bereavement.
14. See page 91.
15. His iconoclasm also threatened both liturgical vesture and differentials in stipend.
16. See Alan Hargrave, *But Who Will Preside?* Grove Worship Series 113, Grove Books, 1990. Alan was sardonic because the South Americans had not been invited to the USA to comment about the international implications when the 1976 General Convention was rocking the Anglican boat with the ordination of women. This South American reaction might also relate to General Convention's actions in August 2003.
17. See Chapter 19 for how this came about.
18. Some information which was relevant but not available to us was that one section of ACC-6 in Nigeria in 1984 had in fact reported on 'Presidency at the Eucharist' and had both recorded that lay presidency actually occurs in the Anglican Communion and (while not endorsing that) 'we commend the subject for further discussion at ACC-7 and the Lambeth Conference of 1988.' See *Bonds of Affection, Proceedings of ACC-6, Badagry, Nigeria, 1984*, ACC, 1984, p. 67.
19. *The Truth Shall Make You Free: The Lambeth Conference 1988*, London: Church House Publishing (for ACC), 1988, p. 73.
20. The point about deacons is that women were made deacons but not presbyters in Sydney, so there were a considerable number of them in parish ministry. In the (theologically) neighbouring diocese of Armidale the bishop permitted deacons to preside in April 1996.
21. It was actually jostling for first place with mine on state control, which had taken rather longer to come to the top, but had been crowded out by items which overran their time that week. See pages 224–5.

22. I wrote up the case more fully in *News of Liturgy* for August 1994.
23. *Eucharistic Presidency: A Theological Statement by the House of Bishops of the General Synod*, Church House Publishing, 1997.
24. See Chapter 8, pages 114–6.
25. Curiously, Anglo-Catholics who spoke worried more about that morning's liturgy in York Minister, where two archbishops had in turn 'presided' over word and sacrament – and getting that point right (or wrong) hardly touched lay presidency.

14 The charismatic movement

1. J. E. L. Newbigin, *The Household of God: Lectures on the Nature of the Church*, SCM Press, 1953.
2. This was also stated about Lesslie by Hugh Montefiore in his speech in Synod in February 1982 (see page 196). But perhaps it was Lesslie's writings which led to David du Plessis, a leading American Pentecostalist, being invited first to attend a conference of the International Missionary Council around 1952, and then being asked by Visser 't Hooft to be a member of staff at the Second Assembly of the World Council of Churches in Evanston in 1954. David du Plessis is usually reckoned to have been the first ecumenical Pentecostalist.
3. I wrote this up in my *Encountering Charismatic Worship*, Grove Booklet on Ministry and Worship 51, Grove Books, 1977.
4. One astonishingly unlikely witness to this 'neo-Pentecostalism' was Philip Hughes, the sternly Calvinist editor of *The Churchman*, who visited California in 1962, and wrote a highly laudatory editorial.
5. It was John Collins who went on in 1980 to bring a revolutionary new ministry to Holy Trinity, Brompton, and the whole world knows where that has led.
6. There were charismatics at the Keele Congress in 1967, but no mention of them or their doctrines and spirituality appears in the otherwise ground-breaking Congress Statement.
7. James Dunn, *Baptism in the Holy Spirit*, SCM Press, 1970.
8. Tom Walker, *Open to God*, Ministry and Worship 38, Grove Books, 1976 – often reprinted; C. O. Buchanan, *Encountering Charismatic Worship*, Ministry and Worship 51, Grove Books, 1977.
9. See page 164 for a further reference to these meetings.
10. This of course was the (relatively) sober truth. A week before the 1978 Lambeth Conference (but after the July 1978 debate in General Synod) a great 'renewal' conference had been held in Canterbury, and had led to the described result – and I published the account in Michael Harper (ed.), *A New Canterbury Tale*, Grove Books, 1978. The cover picture showed Bill Burnet, then Archbishop of Cape Town, teeing them up for the dance. And they danced – I was there. Richard Hare in his Synod speech told members to order the booklet from Grove Books, and added an incorrect telephone number to help them do so.
11. The form of words was carefully shaped, as the diocesan motion on infant baptism which I had carried in the Synod two years before had ended up in a somewhat pathetic one-man report which had been left in limbo rather than

debated (see page 44). So this time I was after a second, properly resourced, debate.

12. A larger account is given in the report written later, *The Charismatic Movement in the Church of England*, CIO, 1981.

13. Colin Craston had just come from the ACC in Newcastle-upon-Tyne (ACC-5), which had passed a resolution asking the secretary-general of the ACC to request member Churches 'to report on the incidence, progress and significance of spiritual renewal, including the Charismatic Movement ...' The word, and perhaps the heart, were around. This led on to five – yes, just five – provinces responding by ACC-7 in 1984, and to Colin Craston editing a pan-Anglican symposium in preparation for the 1988 Lambeth Conference: *Open to the Spirit: Anglicans and the Experience of Renewal*, ACC, 1987.

14. Josephine Bax, *The Good Wine: Spiritual Renewal in the Church of England*, CIO, 1986, p. 217.

15. *We Believe in God*, CIO, 1986; *We Believe in the Holy Spirit*, Church House Publishing, 1991.

16. The points are of interest for what they contain and what they omit. Points (a), (b) and (c) reflect the agenda of the movement from the 1960s. Point (d) looks more like the 1970s. Point (e) undoubtedly has John Wimber in view, which identifies the drafting as of the 1980s (and might have included 'signs and wonders'!). Ten years later, we would have had to include being 'slain in the Spirit', alias the 'Toronto Blessing'.

17. For my prediction see my conversation with Hugh Montefiore mentioned in the footnote § on page 3. It had an extra poignancy for me, as I stood in the debate at Alec Graham's request – and was not called.

18. One interesting reference was to the weighty Roman Catholic volume which had just been published, Kilian McDonnell and George Montague, *Christian Initiation and Baptism in the Holy Spirit*, Liturgical Press, 1991. This is strongly theological, though arguably pressing patristic passages into carrying weights I am not sure they will sustain.

19. MERE, *The Way of Renewal*, Church House Publishing, 1998.

15 Homosexual issues and *Issues in Human Sexuality*

1. Rob Marshall, *Hope the Archbishop: A Portrait*, Continuum, 2004, p. 22.
2. Marshall, *Hope the Archbishop*, p. 24.
3. GS Board for Social Responsibility, *Homosexual Relationships: A Contribution to Discussion*, CIO, 1979, p. 37.
4. GS Board for Social Responsibility, *Homosexual Relationships*, pp. 76–7.
5. The fantasy was curiously echoed in the Wakeham report (see Chapter 18), where the proposal of 16 bishops in the 'House [of Lords] for the Future' was based upon this assertion. 'With nearly 25 million baptized members, the Church of England accounts for nearly 80 per cent of the total church membership in England.' (*A House for the Future*, HMSO, 2000, p. 155).
6. *The Nature of Christian Belief* was debated in Synod in July 1986, and was warmly welcomed there – though openly defied by David Jenkins himself.

7. *Issues in Human Sexuality*, Church House Publishing, 1991, 5.2, p. 40.
8. *Issues* 5.22, p. 47.
9. Marshall, *Hope the Archbishop*, pp. 72-7.
10. For chapters on both 'The Challenge of Homosexuality' and 'Lambeth '98' see George Carey, *Know the Truth: A Memoir*, HarperCollins, 2004, pp. 293-333.
11. It is reprinted in Appendix Three of *The Windsor Report 2004*, ACC, 2004, pp. 95-6.
12. See Rupert Shortt, *Rowan Williams: An Introduction*, Darton, Longman & Todd, 2003, p. 65.
13. The voting at Lambeth was, of course, consultative, not legislative.
14. He and I both joined a diocesan working party on cohabitation. We both deprecated on scriptural and other grounds the (heterosexual) living together of the unmarried, and the working party came to relatively conservative (and supposedly un-Southwark-like) conclusions.
15. This was particularly attested in public in the published address he gave to Affirming Catholicism in 1998.
16. There were, no doubt, various other shifts of opinion in England itself. It needs little imagination to recognize that the Archbishop, in taking the letter of the nine so seriously, raised some disquiet in the House of Bishops not just about the propriety of consecrating this particular man, but also about the precedent of nine bishops criticizing in public another's choice of a suffragan. And Rowan Williams did get to the Blackpool NEAC – to lead prayers, but with opportunity to speak to the Congress before praying.
17. *Some Issues in Human Sexuality: A Guide to the Debate*, Church House Publishing, 2003; Joanna Cox and Martin Davie, *A Companion to Some Issues in Human Sexuality*, Church House Publishing, 2003.

16 Church and State

1. But that may well not have been true in inner-urban parishes.
2. The meeting nowadays also includes others on the electoral roll. When Birmingham diocese in 1992 proposed in Synod that *only* electoral roll members should participate in choosing wardens, Gordon Bates, Bishop of Whitby, said we were not entitled to have access to the world's structures unless we gave the world access to ours. If this principle has any substance (which I would deny), then why is the world's 'access' confined to choosing churchwardens (and, arguably, bishops)? But establishmentarians have great difficulty in being consistent, and sometimes do not try. Synod rejected the proposal.
3. *The Lambeth Conference 1978: Preparatory Information*, CIO, 1978.
4. William Franklin on 'Lambeth 1998 and the Future Mission' in *Anglican Theological Review*, Spring 1999, p. 262.
5. The previous ones had been in 1916, 1935 and 1952.
6. This has been well recounted in various biographies (notably George Bell's life of Randall Davidson), but has recently been the subject of a detailed study by a

liturgist: Donald Gray, *The 1927–28 Prayer Book Crisis*, Alcuin/GROW Joint Liturgical Studies 60, 61, SCM–Canterbury Press, 2005, 2006.

7. The Doctrine Commission's original report was *Subscription and Assent to the Thirty-Nine Articles*, SPCK, 1969; and the Preface and Declaration of Assent derived from it are printed in their final, legal form in the main *Common Worship* book (p. xi).

8. The quotation from George Carey on page 246 illustrates exactly this.

9. See my more detailed account in *Cut the Connection*, Darton, Longman & Todd, 1994, pp. 189–93.

10. The bishops turned up in force and went to enormous trouble to tell their Lordships that 1662 was well and flourishing in their dioceses, which I thought doubtful as fact and ill-judged as policy.

11. There was wonderful trouble ahead if such a Bill had become law – for the law of the land would have been contrary to the Canons of the Church of England, and the clergy would not have known which to obey.

12. In March 2006 Chris Bryant MP introduced a Private Member's Bill in the Commons to provide for the ordination of women as bishops. This, of course, was an attempt to amend unilaterally the 1993 legislation (pages 173–4 above), showing that some Parliamentarians do not consider themselves bound by the constitutional conventions which were supposed to accompany the use of Measures to enact ecclesiastical legislation. The fact that it got nowhere is irrelevant – it ranks with those Prayer Book Protection Bills.

13. I was involved myself in attempting to reform the appointment of bishops (again), see Chapter 18.

14. It briefly stood first, but was overtaken by a newcomer shooting from bottom to top – see Chapter 13.

15. John Moses, *A Broad and Living Way*, Canterbury Press, 1995; Paul Avis, *Church, State and Establishment*, SPCK, 2001.

16. In *Cut the Connection* I did try to take head-on the writings of establishmentarians, viz. the arguments of Hugh Craig, John Habgood, Enoch Powell, Michael Alison and Frank Field.

17 Political structures and the Single Transferable Vote

1. C. O. Buchanan and Peter Dawes, *Proportional Representation in Church Elections*, Falcon Books, 1969.

2. 'Fraudulent message'? Yes, because it is an undeclared 'con' – an opinion poll tells you that party X who held the seat last time, a party you loathe, can be defeated not, unfortunately, by voting for party Y, your favoured lot, but instead by switching to party Z. The con lies in the poll kidding you that you can know how everyone else is going to vote before you, the privileged last one in the line making up your mind after everyone else, deliver the casting vote that settles it. That is bad enough, but if there are four credible parties, and they seem evenly split, then *how* to choose the one that will keep out the most unwanted one is simply a lottery. That is part of the insoluble problem facing voters who are being urged to keep out the BNP – even if

they buy that as the priority to be observed, they may still have no idea how to do it.

3. This is not intended to be a full explanation, nor even to handle what are nowadays called FAQs. But STV is sometimes dismissed as 'complicated'. For the voter it is precisely as complicated as '1', '2', '3' – and critics who cite complexity are usually silenced when reminded that the Irish (North and South) have no problems with it, but somehow manage to put the candidates in order of preference.

4. It is part of the story in Chapter 18.

5. Still 24 February in those far-off times.

6. At the time Harold Wilson was about to leave an almost hung parliament, in which Jim Callaghan was later rescued briefly by the 'Lib-Lab' pact. Mervyn was supporting two mutually incompatible scenarios simultaneously.

7. In October 1983 I contributed my only 'Ethics' title to the Grove Ethics Series, no. 53: *The Christian Conscience and Justice in Representation.* Illustrated from the distorted 1983 election results, it is still available. The arguments which I am itching to set out extensively here (and did include in my speech on 8 November that year) are there in the booklet.

8. In my early days as a bishop, I was invited to become an honorary vice-president of the Electoral Reform Society, and I have pursued the cause as a justice issue. Just after retiring I became the president of the Society and am taking an appropriate role in the Society's organization and business.

9. See Chapter 18.

10. A most curious, tangential though probably inadvertent, reflection upon the Synod's espousal of justice in representation has come from Tony Blair's appointment of the Second Estates Commissioner, the overtly political appointment by the government of the day of their representative on the Church Commissioners with an ex officio seat on Synod – and *faute de mieux,* the Church of England's nearest approach to an official representative in the Commons. Since the Labour victory in 1997 this office has been held by Sir Stuart Bell, who, wearing another hat, has been convenor of the House of Commons 'first-past-the-post' group!

18 The appointment of diocesan bishops

1. See Romans 3.8: 'And why not say (as some people slander us by saying that we say), "Let us do evil so that good may come"? Their condemnation is deserved!'

2. Technically, suffragans are appointed by the monarch on the advice of the Prime Minister. The Prime Minister receives two names from the Archbishop of the Province, who has himself received them from the diocesan bishop of the diocese with the vacancy. But, unlike the procedures for diocesans, there is an iron-clad convention that the Prime Minister forwards to the monarch only the first name of the two. That person has already been approached by the diocesan bishop concerned, and has accepted the appointment. But number two may not even have been informed his name has gone forward – and it is unimaginable it would ever come into play unless number one died while the letter from the Archbishop to the Prime Minister was in the post.

3. As, e.g., in the twentieth century, David Lloyd George, Alec Douglas-Home and Jim Callaghan.
4. *Church and State 1970*, pp. 29–30.
5. *Church and State 1970*, p. 35.
6. *Church and State 1970*, p. 36.
7. *Church and State 1970*, p. 42.
8. There had been three very odd and arbitrary appointments to sees in 1971–3; Eric Kemp began his speech, 'Nothing that I say . . . should be taken as being in any way a reflection on any individual.' For my money, that gave away something about recent choices by Ted Heath.
9. When Hugh Montefiore retired in 1987, I wrote to Downing Street to urge making him a life peer (something his obituarists later wished for him). But Margaret Thatcher had a different view of bishops from that of Tony Blair, who did make David Sheppard a life peer.
10. This is exactly the same point about STV as that which I make more largely on page 146.
11. The ring of certainty here arises from conversations with Robert Runcie, along with knowledge of Margaret Thatcher's doings in particular cases.
12. The issue of the method of resignation was uncontroversial, and came into use in my own life later.
13. In the nearly four years Margaret Thatcher continued as PM, did CAC ever send Jim Thompson's name to her again? If they did, and she went for number 2 again, then clearly her power to block someone she had 'taken against' was total. But if they did *not* send his name again, then it is even worse, for they were not functioning freely, but her shadow was cast over their deliberations and choices. The moment John Major succeeded her, up came Jim Thompson's name, and he went to Bath and Wells.
14. In early 2006 Gordon Brown (himself from Scotland) was heard to say that he did not think Prime Ministers should have this discretion (and, *sotto voce*, he did not want to exercise it, if and as he became Prime Minister). While legislation for the Church of England should not be initiated in Parliament, it is fine for a PM to revisit this 30-year-old convention. But how shameful that Archbishops wait for Prime Ministers to make the first move in such revisiting. Can the convention really bind us to total silence and compliance, but leave Prime Ministers free to reopen it when they wish?
15. How 'not irrelevant'? See page 239 – he was always conservative.
16. George Carey, *Know the Truth: A Memoir*, HarperCollins, 2004, p. 109.
17. I have not gone into details here, but the State part in vacancies at Canterbury was greater than in others, as the Prime Minister nakedly appointed the chair of the CAC.
18. *Working with the Spirit: Choosing Diocesan Bishops*, Church House Publishing, 2001.
19. It was only those whose names were *not* going to the PM who were to be debriefed. So anyone notified he was being considered, and then neither offered a debrief, nor offered the see, would have known his name had gone to the PM and not been chosen. The proposal fell out of sight.
20. A sensible new provision has been that within the vacancy-in-see committee

persons should become candidates only by being proposed and seconded by others. This has inevitably reduced the field of candidates, and has thus given a better chance of not having several persons tied with each other on the first count with simply one first preference each (their own!), and thus having to be eliminated or not by lot.

21. But about bishoprics matters were more relaxed in time past. In 1886 the clergy of East London sent a letter to Walsham How, their local suffragan, thanking him for turning down the see of Manchester. Or in 1958, Mervyn Stockwood had a kind of consultation in Cambridge to consider whether he should accept Southwark: see Michael de la Noy, *Mervyn Stockwood: A Lonely Life*, Mowbray, 1996, p. 100.

22. *A House for the Future*, HMSO, 2000.

19 The Anglican Communion

1. See Chapter 6 note 7, page 295.
2. See Frank Sugeno and Philip Turner (eds), *Crossroads are for Meeting* (SPCK/ USA, 1986), for the edited papers of this celebration of the mission of worldwide Anglicanism.
3. The 30 years of such travel would not have been possible earlier. Easy air travel was just getting under way.
4. The last archbishop who was not already an English diocesan bishop was John Tillotson, appointed in 1691.
5. Curiously, Mrs Thatcher's first and last episcopal appointments were Robert Runcie in 1979 and George Carey in 1990.
6. Colin Podmore raises fascinating precedents of Archbishops of Canterbury pushing out slightly the boundaries of their powers. See Podmore, *Aspects of Anglican Identity*, Church House Publishing, 2005, pp. 72–3.
7. A notable exercise of that discretion was when Geoffrey Fisher declined to invite Fred Morris, Bishop of the 'Church of England in South Africa', to the 1958 Lambeth Conference.
8. This is quoted from the (then just published) ACC-7 report from Singapore, *Many Gifts, One Spirit*, ACC, 1987, p. 75.
9. This is also quoted from the ACC-7 report, and was apparently ignorant of the (then informal) IALC, which held its second meeting that same month in 1987 and applied for ACC recognition.
10. See *The Truth Shall Make You Free: The Lambeth Conference 1988*, Church House Publishing for ACC, 1988, Mission and Ministry, paras 184–5, p. 68.
11. I refer to the statement in Chapter 5, on page 62. I published the statement with my own commentary as *Lambeth and Liturgy 1988*, Grove Worship 106, Grove Books, 1989.
12. See David Holeton (ed.), *Liturgical Inculturation in the Anglican Communion*, Alcuin/GROW Joint Liturgical Study 15, Grove Books, 1990.
13. See page 66.
14. I did, of course, publish the text of our draft in *News of Liturgy* in September 1998.

15. For the text of this, see pages 210–211.
16. The Lambeth Commission on Communion, *The Windsor Report*, Anglican Communion Office, 2004, pp. 23–5.
17. The Americans are well used to split votes ... not only in the Supreme Court and the Senate, but also, *inter alia*, in Florida, the State of the hanging chads.
18. How to count the Church of England itself is a conundrum which I air a little more in Chapter 16.
19. A quotation from GS 1570.

Index

Note: Members of the House of Laity are identified by the abbreviation HL, and of the House of Clergy by HC. The abbreviations Abp and Bp are used for Archbishop and Bishop respectively. Page references in *italics* indicate brief biographies in Appendix A.